The Art of

Fashion

Draping

The Art of Fashion Draping

THIRD EDITION

Connie Amaden-Crawford

Fairchild Publications, Inc. / New York

Third Edition, Copyright © 2005
Second Printing, 2005
Third Printing, 2007
Fairchild Publications, Inc.
Second Edition, Copyright © 1996
Capital Cities Media, Inc., a Capital
Cities/ABC Inc. Company

First Edition, Copyright © 1989
Capital Cities Media, Inc., a Capital
Cities/ABC Inc. Company

Library of Congress Catalog
Card Number: 2004106414
ISBN: 1-56367-277-4
GST R 133004424

Printed in the United States of America

Executive Editor:
Olga T. Kontzias

Acquisitions Editor:
Joseph Miranda

Assistant Acquisitions Editor:
Jason Moring

Art Director:
Adam B. Bohannon

Director of Production:
Priscilla Taguer

Associate Production Editors:
Elizabeth Marotta and Beth Applebome

Assistant Editor:
Suzette Lam

Publishing Assistant:
Jaclyn Bergeron

Copy Editor:
Monotype Composition Co.

Interior Design:
Dutton & Sherman Design

Chapter Opening Illustration:
Kichisaburo Ogawa

Cover Design:
Adam B. Bohannon

Cover Illustration:
Julie Johnson

Contents

Extended Contents

Preface

The third edition of *The Art of Fashion Draping* has been reorganized and expanded for fashion design professionals and students.

It has been revised with the following objectives in mind:

- To appreciate the importance of the grain of fabric in relationship to the desired design.

- To manipulate fabric on a three-dimensional form and obtain harmony and balance between the fabric and design.

- To stimulate creativity by feeling and sculpting with fabric.

- To develop a keen sense of proportion and placement of style lines.

- To evaluate the fit, hang, and balance of garments on live models.

- To create foundation patterns for the basic bodice, skirt, shift, and sleeve from which other more complicated designs with details such as collars, yokes, and cowls may be designed.

The opening of key chapters includes a definition, theory, and principles section to guide the student into understanding the use and variations of the most common blocks/slopers. I have maintained my original concept of step-by-step written instructions accompanied by illustrations to outline the principles involved in draping fabric on the dress form. However, in response to the comments from users of the second edition, all the sleeves, skirts, bodice variations, and dresses have been placed into their respective chapters for less confusion. The third edition maintains the techniques and styles in each part and are aimed at learning draping skills from beginning to intermediate to advanced to stimulate an endless variety of ideas. For the sake of time, some technical work is accomplished using flat pattern drafting methods. However, the designs developed from flat patternmaking would not be complete unless they were checked for balance, fit, and hang in muslin and draped directly on the dress form. Instructions and illustrations on how to transfer the finished drape into a complete pattern are included for all projects.

Organization of the Text

Chapter 1 in Part One begins with an overview of several couturiers and designers in the fashion world to illustrate how they followed their own inspiration and hard work in creating women's clothing to express personal views of fashion, style, and beauty. Chapter 2 has a discussion of the tools and equipment necessary for all designers. A full-size illustration of the dress form and its components is provided in Chapter 3. As in the previous edition an arm pattern, which when sewn and stuffed with polyfill can be attached to the dress form to drape sleeves, is included. Instructions of the

preparation of this fabric arm are now listed on page 14. The elements of fabric, particularly acquiring an understanding of the principles and elements of design in relation to grain and balance for draping fabrics, are discussed in Chapter 4. A short glossary of important draping terminology completes this section.

Chapters in Part Two are the foundation for a sound understanding of manipulating, molding, and shaping fabric into basic garments on the dress form. Each chapter in Part Two completes the draping skills for basic garments—the bodice, skirt, shift (torso), and sleeve, and their variations. The sense of seeing and feeling a simple design, which cannot be achieved by creating patterns flat on the table, is accomplished. The steps discuss how to drape the fabric from neck to hem, maintaining a smooth and easy-flowing design, while at the same time not overworking a piece of fabric. Instructions for the basic sleeve are also included in this section. Here, to save time and maintain accuracy, the basic sleeve is drafted. Sleeves are pinned and checked for bal-

ance, fit, and hang when the garment is placed on the dress form. Step-by-step principles discussed in Part Two enable students to understand: accurate placement of the grain and darts, tucks, and pleats on the figure; necessary ease amounts; and the waistline, side seam, dart, and armhole balance of the flat pattern.

After mastering the basic principles of draping explained in Part Two, the designer can continue with the intermediate projects in Part Three, such as: bodice variations, shirt and kimono designs, princess shapes, and raglan sleeves. Draping principles for collars—basic and fashion-oriented—and pants are covered. Part Three also includes draping of asymmetric designs—introducing the student to more advanced designs. Projects in Part Three encourage the students to identify which draping steps are most flattering to the various figures, while at the same time allows them to continue to refine their ability to handle pliable fabrics. Projects explore how to define styles and silhouettes over the bust, hip, and waist and how to utilize folds, darts, pleats, princess seams, and fullness to emphasize the design.

Designers derive a great deal of pleasure and satisfaction when creating original styles. The chapters in Part Four apply the information discussed in previous parts to more unusual and complicated cuts. Students approaching the draping projects in this section must understand thoroughly the basic and intermediate principles covered earlier. All the draping projects in this section discuss how to retain the figure's most pleasing attributes and how to emphasize them through subtle illusion. Designs are more challenging and work toward the entire effect while paying attention to the most minute details. Draping bias and sculptured dresses, the bustier, and design details such as midriffs, cowls, ruffles, and flounces are discussed and illustrated. As a result of the fibers and construction in knit fabrics, the designer must use a great deal of finesse and be expert in technique to accurately drape these styles. A chapter is devoted to the step-by-step guidelines for draping such knit designs as the sleeve, halter, bodysuit, and leotard.

Acknowledgments

I wish to express appreciation for the assistance, information, and love given to me by colleagues, students, and friends. Their many ideas and suggestions have been useful in presenting this text. My grateful appreciation to the following: Mary Stephens, Moira Doyle, and Alice Kaku at the Fashion Institute of Design and Merchandising, for the continued input of this text. A special thank you to Jimmy Hebert for teaching me Photoshop and the great input on the fashion illustrations.

My deepest appreciation to Tiffin Dove and Kelle Schaeffel for their untiring efforts in drawing the technical illustrations.

A book of this quality and professionalism could not be possible without the guidance of the staff from Fairchild Publications. This staff includes Olga Kontzias, Liz Marotta, and Beth Applebome. Also guiding this project and adding to the book quality is Susanne Viscarra of Monotype Composition Co.

A very warm and loving thank you to my husband, Wayne, for so much patience and help while writing this book.

I wish to thank reviewers selected by the publisher to read the second edition: Janet Hethorn, University of California–Davis; Paula Sampson, Ball State University; Carolyn Schactler, Central Washington University; and Elaine Zarse, Mount Mary College–Milwaukee.

Connie Amaden-Crawford
Sedona, Arizona
2004

The Art of
Fashion
Draping

Part One

Practical Draping Skills

Many designers prefer to use draping methods to create their original designs. A designer can easily see the proportion, fit, balance, and style lines of a design, exactly as it will look on the bodice. Working with actual materials gives a designer greater inspiration and a better indication of the flow and performance of a fabric.

The chapter on "Fashion Influences" reviews who influenced and established draping as a key tool for the greatest of the past designers, as well as the newest designers of today. Part One also identifies the appropriate tools and equipment for draping, defines grain and its relationship to the design, and lists terms and basic principles applicable to the development of draped garments. The importance of the dress form to draping is also illustrated and discussed in this section.

The material covered in Part One is applicable to any of the projects in this text and will result in the accurate and professional production of draped garments.

Chapter One

Fashion Influences

This chapter begins with a history of fashion influences and the designers who inspired, set the trends, and influenced fashion for many years to come. The information presented on these designers is not lengthy, but it has been carefully chosen to illustrate the importance of these great designers. From this group of designers came the innovators who have made fashion an artistic lifestyle and business.

Fashion Influences

The Evolution of Design

The new millennium is officially here. What better way to begin this new edition than to take a look into the past to understand the evolution of fashion and design.

The roots of clothing and primitive sewing techniques can be traced as far back as prehistoric man when hides, fur, and vegetable or animal fibers were woven into primitive tunics.

In 3000 BC, the Egyptians of the Old Kingdom—both males and females—draped a loincloth, which they wrapped several times around their bodies. Later in history, the Egyptians developed various characteristic ways of putting premeasured fabric pieces onto the body. Different graceful drapes and styles were held in place with clasps, allowing the ends to hang freely.

The Romans later developed the first patterns. Two premeasured semicircular, oval-shaped patterns were adapted from the Greeks. The pattern pieces, which were two times the person's height and three times the person's width, were sewn together and draped over the body. We know this style today as the toga.

In the 3rd and 4th centuries, changes in clothing were most often conceived in response to military demands. During this period, the premeasured fabric pieces and simple pattern shapes became more intricate. First, necklines were added, creating a chemise-type garment; simply styled armholes and short breeches followed, allowing a closer fit and greater movement for soldiers on horseback.

The clothes worn up to the 13th century remained quite simple in shape and fairly crudely constructed. Throughout the Middle Ages, clothing varied little from that of previous centuries. Men's and women's garments remained very similar. At the beginning of the 16th century, men's fashions became more intricate—trims, padding, and additional pieces were added. Buttons grew in popularity, both as a means of displaying wealth and as a necessity for fastening form-fitted clothing. Armholes became more oval, allowing for a premeasured sleeve and different shapes of hoods, capes, and collars. Breeches were more intricately styled and more carefully measured and fitted to a human body. Women's clothing was transformed into a separate skirt and bodice. Over time, tailors became more skilled and developed flat pattern methods.

By the early 1800s, manuals outlining the geometrical rules of pattern skills had been written. Pattern blocks (slopers) were being adapted. By 1863, paper patterns were sold for the first time in large scale by Butterick Publishing Company.

Designers Who Shape Fashion

Fashion, as a part of history, repeats itself and is defined as the prevailing style in clothing of any given time. Clothing became relatively easy flowing by the 20th century after the corset was discarded. **Madeleine Vionnet** and **Alix Grès** were the first couture designers to create designs with the live, moving body in mind. Their designs were very carefully conceived, and the most memorable designs resembled classical sculptures. As consumers, we cannot help being affected by the glamour of fashion and the superstar status of many runway models. Areas of the body are emphasized one year and forgotten or hidden the next. In addition, ethnically influenced styles come and go as the global arena changes. The ups and downs of the economy correlate to the ups and downs of skirt lengths. What you thought looked old-fashioned or dowdy on your mother, you end up coveting as an adult.

"The key to all design is an interest in fabric."
— **Giorgio Armani**

The couture designers of the last century can be credited with developing techniques that greatly influenced the treatment of fabric and design. Along the way, couture designers handled fabrics in such a manner that altered the elemental techniques into new applications for designing. These designers understood the visual elements of fabric manipulation and the need to arrange it into a pleasing composition. As you read the following information about these designers, it is important to realize that each combined his or her experiences, skills, and talents to become a leader in the fashion world. Not one of these designers started "at the top" and became famous overnight. As described below, this author is featuring the following designers' skills, along with their talents, to help a new and upcoming designer understand the importance of draping in creating the designs of the future.

Charles Worth was born an Englishman in 1826. At age 20, he left London for Paris where he met his beautiful wife. He began designing dresses for her; she modeled them and attracted more and more prominent women as clients. In 1860, at the age of 32, his design studio became known as the House of Worth. His couture house became the model for all future couture houses that established standards to the design and construction of the newest designs in clothing. At one time his clientele included nine "crowned heads." Worth was the innovator of the presentation of gowns on live mannequins. He became famous for the princess-cut dress and the elimination of crinolines.

"Couture designers have followed their own inspiration, using the medium of women's clothing to express personal views of fashion, style, beauty, and life."
—**Nancy Mitford**

Madeleine Vionnet was the first couturier to work by draping directly on a live model in the 1920s. She personally draped and cut designs on a half-scale wooden mannequin. Her inventive bias draping techniques lent charm and grace to garments that women with any figure could capture in their clothes. Vionnet was known for classical drapery, cowls or halter necks, handkerchief-point hems, and faggoted seams. She used smaller areas that the designer could control. This, and her special treatment of bias fabrics, allowed bias designs to cling away from bulges, but nicely mold the curves. Another incredible feature of her clothes is that after many years the bias hemlines remained parallel to the floor. Her years of hard work transformed a technique into something special.

Sheer lame dress by Madeleine Vionnet, 1937 (© Condé Nast Archive/Corbis).

Madame Alix Grès, a designer in the thirties, used her fine arts talents, especially sculpting, to work directly on a live model. Her superb craftsmanship created statuesque Greek-draped evening gowns with graceful folds down to the floor. She is also credited for creating cowled black jersey day dresses, asymmetric drapes, bias-cut caftans, and loose topcoats with hoods and batwing sleeves.

"Find just that elegant detail that would make the dress be a client's favorite."
—**Nina Ricci**

Nina Ricci, a Paris couture designer in the thirties and forties, also worked directly on a mannequin to achieve the maximum lightness, appeal, and elegant detail. She was skilled in draping the surplice and crossed-over

Dress by Nina Ricci, Spring/Summer ready to wear, 1996 (© Corbis/Sygma).

treatment of the bodice. Both day and evening dresses drew attention to the figure with revealing styles that featured much drapery and shirring.

"Fashion is not something that exists in dress only. Fashion has to do with ideas, with the way we live, with what is happening."
—Coco Chanel

Gabrielle "Coco" Chanel earned her fame by creating designs that were "exquisitely simple" from the 1920s to the 1970s. Working directly on her mannequins, she created designs that would be easy to move in and be recognizable. Chanel refined the vision of creating future and retrospective couturier designs by using cloth and creating the perfect balance to detail, as well as the use of accessories.

"Women think about all colors, but not the absence of color. I say that black offers everything. White also. They are of absolute beauty. Put women in white or black and one sees nothing but them."
—Coco Chanel

Cristobal Balenciaga, designer from 1937 to 1968, was known as the couture designer who could design, cut, sew, and fit a whole garment. He was revered as the "Master" by his staff. With every collection, Balenciaga designed clothes to have an actual shape, as if they had been engineered by an architect. His clothes featured the shape of the woman's body. Balenciaga's construction methods were an art in its own right.

During World War II, with the absence of Parisian fashions, Mainbocher, Claire McCardell, and Gilbert Adrian were able to create their own fashion inspiration for America. Their inventive ideas and use of fabrics gave a new look in dress styles.

Mainbocher was well known for his excellent designs of less formal dinner dresses, evening wraps, and sleeveless dresses with matching jackets. Using the fabric that he had chosen as a starting point and imagining the role a particular design might play in a client's life, he created collections of bias-cut slip dresses made in silks, taffetas, and crepes. A collection of cotton evening dresses, designed in 1932, astonished the Paris community.

"Suitability is half the secret of being well dressed."
—Mainbocher

White chiffon dress by Mainbocher, 1948 (© Genevieve Naylor/Corbis).

Claire McCardell, a top all-American designer of the 1940s and 1950s, is credited for her inventiveness in designing the diaper-wrap one-piece bathing suit and the bareback summer dress. She also popularized "separates"—skirts, blouses, pedal pushers, and sweaters—as the "American Look."

And, **Gilbert Adrian** won his fame by designing clothes for the movies and for stars such as Joan Crawford. His exaggerated shoulder look became the most prevalent fashion of the forties. Adrian was also influential in creating the "little black dress" with the most amazing draped twists.

Dress designed for Joan Crawford by Adrian, 1936 (© Bettman/Corbis).

At the same time, **Hubert de Givenchy** produced collections that gave the mood of sober elegance. He was noted for clothing of exceptional workmanship, masterly cut, and beautiful fabrics. He opened his own couture house in 1952. His clientele included many elegant women of the century, including Audrey Hepburn, Jacqueline Kennedy Onassis, and the Duchess of Windsor.

"Good tailoring is very subtle tailoring. You don't see the workmanship—you feel the fit, the careful balance of the rhythm of the sentence."
— **Gay Talese**

Dress by Givenchy, Fall 2004 (Courtesy of Fairchild Publications, Inc.).

Each designer would explore the fabric weight and pliability of their fashion fabric and transform a technique into something special. Many times, the fabric would take designers on a journey that was unexpected and produced a unique result. For instance, in the 1970s, **Issey Miyake** explored new design concepts by using wrapping, fastening, and tying techniques that were based on Japanese tradition for his designs. His loose, almost formless clothes created draped designs utilizing the perfect space between the body and the garment.

"Women and men need a modern system of clothes that saves time, that makes them look and feel confident, and pulls it all together."
— **Donna Karan**

Designers are able to create beautiful effects through color and texture, which create light and shadows. The collections on the runways directly influence the designs of the future. "Realist" designers, such as **Norma Kamali, Perry Ellis,** and **Miyake,** created new elements of sportswear by using very ethnic and pop influences. For instance, **Norma Kamali** transformed everyday knit fabrics into spirited knit designs. Her body-conscious and adventurous designs gave a new direction in ready-to-wear clothes that still influences designs of today.

"Sportswear allows me to do anything."
— **Perry Ellis**

With fashion and styles forever changing, it may only be the finishing touches that are new, while the basic pattern and silhouette remain the same. The secret is knowing those basics and being able to mix

and match those details, as well as understand the designs. According to *Vogue,* **Nicolas Gesquière,** the shy power at Balenciaga, is Generation X's leading fashion designer. His latest collection includes jersey cocktail dresses with swags of lace, dotted swiss, and raw-edged ruffles and pearl garlands, combined with Arab kaffiyeh and cinched together with prize fighter belts. The effect is strange, sexy, and makes a statement. According to Agular, "Nicolas is the only designer who has been able to truly breathe new life into the eighties resurgence." A creative designer, such as Gesquière, takes all his skills (his internships started at age 14) and turns them into the freshest spins and gets it right.

"Fashion is about selection, editing. You have to be very severe in your selection, so you keep something to yourself—even in the way you present yourself."
— **Nicolas Gesquière**

Gone are the days of one or two distinct fashion looks. The job of getting dressed and being fashionable has gotten harder. Dress codes have been relaxed. Most aspects of our lives can be adapted for any look you like, whether from the past, present, or future, and still be fashionable. This is provided you get the proportions right and bring it in line with current styles.

Throughout this text, you are encouraged to make *discoveries of your own.* Remember, fabric is a sculpturing tool in relating the design to the body. Deciding which fabric will work best for a style comes from experience and observation, as well as trial and error. Considering the texture, weight, and print as well as the color patterns helps in the selection of the most appropriate fabric to complement the appearance, durability, maintenance, and comfort of a garment. Fabric quality and suitability is important because it will determine the appearance, durability, maintenance, and comfort of the finished garment.

You can transform a technique into something special, depending upon the technique, stitching, placement of fabric grain, and placement of seamlines. You can fashion the couture design of tomorrow. Create a spirit of adventure. Invent your own modifications and explore what would happen if you used a similar draping technique, but placed it in an unconventional place. Explore design concepts by testing the behavior of fabric.

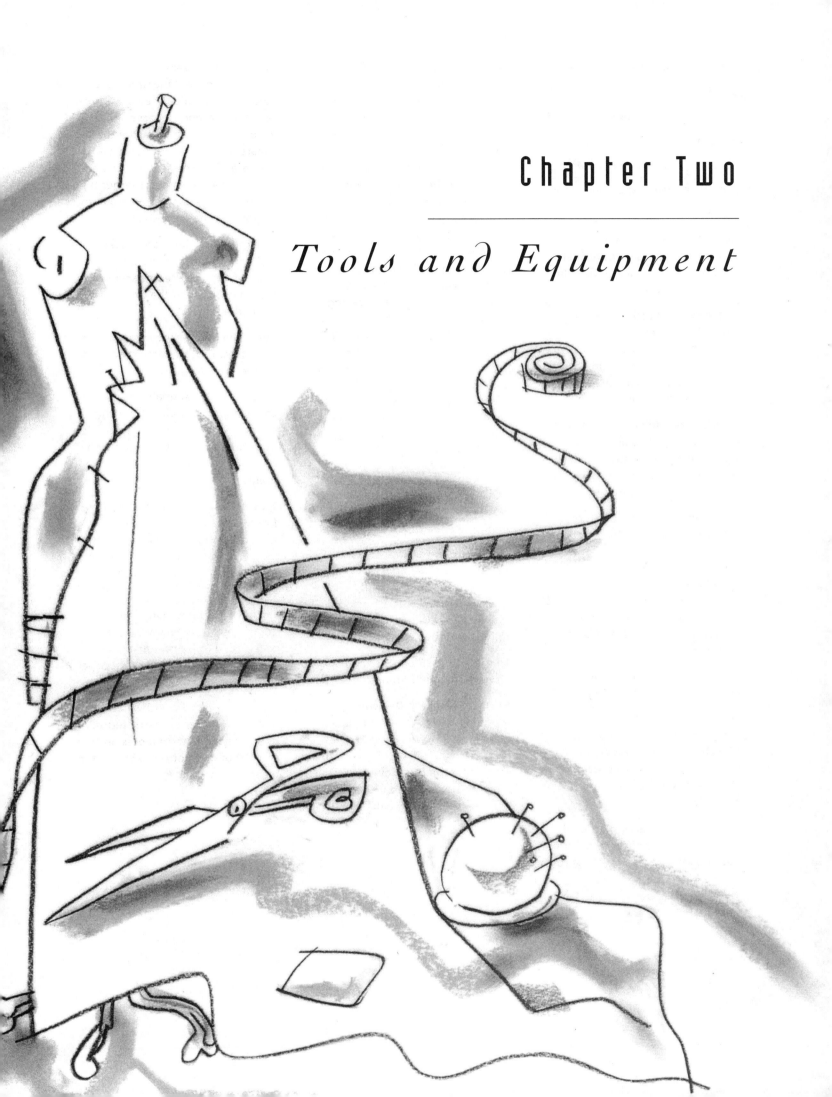

Chapter Two

Tools and Equipment

A few basic supplies are needed for any draping project. Draping tools are necessary to drape, measure, mark, and draft designs. Keep all necessary supplies on hand and keep them neatly together to use at any time.

Awl A pointed metal instrument used for punching holes for belt eyelets and other clean, sharp holes in fabric or leather.

18-Inch Clear Plastic Ruler A 2-inch wide ruler divided into 1/8-inch grids. It is clear and perfect for truing and adding seam allowances. Available through C-Thru Ruler Co.

French Curve Ruler An irregular curve with an edge describing a spiral curve used to shape and curve edges of curved collars, necklines, crotch seams, and armholes.

Hip Curve Ruler A 24-inch ruler with a long, slightly shaped curve that finishes with a strong circular shape. This ruler is marked in both inches and centimeters, along with fractional measurements. It is used to shape lapels, seams, flares, godets, princess lines, and pant crotch seams.

Iron A steam-and-dry iron used to smooth and aid in blocking muslin.

Ironing Board A flat, adjustable board about 54 inches long by 15 inches wide that tapers to 6 inches at one end to provide a stable, soft surface on which to iron or press.

L-Square A metal or plastic ruler with two arms of different lengths meeting at right angles. These rulers are marked in both inches and centimeters, along with fractional measurements.

Muslin An inexpensive fabric, on which the grain and crossgrain are quite visible, used to drape garments made of woven goods. The quality and hand of the muslin should represent the texture and characteristics of the actual fabric chosen for the garment design. *Soft muslin* will simulate the draping quality of natural or synthetic silk, lingerie fabric, and fine cottons. *Medium-weight muslin* will simulate the draping quality of wool and medium-weight cottons. *Coarse muslin* will simulate the draping quality of heavyweight wools and cottons. Also, *canvas muslin* will simulate the draping qualities of such heavyweight fabrics as denim, fur, and imitation fur.

Garments made of *knitted fabrics* should be draped in less expensive knit fabric. However, the sample knit should have the same stretch value as the fabric selected for the finished garment.

Notcher A punching tool used to mark the edge of a sloper or paper pattern.

Pattern Drafting Paper Strong, white drafting paper, with 1-inch grids of pattern dots, of a good quality and thickness. Available in rolls of various widths.

Pencils Soft 2B or 5H pencils used in developing muslin patterns.

Pin Cushion or Pin Dispenser A sewing tool that keeps pins organized in a convenient place. The most common pin cushion is in the shape of a tomato. However, other types and sizes are available. Choose the pin cushion that will be easiest to use.

Scissors and Shears Shears are usually 4 to 8 inches long and made of steel. Bent-handled shears are excellent for easy and correct cutting. A 3- to 6-inch scissor is smaller than shears. The difference between shears and scissors is that one handle on a pair of shears is larger than the other. The handles on a pair of scissors are the same size.

Straight Pins Satin dressmaker pins #17 with sharp tapering points that will not rust are used to anchor muslin or fabric to the dress form while draping.

Style Tape A narrow, woven tape that is used to delineate style lines on the dress form.

Tailor's Chalk A small piece of chalk, approximately 1 1/2-inch square, with two tapered edges. It is used to mark lines temporarily on garment hems and other alteration points.

Tape Measure A flexible, narrow, firmly woven, 60-inch reversible tape marked with measurements indicating both inches and metric terms used to take dress form, muslin, and body measurements.

Tracing Wheel A sharp, spike-edged, circular wheel with a handle that is used to transfer markings from the drape to the pattern paper.

Yardstick A wooden or metal ruler 1 yard in length (36 inches) that is marked in inches or metric terms. An aid for laying pattern pieces on the straight of grain of the fabric or for measuring hem lines.

The Dress Form

The dress form is used to manipulate flat fabric to fit the curves of the body accurately. It is used to visualize what a pattern should look like in relationship to the figure.

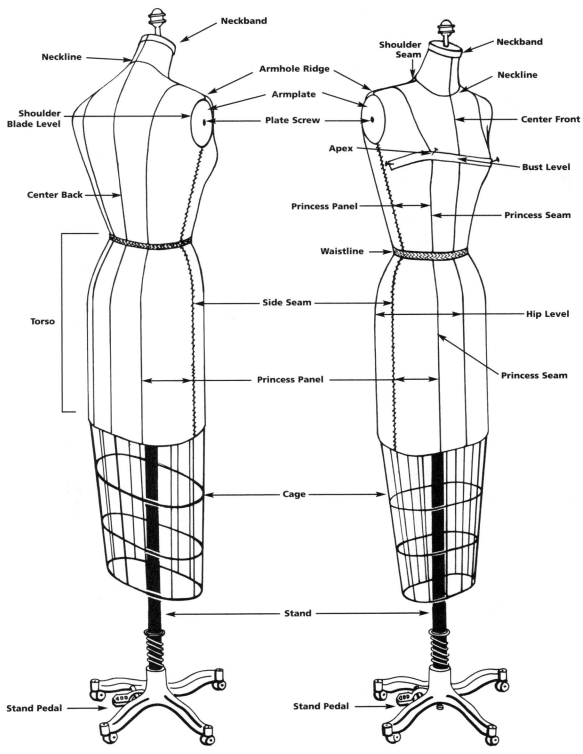

A variety of dress forms are available in standard sizes for junior and missy figures, as well as for children's and men's. Some manufacturers use "special dress forms" for their customers, depending on the type of clothes designed, the fit required, and the figure shape necessary. Illustrated here are some examples of forms other than the standard ladies' size 8 or 10 used for the various garments headed for the retail marketplace.

There are several types of dress forms on the market and several manufacturers of dress forms used by designers. The most commonly used dress form for both the novice and the designer/manufacturer is the muslin-padded dress form (see illustration). This form, set on a movable, height-adjustable stand, duplicates the human body shape. It is firm, yet resilient, and does not resist pins. The right and left sides are exactly alike.

Garment manufacturers use this type of dress form to drape and perfect most basic blocks and original designs. Sample garments are fitted, checked, and corrected on this same form. Therefore, much care and thought is given as to which model, size, and proportion of dress form should be purchased. Manufacturers must be selective because their basic patterns and subsequent designs are proportioned to fit many customers without involving too many alterations.

The dress form illustrated follows the measurements of a particular size and type of figure for an individual or specific manufacturer. Dress forms are updated every year according to government standards and silhouette changes. However, any newly purchased dress form should be tested and checked for alignment, relationship, and balance of the shoulder and side seams.

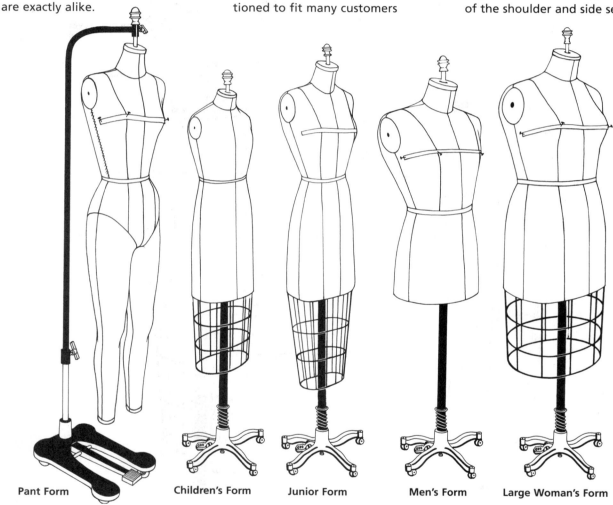

Pant Form   **Children's Form**   **Junior Form**   **Men's Form**   **Large Woman's Form**

Dress Form Manufacturers

Dress Rite Forms
3817 N. Pulaski
Chicago, IL 60641

Fabulous Fit/Royal Forms
P.O. Box 1648
New York, NY 10013

Global Model Forms
P.O. Box 1214
North Baldwin, NY 11510

Modern Model Form
A Division of Bernstein Display
30 W. 29th Street
New York, NY 10001

Superior Forms
Richard the Thread
8320 Melrose Avenue
West Hollywood, CA 90069

Wolf Form Company, Inc.
P.O. Box 510
17 Van Nostrand Avenue
Englewood, NJ 07631-4309

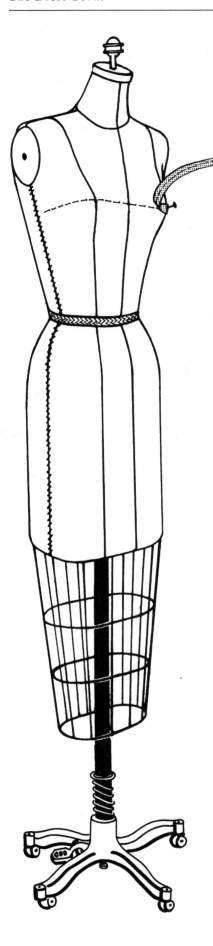

Attaching the Bustline Tape

In many cases, the dress form needs a bustline tape in order to achieve a correctly fitted drape. This bustline tape represents the same fit on the dress form as a bra does on the human body. This tape is sometimes referred to as the *bra tape*.

1. Pin the bustline tape to the dress form in the middle of the princess panel on the left side of the dress form.

2. Drape the bustline tape tightly across the bustline. Do not secure tape at center front.

3. Finish pinning the bustline tape, across the front only, in the middle of the princess panel on the right side of the dress form.

NOTE: The tape should be tight and pinned securely.

4. Pin and crossmark the apex on the bustline tape. (The apex is the highest point of the bustline at the princess seam.)

Balancing the Armhole

The armhole side seam and the armplate screw level should be in perfect alignment.

Shift the shoulder and side seam positions if they need adjusting. Draw the new lines with a dark pen.

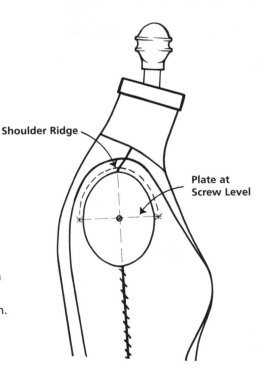

Shoulder Ridge

Plate at Screw Level

Preparing the Arm

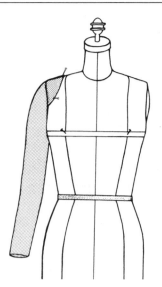

An arm is often not included with the dress form. An arm pattern is included on these pages. This arm, when cut, sewn, stuffed, and attached to the dress form, will allow you to check the drape of sleeves. By following the instructions, you will be ready to drape and check-fit many types of sleeves.

1 **Cut arm pattern pieces** out of heavy muslin and transfer all notches and dart drill hole. Be sure to follow the grainlines when placing the pattern pieces onto fabric.

a. **Cut 1 arm pattern.**

b. **Cut 2 shoulder stay patterns.**

c. **Cut 1 top arm circle pattern.**

d. **Cut 1 wrist arm circle pattern.**

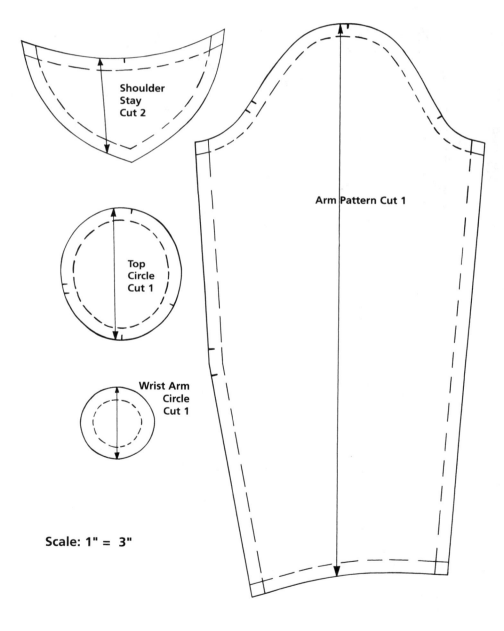

Shoulder
Stay
Cut 2

Top
Circle
Cut 1

Wrist Arm
Circle
Cut 1

Arm Pattern Cut 1

Scale: 1" = 3"

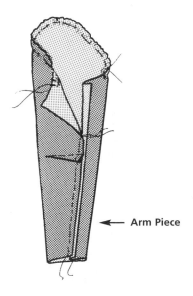

← **Arm Piece**

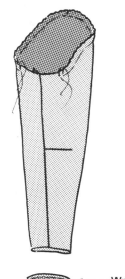

← **Wrist Arm Circle**

2 **Sew the arm piece.**

a. Crimp the cap of the arm.

b. Sew the elbow dart and the underarm seam. Be sure to sew the underarm together, so it will fit the **right side** of the dress form when the arm is completed.

3 **Turn the arm correct side out.**

4 **Sew the wrist area of the arm.**

a. Clip and press under (to the inside) the wrist seam allowance of the arm.

b. Clip and press under the seam allowance of the wrist arm circle (smaller circle).

c. Hand sew the wrist arm circle (smaller circle) to the bottom at the wrist level of the arm. Be sure the wrist level at this stitchline remains 7 inches.

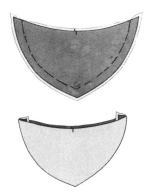

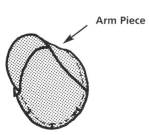

Arm Piece

5 **Sew the shoulder stay.**

a. Sew the outer edges of the shoulder stay (pointed edge).

b. Turn the stay correct side out.

6 **Sew the shoulder stay to the larger circle (top arm circle), matching shoulder position notches.**

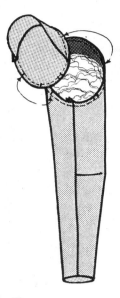

7 Sew the shoulder stay with the attached larger circle (top arm circle) to the cap of the arm.

a. Place the shoulder stay between the arm cap (previously crimped) and the larger circle.

b. Stitch the shoulder stay to the arm cap from the edge of the shoulder stay across to the opposite edge of the shoulder stay.

8 Fill the arm with polyfill. Be careful not to overstuff, as the arm may become distorted.

9 Match the bottom area (unsewn section) of the larger circle to the underarm section of the arm (notched area). Hand sew the underarm section of the arm to the lower section of the larger circle, matching stitchline to stitchline.

10 Pin the arm to the right side of the dress form when the arm is completely sewn.

Chapter Three

Elements of Fabrics, Draping Principles, and Fitting Methods

Elements of Fabrics

The approach to dressing and the new technological age have introduced fabrics that are flatter, crisper, smoother, firmer, and stretchier than ever before. These versatile fabrics fit the lifestyles and the moods of the new fashion age.

Fabrics and clothes should relate to our lifestyles and our need for greater variety and diversity in dressing. Thus, clothes for our active lifestyles are made of many different stretch knits. All around us, sportswear garments are made of denim, single knits, and a variety of woven cottons and synthetics. Sheer, see-through fabrics capture the body's sleek line, while tulle, organ-za, and sheer cottons and knits are used for discreetly revealing effects. Special evening fabrics, such as chiffon, crepe de chine, silk, voile, and brocade, capture the elegant lifestyles of today's women. In contrast, linen, seersucker, homespun plaids, natural cottons, corduroy, woolens, and a variety of woven synthetics are appealing fabrics for realistic, durable, and longer-lasting quality clothes.

Before beginning any draping steps, consider the large selection of available fabrics. The fabric selected for a garment greatly influences the finished look. A good designer is not only aware of the fiber content, weave, and finish of a fabric, but analyzes and understands its structure and characteristics to create the proper ease and balance of the garment or pattern drape.

Selecting a fabric of correct quality and suitability is important because it will determine the appearance, durability, maintenance, and comfort of the finished garment. A designer selects the fabric with the following criteria in mind: color, texture, hand, weight, comfort, and price.

Approach each design with a positive attitude and a clear fashion sense.

Fibers

The various fibers used and the methods by which these fibers are put together define the differences among fabrics. Fibers are either natural or manufactured. Natural fibers include cotton from the cotton plant, flax that is processed into linen, wool from sheep, and silk from the silkworm. Manufactured fibers are not found in nature and are produced using different combinations of chemicals. Manufactured fibers include acrylic, nylon, polyester, rayon, and spandex.

Fibers possess certain basic properties or characteristics. A designer must understand these properties to determine if the fabric made from these fibers is suitable for a specific design. The fiber content in a fabric will change the performance and drapability qualities of the fabric.

A major development of the 1990s is the production of microfibers. These are manufactured fibers that are thinner than a human hair or a strand of silk. Because fabrics produced from microfibers are very soft and drapable, nylon or polyester fibers can, for example, be produced to look and feel like silk.

Fabrics can be made entirely of the same fiber or by blending or combining different fibers. This is done when no single fiber possesses all of the properties required to make the most desirable fabric. For example, one of cotton's unfavorable features is that it wrinkles easily. However, if polyester, which possesses excellent wrinkle resistance, and cotton are combined, the fabric will wrinkle less and still maintain the most favorable properties of cotton, such as its absorbency and softness.

It is not only the properties of a fiber that determine the fundamental properties of a fabric. Other components, such as yarns, fabric construction, colorization, and finish, also govern how the fabric will ultimately perform. If a property of any component is changed, then the properties of the fabric will change.

Fabric Construction

Although several construction methods are used, the two basic methods of producing fabrics—weaving and knitting—are the most pertinent for this discussion. Woven fabrics are made by interlacing yarns, while knitted fabrics are made by interlooping yarns. Different methods of interlacing and interlooping yarns, variations in fiber content, and yarn character influence the fabric structure.

Woven Fabrics

Woven fabrics are formed by interlacing yarns in a *plain weave, twill weave,* or *satin weave.* Some common woven fabrics are cotton, linen, denim, poplin, broadcloth, gingham, sharkskin, corduroy, wool, chambray, and rayon gabardine. An important characteristic of all woven fabrics is that they fray at the cut edge. The looser the weave, the more the cut edge frays. Loosely woven fabrics are usually less durable. When testing the straightness of the cut ends, the crosswise and lengthwise yarns should run at right angles.

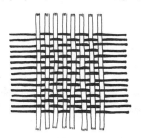

Plain Weave   Each thread passes over and under each of the threads going in the opposite direction.

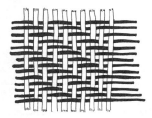

Twill Weave   The fabric has diagonal lines. Yarns cross at least two yarns before going under one or more yarns.

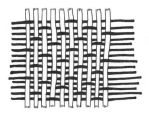

Satin Weave   Thread goes over one and under several yarns to create greater luster on the right side of the fabric.

Knitted Fabrics

Knitted fabrics are formed by interlooping yarns. The most common knits are flat jersey, purl, and rib (better known as weft knits). These knits stretch more in width than in length. Double knits are also weft knits; they are firmer and heavier and have less stretch and more resilience than single knits. Tricot and raschel knits are well-known warp knits. These warp knits have less stretch than weft knits and tend to be run resistant.

The most common characteristic of a knitted fabric is its capacity to change its dimensions by stretching. The amount and direction (one-way or two-way) of stretch varies according to the knitting process. New stretch yarns, manufactured fibers, and double-knit construction have helped to develop and produce knit fabrics that retain their comfort, shape, and size. Stretch fabrics are developed by means of textured yarns, spandex fiber yarns, or chemical treatment of cotton or wool fibers.

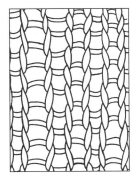

Single Knit   One set of needles is used to form loops across the fabric width.

Double Knit   Two sets of needles are used to give both sides of the fabric a similar appearance.

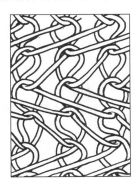

Tricot Knit   Several loops are formed in a lengthwise direction.

Understanding Grainline and Crossgrain

Draping skills are acquired with patience and practice. Practice *smoothing* the fabric over the dress form with a light and skillful touch of the hand. Avoid stretching the fabric. The fabric must be premeasured and have correct grainline and crossgrain drawn on the fabric piece.

Lengthwise Grain (Straight of Grain)

The **lengthwise grain** of the fabric is always parallel to the selvage of the fabric goods and is also sometimes referred to as the **warp.** The **selvage** is the firmly woven edge running the length of the fabric on both sides. The strongest threads run in the lengthwise direction and have the least stretch.

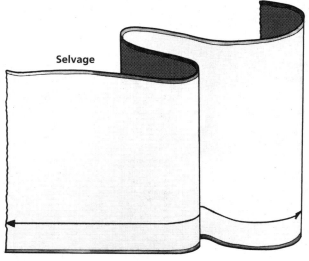

Selvage

Lengthwise Grain

Crosswise Grain

The **crossgrain** is easily recognized as the weave that runs perpendicular to the lengthwise grain of the goods from selvage to selvage. These crossgrain yarns are sometimes referred to as the "filling" yarns and are better known as the **weft.** The crossgrain has slightly more give than the straight of the grain in fabrics. When draping, the crosswise grain usually lies parallel to the floor.

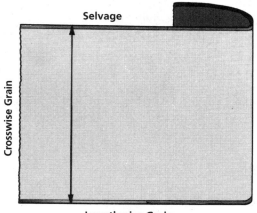

Selvage

Crosswise Grain

Lengthwise Grain

True Bias

To find **true bias** easily, fold the grain of the goods to the crossgrain of the goods to create a perfect 45-degree foldline. Bias fabric always gives and stretches a great deal more than the grain or crossgrain of the goods. Bias is used when a design requires draping contours over the body without using darts.

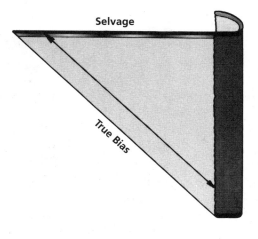

Selvage

True Bias

Hand, Appearance, and Texture of Fabrics

The feel of a fabric is referred to as the *hand.* The *appearance* is the flexibility of the fabric. *Texture* refers to the weight, body, or drape of fabrics. Texture is created by different types and combinations of fibers, yarns, and methods of construction, as well as colorings and finishes.

Regardless of hand, appearance, and texture, fibers are usually twisted together to form yarns, which are then woven or knitted to form a fabric. Color is applied by either dyeing or printing. Finally, a finishing technique, usually chemical, is applied to improve the performance and provide fabric characteristics that are suitable for the end use and desirable to the customer.

Testing the Fiber Content

If the fiber content is unknown, a simple burn test can be performed. By identifying the ash, the fiber content can be determined. Hold a small swatch of fabric with a pair of tweezers. Touch this fabric with a lighted match. When cotton, linen, or rayon is burned, the ash is feathery and floats away. The ash will disintegrate. Wool burns slowly. The ash is easily crushed, feels crispy, and turns to soot. Burning wool also has a distinctive odor. Burning silk is similar to that of wool; however, the ash formed feels more delicate. Most synthetics react and burn in the same manner. Some synthetics drip when burned and are very hot. When the ash cools, it can be crushed easily with the fingers, but cannot be brushed off.

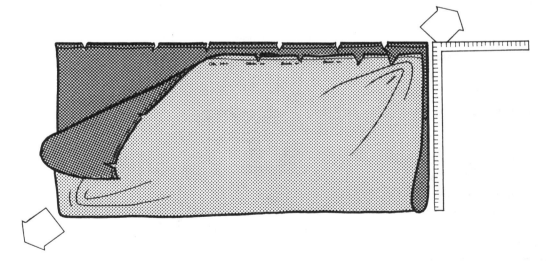

Blocking

Before beginning the draping process, check the fabric to determine if the lengthwise and crosswise threads have distorted from a 90-degree alignment. Blocking is the process of ensuring that the lengthwise and crossgrain threads are at right angles to each other. If the threads of the fabric are not at perfect right angles, the fabric must be realigned or put on grain by blocking.

Fabric grain can be straightened (or "blocked") by folding the fabric from selvage to selvage. Clip the selvage about every 2 inches to relax the lengthwise grain. Pin all the fabric edges together (excluding the folded side). Gently pull on the true bias for a few moments. Repeat this stretching process a few inches away until the fabric is straight and the crossgrain threads are at a 90-degree angle from the lengthwise threads.

Draping Principles

Learning Draping Skills

The techniques by which a designer works to develop a line may vary. This section of the chapter focuses on the designer who chooses to work with muslin or fabric, using a dress form or live model, draping and pinning the pieces together to get the desired style.

The guidelines in this text will direct you in cultivating an awareness of current fashion and silhouettes and help you analyze each design. This will assist you in observing and processing the details of each line in order to acquire a knowledge of fashion that will stimulate your draping and style sense and help you to acquire your own fashion look. The importance of draping a garment artistically to give a sense of excitement takes practice and talent. The results can be quite rewarding.

When draping, one can literally see a design take shape. This text gives draping principles and procedures to enable students to learn the process easily. The handling and use of various fabrics and how to convert original designs into finished garments are illustrated. From the first stage of draping and true- ing basic designs to advanced dress and bias designs, step-by-step demonstrations are illustrated. These steps are consistent through- out the text to help students under- stand the principles of draping.

Draping is the oldest means of creating clothing. It is an art form in fabric. A design is only as exciting as the fabric that makes it. The fabric must inspire you. Many times, the texture and color of the fabric will be the source of inspiration and greatly influence the design. Once the designer has chosen the fabric, the designer is ready to create a

specific style, keeping a pleasing combination of correct proportion, balance, and detail in mind.

Draping a finished design on a dress form or on a live figure is supe- rior to relying exclusively on a flat pattern for a number of reasons.

- Draping assures a proper fitting garment by allowing the designer to actually see how the style falls on the dress form or body.

- Draping allows for experimenta- tion with design features such as yokes, collars, and sleeves.

- Draping enables the designer to see the best placement of layers, pockets, trims, and buttons.

- Draping creates the opportunity to rotate darts or move a seam so that it enhances the line of the garment.

Principles of Balanced Patterns

All designs have a definite relationship with the figure that enables them to hang straight up and down and have crossgrains parallel to the floor. The grainline and crossgrain alignment, in addition to the side seam angle, allows the designer to maintain the correct balance between the front and back of the garment. The garment will twist, drag, or pull when worn if the pieces are not on the correct grainlines and crossgrains.

Outlined in this text are guidelines for understanding and recognizing the key elements of a draped design in order to produce a correctly made style. These principles will enable the designer to achieve a correct hang and fit in the simplest manner and most efficient amount of time.

Maintaining Balance (Plumb Theory)

The following principles should be followed when draping a new design:

- The center front and center back are on perfect grain.

- The bust level line of the front pattern is on perfect crossgrain, allowing the area below the bust level to hang straight up and down.

- The shoulder blade level line of the back bodice is on perfect crossgrain, allowing the area below the shoulder blade level line to hang straight up and down.

- On the front bodice, the center of the princess panel line (centered distance from the bust point to the side seam) is on perfect grain and is parallel to center front. This ensures that the side seam maintains the same angle as the back.

- The armholes must resemble a horseshoe shape. The armholes should also balance—measurement of the back armhole should be 1/2 inch more than the front armhole. The correct shape and balanced amount ensures that the sleeves hang properly.

- The front waistline distance is 1/2 inch larger than the back waistline distance.

- The side seams should be at the same angle, while the center front and center back are parallel. Also, the side seams should be the same shape and length.

NOTE: Balancing a pattern ensures that the garment side seams will hang straight up and down and lie correctly on the body or dress form. This also ensures that the garment is not pitching forwards or backwards.

Balancing a design ensures that the garment side seams will hang straight up and down and lie correctly on the body or dress form.

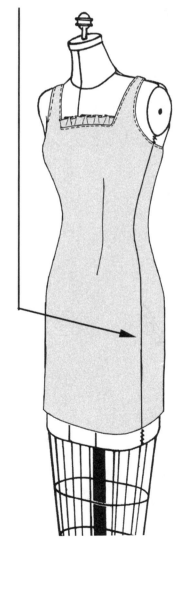

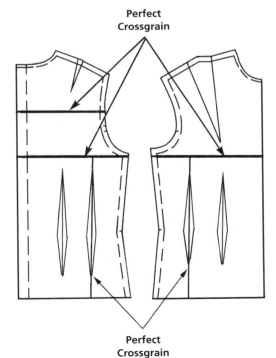

Perfect Crossgrain

Perfect Crossgrain

Draping Fabric on the Dress Form

Draping skills are usually learned on a dress form. The following principles of standard draping skills help create consistency in draping.

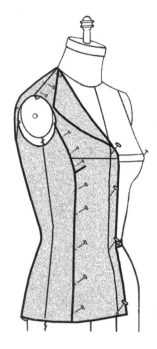

When both sides of the design are the same:
It is almost impossible to drape two sides identically. Therefore, each design is traditionally draped on one side of the dress form. The right side of the front dress form is used to drape the front garment, and the left side of the back dress form is used to drape the back garment. Although the procedure may vary, this is the "standard" rule when fitting and draping a symmetric design.

When the design is asymmetric:
As designs get more complicated, asymmetric designs are a great learning tool for creating fabulous dresses, skirts, and blouses. The left and right sides of these particular designs are draped individually.

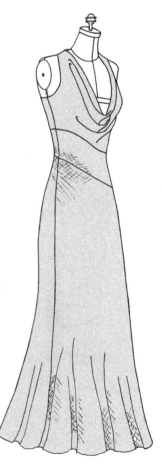

When draping bias designs:
Designs that are created to mold the body or give decorative effect in draping soft folds are usually draped on the bias. These designs are typically draped to both sides of the dress form to accurately get the effect of the bias. Bias designs have great elasticity. They can be molded to the body to create roundness or curviness without darts to create the shaping. Use fabric on the bias for draping soft folds, such as cowls.

Principles and Elements of Design

Gone are the days of one or two distinct fashion looks. The job of getting dressed and being fashionable has gotten harder. Dress codes have been relaxed. Most aspects of our lives can be adapted for any look, whether from the past, present, or future, and still be fashionable, assuming the proportions are right and in line with current styles.

Clothing is three-dimensional, which means it is perceived in the round. As we visualize some of our designs on paper or view them from catalogs and magazines, it is important to remember that this viewpoint is only a two-dimensional shape.

Three components that are vital to creating a successful garment are:

• The garment should be suitable to the style, image, age, occasion, and lifestyle needs.

• The garment should be made with the desired quality levels both in fabrication and construction.

• The garment should possess the necessary aesthetics needed for the design, both in color and detailing.

The fundamental concept of designing new styles is achieved by creating a pleasing combination of all the elements of good design. These elements are: color, value, line, shape, and fabric texture. Keep these features in mind as you are creating new styles.

Color   The first element that people respond to, often selecting or rejecting a garment, is color appeal. Classic colors play a strong role because many people associate various colors with the seasons and holidays. Spring clothing is associated with pastels and garden flowers; fall colors are associated with earth tones and autumn leaves; summer is associated with vivid bright colors and pure white. In addition, glamorous, rich jewel tone colors and bright white are associated with winter garments.

Value   The use of lights and darks is referred to as value. Lighter values are called *tints;* they stand out in the color palette. The darker values are called *shades;* they recede visually in the color palette. The strongest value contrast is pure white against pure black.

Line   The subdivisions created by seams and other design details such as pleats, tucks, and openings are referred to as line.

Shape   The outline of the garment minus the detail is known as the silhouette shape. The shape is what is noticed from a distance. Fashion cycles will concentrate on and feature a specific shape.

Fabric and Texture   Fabric is a sculpturing tool in relating the design to the body. Deciding which fabric will work best for a style comes from experience and observation, as well as trial and error. Considering the fabric quality, texture, weight, and print, as well as the color patterns, helps in the selection of the most appropriate fabric to complement the appearance, durability, maintenance, and comfort of a garment.

Draping Procedure

Whether a designer uses sketches to work from or has a vision in his or her mind, the eyes and hands dictate the line and shape of the fabric. The hands should be free to caress and form the fabric into shape. Learn to use your hands to smooth and manipulate the fabric over the dress form until the fabric eases into position. Feel the design with your fingertips. Manipulate the fabric until the design is what you want. Refine the design, perfect the fit, true up the pattern, and duplicate the second side.

There are some designers who develop their creations by draping directly in the fabric they plan to use for the finished garment. This is most common when draping very soft fabrics or knit designs. And yet, others, especially beginners, use various weights of muslin to develop the initial design. When using muslin, it is important to select a weight that is similar to the fabric of the finished design. Incorrect fabric weight can result in a garment that hangs differently on the figure, resulting in fitting problems.

As you apply the principles of design to each garment, the following guidelines will be done quite consciously, but after long experience, instinctively. Learn to acquire the technical skills in draping that make it possible to carry a design through to completion. When enough experience is acquired, the necessary background for designing will become effortless in creating any original design you can imagine.

Draping Steps

1. Analyze the creative elements of the design. Identify the design details such as body style, style-lines, neckline detail, collars, plackets, garment openings, darts, pleats or fullness variations, garment length, and sleeve types. Determine the draping techniques required for this particular design. Decide how you wish to place the grain of the fabric. Plan the draping sequence.

2. Measure and prepare the approximate length and width of the fabric for the design you have in mind. Draw in the grainline of the fabric.

3. Align and anchor the fabric for the beginning steps, starting with the chosen grainline.

4. After the fabric has been properly aligned on the dress form, work around the figure. You may arrange the fabric in any position, radiating from the apex. Pin the fabric into any silhouette seams, darts, graceful folds, gathers, or drapery for each particular design. Manipulate dart excess, adding fullness and contour draping within the design process. As each design is created, the grainline and crossgrain should be carefully maintained. This grainline and crossgrain alignment allows you to maintain the correct balance between the front and back of the garment.

5. Trim, clip, and cut the excess fabric around the styled area as each section is draped. Continue to check the grain, wrinkles, bulges, gapping, or strain that needs corrections. Keep all grainlines balanced. Otherwise, there will be pulling or puckering when the garment is finished.

6. When the design is completed, remove the fabric from the dress form. True up all lines with the various drafting rulers. Make sure that all dart legs and corresponding style seams match in length.

7. Pin the finished design together and recheck the fit.

Design Development

Much pleasure can be derived from creating original designs. Remember to choose each design with the intention of saturating your mind with general impressions of current fashion trends and silhouette shapes and, at the same time, analyze the subtle fashion changes that influence them, such as trim detail, style lines, and neckline shapes. You must observe and analyze the details of each line and cut in order to acquire a knowledge of fashion and style information. Remember, there are three components that are vital to creating a successful design.

Each year fashion magazines present new trends. As you analyze these newest designs, you are looking at the art of designing new styles, which is represented by creating a pleasing combination of all the elements of good design. Spend time researching various predictives and magazines or visit boutiques to inspire your imagination and create and stimulate the learning process of designing through draping. The knowledge you acquire will provide you with the way to execute all of your creative ideas in an endless variety of designs.

Identify the Design Details

- **Body Style:** basic, princess, dartless, sheath, jacket, knit, sculptured, etc.

- **Stylelines:** princess seams, yoke seams, etc.

- **Neckline Detail:** front or back—high neck, low neck, "V" neck, square neck, etc.

- **Darts or Pleats:** one, two, multiple, etc.

- **Fullness Variations:** from shoulder, from waistline, radiating fullness from side seam, from styleline, or from template design feature

- **Garment Length:** mini, traditional knee length, mid calf, demi-princess, or full length

- **Garment Openings:** front, back, side, double breasted, or none

- **Sleeve Types:** short, long, cuffed or not, bell shape, shirt style, bishop style, or coat style

- **Accent Pieces:** collars, cuffs, plackets, pockets, waistbands, etc., to create the finished look

Apply the Principles of Design

You can add dozens of style options to your basic drapes for exciting new styles with a perfect fit. Then, of course, this would lead you to concentrate on the most important characteristics of every garment. This may be the various stylelines, trims, and shape of the sleeves, and whether skirts are pencil-slim or bell-shaped, short or long, or flared at the side, front, or back.

Finishing Touches Create New Looks

With fashion and styles forever changing, it may be the finishing touches that are new, while the overall line may remain the same. The secret is knowing your basics. The underlying principles of carrying out each design are necessary to practice.

Evaluating a Finished Design

The overall flow and silhouette shape of each design can only be evaluated on a moving person. Therefore, each company experiments by trying its sample garments on models who are typical of the company's customers. Each company evaluates the fashion appeal elements of each design and its suitability for their customers. The garment's overall look may create styles that are meant to be snug and close fitting, while others are meant to be very full and loose. The amount of ease depends upon the fashion trend and each particular design.

There are many aspects of a garment that must be checked and, if necessary, adjusted. Clothes that fit well look attractive and are comfortable to wear without any obvious pulls and wrinkles. The center front, center back, and side seams should hang straight. The darts should taper smoothly toward the fullest part of the body. The sleeves should be comfortable when the arms are lifted and moved. The pants and skirt styles fit comfortably when the model stands, sits, stretches, bends, or walks. The design details, such as collars and pockets, are flattering to the figure. The garment should conceal the figure problems, flatter the face and body, and be pleasingly proportioned.

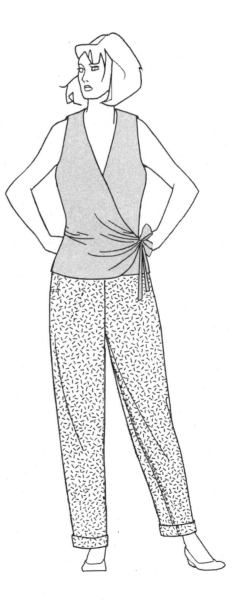

Making a Sample Garment

After the design has been draped in muslin or fabric, the pattern is transferred to pattern paper. The pattern is rechecked to be sure that all seams and notches are correct. The pattern should also have all the pattern symbols that will allow it to be accurately cut and sewn.

Fitting a Sample Garment

Using the completed paper pattern, a "sample garment" is cut and sewn. This sample garment is then fitted on a live model who represents the typical customers of that company. The live model helps the designer see if the garment hangs correctly and has the desired fit, feels comfortable, and adjusts naturally to the activities of the wearer.

Check the Overall Look

Starting from the shoulders, work down and check the grain, darts, and stylelines. Check to see if there is enough ease within the style—is there enough or too much? Will the pants and skirts fit when the model sits or walks? Then proceed to the neckline and check the style features of the neckline, collar, and sleeves. For instance, will the sleeves feel comfortable when the arms are lifted? And, lastly, check the positions of the buttons and buttonholes, pockets, and trimmings. Almost always, the sample will need to be made at least two or three times.

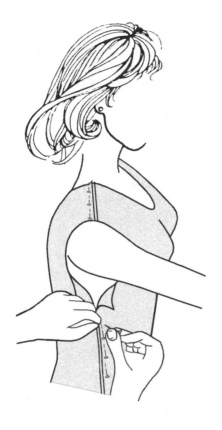

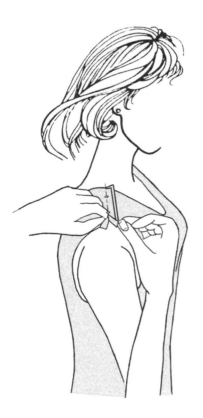

Check the Side Seam Balance, Garment Ease, and Front-to-Back Balance and Grainlines

● **Ease Amount:** Each design has the amount of ease that would be necessary to give the overall look of the design.

Fitting Correction: At this time, the design should be checked for the desired amount of ease wanted for that particular style. Readjust the ease amount by repinning the side seams looser or tighter.

● **Balance Front to Back of the Design:** The front waist measurement of garments is 1 inch larger than the back waist measurement (1/2 inch from center front to the side seam). This difference allows the garment to hang correctly from side seam to side seam.

Fitting Correction: To make the front larger than the back, you will need to add or subtract the side seam and readjust the armholes (see armhole balance below).

● **Balance Side Seams and Grainlines:** If the garment is pulling or twisting from the side seam, this is usually an indication that the side seams and grainlines are not balanced. The front and back side seams should be the same angle off the straight of grain while keeping center front and center back parallel to grain. Also, the side seams should be the same shape and length.

Fitting Correction: To balance side seams and align grainlines, pin the front underarm/side seam corner to the back underarm/side seam corner. At the underarm corner pin, pivot the front pattern until the center front and the center back positions are parallel.

When checking a dartless design, once the garment is balanced, the crossgrain lines at the underarm level should be perfectly parallel to the floor. This allows the area below the bust level line to hang straight up and down, making sure it does not pitch to the front or the back.

NOTE: If the side seams are balanced and the design is still twisting when it is placed on the model, then the problem needs to be corrected by releasing the shoulder seam.

Check the Shoulder Fit and Hang of the Design

● Once the garment is checked at the side seam for ease, balance, and shape, the garment hang from the shoulder and bust should be checked. The shoulder shape must be identical to the body in order for a garment to hang correctly. Just five degrees off in the shoulder slope makes a difference. Each design should hang straight up and down without any wrinkles, sagging, or pulling when placed on a body.

Fitting Correction: If the above problems occur, it will be necessary to open and adjust the shoulder seams to allow the garment to hang properly. For example, the shoulder seam in the back may need an additional amount, while the front will require shortening.

NOTE: If there are major adjustments on the shoulder seam, this adjustment may change the shape of the armhole, making it too large or too small. See the next step for checking armholes.

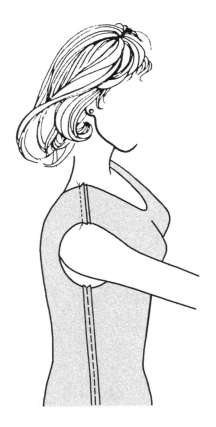

Check for Armhole Balance and Fit

- **Armhole Shape:** Each armhole must resemble a horseshoe shape. The armholes should start at the shoulder joint at the top of the arm, pass through the mid-armhole area, and continue down to the underarm at the side seam.

- **Armhole Balance:** The armholes should balance front to back. In other words, the back armhole measurement should be 1/2 inch longer than the front armhole measurement.

- **Armhole Ease:** The armhole at the side seam should fit comfortably under the armpit, including the desired ease necessary for that particular design. The armhole should fit with enough ease to allow the arm to move freely without binding or gapping.

Fitting Correction—Shape: If the armhole is scooped in too far at the front or back mid-armhole area, the sleeve will pull at this point. Pulling is also an indication that the armholes are not balanced. Also, if the armhole is too high at the armpit, the sleeve will bind.

Fitting Correction—Gapping: A gapping armhole can usually be traced to inadequate shoulder darting and/or shoulder shaping.

(Refer to Trueing the Basic Bodice Armhole on page 61.)

NOTE: The correctly balanced and shaped armhole ensures a properly hanging sleeve. This is why the armholes must be shaped and fitted correctly before checking the sleeve.

Armhole Styles Control Various Looks in Sleeve Design

- **Shorter shoulder length and a smaller overall armhole gives the bodice a youthful look.**

  Fitting Correction: Raise the underarm seam at the armpit up 1/4 inch to 1/2 inch. Also, move the armhole seam at the shoulder in toward the neckline. Using a French curve, reshape the armhole.

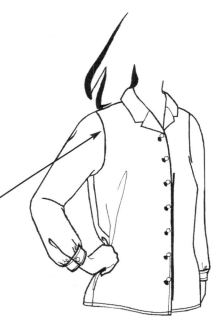

- **A sporty, casual look allows greater sleeve movement by lowering the armhole and extending the shoulder length.**

  Fitting Correction: Lower the underarm seam at the armpit 1 to 1 1/2 inches. Also, move the armhole seam at the shoulder out 1 to 2 inches. Using a vari-form ruler, reshape the armhole, resulting in a very shallow shape. Also, readjust the sleeve that will give a shorter cap and a longer underarm seam (refer to pages 134–137 to make a shirt sleeve).

Check the Sleeve Fit

- The sleeve cap covers the top of the arm at the shoulder joint and smoothly covers the upper arm. The sleeve grainline should fall straight down in the center of the arm and curve slightly forward below the elbow. If the sleeve droops, the sleeve will look sloppy. If the sleeve is too tight, it will impede the movement of the arm and the fabric will pull. The cap of the sleeve must have a small amount of ease in woven fabrics to allow for arm movement (3/4 to 1 1/4 inches). This ease amount will be ease-stitched into the armhole without gathers.

Fitting Corrections:

- If the sleeve is lowered, a more comfortable fit will result, providing that the sleeve has been adjusted and fitted into this new armhole (see below).

- If the fitting model cannot move her arm forward or raise her arm comfortably, this indicates that the underarm section of the sleeve needs to be raised (refer to page 130–133, Adjusting a Sleeve for More Arm Movement).

- If the sleeve cap is too tight, add about 1/2 inch to the back cap, blending it from nothing at the quarter fold back to nothing at the center of the sleeve. This extra amount of back cap fullness allows the sleeve to move forward easier and allows for a fuller cap, especially for arms that are fatter or more muscular. Refer to page 128 for draping the sleeve to check fit.

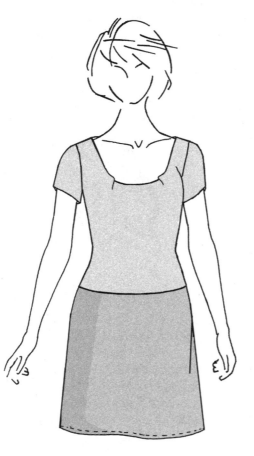

Check Gapping Necklines

- A neckline that gives extra fullness and gaps must be corrected. Because the neckline frames the face and is the focal point on a garment, it is imperative that the necklines fit properly.

Fitting Correction: A gapping neckline indicates that there is too much width across the front from shoulder seam to shoulder seam. Pinch in a curved dart from the neckline to the middle of the armhole. Slash and close the dart when the muslin is removed from the fitting model. With this draping approach, the neckline is made tighter and brings in the shoulder seam toward the neckline.

Other Fitting Considerations

- Sometimes adjustments are needed in the style lines, shoulder widths, and dart positions. Bust darts should point to the fullest part of the bust. Necklines should fit snugly without gapping. If you have a gapping neckline, this will also need to be corrected (see above).

Check the Fit of the Skirt

Because the skirt hangs from the waist, it is obvious that the waistline controls the hang of the grainline and crossgrains. Therefore, when the skirt drape is fitted on the model, the grainline and crossgrain need to be aligned perfectly to the center front and center back of the body. At the same time, the crossgrain and side seams need to be aligned to the body.

● **Check the Balance:** Check the balance of the skirt by placing a pin at the side/waist corner. Pivot the front skirt until the center front is parallel to the center back of the skirt. The skirt front should be 1/2 inch larger than the back skirt. If

this is not the case, adjust the pattern.

● **Align the Grainlines and Crossgrains:** Place the balanced skirt on the model and align the grainlines. At the same time, align the crossgrain at the hip line, making sure that the skirt hangs straight up and down. Also, align the side seam to hang at the side seam of the model.

● **Check Waistline:** Once grainline and crossgrain are aligned, smooth the fabric around the waistline of the model and readjust the waistline of the garment to match the waistline of the model.

Check the Fit of Pants

The fitting of the pant has several items that need to be addressed. The waist and crotch shapes control the overall look. In general, it should be well balanced and hang without wrinkles, sagging, or pulling.

● **Sew a Sample:** For the first pants fitting, it is suggested that the design be sewn in muslin. Also, allow an extra inch on the waistline seam. Stitch the pant with a basting stitch.

● **Align Hip Level and Crotch Level:** NOTE: It may be necessary to release the waistband. Align the hip level and crotch level of the pants parallel to the floor. Position the pants crotch to a comfortable wearing position. Be sure to keep the pant "hang" straight up and down. Do not let the pants twist.

● **Back Crotch Smile:** If the back crotch area shows a "smile" in the fabric, just below the tush, this is an indication that the back crotch, at the deepest point of the curve, needs to be scooped in. Drape the

back crotch in about 1/2 inch. You will see the "smile" disappear.

● **Front Crotch Pull:** If the front crotch area shows a "pull" at the curved point of the front crotch, this is an indication that the front crotch shape needs to be a softer curve. Blend the curve out about 3/8 inch.

● **Mark the Waistline:** Once the crotch line is correct, you will be able to mark the waistline at the waist of the model. Tie string or twill tape around the waistline of the pant where you want to wear the pants. Align darts or pleats or evenly distribute any fullness around the waistline. Mark the waistline with a pencil or felt tip pen.

● **Reshape the Legging and Hip Side Seam:** This is a personal preference as to the shape of the design you would like for each styled pant. Pin and shape the side seam to your desired shaping. Pin the inseam to your desired shaping. Many times the inseam does not need any extra shaping.

Chapter Four

Draping Terminology

Notching Theory

Notches are the "road signs" that inform an operator which garment piece sews to which piece. Each notch is noted with a pencil marking on the finished drape. Notches help to identify where pattern pieces should be matched. If the garment is properly notched, the operator can sew together a garment design quickly and correctly. Therefore, it is important that a patternmaker understands why and where to place notches on a pattern.

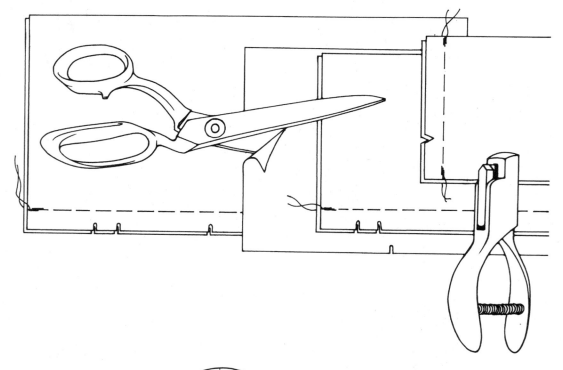

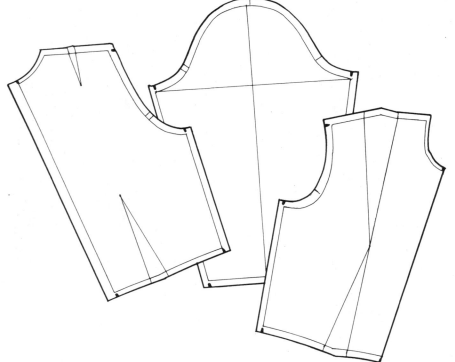

Seam Allowance Notches

Manufacturers save money by having as few notches as possible within the finished pattern. To use fewer notches, do not notch the seam allowances of the pattern. Because sewing operators always know how much seam allowances are within the garment, this is readily accepted.

Many times a student has difficulty learning where notches are to be placed on a drape or a complete pattern.

Notching Guidelines

The following rules and guidelines will help the patternmaker correctly place a sufficient number of notches to help guide the placement of notches and enable the operator to sew together the garment.

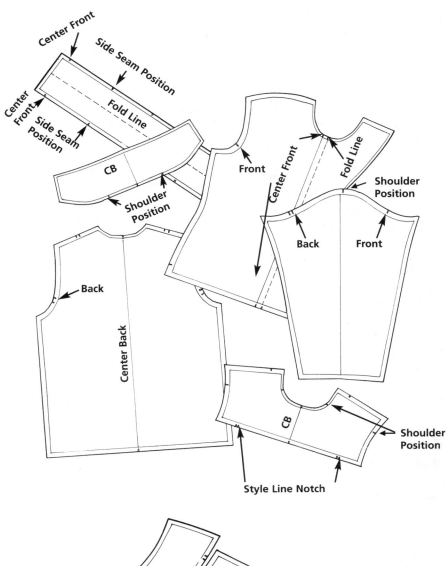

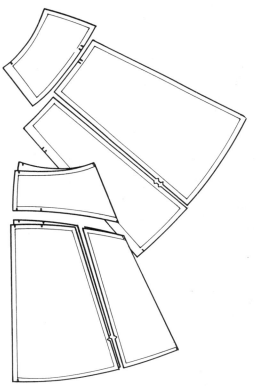

Always Notch

Center Front Positions All center front locations of blouses, bodices, skirts, and pants should be notched.

Center Back Positions All center back locations of blouses, bodices, skirts, pants, and collars should be notched.

Shoulder Positions All shoulder positions of collars, sleeves, and yokes should be notched.

Side Seam Positions All side seam positions of waistbands should be notched.

All Foldlines Hems, pleats, darts, and foldlines of attached facings are common areas where foldline notches are necessary.

Identify Front Pattern Pieces Single notch.

Identify Back Pattern Pieces Double notch.

NOTE: When pattern pieces look very similar and both have a center fold, the center fold notches will identify all front positions with a *single notch* and the center back position with a *double notch*. A typical garment needing this type of notching is a pull-on blouse, an elastic waist skirt, or a top-and-under collar.

Guidelines for Notching Stylelines

After fully understanding which positions always need to be notched, the patternmaker must apply the following guidelines to correctly notch all stylelines:

- A notch must match a notch or seamline.

- Notch the pattern so it can be identified as *front* or *back*.

- Do not center the notches in a styleline.

- Do not allow the pattern pieces to flip.

- All stylelines must be notched so they say "sew me to me."

Glossary of Draping Terms

The following is a useful source of terms related to draping garments. These terms should be helpful to the educator as well as the student and design room professional in offering a quick reference to achieve a desired draping technique. Each term is defined to offer a quick understanding of the facts.

Apex   The highest point of a bust on a dress form or live model. In draping, the apex is a reference point for establishing the crossgrain position on the front bodice muslin.

Balance   The matching of grains and adjacent pattern sections. When trueing, lines on patterns should correspond with lines and measurements on the figure. All patterns have a definite relationship with the figure that enables the garment to hang straight up and down (plumb) and be parallel to the floor. The garment will twist, drag, or pull when worn if the pieces are not on the correct grainlines and crossgrains.

Armhole Balance   This allows a set-in sleeve to hang slightly forward and follow the curvature of the arm. To achieve this balance, the back armhole should measure 1/2 inch larger than the front armhole and have a "horseshoe" shape. This extra 1/2-inch back armhole distance also keeps the back bodice distance extended to the front shoulder seam, keeping the shoulder blade level at a perfect crossgrain.

Pant Leg Seam   The back pant leg at the ankle/hem should measure at least 1 inch more than the front leg ankle. This 1-inch difference allows a correct blend into the longer back crotch distance. Otherwise, the legs of the pants will twist and pull.

Pants Crotch Seam Balance   The back crotch measurement should measure 2 inches longer than the front crotch. This will prevent pants from pulling or sagging.

Perpendicular Line   The front bust level of the body, the shoulder blade level on the body, and the hip level on the body should be parallel to the floor. The crossgrains of garments should always be on these lines. Otherwise, the garment will drag and pull downward or upward.

Plumb Lines   The center front of the body and the center back of the body should always be vertical to the floor. Therefore, the grainline of the garment should be parallel to these lines. Otherwise, the garment will twist or pull.

Side Seam Balance   The front and back side seams should be the same shape and length. In a fitted bodice, side seams and flared skirt side seams should be the same angle off the straight grain. To drape a torso, shift, or fitted skirt, the side seam should be parallel to the center front/back grain.

Waistline Balance   The front waist measurement of garments is 1 inch larger than the back waist measurement. This difference allows garments to hang correctly from side seam to side seam.

Bias   A line diagonally across the grain of the fabric that offers the greatest stretchability. True bias is at a 45-degree angle.

Blend   A technique that helps form a smooth, continuous line or smoothly shapes discrepancies of marks or dots made on the muslin drape. Sleeve seams, princess lines, waistlines, and skirt gores are the most common seams needing blending.

Block   A technique to shape the fabric by pulling and realigning it on grain while pressing with steam.

Break Point   The point of a controlled turn, roll, or flare, usually relating to lapels, shawl collars, revere collars, and notched collars.

Center Back   A defined place that indicates the exact center of the pattern or garment in relation to the true center back of a figure.

Center Front   A defined place that indicates the exact center of the pattern or garment in relation to the true center front of a figure.

Clip   A small cut into the seam allowance that extends almost to the stitch line. It is used on curved seams to release strain and help the seam lie flat when turned, as in necklines, or in corners of squared seams, as in collars, facings, and necklines.

Concave Curve   An inside curved seam forming an inward arc, as in armholes and necklines.

Convex Curve   An outward curved seam forming a rounded curve, as on the outer edge of scallops, caplets, Peter Pan collars, and shawl collars.

Crease   Folding and finger pressing the fabric along the grain or structural line.

Crossmarks   A mark or set of marks placed on a drape or pattern to indicate the point at which corresponding pieces or garment sections (style lines, shoulder, yokes, collars, front, or back) are to be matched, shirred, or joined.

Crotch Seam   The curved seam that is formed at the point where pant legs meet.

Cut in One   Two or more pattern sections that are cut as one piece, such as an attached front facing with the bodice or blouse front, or a sleeve with a bodice.

Dart   To take up excess fabric of a specified width and taper it to nothing at one or both ends. Used to aid in fitting the garment over the body curves.

Dart Legs   The stitch line on both sides of the dart.

Dots   A pencil mark placed on a draped muslin or fabric to record the seam lines or style lines. Used as the guide mark for trueing.

Ease   The even distribution of slight fullness when one section of a seam is joined to a slightly shorter section without forming gathers or tucks. Used to shape set-in sleeves, princess seams, and other areas.

Ease Allowance   The amount of excess fabric added to the draped pattern to make garments more comfortable and allow for easier movement.

Fabric Excess   The amount of extra fabric manipulated into designated areas (such as shoulder, waist, and side bust) to help create body shape and garment style lines.

Fold   A fabric ply that doubles back on itself, thereby forming an underlay to create darts, pleats, tucks, or attached facings.

Gather   To draw up fabric fullness on a line of stitching.

Grain   See Chapter 3, page 20.

Guide Lines on Muslin   Directional lines and markings that indicate the grain, crossgrain, center front, center back, shoulder blade, bust level, apex, hip level, and side seam. These lines are drawn on the prepared muslin to facilitate correct draping.

Master Pattern   Basic pattern, made from specific measurements, that is used as a template for tracing rather than cutting. It may be used to develop other patterns.

Match   To bring notches or other construction markings on two pieces together.

Muslin Shell   A basic sample garment made from muslin fabric as an aid during the styling and fitting processes.

Notch   See Notching Theory, pages 36–37.

Panels   A premeasured piece of muslin used to drape a specific design. These premeasured pieces are usually 4 to 10 inches larger than the finished length and width of the pattern piece. If a piece is too large, the weight of the fabric panel may cause an inaccurate drape.

Pivot   The shifting or moving of a pattern from a marked position toward a designated guide line.

Ply   One layer of fabric when laying out fabric to be cut. (pl: plies)

Princess Panel   The area of the dress form that extends from the princess seam to the armhole and side seams.

Seam   Two or more edges of fabric are held together and sewn using a variety of stitches. Seams should be well constructed and appropriate for the fabric, type of garment, and location on the garment.

Seam Allowance   The amount of fabric allowed for seams in joining together sections of a garment. Seam allowances must be added to any edge that is to be joined to another. The width of the seam allowance depends on the location of the seam and the price range of the manufacturer.

Collars, Facings and Necklines, Armholes, and Other Curves   These elements require seam allowances ranging from l/4 to 1/2 inch. This allowance saves time in trimming these areas after sewing the seam.

Stitched Seam   Garments that require a specially stitched seam, such as those made of knit fabrics or sleepwear, require seam allowances from 1/4 to 1/2 inch.

Traditional Seam Allowances   Elements such as shoulder seams, style lines, and side seams require an additional 1/2 to 1 inch seam allowance.

Zipped Seams   These seams, which require zippers and are used for fitting and/or alterations, require a 1 inch seam allowance.

Selvage   The narrow, firmly woven finished edge along both lengthwise edges of the fabric that does not ravel.

Shirr   A technique to gather up fabric on the stitch line where fullness in the garment is desired. Shirring is sometimes thought of as multiple rows of gathers.

Side Seam   A defined place on a pattern or garment that indicates the point at which the front and back of a garment is sewn together.

Slash   A straight cut (longer than a clip) from the outer edge of the fabric into the style line of the garment. A slash is made to relieve tension in the muslin, which allows the drape to fit around the curves of the body.

Squared Line   A straight line drawn perpendicular from another line. An L-square ruler is usually used to create a perfect perpendicular line.

Stitch Line The line designated for stitching the seam, generally 5/8 inch, 1/2 inch, or 1/4 inch from the cut edge of patterns.

Style Lines Any seam line other than shoulder seams, armhole seams, or side seams. A style line usually runs from one point of a garment to another point. For example, a yoke runs from side seam to side seam; a shoulder princess seam runs from shoulder seam to waistline seam.

Transferring The process of pinning and tracing all the fabric markings onto the pattern paper. Some designers prefer to transfer and true up muslin drapes on the dotted paper.

Trim (Cut) To cut away excess fabric and make the seam narrower after it has been stitched. Also, to remove or eliminate bulk and excess fabric in corners at any point before turning.

Trueing The process of blending the markings, dots, and cross marks made during the draping process. Trueing establishes continuous seams, style lines, darts, or dart variations. Some designers prefer to transfer and true up muslin drapes on the dotted paper, while others prefer to true up directly onto muslin. See pages 56–62 for instructions on the process of trueing.

Underlay The underside of a draped design that is made when establishing darts, pleats, and extensions.

Vanishing Point The tapered, finished point of a dart.

Part Two

Basic Foundation Patterns

When a manufacturer develops a new clothing line, one of the first requirements is a set of foundation patterns (blocks). These foundation patterns, which should match the proportion, size, and fit of the target customers, are created by draping fabric onto a professional dress form. Because of the importance of these patterns, sufficient time should be allowed to drape, fit,

readjust, and refit before a finished set of patterns is prepared.

This unit illustrates various draping methods to create the foundation patterns for the basic bodice, skirt, and shift. Understanding the many uses and applications of these foundation patterns is an important key to good design theory. These foundation patterns provide the designer and

manufacturer with a constant fit and silhouette, ease allowance, armhole size, waistline measurement, and desired length. Correct use of these foundation patterns will help save valuable time in both fittings and patternmaking. Once the basic skills have been mastered, other designs will be easier to develop.

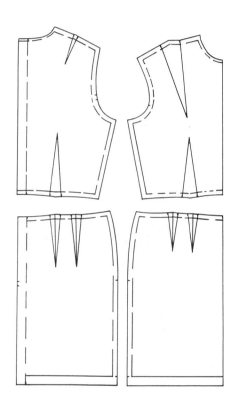

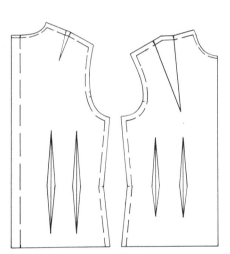

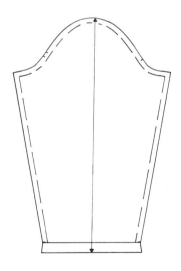

The **basic bodice and skirt slopers** are the most common foundation patterns used to create a three-dimensional design from a flat pattern. These slopers are used to develop other foundation patterns. Darts, tucks, style lines, or gathers can also be created by readjusting the dart areas of these foundation patterns.

The **shift/torso bodice sloper** is a hip-length bodice with a shoulder or side bust dart and sometimes with waistline fisheye darts. This versatile foundation pattern is used to design blouses or dresses that require a fitted armhole. It is also used to make flat pattern designs, which have no waist fitting seams, with a straight-tapered or flared side seam fit. Dart areas on these foundation patterns can also be converted into tucks, style lines, or gathers.

For the sake of time, the **basic sleeve sloper** is created using the pattern drafting method. However, this design is not complete until it is checked for balance, fit, and hang directly on the dress form. See pages 14–16 for a pattern for a sleeve form and instructions to prepare the arm. The chapters include details on how to transfer the finished drapes into complete patterns.

Chapter Five

Basic Bodice Blocks/Slopers

By studying the various draping steps in this chapter, the designer should be able to:

• Recognize grain and crossgrain of fabric in relationship to the bust level line, shoulder blade level, and direction and placement of darts.

• Take a flat piece of fabric and make it fit the curves of the body.

• Manipulate and shape a flat piece of fabric to create darts.

• Develop the correct amount of ease allowance, armhole size, waistline shape, measurement, and balance.

• Check and analyze the results of the draping process in order to analyze the fit, hang, balance, proportion, and true up.

Basic Two-Dart Bodice Sloper

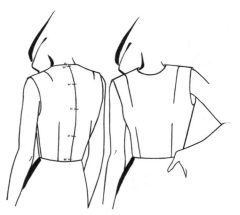

Front and back basic bodices use darts to control a fitted waist seam. Darts are the key to the fit of a woman's individual figure. Designs emphasizing a fitted silhouette may be achieved when using this darted, waist seam basic pattern.

The basic block pattern is also used to make other basic patterns or garment designs. It is important, therefore, to drape carefully and accurately.

The Fitted Waist-Seam Bodice Block/Sloper

Definition, Theory, & Principles

When a manufacturer develops a new clothing line, one of the first requirements is a set of foundation patterns (blocks). These foundation patterns should match the proportion, size, and fit of the target customers. They provide the designer and manufacturer with a constant fit and silhouette, ease allowance, armhole size, waistline measurement, and desired length. As draping skills are learned throughout this text, a greater variety of foundation patterns (blocks) are developed by draping. One will experience the method of making correctly fitting blocks and designs by draping, rather than making blocks through a flat pattern method. As one drapes either a block or a complete design, the draping techniques will allow correct fit, ease, and proportion much more quickly.

To help students learn the theory and principles of the various foundation patterns (blocks), a "Definition, Theory, & Principles" section has been placed in the introductions to the most commonly used foundation patterns. These guidelines will help one choose which block is needed to develop various designs. Correct use of these foundation patterns will help save valuable time in both fittings and patternmaking.

Definition

The **fitted waist-seam bodice block/sloper** is also known as the **basic bodice.** A front and back basic bodice uses darts to control a fitted waist seam. Darts are the key to the fit of a woman's individual figure. Designs with a fitted waist-seam silhouette may be made when using this darted waist-seam basic pattern. This basic block pattern is also used as the guiding pattern to make other basic patterns.

In addition, the basic block is the most common foundation pattern used to make a flat pattern design into a three-dimensional design. Also, because most pattern theory begins with the many usages of this basic block, it is also the block most often used to teach basic pattern skills.

Variations of the Basic Bodice Block

1. The most common version of this block has a shoulder and waist dart with the waist-fitted seam. This is also the block to make other blocks. This basic bodice block creates a waist dart by picking up the excess fabric between the center of the princess line and center front. With the waist dart in place, the contour of the waistline controls the shape and the side seam placement, thus allowing the excess fabric to be placed into the shoulder dart, which controls the bust cup. This balanced pattern now allows the side seams to be free of any darting, enables the subsequent blocks to have squared or shaped side seams, and will allow the garment to hang straight up and down.

2. Another version is the side bust dart and waist dart with the waist-fitted seam. Once the shoulder/waist basic block is made and the side seams are checked for balance, then the shoulder dart amount may be moved into the side bust area.

3. Another version is a wide single waist dart with the waist-fitted seam. This style of block is also known as the one-dart basic front bodice. This one-dart basic bodice is made by draping the shoulder and waistline excess into the waistline fullness, resulting in one single dart at the waistline. A patternmaker may prefer to use this sloper to manipulate darts rather than using the basic two-dart sloper. This choice is usually made when the patternmaker will save time by starting with the one-dart block.

Theory

All three versions of the basic block (**shoulder and waist dart, side bust dart,** and **single waist dart** with the waist-fitted seam) may be used when:

- The design has a fitted waist seam.

- The dart amount has been converted into tucks, stylelines, or gathers or simply kept as a dart somewhere within the design.

The shoulder and waist dart version must be used when making another block. When the front and back side seams are at the same angle, the side seams may be aligned perfectly from the grainline, starting from the underarm corner. Therefore, when this new pattern is cut out of fabric and is placed on a figure, the garment will hang straight up and down and the hems will be parallel to the floor.

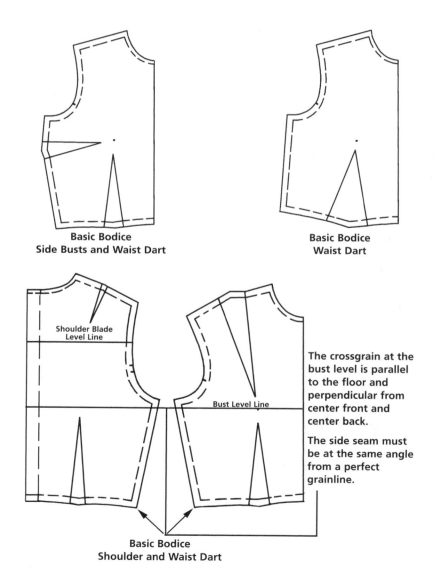

Basic Bodice
Side Busts and Waist Dart

Basic Bodice
Waist Dart

Shoulder Blade
Level Line

Bust Level Line

Basic Bodice
Shoulder and Waist Dart

The crossgrain at the bust level is parallel to the floor and perpendicular from center front and center back.

The side seam must be at the same angle from a perfect grainline.

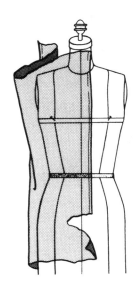

1 **Measure the length for the front bodice** along the straight of grain from the neckband to the waist and add 5 inches.

Snip and tear the fabric at this length.

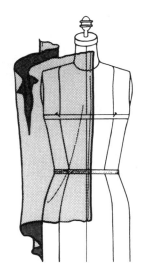

2 **Measure the width for the front bodice** along the cross-grain from the center front of the dress form to the side seam at the bust level and add 5 inches.

Snip and tear the fabric at this width, then block and press the fabric.

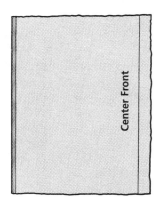

3 **Draw the center front grain-line** 1 inch from the torn edge and press under.

NOTE: The selvage is toward your left hand and the torn edge is toward your right.

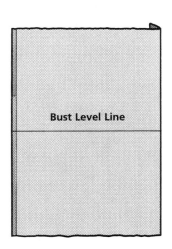

4 **Draw a perfect crossgrain line that will represent the bust level line.** With an L-square ruler, draw a perfect crossgrain line in the center of the fabric panel.

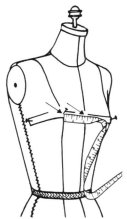

5 **a. Measure the apex** on the dress form the distance from the center front to the apex.

b. Measure and crossmark the apex this distance on the bust level of the fabric.

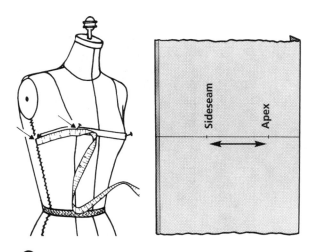

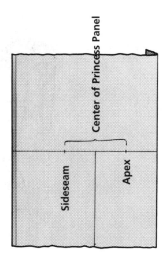

6 **a. Measure from the apex to the side seam** at the bust level on the dress form and add 1/8-inch ease.

b. Measure and crossmark this side seam distance on the bust level of the fabric.

7 **a. Draw the center of the princess panel line.** Divide in half the distance from the apex to the side seam at the bust level.

b. Draw a line parallel to the center front grainline at this divided position, squaring down from the bust level, using an L-square ruler.

Notes

Basic Back Bodice: *Preparing the Fabric*

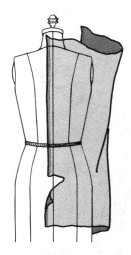

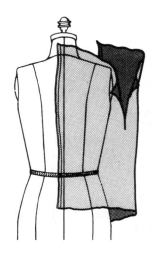

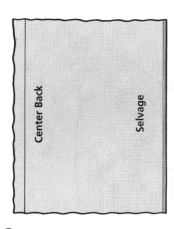

1 **Measure the length for the back bodice** along the straight of grain from the neckband to the waist and add 5 inches.

Snip and tear the fabric at this length.

2 **Measure the width for the back bodice** along the cross-grain from the center back seam to the side seam at the underarm and add 5 inches.

Snip and tear the fabric at this width.

3 **Draw the center back grainline** 1 inch from the torn edge and press under.

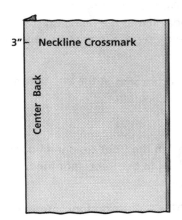

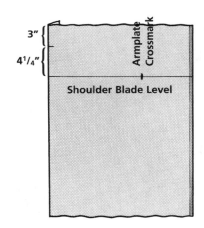

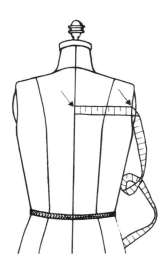

4 **Crossmark the center back neckline position** 3 inches below the top of the fabric on the center back grainline.

5 **Draw the shoulder blade level line.**

a. Measure down 4 1/4 inches from the back neckline mark.

b. Draw a perfect crossgrain line, using an L-square ruler at this 4 1/4-inch position.

NOTE: This 4 1/4-inch measurement represents one-fourth of the distance from the center back neck to the waist for a size 8 or 10.

6 **a. Measure the distance from center back to the armplate** at the shoulder blade level of the dress form.

b. Crossmark this back shoulder distance on the fabric at the shoulder blade level line.

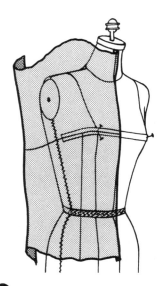

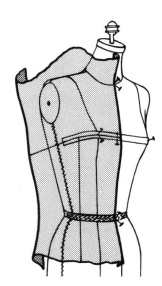

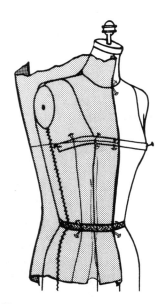

1 **Pin the apex mark** on the fabric to the apex position on the dress form.

2 **Pin the center front grainline fold** of the fabric to the center front position of the dress form.

Anchor pins at center front neck and center front waist. An additional pin may be needed at the bust level tape.

3 **a. Put a pin on the center of the princess panel position at the waistline** on the dress form and use it as a guide for the following steps.

b. Pin the center of the princess panel line of the fabric exactly in the center of the princess panel of the dress form.

c. Anchor pins at the waistline and the crossgrain.

4 **Pin the front crossgrain parallel to the floor** (not the bust level tape).

NOTE: The reason for centering the princess panel line is to verify that the crossgrain line is perfectly aligned. Check that the lengthwise grain is parallel to the center front and that the crossgrain is parallel to the floor.

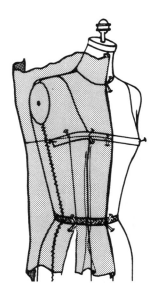
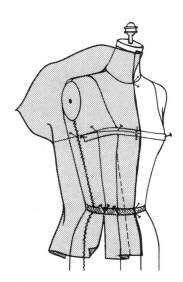
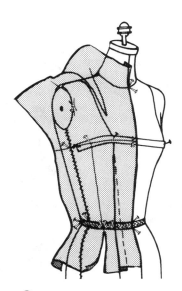

5 **Clip the waistline fabric at the center of the princess panel** from the bottom edge up to the waist seam tape.

NOTE: Overclipping the waistline will result in a tight waistline fit and the lack of necessary ease. See page 63 for correct finished ease.

6 **Pin and drape the front waist dart.** The excess fabric that falls between the center of the princess panel and the center front waist position will become the front waist dart. Be careful not to overstretch the waistline or the rib cage area.

a. Crossmark the princess seam at the waistline. Smooth the fabric from center front to the princess seam at the waistline and crossmark. Crease the fabric at the waistline/princess seam crossmark.

b. Pin the excess fabric on the princess seam. The excess fabric is creased at the princess seam crossmark and folded toward the center front. Taper the dart to nothing toward the bust apex.

7 **Smooth and drape the remainder of the waistline.** Smooth the fabric across the waist tape until the fabric passes the side seam. Pin at the side seam/waist corner. Leave a 1/8-inch pinch at the waistline. Also, do not mold the rib cage area.

8 **Pin and drape the side seam and the beginning of the shoulder.**

a. Smooth the excess fabric past the side seam. Be careful not to pull or mold the fabric across the rib cage area.

b. Smooth the fabric up and over the dress form armplate to the shoulder. Create a 1/4-inch–1/4-inch pinch at the screw level (middle at ridge) of the armhole. This ensures that the armhole does not become too tight. Pin in place. Leave all excess fabric in the shoulder area.

NOTE: It is not necessary to make the 1/4-inch–1/4-inch pinch if using a foam form or any amount of arm.

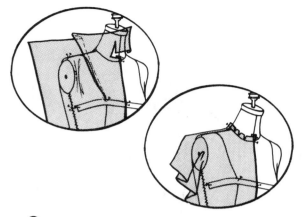

9 Drape the front neckline. Trim and clip the neckline at intervals. Smooth the excess fabric around the neck area.

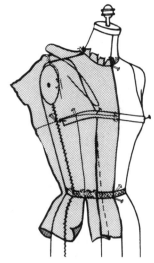

10 Drape and smooth the fabric over the shoulder/neckline seam of the dress form to a point just past the princess seam. Pin in place. Crossmark the princess seam and the shoulder.

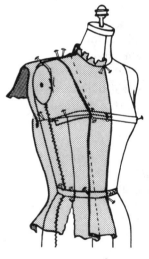

11 Drape the front shoulder dart. The excess fabric that falls between the shoulder/neckline and the shoulder/armhole area will become the amount of excess fabric in the shoulder dart. The larger the bust, the larger the dart; the smaller the bust, the smaller the dart.

a. Crease the fabric at the shoulder/princess seam crossmark.

b. Pin the excess fabric on the princess seam. The excess fabric is folded at the princess seam crossmark and folded toward the center front neck. Taper the dart to nothing toward the bust apex.

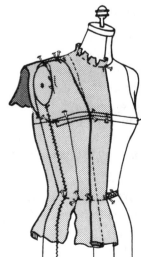

12 Mark all key areas of the dress form to the fabric.

a. Neckline: Crossmark at center front neck and at neckline/shoulder corner. Lightly mark remainder of neckline.

b. Shoulder seam and shoulder dart: Lightly mark shoulder seam and crossmark shoulder dart and shoulder ridge corner.

c. Armplate:
  • Top at shoulder seam ridge.
  • Middle at screw level.
  • Crossmark bottom at side seam.

d. Side seam: Lightly mark.

e. Waistline and waist dart: Crossmark at center front waist, side seam waist, and both sides of the dart.

Basic Back Bodice: Draping Steps

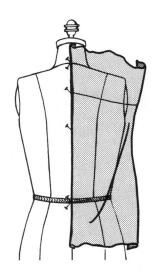

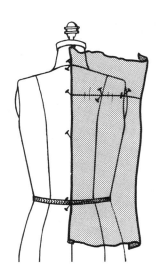

1 **Pin the center back grainline** fold of the fabric to the center back position on the dress form.

2 **Align the neckline position mark** of the fabric to the center back neck position on the dress form.

3 **Pin and drape the back cross-grain line** of the fabric to the shoulder blade level on the dress form. Pin the armplate crossmark 1/4 inch away from the plate (at the armhole ridge). Distribute the excess ease along the shoulder blade level.

NOTE: This line is correctly draped when the drape hangs freely and evenly without any drag or pulled-down look. Also, the lower edge of the drape should hang parallel to the floor.

4 **Pin and drape in the back waistline dart** 7 inches long by 1 1/4 inches wide, as follows:

a. Smooth the fabric toward the side seam until the fabric passes the princess seam. Place a crossmark at the princess/waist seam.

b. Measure and crossmark the waistline 1 1/4 inches toward the side seam from the princess seam/waist crossmark.

c. Measure and crossmark 7 inches up at the middle of the dart, remaining parallel to center back (on grain). Refer to the illustration.

d. Fold the back waistline dart in place. At the waistline, fold the princess seam crossmark to the 1 1/4-inch crossmark. Taper the dart to nothing at the 7-inch mark.

NOTE: The waist dart increases or decreases in width and length as sizes get larger or smaller from a standard size 8 or 10.

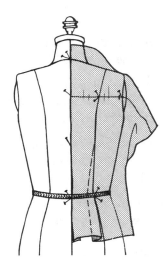

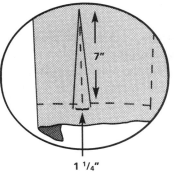

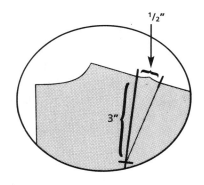

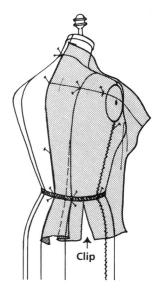

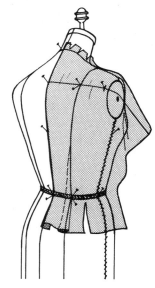

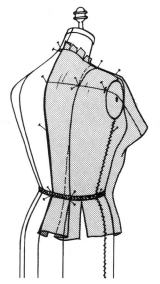

5 Clip, smooth, and drape the waistline.

a. Clip the waistline fabric at the center of the princess panel up to the bottom of the waist seam tape.

NOTE: Overclipping the waistline will result in a tight waistline fit and the lack of necessary ease.

b. Smooth the fabric across the waist tape until the fabric passes the side seam. Pin at the side seam/waist corner.

6 Drape the back side seam.
Smooth the fabric past the side seam and flat over the dress form. Be careful not to mold or distort the back rib cage area. Pin in place.

7 Clip, smooth, and drape the back neckline.

a. Carefully trim the excess fabric around the neck area, clipping at intervals.

b. Smooth the fabric over the shoulder/neckline area of the dress form and pin in place.

8 Drape in the back shoulder dart, 3 inches long by 1/2 inch wide:

a. Smooth the fabric over the shoulder seam, starting at the neckline and moving toward the princess seam, and crossmark.

b. Measure toward the armhole 1/2 inch from the princess seam at the shoulder (width of back shoulder dart) and crossmark.

c. Measure down 3 inches on the princess seam from the shoulder seam and crossmark.

d. Fold the back shoulder dart in place. Fold the fabric from the princess seam crossmark to the 1/2-inch crossmark. Taper the dart to nothing at the 3-inch crossmark.

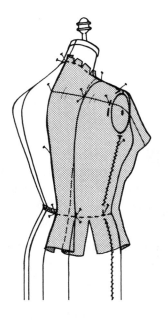

9 **Mark all key areas of the dress form to the fabric.**

a. Neckline: Crossmark at center back neck and at neckline/shoulder corner. Lightly mark remainder of neckline.

b. Shoulder seam and shoulder dart: Lightly mark shoulder seam and crossmark shoulder dart and shoulder ridge corner.

c. Armplate:
- Mark top at shoulder seam ridge.
- Mark middle at screw level.
- Mark bottom of the plate at the side seam crossmark.

d. Side seam: Lightly mark.

e. Waistline and waist dart: Crossmark at center back waist, side seam waist, and both sides of the dart.

Notes

Trueing the Basic Two-Dart Bodice Drape

Some designers prefer to transfer and true up muslin drapes on the dotted paper. Others prefer to true up directly onto muslin. This author recognizes that there is more than one way of creating a design. Illustrations of steps 2 through 10 are examples of the trueing process on the actual muslin drape.

Back

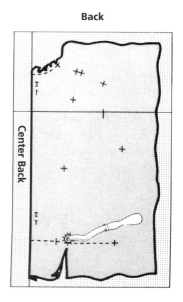

Front

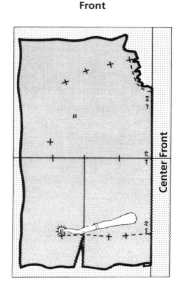

1 **Remove the fabric from the dress form and lay it flat on the table.** If you are planning to true up the fabric onto paper complete the following steps:

a. Draw in the straight of grain and crossgrain on the pattern paper. Place the fabric on top of the paper, matching the straight of grain and crossgrain.

b. Transfer all the fabric markings using a trace wheel.

Back

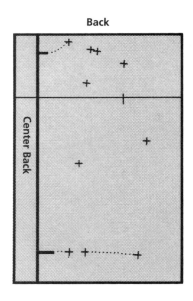

Front

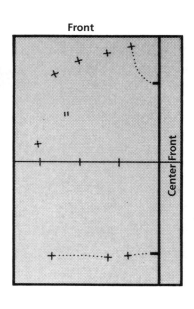

2 **Draw a short 90-degree angle at:**

a. Center front neck **(1/4 inch)**

b. Center front waist **(1/2 inch)**

c. Center back neck **(1 inch)**

d. Center back waist **(1 inch)**

Back

Front

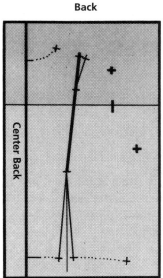

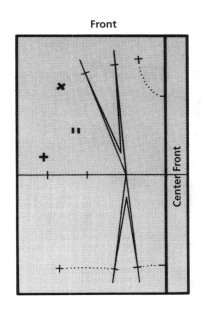

3 Draw in the four darts using a straight ruler.

a. Front waist dart: Locate the center of the dart at the waistline crossmarks. At this center position, extend a grainline to the apex. If necessary, recenter the dart until it is on grain. Draw the dart legs 1 inch from the apex through the waist dart crossmarks. The center of the dart should be on the grain.

b. Front shoulder dart: Draw the dart 1 inch from the apex through the shoulder dart crossmarks.

c. Back waist dart: Locate the center of the dart at the waistline crossmarks. At this center position, extend a grainline the length of the dart (new vanishing point). Draw lines from the vanishing point (point of the dart) through waist dart crossmarks.

d. Back shoulder dart: The vanishing point of the back waist dart goes through the shoulder dart crossmarks nearest the neckline. This line will not be exactly on the original princess markings. Measure down 3 inches on the vanishing point line and connect the other shoulder dart crossmark.

Back

Front

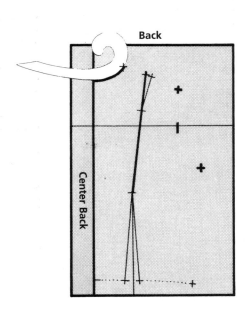

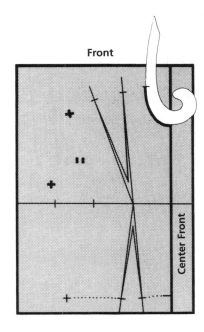

4 Draw in the front and back necklines using a french curve ruler, as illustrated. Be sure to blend lines smoothly into the 90-degree angle at center front and center back necklines. Connect the crossmarks at the shoulder seam.

Back   **Front**

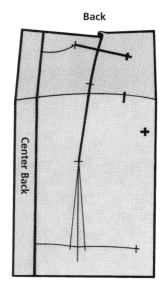
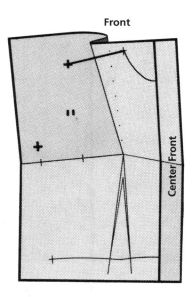

5 Draw in the front and back
shoulder seams. Fold the
shoulder darts into position.
Using a straight ruler, blend from
the shoulder neck corner to the
shoulder ridge corner in one
continuous line.

Back   **Front**

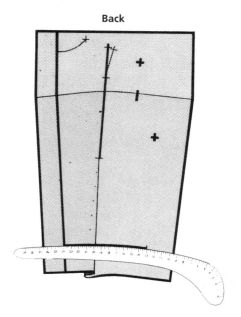
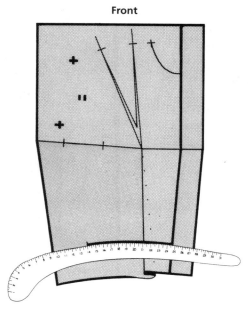

6 Draw in the front and back
waistline. Fold the waist dart
closed. Using a hip curve ruler,
blend the waistline smoothly from
center front to the side seam.
Then blend the waistline from
center back to the side seam.

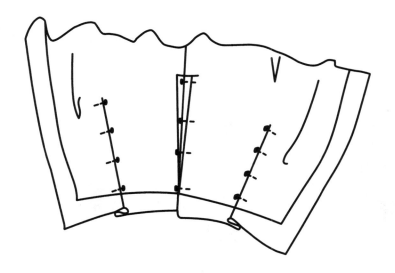

7 Check the waistline curve. Pin the trued side seams together. The waistline should be drawn in one continuous, smooth line. If this is not the case, the drape is probably incorrect.

Sometimes a slight readjustment is needed to get a smooth continuous curve. This is done by lowering the side seam/waist corner 1/4 inch. If this does not solve the problem, check the drape for accuracy by redraping and rechecking all draping steps.

8 Check the front to back waistline distance (waistline balance).

a. Measure from center front to the side seam.

b. Measure from center back to the side seam.

The front waistline should be 1/2 inch longer than the back measurement. If this is not the case, readjust the side seam at the waistline by adding and subtracting the difference.

9 Draw in the front and back side seam positions. Using a straight ruler, connect the crossmark at the armplate/side seam to the side seam/waist crossmark.

Back   **Front**

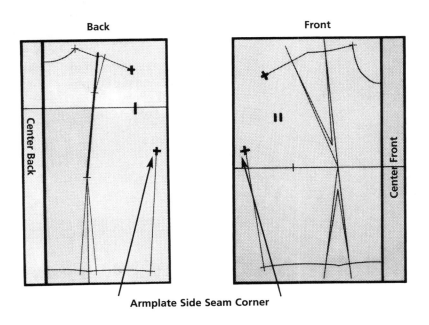

Center Back

Center Front

Armplate Side Seam Corner

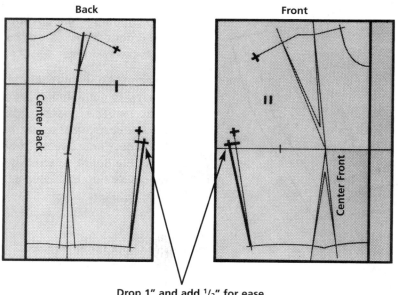

Back **Front**

Center Back

Center Front

Drop 1″ and add ¹/₂″ for ease

 Add side seam ease.

a. Drop the front and back side seams 1 inch. At the underarm/side seam position, drop and crossmark the side seam 1 inch from the armplate/side seam crossmarks.

b. Add 1/2 inch body ease to the front and back side seam/armhole corner and crossmark.

c. Draw in a new side seam for both the front and back. Connect the 1-inch crossmark with the 1/2-inch ease crossmark and draw in a new side seam. Connect them to the original side waist corners.

NOTE: The front and back side seams should be the same angle off straight grain (balanced). If this is not the case, there has been a draping error.

Designer's Custom Fashion Ease: In some years, fit is snug, while in other years, fit is very loose. Because fit varies, the ease amount may be less or more, depending upon the fashion ease of the season. Also, note that when trueing bustiers, sleeveless dresses, and knits, the ease amount is not included. Refer to the chapters on these types of garment.

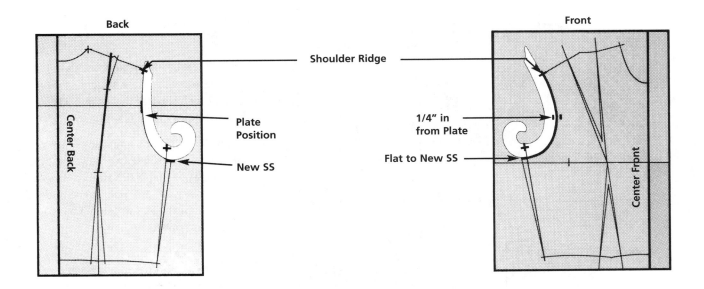

Back · Shoulder Ridge · **Front**

Center Back · Plate Position · 1/4" in from Plate · Center Front

New SS · Flat to New SS

11 **Draw in the back bodice arm-hole.** Using a french curve, connect the following positions and place the ruler down, as illustrated:

a. Shoulder back ridge corner.

b. Plate position at the screw level. Square and draw in a line 1 1/4 inches down from the shoulder blade back crossmark position.

c. The new side seam, at the 1-inch drop position.

The back armhole line should blend parallel to the grain at the screw level armhole mark. The french curved ruler blends at a slight angle at the side seam underarm position. Only the front blends in flat at this position.

12 **Draw in the front bodice arm-hole.** Using a french curve, connect the following positions and place the ruler down, as illustrated:

a. Shoulder ridge corner.

b. 1/4 inch toward center front from the front plate position at the screw level.

c. The first side seam at the 1-inch drop position. Be sure this front armhole line blends in flat for 1/2 inch at the underarm position.

13 **Add seam allowances to all seams** and trim excess fabric.

14 **Establish armhole notches.** Place the armhole notches. The front armhole notch (single) and the back armhole notches (double) should be placed one-third of the armhole distance up from the side seam (about 3 inches).

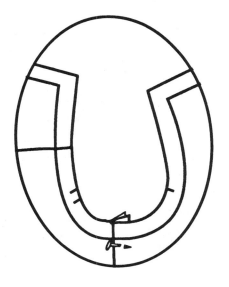

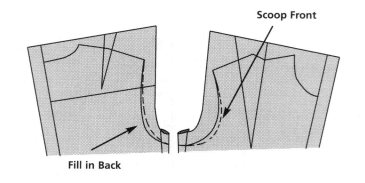

Scoop Front

Fill in Back

———————— OR ————————

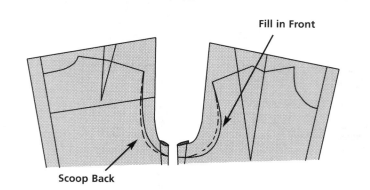

Fill in Front

Scoop Back

15 **Balance the armhole.**

a. Measure front and back armhole.
The front armhole should measure 1/2 inch shorter than the back armhole.

b. Correct front and back armhole.
To make the front or back armhole longer, reshape the front armhole by removing 1/4 inch at the middle of the armhole, shaping back to its original corners at the top and bottom.

To make the front and back armhole shorter, add 1/4 inch at the midarmhole area and again reshape to its original corners at the top and bottom.

NOTE: If the armhole does not balance by removing or adding 1/4 inch, an error was probably made while trueing or draping the armhole.

Notes

Pin and Check Final Proof of Bodice Drape

After completing and trueing up the fabric drape, pin the finished design together. All pins should be perpendicular to the seamlines. This design drape usually represents one half of the design and is placed on the right side of the dress form. Pin the front drape to the back drape, matching shoulder and side seams very carefully.

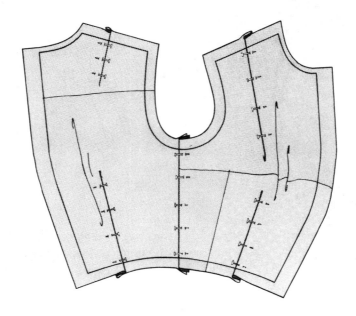

Checklist

A careful check of the finished drape serves several purposes. It may show inaccuracies or errors in the fit. A well-fitted garment looks comfortable and is proportioned naturally to the figure, with the amount of ease that is consistent with current fashion and garment style. Check the ease amounts and balance; then analyze the design concept against the list below. Any changes or corrections can be made at this time.

Evidence of lack of ease:

☐ Bodice is drawing across the bust or shoulder blade level.

☐ Waistline may be too tight.

☐ Bodice molds tightly to the body.

☐ Side seam pulls or twists away from the side seam of the dress form.

Evidence of excess ease:

☐ Shoulder seams appear too long.

☐ Folds or gapping forms across the chest.

☐ Folds or gapping forms into the neckline.

☐ Folds or gapping excess forms at the armhole.

Correct amount of ease:

☐ 1/2-inch pickup ease at the side seam/armhole intersection.

☐ 1/8- to 1/4-inch ease across the front chest area without pulling the front armhole.

☐ 1/8- to 1/4-inch ease across the back shoulder blade level without pulling the back armhole.

☐ 1/4-inch ease at each quarter of the waist.

☐ Draped side seams align with the dress form side seam.

☐ Side seams drape together without pulling, twisting, or distorting.

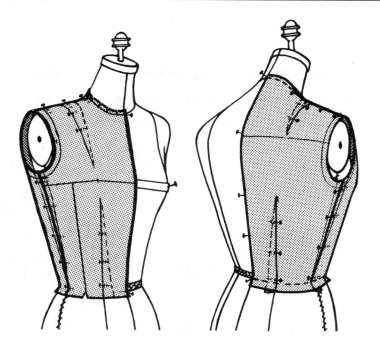

Correct balance and proportion:

☐ Front and back grainlines hang straight and are perpendicular to the floor.

☐ Front and back crossgrains are perfectly level to the floor.

☐ Bodice front darts are pinned in properly:

☐ 1 inch from the apex (vanishing point) to the shoulder crossmarks.

☐ 1 inch from the apex (vanishing point) to the waistline crossmarks.

☐ All darts are folded in the correct direction (toward the center).

☐ Shoulder seams match correctly.

☐ Side seams match and are the same length.

☐ The drape hangs freely on all seamlines, without any pulling or twisting.

☐ The armhole shape is correct. The armhole at the side seam is dropped the required amount from the plate and resembles a horseshoe shape.

☐ All trued lines are smooth and clean, with the correct amount of seam allowances.

☐ The overall look of the drape is neat and pressed.

NOTE: If the drape does not hang properly, unpin all joining seams and redrape the front and back independently. Be careful not to pull, stretch, or hold the fabric.

Sewing a Final Muslin Proof

It is advisable to sew together complete muslin samples of the basic bodice and skirt. (The skirt drape is shown on pages 85–94.) Muslin samples enable the designer to check the fit, balance, and hang of the two pieces as one unit.

Once the muslin samples are proven accurate, use them as basic patterns for the development of a variety of styles.

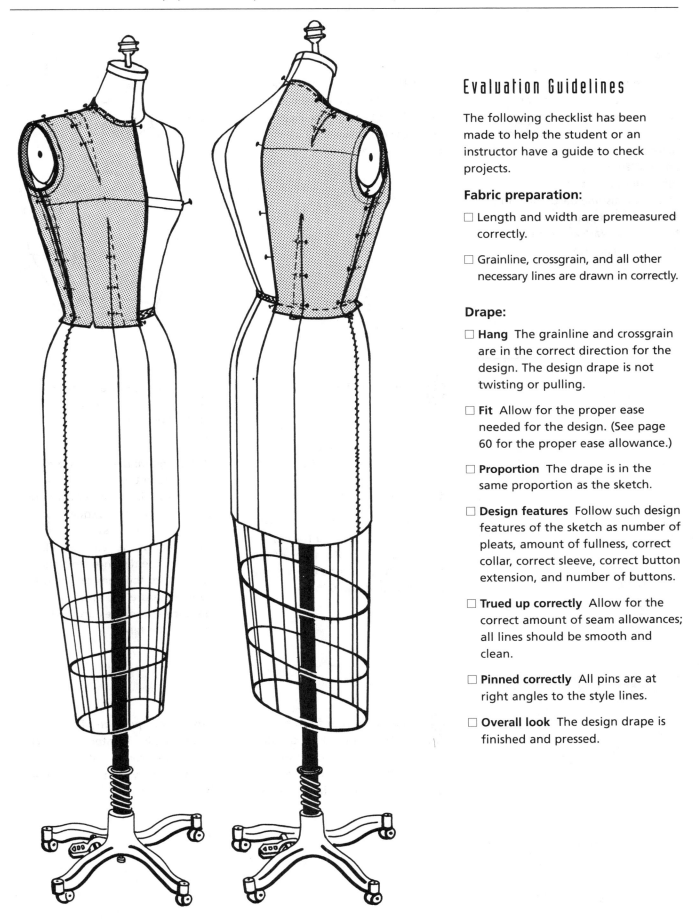

Evaluation Guidelines

The following checklist has been made to help the student or an instructor have a guide to check projects.

Fabric preparation:

☐ Length and width are premeasured correctly.

☐ Grainline, crossgrain, and all other necessary lines are drawn in correctly.

Drape:

☐ **Hang** The grainline and crossgrain are in the correct direction for the design. The design drape is not twisting or pulling.

☐ **Fit** Allow for the proper ease needed for the design. (See page 60 for the proper ease allowance.)

☐ **Proportion** The drape is in the same proportion as the sketch.

☐ **Design features** Follow such design features of the sketch as number of pleats, amount of fullness, correct collar, correct sleeve, correct button extension, and number of buttons.

☐ **Trued up correctly** Allow for the correct amount of seam allowances; all lines should be smooth and clean.

☐ **Pinned correctly** All pins are at right angles to the style lines.

☐ **Overall look** The design drape is finished and pressed.

One Dart Block, Front

The one-dart basic bodice is a front bodice that is draped, starting from center front and aligning grain and crossgrain. The drape is then manipulated up and around the shoulder and the armhole, down past the side seam, finishing at the waistline to create a waistline dart. The dart allows the flat pattern to control a fitted waist seam and create the amount of cup size for the customer.

NOTE: This one-dart basic bodice block should not be used to make other blocks because the front and back side seams are not at the same angle.

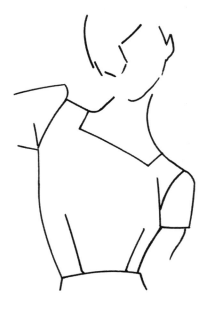

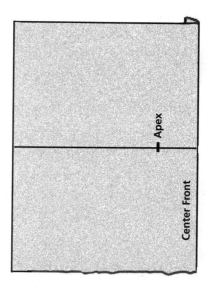

1 **Prepare the fabric.**

a. Length: Measure the length for the front bodice along the straight of grain from the neckband to the waist and add 5 inches. Snip and tear the fabric at this length.

b. Width: Measure the width for the front bodice along the crossgrain from the center front of the dress form to the side seam at the bust level and add 5 inches.

c. Grainline: Draw a center front grainline 1 inch from the torn edge of the fabric. Fold under this 1-inch amount.

d. Crossgrain: Draw a perfect crossgrain line in the center of the panel. This line represents the bust level line. With an L-square ruler, draw a perfect crossgrain line in the center of the fabric panel. Measure the distance from the center front to the apex on the dress form. Measure and crossmark this distance as the apex on the bust level of the fabric.

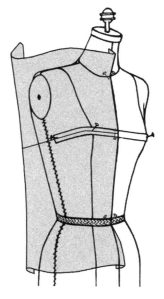

2 **Drape the center front bodice.** Pin the apex mark on the fabric to the apex position on the dress form. Pin the center front grainline fold of the fabric to the

center front position of the body. Anchor a pin at center front neck and center front waist. An additional pin may be needed at the bust level tape.

3 **Clip and drape the front neck-line and shoulder.** Trim and clip the front neckline at intervals. Smooth the excess fabric around the front neck area. Smooth the

fabric upward and across the upper chest area and over the shoulder. Pin the shoulder just past the shoulder seam at the shoulder/neckline and the shoulder/armhole area.

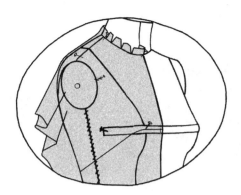

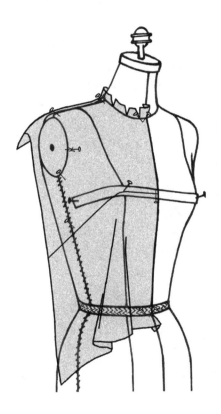

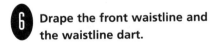

4 **Drape the armhole.** Continue to smooth and drape the fabric around the armhole plate, creating a 1/4-inch–1/4-inch pinch at the screw level of the armhole ridge. This ensures that the armhole does not get too tight and allows room for the muscle of the arm area. Place a pin at the underarm/side seam.

NOTE: Do not trim the fabric around the armhole, as you will have a tendency to stretch the armhole too tight.

5 **Drape the side seam.** Smooth the fabric underneath the arm-plate and across the side seam area. The excess fabric will fall into the waist area from the apex. Pin the side seam area.

NOTE: The crossgrain will be angled downward from the apex pin toward the side seam.

6 **Drape the front waistline and the waistline dart.**

a. Trim and clip the waistline at 1-inch intervals up to the waistline tape.

NOTE: It may be necessary to trim the excess within 1 inch of the waistline.

b. Allow all excess fabric to be pinned at the princess seam on the waistline toward center front. Crease the dart excess inward toward center front from the apex (tip of the bust) down to the waist-line tape.

NOTE: The amount of fullness (dart excess) in the waist dart depends upon the bust size (the larger the bust, the more fullness is created).

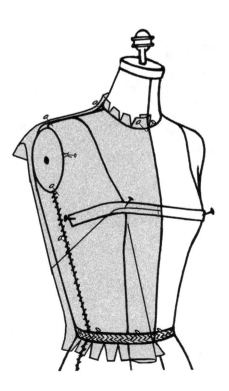

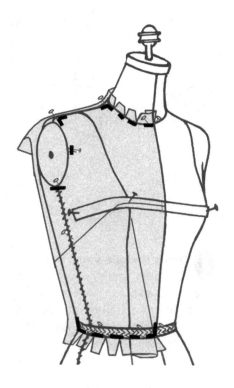

7 **Mark all key areas.** Mark all key areas of the dress form to the fabric.

a. Neckline: Crossmark at center front neck and at the neckline/ shoulder ridge corner.

b. Shoulder seam: Lightly mark the shoulder seam and crossmark the shoulder/ridge corner.

c. Armplate:
- Mark top at shoulder seam ridge.
- Mark middle at screw level.
- Crossmark bottom at the side seam.

d. Side seam: Lightly mark.

e. Waistline and waist dart: Crossmark at center front waist, side seam waist, and both sides of the dart.

8 **Drape the back bodice.** Follow the same draping steps as for the basic back bodice, illustrated on pages 53–55.

9 **Remove the drape from the dress form.** Remove the fabric from the dress form and true up all seams. Follow the trueing directions for the one-dart block on the following pages.

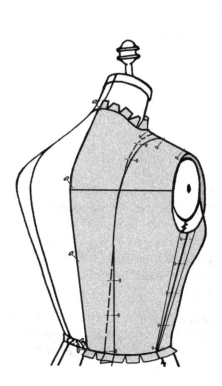

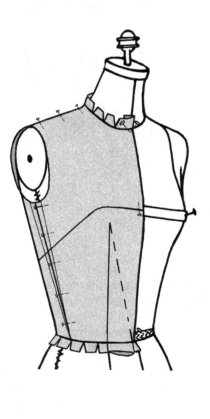

One-Dart Block: *True and Balance the Front and Back*

This trueing process is similar to that used to true the two-dart basic block. However, this method of developing a one-dart block does not allow the side seams of the front and back to be checked for hang, balance, and proportion. But, the seam lines on the finished drape should match and correspond with measurements on the figure.

1 **Draw in the front and back waistline darts.** Draw the front dart legs from the apex (tip of bust) to the waist dart crossmarks. Also, draw in the back waist dart.

2 **Draw a short 90-degree angle at:**

a. Center front neck **(1/4 inch).**

b. Center front waist **(1/2 inch).**

c. Center back neck **(1 inch).**

d. Center back waist **(1 inch).**

3 **Draw in the shoulder seams and match front to back distances.** Draw in the front and back shoulder seams. Using a straight ruler, blend from the shoulder neck corner to the shoulder ridge corner in one continuous line.

4 **Draw in the front and back necklines.** Use a french curve ruler as illustrated. Be sure to blend the lines smoothly into the 90-degree angle at center front and center back necklines. Connect the crossmarks at the shoulder seam.

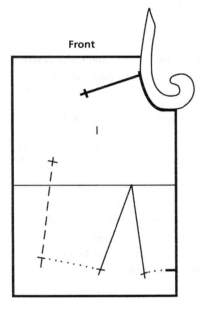

Front

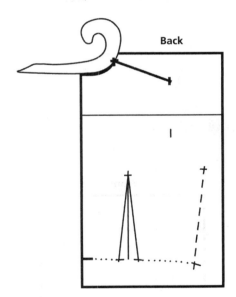

Back

5 **Draw in the front and back waistlines.**

a. Fold the front waist dart closed. Using a hip curve ruler, blend the waistline smoothly from center front to the side seam.

b. Fold the back waist dart closed. Using a hip curve ruler, blend the waistline smoothly from center back to the side seam.

6 **Measure and check the waist-line distance and balance.**

a. Measure from center front to the side seam on the waist seam.

b. Measure from center back to the side seam on the waist seam.

c. The front waistline should be 1/2 inch longer than the back waistline measurement. If this is not the case, readjust the side seam at the waistline by adding and subtracting the difference.

NOTE: For fuller, mature figures, the front waistline should be 1 inch longer than the back waistline measurement.

Front

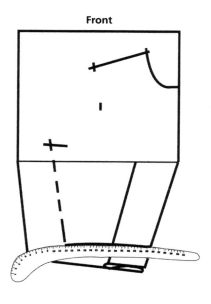

Back

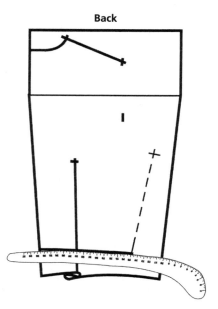

Front

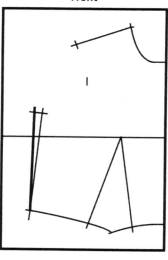

Back

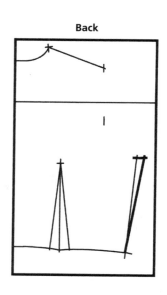

7 **Draw in the front and back side seams.**

a. Draw a temporary side seam by connecting the underarm/side seam crossmark to the waistline/side seam crossmark.

b. Add 1/2-inch body ease to the front and back underarm/side seam corner. Add no ease to the waistline.

c. Draw in a new side seam by connecting the 1/2 inch ease crossmark to the original side seam/waist corner. Do this on both the front and back.

8 **Check the waistline curve.**

a. Pin the front and back waistline darts closed. Then, pin the front and back side seams together.

b. The waistline should illustrate a continuous, smooth line. If this is not the case, lower the side seam/waist corner 1/4 inch to get a smooth continuous curve.

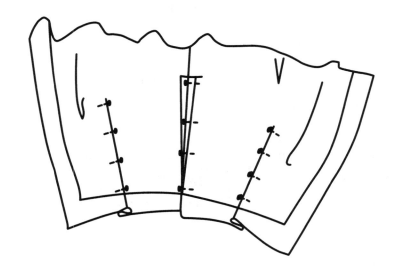

9 **Draw in the front armhole.**
Using a french curve ruler, connect the following positions and place the ruler down as illustrated:

a. Shoulder front ridge corner.

b. Midpoint crossmark of the armhole.

c. The front side seam/armhole corner.

NOTE: Be sure this front armhole line blends in flat with the 1/2 inch ease.

Front

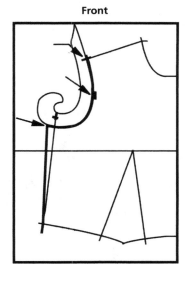

10 **Draw in the back armhole.**
Using a french curve ruler, connect the following positions and place the ruler down as illustrated:

a. Shoulder back ridge corner.

b. Midpoint crossmark of the armhole. To ensure accuracy, this crossmark should be parallel to center back for 1 1/4 inches.

c. The back side seam/armhole corner.

NOTE: The back armhole line should blend parallel to the grain at the midarmhole point. Also, the french curve ruler blends at a slight angle into the side seam/armhole corner.

Back

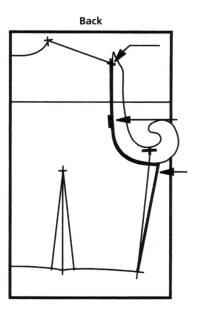

Convert the One-Dart Block into a Two-Dart Block and Check Balance

Because of the wide dart pickup of a one-dart block, it cannot be checked for side seam balance to a back block. Nor can it be checked for correct hang. Therefore, once the two-dart block is converted and all balances are checked, then this block may be repositioned into a one-dart block to save time when making waist-fitted designs. When converting the one-dart block into a two-dart block, it is important to reposition darts with the correct amount of dart pickup. At the same time, the side seams should be at the same angle from a perfect grainline and should be free of any existing dart. Therefore, the second dart should be positioned at the shoulder. This method of developing a two-dart block allows the side seams of the front and back to be checked for hang and balance between the front and back of the garment.

 Prepare the front bodice pattern to make a shoulder dart.

a. Draw in the center of the princess panel line. Fold the side seam to the front dart leg nearest to the side seam. Draw a line at the center fold of this position. This is the center of the princess panel line.

b. Draw another line from the apex to the middle of the shoulder seam. This is the position for the shoulder dart.

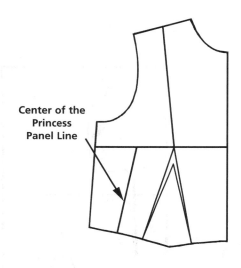

Center of the Princess Panel Line

Pivot a portion of the waist dart into the shoulder. At the same time, place center of the princess panel line parallel to center front.

2 **Pivot a portion of the waist dart into the shoulder to make a shoulder dart.**

a. Cut the waist dart (leg nearest the side seam) from the waistline up the apex.

b. Cut the shoulder dart line from the shoulder seam down to the apex.

c. Pivot the waist dart smaller from the apex until the center of the princess panel line is perfectly parallel to the center front (on grain). The excess automatically relocates into the shoulder dart area.

NOTE: The larger the cup size, the larger the shoulder dart. Conversely, the smaller the cup size, the smaller the shoulder dart.

d. Draw in a new shoulder dart and a new waist dart.

3 **Balance the front and back side seams.**

a. Pin the front waist corner to the back waist corner.

b. From the side seam/waistline corner pin, pivot the front pattern until the bodice center front and the bodice center back positions are parallel.

c. Check the front and back side seam locations. The front and back side seams should meet. If this is not the case, add and subtract the side seams until they meet.

4 **Check armhole balance.**
Measure the front armhole and back armhole. The back armhole distance should be 1/2 inch longer than the front armhole measurement. If this is not the case, re-adjust the midarmhole distance. Refer to page 127 for more detailed instructions of balancing an armhole.

5 **Pin and check the pattern.**
After completing the two-dart bodice pattern, add seam allowances and pin the finished design together.

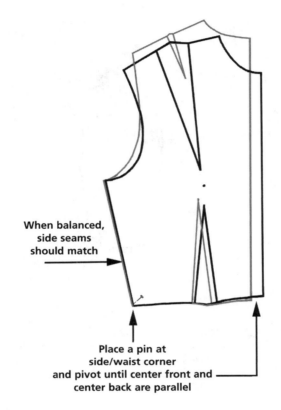

When balanced, side seams should match

Place a pin at side/waist corner and pivot until center front and center back are parallel

Custom Draping

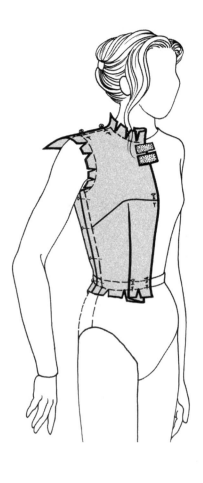

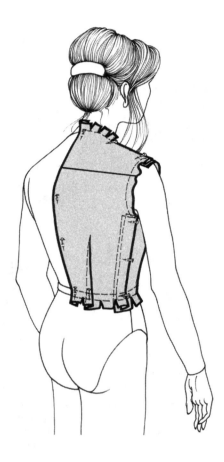

Bodice Front and Back

A custom-draped bodice pattern is created by draping directly onto a live model or the client's body. This method of draping directly onto the body allows all proportions of the body to be accurately sized: bodice length, cup size, apex location, and waistline stance. This method of draping is especially helpful when the model is not the shape of a typical dress form. Draping directly on a figure also eliminates numerous fittings for such clients.

A custom bodice pattern may be used as a template from which other patterns are developed into original styles. This customizing feature eliminates many hours of adjusting designs on future styles because the specs are the same on the pattern as on the model.

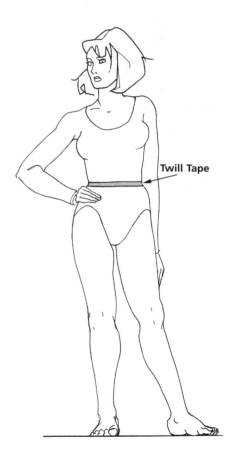

Twill Tape

Preparation

For best results, have the client wear undergarments or a leotard and remove her shoes. Tie a wide string or twill tape snugly around the waistline. The waistline is where the string settles nicely in the waist area.

Be careful that the client does not look down during the draping process.

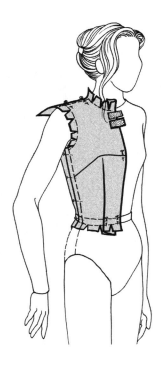

Front Bodice Drape

Drape the Front Bodice

The front bodice master pattern is draped, starting from center front and aligning grain and crossgrain. The drape is manipulated up and around the shoulder and the armhole, down past the side seam, finishing at the waistline to create a waistline dart. The dart allows the flat pattern to control a fitted waist seam and create the appropriate amount of cup size for the customer.

 Prepare the paper.

NOTE: With custom drapes, it is advisable to drape in alphabet paper. This ensures that there is no stretching as the drape is being developed.

a. Length: Measure on the live model from the top of the neck to below the waist. Add 5 inches. This is the length for the paper.

b. Width: Measure on the live model from the center front to the side seam area. Add 5 inches. This is the width for the paper.

c. Grainline: Draw a center front grainline 1 inch from the edge of the paper. Fold under this 1-inch amount.

d. Crossgrain: Draw a perfect crossgrain line in the center of the panel. This line represents the bust level line.

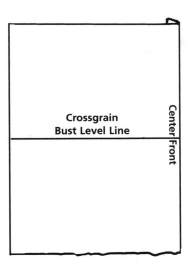

Crossgrain
Bust Level Line

Center Front

 Drape the center front bodice.

a. Tape the center front grainline fold of the paper to the center front position of the body.

b. Pin the center front at the bustline level. Anchor the pin into the bra.

c. Pin the center front waist. Anchor the pin into the waist tape.

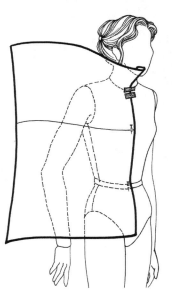

Clip and drape the front neckline.

a. Trim and clip the front neckline at intervals. Smooth the excess paper around the front neck area.

b. Pin the shoulder to the leotard at the shoulder neckline area.

 Drape the shoulder.

a. Smooth the excess paper over the shoulder.

b. Pin the shoulder to the leotard at the shoulder armhole area.

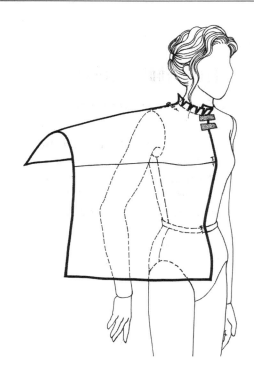

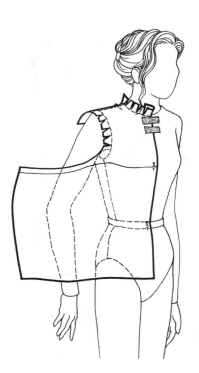

 Drape the shoulder and armhole.

a. Continue to drape the paper around the armhole. Trim and clip at intervals around the armhole area.

b. Smooth the paper underneath the arm.

 Drape the side/waistline area.

a. Smooth the paper underneath the arm and across the side seam area. The excess paper will fall into the waist area from the apex. The amount of this fullness depends upon the bust size (the larger the bust, the more fullness is created).

b. Pin the side seam area to the bra of the customer and the leotard.

7 Drape the front waistline and the waistline dart.

a. Trim and clip the waistline up to the waistline tape.

b. Crease the dart excess from the apex (tip of the bust) down to the waistline tape. Pin the dart excess at the waistline tape.

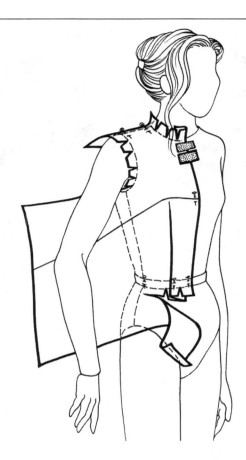

8 Drape the front side seam.

a. Trim the side seam area, leaving at least 2 inches of excess.

b. Secure pins at the underarm area and at the waistline tape.

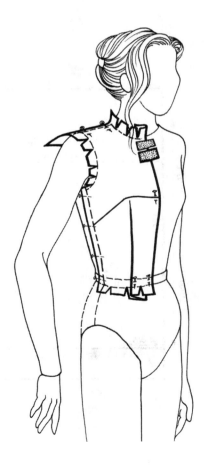

Back Bodice Drape

Drape the Back Bodice

The back bodice master pattern is draped, starting from center back and aligning grain and crossgrain.

The drape is manipulated across the back waist tape, up past the side seam, and up and around the armhole, finishing over the shoulder. The back waistline dart allows the flat pattern to control a fitted waist seam.

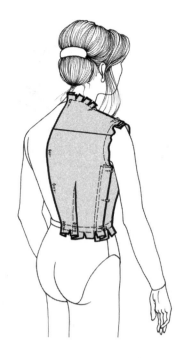

 Prepare the paper.

a. Length: Measure on the live model from the top of the neck to below the waist. Add 5 inches. This is the length for the paper.

b. Width: Measure on the live model from the center back to the side seam area. Add 5 inches. This is the width for the paper.

c. Grainline: Draw a center back grainline 1 inch from the left edge of the paper. Fold under this 1-inch amount.

d. Neckline crossgrain: Draw a short (1 inch long) crossgrain 3 inches from the top of the paper. This represents the center back neckline position.

e. Shoulder blade level crossgrain: Draw a perfect crossgrain line 4 inches below the neckline cross mark. This line represents the shoulder blade level line.

f. Temporary waistline crossgrain: Measure on the customer from center back neck down to the bottom of the waist tape. Transfer this distance to the paper. Draw a perfect crossgrain line at this waistline position.

g. Prepare back waist dart:
- On the temporary waistline, measure over from center back 2 3/4 inches and crossmark.
- Measure and crossmark 1 1/4 inches from the first crossmark (toward the side seam). This is the width of the back waistline dart. (Refer to illustration.)
- Measure and crossmark 7 inches up at the middle of the dart, remaining parallel to center back, on grain. (For shorter clients, use 6 inches.)

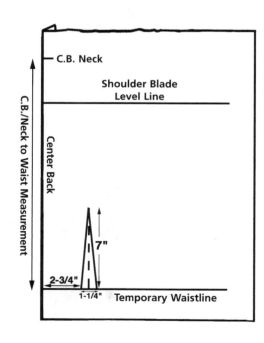

Drape the center back bodice.

a. Tape the center back grainline fold of the paper to the center back position of the body. Feel for the backbone to align the center back position accurately.

b. Align and pin center back at the neckline and the shoulder blade level. Anchor a pin into the bra at center back.

c. Align and pin the back waistline crossmark to the waist tape. Anchor the pin into the waist tape at center back (bone).

Drape the back waistline dart.

a. Pin and drape in the back waistline dart 7 inches long (6 inches for shorter bodies) by 1 1/4 inches at the waistline. This was premeasured in step 1.

b. Taper the dart to nothing at the 7-inch mark.

c. Anchor a pin into the waist tape at the waistline dart.

4 **Drape the remainder of the back waistline into the side seam.**

a. Smooth the excess paper over the waist tape toward the side seam, being careful not to pull downward or upward.

b. Have the client lift her arm slightly. Fold under the paper at the side seam. Tape the back side to the front side seam.

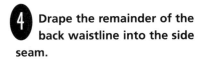

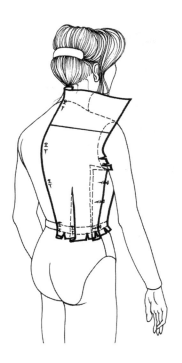

Clip and drape the back neckline.

a. Trim and clip the back neckline at intervals. Smooth the excess paper around the front neck area.

b. Fold the paper under at the shoulder area, matching the front shoulder to the back shoulder. Tape the back shoulder to the front shoulder.

 Drape the back armhole.

a. Continue to trim and clip the paper around the back armhole.

b. The back armhole will have a definite amount of ease left near the shoulder blade line. *Do not drape this ease out.*

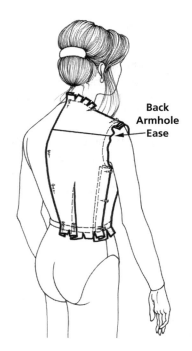

Back Armhole Ease

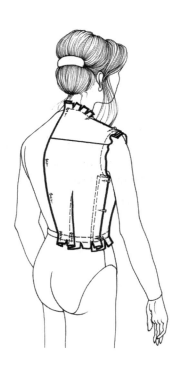

7 **Mark all necessary areas.** Using a color marking pen, mark the following areas:

a. Front and back **waistline** at the bottom of the tape.

b. Front and back **side seam.**

c. Front and back **neckline.**

d. Front and back **shoulder seam.**

e. Front and back **armhole:**
  • Shoulder ridge.
  • Middle of front and back armhole (paper will have automatically creased at this midpoint area) .
  • Underarm area (lowest point where sleeve will be attached).

f. Front waistline dart.

g. Apex.

8 **True the front and back pattern.** Refer to pages 69–71 for the directions in trueing the front and pages 56–61 for the back custom drape.

Chapter Six

Basic Skirt

By studying the various draping steps in this chapter, the designer should be able to:

• Recognize the grain and crossgrain of a fabric in relation to the hipline of a pattern.

• Take a flat piece of fabric and make it fit the curves of the body.

• Check and analyze the results of the draping process for proper ease, fit, and hang.

• Transfer the drape onto paper and true up the basic skirt pattern.

• Drape and shape a fitted waistline with two darts and straight side seams.

• Develop a one-dart waistline skirt and a shirred waistline skirt from the two-dart basic skirt.

The Basic Skirt Blocks: Definition, Theory, & Principles

Definition

A basic two-dart straight skirt is a fitted skirt with seams parallel to the center of the skirt. This skirt has a fitted waist area in which the excess fabric above the hip line is controlled by waistline darts.

This skirt is considered the most important of all skirt drapes because of its versatility in creating many different patterns. The designs created from the basic straight skirt must have a use for the waistline darts. This means that the waistline darts need to be converted into gathers, tucks, styled pleats, yokes, or style-lines or simply kept as darts.

The following section demonstrates how to drape a basic straight skirt. Information is also given on transferring the drape onto paper and trueing this skirt pattern. A variety of designs can be made by using these skirt blocks.

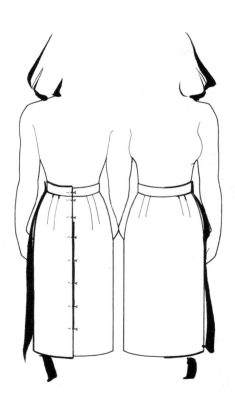

Variations of the basic skirt blocks:

- **One-dart basic skirt:** The one-dart basic skirt is fitted, with seams parallel to the center of the skirt. This skirt has a fitted waist area in which the excess fabric above the hip line is controlled by one waistline dart.

- **Flared (A-line) skirt:** The flared (A-line) skirt is fitted in the waist and hip area with flares falling from the bottom of the hip. The waistline seam has a distinctive semicircular curve. When the waistline curve is sewn into a straight waistband or waistline seam, the lower section flows evenly and smoothly over the hip.

Theory

The basic skirt block and its variations may be used when the following apply:

- The designs created from the basic two-dart straight skirt must have a reason to use both darts. This means that both darts need to be converted into tucks, gathers, styled pleats, yokes, flares, or style lines, or simply kept as darts. Usually the skirt design keeps the side seams parallel to the center of the skirt, unless the darts are pivoted out into flares.

- The one-dart basic skirt is used when the design requires that only one dart be converted into another dart location, a tuck, a styled pleat, a style line, or a limited amount of gathers. Tucks, pleats, and style lines can be created from readjusting areas of this foundation pattern.

- The designs created from the flared (A-line) skirt usually have a definite A-line or circular silhouette. Style lines, waistbands, a variety of pockets, and different hem lengths can easily be adapted to create a combination of designs from this basic foundation pattern.

Principles: Analyzing the Skirt Blocks

The skirt blocks are used to create new designs for a variety of skirts. It is important to analyze the block to insure that the following items are correct. If one of these items is wrong, the designs made from this block will not fit properly, and they will twist, drag, or pull.

• All pattern pieces have a definite relationship with the figure that enables them to hang straight up and down and be parallel to the floor. This grainline and crossgrain alignment, in addition to the side seam angle, allows the designer to maintain the correct balance between the front and back of the garment.

• The center front and center back are on perfect grain.

• The hip level line of the front and back skirts are on perfect crossgrain, allowing the area below the hipline to hang straight up and down.

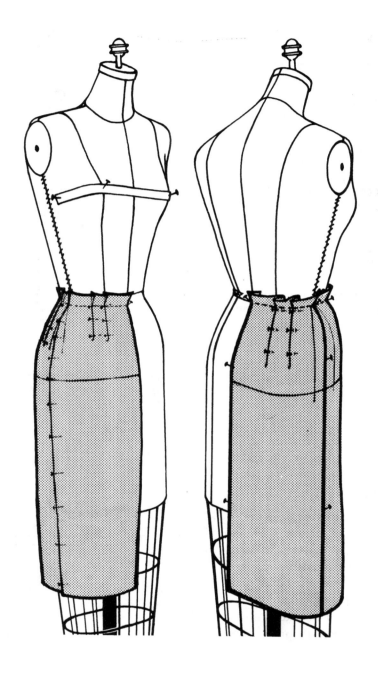

Basic Skirt: *Preparing the Dress Form*

1 **Establish the hip level on the dress form.** Measure down 7 inches from the waistline on the center front of the dress form. This is the hip level.

2 **Place twill tape** (or measuring tape) parallel to the floor at this position. Place pins on the dress form at this hip level and remove the tape.

Basic Front and Back Skirt: *Preparing the Fabric*

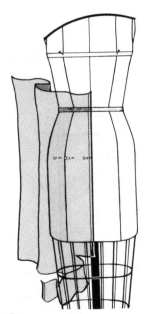
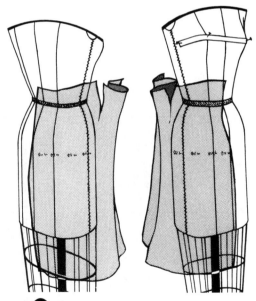

1 **Measure the length** (along the straight of grain) for the front and back skirt from 2 inches above the waist to the bottom of the dress form. Add 4 inches. Snip and tear the fabric at this length.

2 **Measure the width** (along the crossgrain) for the front and back skirt at the hip level from center of the dress form to the side seam. Add 3 inches. Snip and tear the fabric at this width.

3 Draw the center front and center back grainlines on the fabric 1 inch from the torn edge and press under.

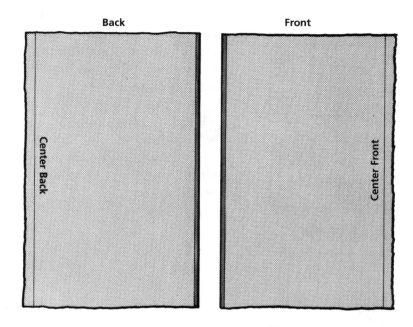

4 Mark the center front waist position. Measure down 2 inches from the top of the fabric at the center front fold. Pencil in a waistline mark at this position.

5 Draw the crossgrains for the front and back skirt.

a. On the skirt front, measure down 7 inches from the waistline mark. Using an L-square ruler, draw the perfect crossgrain on the skirt front.

b. On the skirt back, measure down 9 inches (on the center back grainline) from the top of the fabric. Using an L-square ruler, draw the perfect crossgrain on the skirt back.

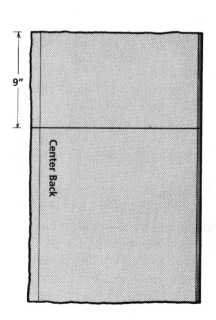
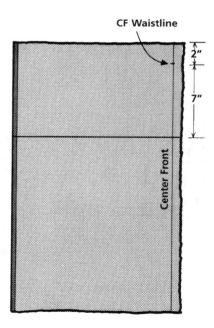

Front

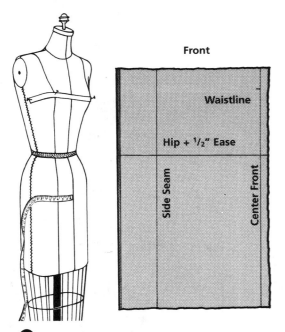

Waistline

Hip + 1/2" Ease

Side Seam

Center Front

Back

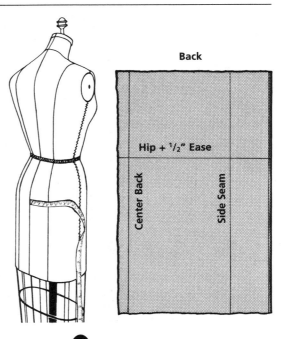

Hip + 1/2" Ease

Center Back

Side Seam

6 **Determine the front side seam.** Measure from center front to the side seam (at the hip level) and add 1/2 inch for ease. Transfer this measurement to the fabric. Using this mark, draw a side seam perfectly parallel to the center front grainline.

7 **Determine the back side seam.** Measure from center back to the side seam (at the hip level) and add 1/2 inch for ease. Transfer this measurement to the fabric. Using this mark, draw a side seam perfectly parallel to the center back grainline.

8 **Draw a secondary side seam line.** Measure 3/4 inch toward center front/back from the side seam on both the front and back skirts. This line will be used to help drape in the waistline.

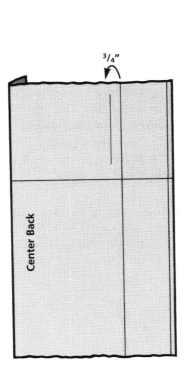

3/4"

Center Back

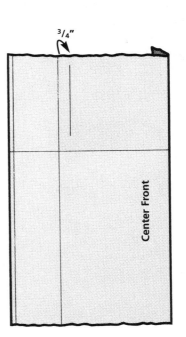

3/4"

Center Front

Basic Front Skirt: Draping Steps

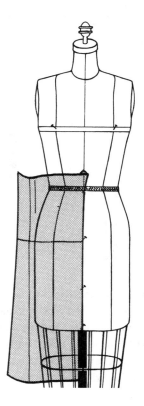 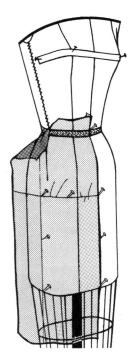 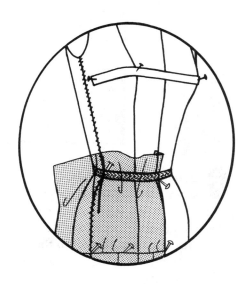

1 **Pin the center front grainline** fold of the fabric on the center front position of the dress form, matching the crossgrain of the fabric to the hip level line on the dress form.

2 **Smooth and pin the crossgrain** of the fabric, evenly distributing the ease across the dress form to the side seam.

Be sure the fabric crossgrain is parallel to the floor. The side seam of the skirt drape should fall exactly on the side seam of the dress form when the crossgrain is placed perfectly.

3 **Pin the side seam** (below the hip level) to the dress form.

4 **Pin the front 3/4-inch line** to the side seam/waist corner of the dress form.

NOTE: When this side seam/waist corner is draped correctly, a slight gap will occur automatically at the side seam above the hip level.

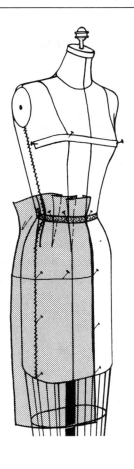

5 **Drape in two darts at the front waistline.** The excess fabric that falls between center front of the dress form and the pinned 3/4-inch mark on side seam will become the front waist darts.

a. Drape in the first dart (the first half of the excess fabric) on the princess seam.

• **Crossmark the princess seam at the waistline.** Smooth the fabric from the center front to the princess seam. Crossmark and crease the fabric at the princess seam/waist.

• **Pin the excess fabric on the princess seam.** The excess fabric is folded at the princess seam crossmark and folded toward center front. Taper the dart to nothing down toward the hipline.

b. Drape in the second dart (the remaining half of the excess fabric).

• **Measure over on the waistline 1 1/4 inches from the first dart.** Place a waistline crossmark at this position. Crossmark and crease the fabric at the waistline crossmark.

• **Pin and drape the excess fabric on the waistline crossmark.** The remaining amount of excess fabric is creased at the second crossmark and folded toward center front. Taper the dart to nothing down toward the hipline.

Basic Back Skirt: Draping Steps

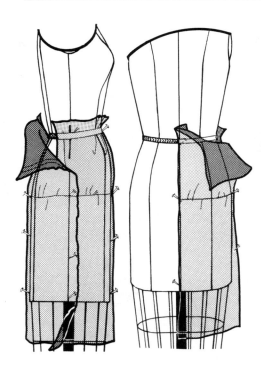

1 **Match the back side seam at the hip level to the front side seam at the hip level.** The side seams should match and be perfectly parallel to each other.

2 **Smooth and pin the crossgrain of the fabric,** evenly distributing the ease across the dress form.

3 **Pin the center back grainline** fold of the fabric to the center back seam of the dress form.

4 **Drape and pin the back 3/4-inch line** of the fabric to the side seam/waist corner of the dress form.

NOTE: When this side seam/waist corner is draped correctly, a slight gap will occur automatically on the side seam above the hip level.

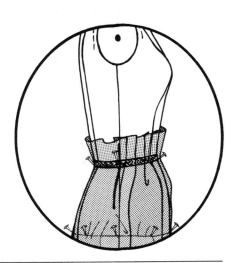

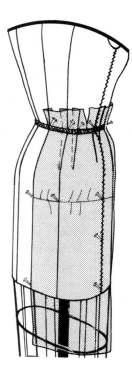

5 **Drape in two darts at the back waistline.** The excess fabric that falls between center back of the dress form and the pinned 3/4-inch mark on the side seam will become the back waist darts.

a. Drape the first dart (the first half of the excess fabric) on the princess seam.

- **Crossmark the princess seam at the waistline.** Smooth the fabric from the center back to the princess seam. Crossmark and crease the fabric at the princess seam/waist.
- **Pin the excess fabric on the princess seam.** The excess fabric is folded at the princess seam crossmark and folded toward center back. Taper the dart to nothing down toward the hipline.

b. Drape in the second dart (the remaining half of the excess fabric).

- **Measure over on the waistline 1 1/4 inches from the first dart.** Place a waistline crossmark at this position. Crossmark and crease the fabric at the waistline crossmark.
- **Pin and drape the excess fabric on the waistline crossmark.** The remaining amount of excess fabric is creased at the second crossmark and folded toward center back. Taper the dart to nothing down toward the hipline.

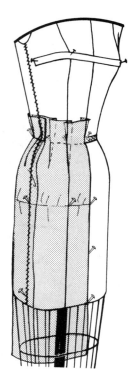

6 **Mark all key areas** of the dress form:

a. Waistline front and back.

b. Darts front and back.

Trueing Basic Skirt Drape

1 Remove the fabric from the dress form and lay it flat on the table. If you are planning to true up the fabric onto paper, complete the following steps:

a. Draw in a straight grainline and the crossgrain at the hip level to match the straight of grain and crossgrain of the fabric on two pieces of paper (one for the skirt front and one for the skirt back).

b. Draw a side seam line. Remeasure the hip and add 1/2 inch ease. Transfer this measurement to the paper. Draw a side seam line at this position parallel to the grainline. (Do this for both the front and back skirts.)

c. Place the fabric drape on top of the paper, matching the straight grains and the crossgrain hip levels. The side seamlines should match automatically.

d. Transfer the waistline, darts, and side seam markings onto the paper, using a trace wheel.

2 Draw a short 90 degree angle at:

a. Center front waist **(1/2 inch)**

b. Center back waist **(1 inch)**

3 Draw the front and back waist darts.

a. Locate the center of each dart.

b. Draw the center dart line. Using a straight ruler, draw a line for the center of each dart parallel to the grainline. The length of the front darts is 3 1/2 inches. The length of the back darts is 5 1/2 inches. The bottom of each dart line is known as the vanishing point.

Back

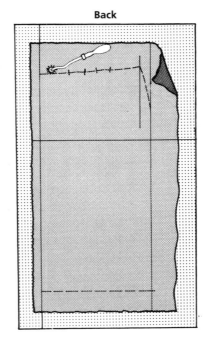

Front

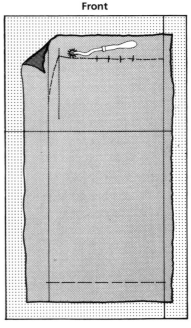

Back Waistline

Back

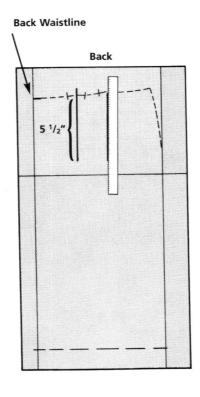

5 1/2"

Front Waistline

Front

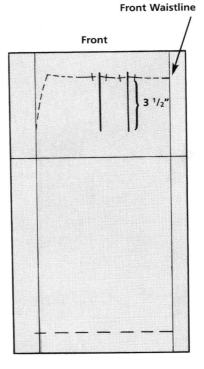

3 1/2"

Back   **Front**   **Back**   **Front**

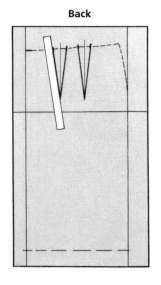 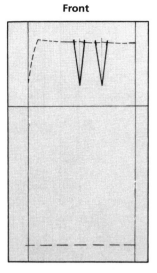   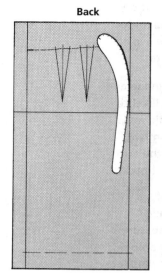 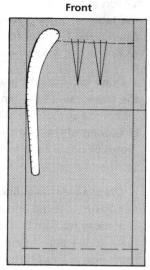

4 **Draw in the outer dart legs.**
Using a straight ruler, draw
the outer legs of the darts from
the vanishing point to the waistline crossmarks.

5 **Draw the side seams.** Using
a hip curve ruler, place the
straight part of this ruler to the
side seam/waist corner and the
side seam (as illustrated).

Back   **Front**

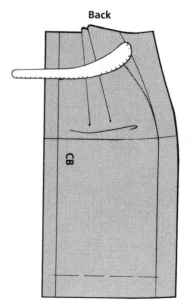 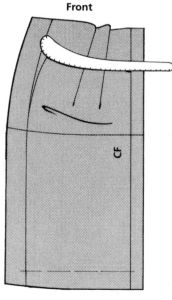

6 **Draw the waistline.** Fold
and pin in the waist darts.
With the darts folded in place, use
the hip curve ruler and draw the
waistline.

7 Check side seams.

a. Pin the front and back side seams together.

b. Measure the side seams from the hip level to the waistline. These measurements should be the same. If they are not, adjust the back waistline/side seam corner to match the front measurement.

NOTE: If these measurements are more than 5/8 inch off, recheck the drape to create a more accurately draped side seam/waist corner.

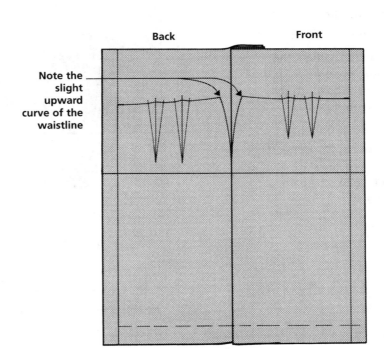

Back Front

Note the slight upward curve of the waistline

8 Check the waistline.

a. Pin the front and back skirt side seams to each other. Pin in the darts.

b. Check the waistline shape. This should be a continuous, smooth, curving line.

c. Match and walk front and back bodice waists to the skirt waists when a bodice is being attached to the skirt. Waistlines should be the same distance when all darts are folded closed.

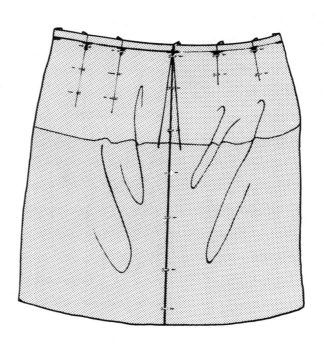

9 **Draw the hemline, with the side seams still pinned.**

a. Measure and crossmark the desired length. Measure from the center back waist down to the desired skirt length.

b. Square a line from center back crossmark, across the skirt to center front of the skirt. This line should be perfectly parallel to the hipline.

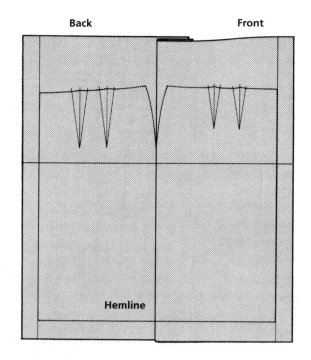

Back   Front

Hemline

Basic Skirt Variations

A basic skirt waistline fullness may also be draped with gathers or a single dart rather than the standard two darts.

Pin and Check Final Proof of Skirt Drape

After completing and trueing up the skirt fabric drape, the finished design should be pinned together. This usually represents half of the design and is placed on the right side of the dress form. The front drape should be pinned to the back drape, matching the side seams very carefully. All pins should be perpendicular to the seamline.

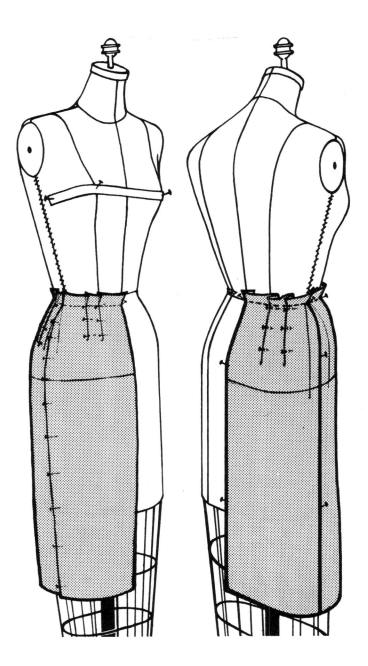

Checklist

A careful check of the finished drape serves several purposes. It may show inaccuracies or errors in the fit. Any changes or corrections can be made at this time.

☐ Front and back grainlines should be straight.

☐ Front and back crossgrains should be perfectly level to the floor.

☐ Hip level ease should be evenly distributed.

☐ All trued lines are smooth and clean.

☐ All trued lines have the correct amount of seam allowances.

☐ The overall look of the drape is neat and clean.

☐ Darts are pinned in place to the vanishing points.

☐ Draped side seams are in alignment with the dress form side seam.

☐ The drape is correctly balanced. The front of the design is in the front and the back of the design is in the back. It hangs freely on all seamlines.

Basic Shift and Empire Designs

The Basic Shift Block: Definition, Theory, & Principles

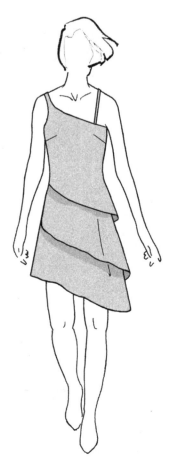

Definition

The shift dress is the most basic of all dress styles. The silhouette has a boxy shape without a waist-fitting seam. The side seams hang away from the body and are parallel to center front.

The waist may be belted, drawn in by using elastic, or slightly fitted by using one or two fisheye darts. Within the silhouette shape, many different styles of pockets, plackets, yokes, necklines, collars, and/or sleeves may be chosen to create the individual style wanted.

The following procedures demonstrate how to drape a basic shift dress. Some variations of this traditional design are also included, such as the empire dress and tiered dresses. One can realize the many creative styles and uses for this basic dress design by mastering the following draping procedures.

Variations of the Basic Shift Dress

- **Fitted silhouette:** Within the silhouette, the waist area may be fitted by using fisheye waistline darts.

- **Slightly fitted silhouette:** Within the silhouette, the waist area may be slightly fitted by using only one fisheye waistline dart that is smaller in width.

- **Fitted silhouette with side bust dart:** The shoulder dart may be pivoted into the side bust dart. This is usually necessary to free the shoulder area of a dart to allow easy styling of yoke and pleats.

Theory

The basic shift block and its variations may be used when:

- The design includes the shoulder dart amount, which may have been converted into tucks, style-lines, or gathers or simply kept as a dart somewhere within the design.

- The design would also have *no* waist-fitting seam.

- The silhouette shape at the waistline may be controlled by release tucks, various fisheye darts, or elastic casing or simply left free to hang without darts.

- A yoke area can also be styled, after which the dart can be converted into gathers, tucks, or release pleats.

Principles: Analyzing the Shift Block

It is important to analyze the design to ensure that the following items are correct. If one of these items is wrong, the designs made will not fit properly and they will twist, drag, or pull.

- All pattern pieces have a definite relationship with the figure that enables them to hang straight up and down and be parallel to the floor. This grainline and crossgrain alignment, in addition to the side seam angle, allows the designer to maintain the correct balance between the front and back of the garment.

- The center front and center back are on perfect grain.

- The bust level line of the front bodice is on perfect crossgrain, allowing the area below the bust level line to hang straight up and down.

- The shoulder blade level line of the back bodice is on perfect crossgrain, allowing the area below the shoulder blade level line to hang straight up and down.

- On the front bodice, the center of the princess panel line (centered distance from the apex to the side seam) is on perfect grain and is parallel to center front. This ensures that the side seam maintains the same angle as the back.

- The front and back waist fisheye darts have picked up the amount of fabric necessary to create the desired fit of a fitted style.

- The shoulder dart has picked up the excess fabric above the bust level line. This controls the bust fullness and maintains the correct cup size.

- The side seam is free of any other dart, which allows the matching and balancing process.

- The armholes must resemble a horseshoe shape. The armholes should also balance—measurement of the back armhole should be 1/2 inch more than the front armhole. The correct shape and the correct balanced amount ensure that the sleeve hangs properly.

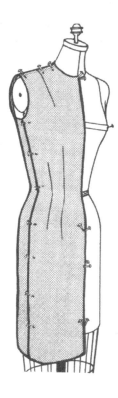

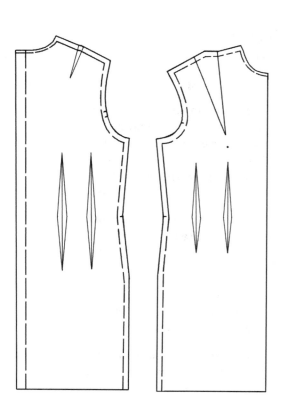

Basic Front and Back Shift: *Preparing the Fabric*

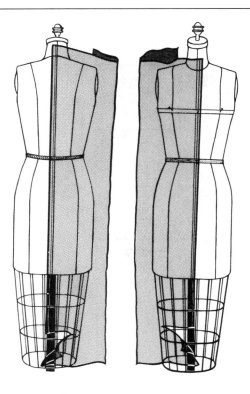

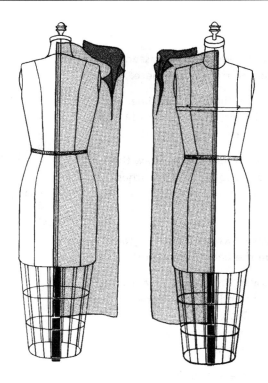

1 **Measure the length** (along the straight of grain) for the front and back from the neckband to the desired length of the shift dress and add 3 inches.

Snip and tear the fabric at this length.

2 **Measure the width** (along the crossgrain) at the underarm level for the front and back from the center of the dress form to the side seam and add 5 inches.

Snip and tear the fabric at this width.

3 Draw the center front and center back grainline 1 inch from the torn edge and press under.

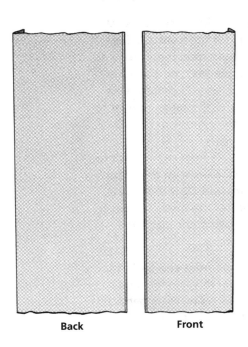

Back   Front

4 Draw two perfect crossgrains on the front fabric piece.

a. Draw in the bust level line. Draw the first crossgrain line 13 inches from the top edge of the fabric.

b. Draw in the hipline. Draw the second crossgrain line 14 inches below the first crossgrain.

5 Draw two perfect crossgrains on the back fabric piece.

a. Draw in the back hipline. Place the front and back fabric pieces side by side. Draw a crossgrain line on the back piece to match the crossgrain on the front piece.

b. Draw the shoulder blade level line. On the dress form, measure the distance from the hip line to the shoulder blade line. Transfer this measurement to the fabric and draw a crossgrain line at this crossmark.

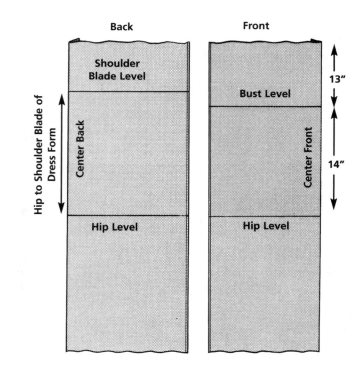

6 Draw the side seams for the front and back fabric pieces.

a. Measure the dress form at the hip level for the front and back.
 • **Measure from center front to the side seam** on the dress form. Add 1/2 inch for ease. Transfer this measurement to the front fabric piece and crossmark.
 • **Measure from center back to the side seam** on the dress form. Add 1/2 inch for ease. Transfer this measurement to the back fabric piece and crossmark.

b. Draw the front and back side seam. From this side seam crossmark, draw a side seam perfectly parallel to the grainline.

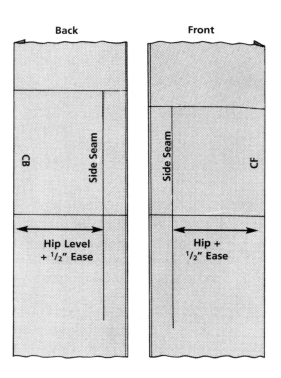

Basic Front Shift: *Draping Steps*

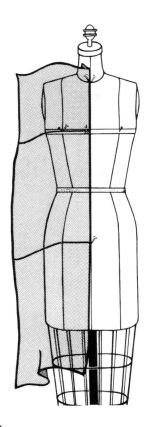

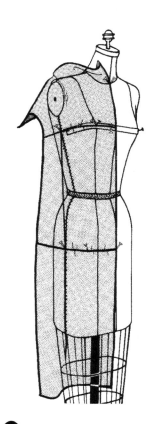

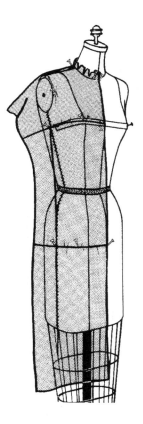

1 **Pin the center front grain-line** fold of the fabric onto the center front position of the dress form.

2 **Align the crossgrains at the bust level and at the hip level.** Anchor pins at center front neck and center front hip. An additional pin may be needed at the bust level tape.

3 **Pin the front crossgrains and the front side seam.** Smooth the fabric across the dress form to the side seam. Pin the side seam. Be sure the fabric crossgrains are parallel to the floor and that the side seam of the pattern is on the side seam of the dress form.

NOTE: Sometimes the dress form tape is crooked; therefore, the crossgrain should be judged by viewing the crossgrain parallel to the floor.

4 Smooth the fabric up and over the dress form armplate to the shoulder. Create a 1/4-inch–1/4-inch pinch at the screw level (middle at ridge) of the armhole. This is to ensure the armhole does not become too tight. Pin in place.

5 **Drape the front neckline.** Trim excess fabric around the neck and clip at intervals. Continue to smooth and pin the fabric around the neck area.

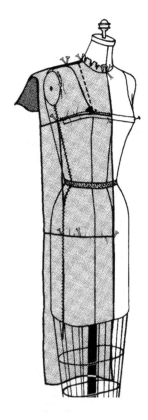

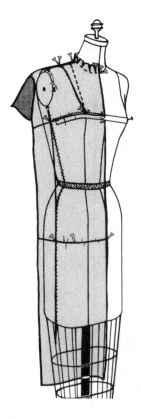

6 Drape and smooth the fabric over the shoulder/neckline seam of the dress form to just past the princess seam. Pin in place. Crossmark the princess seam and the shoulder.

7 Drape the front shoulder dart. The excess fabric that falls between the shoulder/neckline and the shoulder/armhole area will become the amount of excess fabric in the shoulder dart. The larger the bust, the larger the dart; the smaller the bust, the smaller the dart.

a. Crease the fabric at the shoulder/princess seam crossmark.

b. Pin the excess fabric on the princess seam. The excess fabric is creased at the princess seam crossmark and folded toward center front neck. Taper the dart to nothing toward the bust apex.

8 Mark all key areas of the dress form to the fabric.

a. Neckline: Crossmark at center front neck and at the neckline/shoulder corner. Lightly mark the remainder of the neckline.

b. Shoulder seam and shoulder dart: Lightly mark the shoulder seam; crossmark the shoulder dart and shoulder ridge corner.

c. Armplate:
  • Top at shoulder seam ridge
  • Middle at screw level
  • Crossmark bottom at side seam.

d. Side seam: Lightly mark.

Basic Back Shift: *Draping Steps*

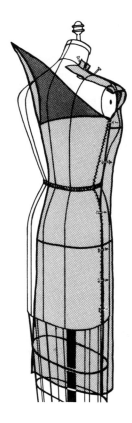 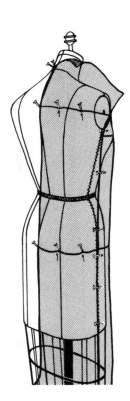 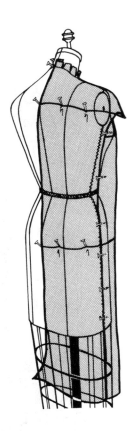

1 **Pin the front and back side seams** to each other, matching the hip level crossgrains.

2 **Pin the center back grainline** fold of the fabric to the center back position of the dress form.

4 **Clip, smooth, and drape the back neckline.** Smooth and pin the back neck area into position.

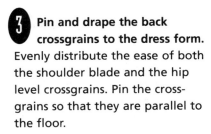

3 **Pin and drape the back crossgrains to the dress form.** Evenly distribute the ease of both the shoulder blade and the hip level crossgrains. Pin the crossgrains so that they are parallel to the floor.

NOTE: If the fabric is correctly draped, there should be no drag between the two crossgrains.

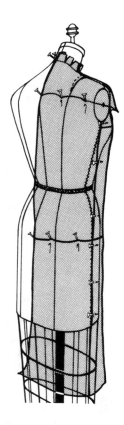
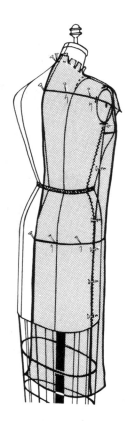

5 **Drape in the back shoulder dart** 3 inches long and 1/2 inch wide, as follows:

a. Smooth the fabric over the shoulder seam from the neckline to the princess seam and crossmark.

b. Measure toward the armhole 1/2 inch from the princess seam at the shoulder and crossmark.

c. Measure down 3 inches on the princess seam from the shoulder seam.

d. Fold the back shoulder dart in place. Fold the fabric from the princess seam crossmark to the 1/2-inch crossmark. Taper the dart to nothing at the 3-inch crossmark.

6 **Mark all key areas** of the dress form to the fabric:

a. Back neckline

b. Shoulder seam and shoulder dart

c. Armplate:
- Top at shoulder ridge
- Middle at screw level
- Bottom at side seam

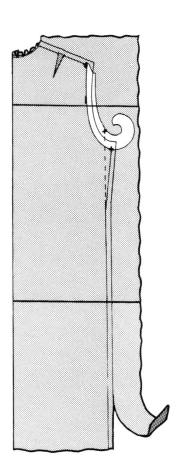

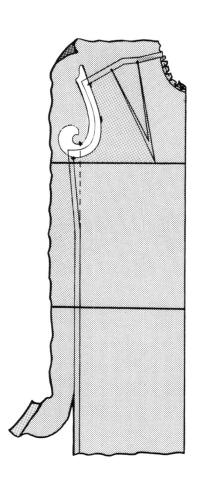

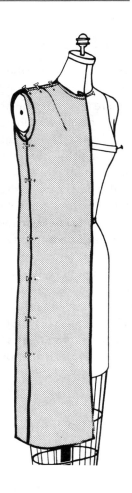

True up the neckline, shoulder, shoulder darts, and the front and back armholes. Remove the fabric drape from the dress form. Add seam allowances and trim excess fabric. Pin darts, side seams, and shoulder seams together.

Return the drape to the dress form and check for accuracy, fit, and balance.

Shift Dresses: *Empire Style*

Preparing the Fabric

Dresses may be divided horizontally at any point on the body. The empire line is particularly well suited to the eased waistline of the demi-fitted shift. It has a high waistline just under the bosom, gradually sloping to the back. The skirt section of this dress may be draped so the side seams are parallel to the grain, or they may be draped to give any degree of flare. The term "empire line" was made popular by Empress Josephine of France, first wife of Napoleon. Her dress had a low-cut neckline, small puffed sleeves, an ankle-length skirt, and a sash tied under the bust. Illustrated here are two examples given for today's look.

Preparation of the Dress Form

Referring to the illustrated design, pin or place style tape for the neckline and the desired empire-style line on the dress form front and back. Also place pins at the hipline of the dress form.

Prepare the Fabric for the Empire Bodice

1 **Length and Width:** Measure the desired length and width of the front and back bodice. Add 4 inches to this measurement. Snip and tear the fabric at this length and width.

2 **Grainline:** Draw the center front and center back grainline 1 inch along the torn edge and parallel to the grain of the fabric. Press under.

3 **Crossgrain:**

a. Draw the front crossgrain at the bustline level (approximately the middle of the fabric piece).

b. Draw the back crossgrain 9 inches below the top of the fabric. This will represent the shoulder blade level line.

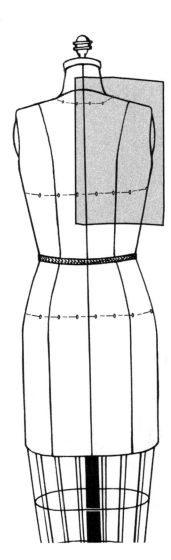
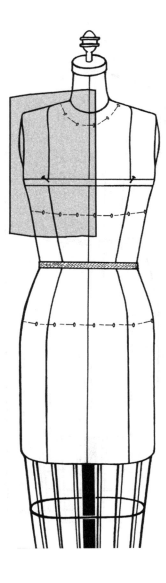

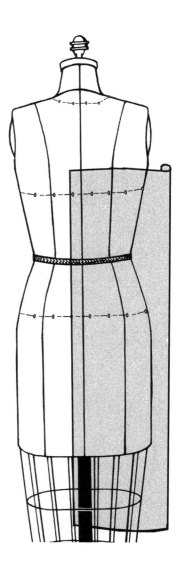

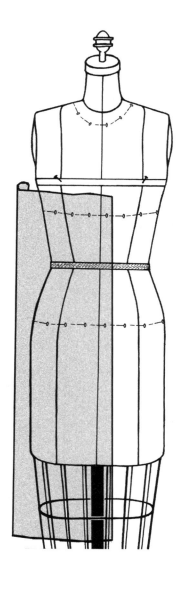

Prepare the Fabric for the Empire Skirt

1 **Length:** Measure the desired length (along the straight of grain) of the front and back skirt sections. Measure from the empire styleline to the desired length and add 5 inches to this measurement. Snip and tear the fabric at this length.

2 **Width:** Divide the fabric piece in half. Fold the fabric piece in half from selvage to selvage. Snip and tear the piece in half lengthwise. One piece will be used for the front skirt, and the other piece will be used for the back skirt.

3 **Grainline:** Draw the center front and center back grainline 1 inch along the torn edge and parallel to the grain of the fabric. Press under.

4 **Crossgrain:** From the top of the fabric edge, draw the front and back hipline crossgrain the distance from the empire styleline to the hipline, plus 4 inches. Draw the crossgrain across the front and back fabric pieces.

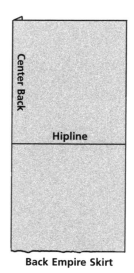

Center Back

Hipline

Back Empire Skirt

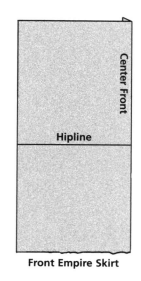

Center Front

Hipline

Front Empire Skirt

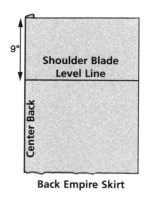

9"

Center Back

Shoulder Blade Level Line

Back Empire Skirt

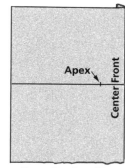

Apex

Center Front

Front Empire Skirt

Basic Foundation Patterns

Draping Steps: Front and Back Empire Bodice

1 **a. Drape front bodice grainline and crossgrain.** Pin center front grainline fold of the empire bodice fabric piece to the center front position of the dress form. Align the crossgrain at the bustline leveland pin in place. Also, anchor pins at the center front neckline position of the design and at the center front empire styleline.

b. Drape back bodice grainline and crossgrain. Pin and drape center back grainline fold of the empire bodice fabric piece to the center back position of the dress form. Align and pin the crossgrain at the shoulder blade level of the dress form. Also, anchor pins at center back neckline position of the design and at the center back empire styleline.

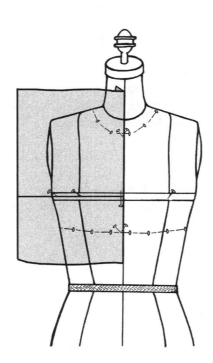

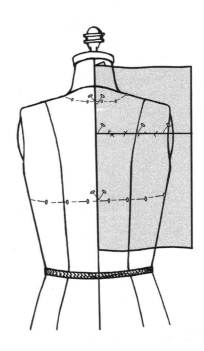

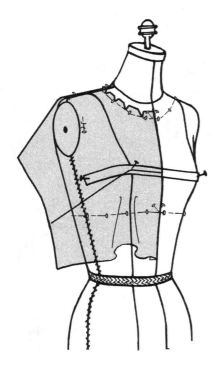

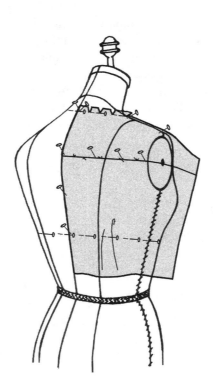

2 **Drape the front and back neckline/shoulder.**

a. Front: Trim, clip, smooth, and pin the front bodice neckline. Drape in a counterclockwise direction, smoothing the fabric over the shoulder and past the armplate. Allow all excess fabric to fall below the empire styleline.

b. Back: Trim, clip, smooth, and pin the back bodice neckline. Smooth the fabric over the shoulder and past the armplate. Some excess fabric will fall below the empire styleline.

c. Match the front shoulder seam to the back shoulder seam.

3 **Drape the front and back armholes and side seams.**

a. Front armhole and side seam: Smooth and drape the fabric around the front armhole of the design, allowing all excess fabric to fall across the side seam and underneath the bust cup at the empire styleline. Pin the side seam area.

NOTE: The crossgrain will angle downward from the apex toward the side seam.

• **For sleeved designs:** Create a 1/4-inch–1/4-inch pinch at the screw level of the armhole ridge. Also, do not trim the fabric around the armhole, as you will have a tendency to stretch the armhole too tight.

• **For sleeveless designs:** Trim, clip, and smooth the fabric around the designed sleeveless armhole. Do not create any ease in the sleeveless armhole. Be careful not to overstitch this armhole.

b. Back armhole and side seam: Drape the fabric from the shoulder blade level line across the back armhole and past the side seam of the dress form. Some excess fullness will fall at the back empire styleline. This excess fullness will be draped into a darting or gathers.

• **For sleeved designs:** A 1/4-inch ease will need to be draped into the armhole near the shoulder blade level line and the back armplate.

• **For sleeveless designs:** Trim, clip, and smooth the fabric around the designed sleeveless armhole. All excess ease will be draped toward the shoulder seam and into the back side seam.

4 **Drape the empire stylelines.**

a. Front styleline design choices: The excess fabric that has accumulated underneath the bust cup may be darted, pleated, or gathered to create your own personal empire design. If a front armhole dart or side bust dart is desired within the design, the excess fabric will be draped into the desired darted area at this time. Drape the remainder of the empire styleline.

b. Back styleline: From center back at the empire styleline, smooth the fabric toward the princess seam. Fold in a 3/4-inch dart. Continue to smooth and drape the fabric across the empire styleline until it passes the side seam. Pin the side seam in place.

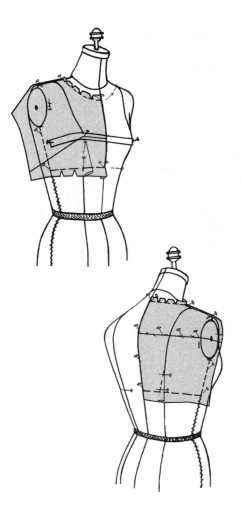

5 **Mark all key areas of the dress form to the fabric.**

a. Neckline: Crossmark at center front neck and at the neckline/ shoulder ridge corner.

b. Shoulder seam: Lightly mark the shoulder seam and crossmark the shoulder/ridge corner.

c. Armplate:
• Top at shoulder seam ridge
• Middle at screw level
• Crossmark bottom at the side seam.

d. Side seam: Lightly mark.

e. Styleline and any styleline details

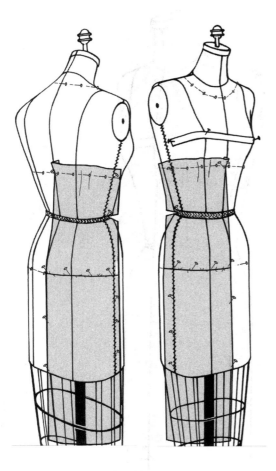

Draping Steps: Empire Skirt

1 **Drape skirt grainlines, crossgrain, and side seam.**

a. Pin the center front grainline fold of the empire skirt fabric piece to the center front and back positions of the dress form. Anchor pins at the center front styleline, at the hipline, and down the center front.

b. Align and pin the hipline crossgrains to the hip level line of the dress form. Smooth and pin the crossgrain of the fabric (evenly distributing 1/4 inch of ease) across the dress form to the side seam.

c. Pin the side seam (below the hip level) to the dress form and at the side seam/styleline.

d. Clip the waistline at the side seam. Continue to smooth the fabric over the side seam of the dress form up to the empire styleline.

NOTE: The shaping and looseness of the waist area are determined by each garment style. Therefore, the waistline area could be loose and away from the body or fitted and kept close to the body. A more fitted waistline needs waist-fitting darts draped into the style. (See steps below.)

2 **Shape the side seams and waist-fitting dart or darts.**

a. Drape the desired shape of the side seam. Mark the side seam. Remove the hipline pins. Pin the front and back side seams together. From the hipline, clip and pin the side seam to the outside for easier shaping. Check the skirt drape for any pulling or twisting. Readjust hang of skirt if necessary and check the desired side seam shaping.

b. With the skirt hanging plumb from the hipline and the side seam draped to your desired shape, drape in the desired darting. The first dart is placed on the princess

seam, starting at the empire styleline. Shape the dart into the waistline and taper to nothing 4 inches below the waistline. If a second dart is desired, place it 1 1/4 inches from the princess seam. The maximum length will be 4 inches from the waistline in the front and 5 1/2 inches in the back.

c. Mark all key areas of the dress form to the skirt fabric.
- Side seam: Lightly mark.
- Darts: Crossmark both sides of all darts and the vanishing points.
- Mark empire styleline and any styleline details.

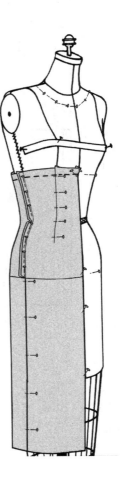

3 **True up the bodice and skirt sections.** After trueing, pin and join the front and back skirt sections to the front and back bodice sections at the empire styeline. Recheck for any twisting or pulling. Reposition darts if necessary.

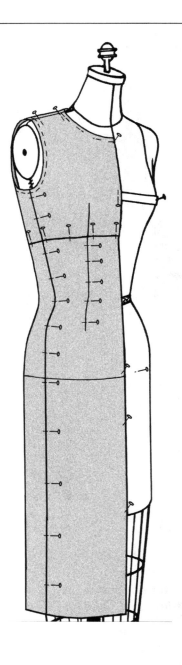

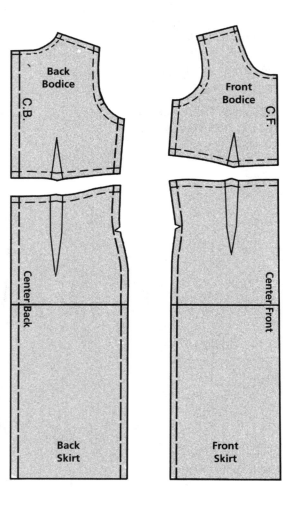

Back Bodice

C.B.

Front Bodice

C.F.

Center Back

Center Front

Back Skirt

Front Skirt

Chapter Eight

Sleeves

Objectives

By studying the various draping steps in this chapter, the designer should be able to:

• Recognize grain and crossgrain of the fabric in relation to the sleeve.

• Take a flat piece of fabric and make it fit the curves of the arm.

• Develop a basic sleeve block with the correct amount of ease allowance, cap size, and measurements.

• Pivot or "walk" the sleeve into the bodice armhole, determine sleeve ease, and place the sleeve cap notches.

• Check the results of each sleeve draft for proper ease, cap shape, fit, hang, and proportion.

• Adjust sleeve or armhole if any part of the sleeve pattern is incorrect.

• Adjust the basic sleeve to allow for more arm movement.

• Convert the basic sleeve into an enlarged armhole to be used with coat sleeves.

• Combine and attach the raglan sleeve to a bodice yoke and achieve an easy sleeve movement.

The Basic Sleeve Blocks: *Definition, Theory, & Principles*

Definition

A sleeve is the section of the garment that covers the arm. The sleeve usually joins the garment in a seam that encircles the arm over the shoulder. There are a number of ways to draft and finish the arm openings of a garment.

Sleeves generally are divided into the following basic types.

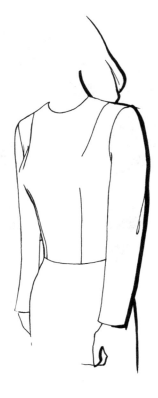

Variations of the Sleeve Blocks

The **basic sleeve** fits into the traditional armhole. This sleeve is sometimes termed a set-in or closed sleeve. The sleeve is completed before it is attached to the armhole. The garment armhole seam circles the arm near the shoulder because the side seams and shoulder seams of the garment are also previously sewn and the sleeve is "set into the armhole," thus the term.

The **shirt sleeve** is placed into a dropped sleeve opening. In the shirt sleeve or open-sleeve method, the sleeve is sewn into an open seam because it is stitched to the armhole while both the sleeve and garment seam remain open.

The **raglan sleeve** includes a portion of the yoke of a bodice or shirt, retaining its original underarm curve in both the bodice and the sleeve. The sleeve is usually cut in two pieces with a shoulder seam. The raglan sleeve sews into a front and back diagonal seam that extends from the armhole up to the neckline. Please refer to Chapter 14 for further discussion on raglan sleeves.

Theory

The **basic sleeve** block may be used when:

• The design has a traditional armhole for a set-in sleeve that extends from the shoulder ridge to the underarm/side seam of the garment.

   The **shirt sleeve** block may be used when:

• The shirt sleeve is placed into a design that includes a dropped sleeve opening.

   The **raglan sleeve** block may be used when:

• The design may or may not have a waist-fitting seam.

• A raglan styleline is within the design.

• The raglan sleeve sews into a front and back diagonal seam that extends from the armhole up to the neckline.

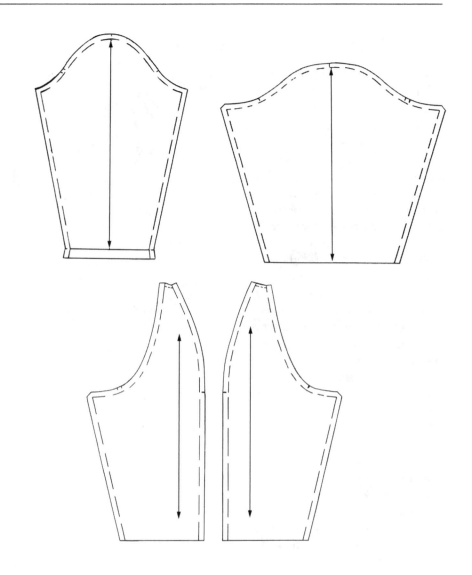

Principles: Analyzing the Sleeve Blocks

The sleeve blocks are used to create a variety of sleeve designs for dresses, blouses, and shirts (refer to theory, above). It is important to analyze the block to insure that the following items are correct. If one of these items is wrong, the designs made from this block will not fit properly, and they will twist, drag, or pull.

• Grainline should be straight and in the middle of the sleeve.

• The crossgrain should be parallel to the floor.

• The sleeve is pivoted or "walked," matching stitchline of the sleeve to stitchline of the bodice armhole, to determine the sleeve cap ease.

• Walking a sleeve into an armhole will show if there is enough cap distance and will determine the amount of ease needed in the cap.

• Walking a sleeve into an armhole will show where to match and place the sleeve cap notches—front, back, and shoulder position.

NOTE: If the ease amount is too much or too little, check the armhole shape of the bodice.

Basic Sleeve Measurement Chart

Before you draft the basic fitted sleeve, study the following five important measurements.

1. Overarm length (distance from the shoulder to the wrist)

Size	6	8	10	12	14
Overarm length	22 3/8"	22 3/4"	23 1/8"	23 1/2"	23 7/8"

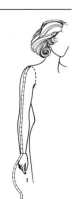

2. Underarm length (distance from the underarm armpit to the wrist)

Size	6	8	10	12	14
Underarm length	16 1/4"	16 1/2"	16 3/4"	17"	17 1/4"

3. Cap height (remaining distance from the underarm armpit to the shoulder)

Size	6	8	10	12	14
Cap height	6 1/8"	6 1/4"	6 3/8"	6 1/2"	6 5/8"

4. Elbow circumference (measurement around the elbow plus 1 inch ease)

Size	6	8	10	12	14
Elbow circumference	9 3/4"	10 1/4"	10 3/4"	11 1/4"	11 3/4"

5. Bicep circumference (measurement around the upper arm plus 2 inch ease)

Size	6	8	10	12	14
Bicep circumference	11 1/2"	12"	12 1/2"	13"	13 1/2"

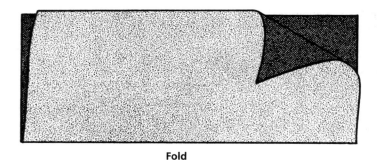

Fold

① **Cut a piece of pattern paper** 32 inches long by 24 inches wide. Fold the paper in half lengthwise.

NOTE: One half of the sleeve is drafted. It is then cut on the fold and opened up to make a full sleeve. Minor pattern changes are then made to show the difference between the front and back of the sleeve.

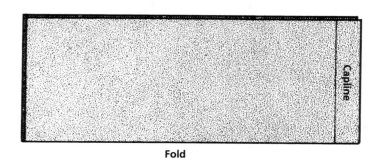

Fold

② **Draw the capline.** With the fold in front of you, draw a perfect crossgrain line 2 inches from the right side of the paper. This is the top of your sleeve, or the capline.

Overarm Distance

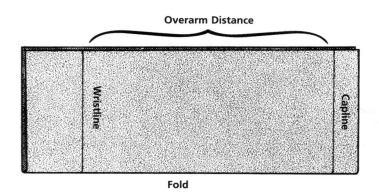

Fold

③ **Draw the wrist level line.** With the fold in front of you, measure down from the top of the sleeve (capline) the desired overarm distance (size 8 is 22 3/4 inches, size 10 is 23 1/8 inches). Using an L-square ruler, draw a perfect crossgrain line up from the fold at this level for the wristline.

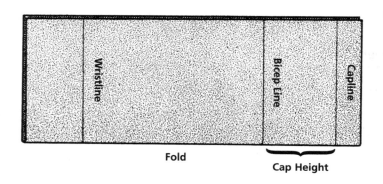

Fold

Cap Height

④ **Draw the bicep line.** With the fold in front of you, measure from the top of the sleeve (capline) the desired cap height (size 8 is 6 1/4 inches, size 10 is 6 3/8 inches). Using an L-square ruler, draw a perfect crossgrain line up from the fold at this level for the bicep line.

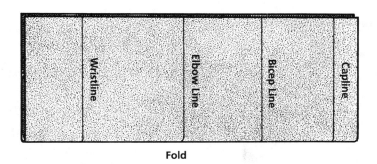

Fold

5 **Draw the elbow line.** With the fold in front of you, divide the distance from the bicep line to the wristline in half. Draw in an **elbow line** 1/2 inch above this halfway point.

One Half of Bicep Circumference

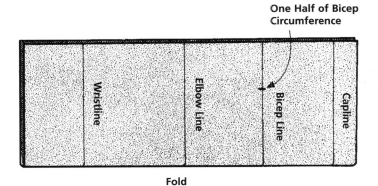

Fold

6 **Crossmark one half of the bicep circumference.**

a. Determine the bicep sleeve circumference needed and add the necessary amount of ease. Divide this amount in half (size 8 is 6 inches, size 10 is 6 1/4 inches).

b. Place a crossmark on the bicep line this distance up from the fold of the paper.

One Half of Elbow Circumference

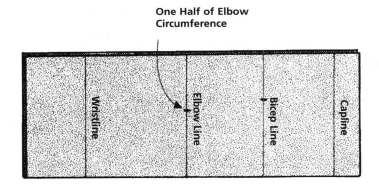

7 **Crossmark one half of the elbow circumference.**

a. Determine the elbow circumference needed and add the necessary amount of ease. Divide this amount in half (size 8 is 5 1/8 inches, size 10 is 5 3/8 inches).

b. Place a crossmark on the elbow line this distance up from the fold of the paper.

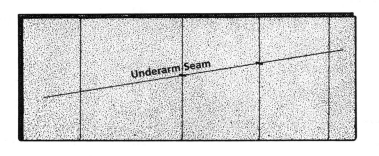

8 **Draw the underarm seamline.** Connect the bicep crossmark and the elbow crossmark. Continue this line straight up until it crosses the top of the sleeve (capline) and down until it crosses the wristline. This line represents the underarm seamline.

Fold of Cap

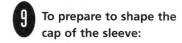

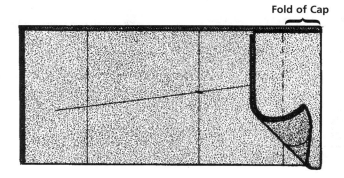

9 To prepare to shape the cap of the sleeve:

a. Fold the cap area in half from the top of the sleeve (capline) to the bicep line.

b. Fold the sleeve in half lengthwise. Place and crease the sleeve foldline to the underarm seamline.

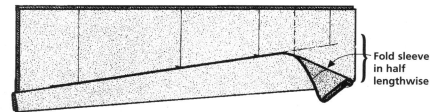

→ **Fold sleeve in half lengthwise**

French Curve Guideline

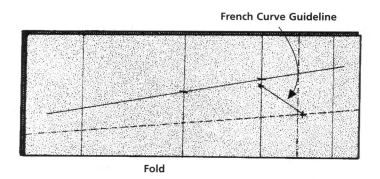

Fold

10 Prepare to draw in the cap shape by establishing a guideline for the french curve.

a. Put a crossmark on the bicep line 1 inch in from the underarm seamline.

b. Put a crossmark on the lengthwise fold 3/4 inch above the point at which the folds of the cap height meet.

c. Lightly draw a line to connect these two crossmarks.

A

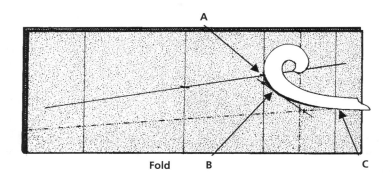

Fold **B** **C**

11 Draw the underarm curve of the sleeve cap. Using a french curve and referring to the illustration, connect positions **A** (underarm seam/bicep line corner), **B** (middle of french curve guideline), and **C** (capline at lengthwise foldline).

All three positions must touch the french curve at the same time.

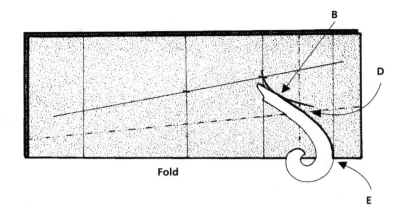

Fold

12 **Draw the top portion of the sleeve cap.** Using a french curve and referring to the illustration, **connect positions B** (middle of french curve guide-line), **D** (crossmark on lengthwise foldline), and **E** (capline at center sleeve foldline). All three positions must touch the french curve at the same time.

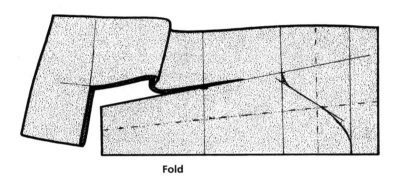

Fold

13 **Cut out the entire sleeve.** With the sleeve still folded in half, cut out the sleeve following the newly shaped cap, the underarm seamline, and the wristline.

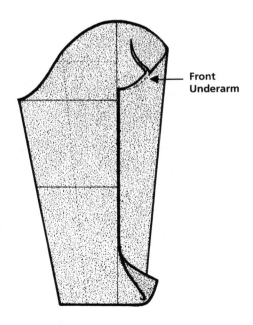

Front Underarm

14 **Reshape the front under arm curve.** Open the sleeve draft and fold the unmarked underarm area in half. Remove 1/4 inch at the middle of this lower curve on the underarm seamline, blending to nothing at the lengthwise quarter fold and the underarm seam. This side represents the front cap/underarm of the sleeve.

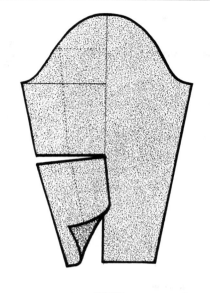

15 **Create the elbow dart and wristline placement.** With the sleeve open, cut on the elbow line to the center foldline of the sleeve. Also cut on the center foldline from the wrist level up to the elbow level. Do not cut through entirely.

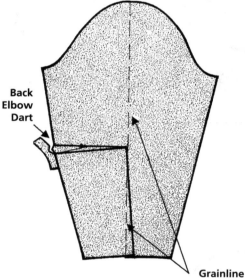

Back Elbow Dart

Grainline

16 **Form the back of the sleeve and the elbow dart.** Lap over the center sleeve line. This will cause an opening at the elbow line. Lap this center line until the elbow dart area is opened at least 1/2 to 5/8 inch.

Tape a small piece of paper underneath the slashed opening. At this slashed opening, draw the dart 3 1/2 inches long and the width of the opening. Fold the dart closed to determine the shape of the dart and trim excess paper.

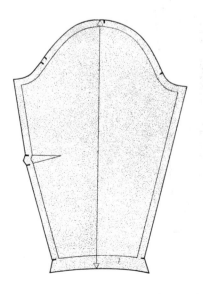

17 **Determine the sleeve cap notches.** Pivot the stitchline of the sleeve cap into the stitchline of the desired armhole. Refer to the pivoting steps on pages 125–126, for a clear example of pivoting technique and notch placement.

18 **Add seam allowance to the sleeve.**

Refer to Walking the Sleeve, page 126, to determine the ease amount. This ease will be "crimped" and evenly distributed from the front (single notch) to the back notches (double notches). The sleeve is now ready for a fitting.

Walking the Sleeve into the Armhole

The silhouette of a sleeve gradually changes from year to year. It may vary from a skimpy short cap to a voluminous puff. It may have a natural shoulder look or a tailored squared look with padded shoulders. In all cases, the sleeve must fit smoothly and yet offer freedom of movement. As a result, each new look must be checked for cap distance, notch placement, and sleeve fit.

To ensure a proper fit, the sleeve must be pivoted to the bodice armhole, matching stitchline to stitchline. This technique is known as "walking the sleeve." Walking a sleeve into an armhole will show if there is enough cap distance and where to match and place the notches and will determine the amount of ease needed in the cap.

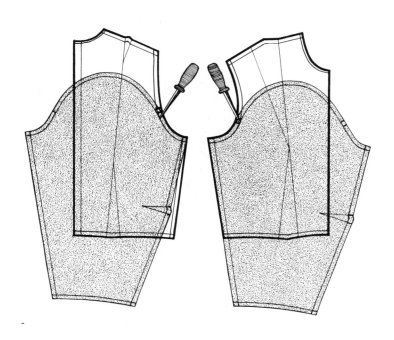

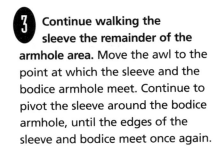

1 **Place the underarm of the sleeve to the underarm of the bodice,** matching the stitch-lines and the side seams.

NOTE: The armhole notches for the bodice have already been established. The front and back armhole notches have been placed 1/3 the distance up from the side seam (about 3 inches). Refer to page 61.

2 **Pivot the sleeve around the armhole.** Starting at the underarm side seam corner, pivot the sleeve around the armhole until the edges of the sleeve and bodice meet. Use a pencil or an awl at the stitchline of the sleeve to hold the sleeve in place. While walking the sleeve, match and pencil in the front and back armhole notches (one on the front and two on the back).

3 **Continue walking the sleeve the remainder of the armhole area.** Move the awl to the point at which the sleeve and the bodice armhole meet. Continue to pivot the sleeve around the bodice armhole, until the edges of the sleeve and bodice meet once again.

4 **Crossmark the shoulder positions.** While walking the sleeve, notch and crossmark on the sleeve cap the front and back bodice shoulder position of the front and back bodice.

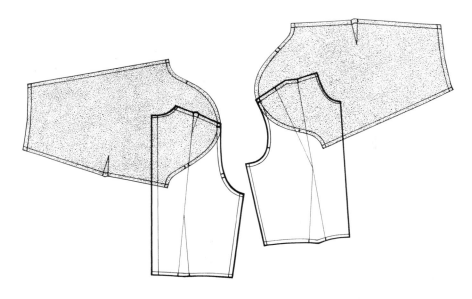

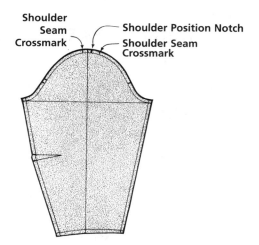

Shoulder Seam Crossmark

Shoulder Position Notch

Shoulder Seam Crossmark

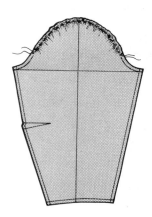

5 **Determine the shoulder position notch of the sleeve cap.** Divide the distance between the shoulder seam crossmarks in half. This center position is the shoulder notch.

NOTE: If the armhole shape is correct, the notch at the shoulder position will fall 1/4 inch toward the front of the grain. If the notch does not fall close to that position, it can be assumed that the bodice drape and/or the armhole shape is incorrect. (The back armhole should measure 1/2 inch longer than the front armhole.)

6 **Determine the amount of sleeve cap ease.** The distance between the shoulder position crossmarks is the amount of ease in the sleeve cap. This amount of ease will be evenly distributed or "crimped" into the sleeve from the front underarm notch to the back underarm notches. Crimp (ease in) the sleeve cap from the front notch to the back notches.

NOTE: The sleeve cap ease should be 1 to 1 1/2 inches. If it is not, there is probably an error in the sleeve draft or, more likely, an error in the bodice armhole true up or drape.

Notes

Balancing the Armhole

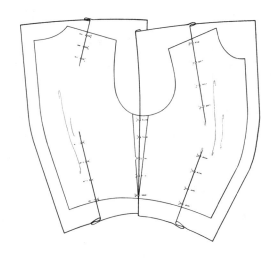

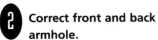

1 **Measure front and back armhole.** The front armhole should measure 1/2 inch shorter than the back armhole.

2 **Correct front and back armhole.**

a. To make the front or back armhole longer: Reshape the front armhole by removing 1/4 inch at the middle of the armhole, shaping back to its original corners at the top and bottom.

b. To make the front and back armhole shorter: Add 1/4 inch at the mid/armhole area and, again, reshape to its original corners at the top and bottom.

NOTE: If the armhole does not balance by removing or adding 1/4 inch, an error was probably made while trueing or draping the armhole.

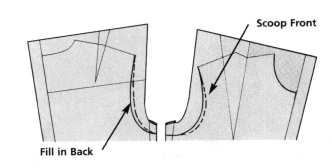

Scoop Front

Fill in Back

──────── OR ────────

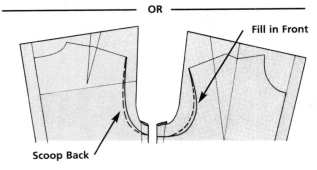

Fill in Front

Scoop Back

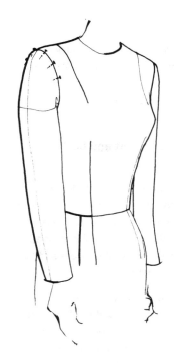

The designer may make pattern adjustments but still retain the original character of the sleeve. Fitting a sleeve into a garment is essential when a new sleeve has been drafted. The fitting allows the designer to compare the flat pattern dimensions with the hang, movement, proportion, and shape of the actual sleeve.

A properly fitted sleeve will provide the designer with the highest-quality garments. Therefore, fittings must be done carefully and accurately.

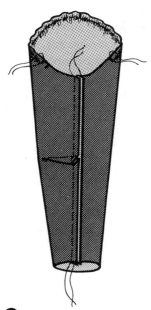

1 **Cut, sew, and crimp the basic sleeve.** Cut the basic sleeve out of fabric. Sew the elbow dart and the underarm seam. Crimp the sleeve cap from the front notch to the back notches.

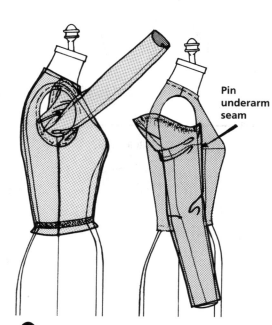

Pin underarm seam

2 **Pin the underarm seam of the sleeve.** Lift the arm to expose the underarm seams and pin the underarm seam of the sleeve to the underarm seam of the bodice armhole. Place the pins parallel to the stitchline, from the front notches down and around to the back notches.

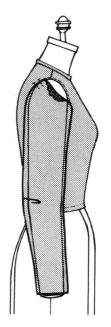

3 **Pin the sleeve cap to the remaining portion of the armhole,** matching the shoulder notch to the shoulder seam of the bodice and all remaining stitchlines.

NOTE: For additional fitting procedures on sleeves, refer to Chapter 3, page 32.

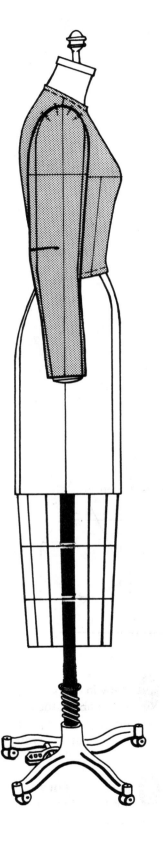

Checklist

Check the sleeve for proper fit and hang.

☐ **Grainline:** The grainline should hang straight and in the middle of the arm. The grainline should fall to the side seam of the dress form.

☐ **Crossgrain:** The crossgrain should be parallel to the floor. It should not pull or sag.

☐ **Hang:** From the elbow level, the sleeve should have a slight forward movement to follow the hang of the human arm.

☐ **Ease:** The sleeve cap should have the correct amount of ease.

NOTE: The amount of ease varies in sleeve styles and among different manufacturers.

Notes for Any Adjustments

Adjust and pin the sleeve cap if any of the above areas are slightly off. Draw any changes on draft.

- If the ease amount is too much or too little, check the armhole shape of the bodice.

- If the sleeve swings too far forward or backward, check the armhole shape of the bodice.

Check sleeve draft for accuracy.

- Position and pin the altered pattern to the original sleeve pattern. Transfer, with a trace wheel, all changes to this pattern and retrue all changes.

NOTE: It would be advisable to make a quick second fitting of the sleeve if there are any changes.

A set-in sleeve sometimes needs a longer underarm seam to allow the arm to move more freely up and down or to allow greater ease of movement forward and backward. To achieve an easier movement in a sleeve, draft a new sleeve from the original set-in sleeve, using the following steps.

Draw in the bicep line

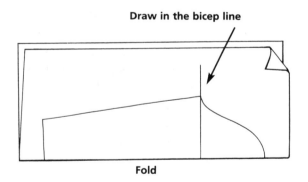

Fold

Draw in the second bicep line

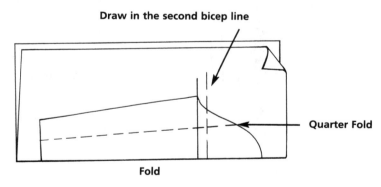

Quarter Fold

Fold

1 Cut a piece of pattern **paper** 32 inches long by 30 inches wide. Fold the paper in half lengthwise.

2 Place the basic block sleeve **(without the elbow dart) on the pattern paper,** matching center of the sleeve (straight of grain) to the paper pattern fold.

3 Draw in the entire sleeve **lightly** from the center of the sleeve cap (fold of paper) around and down to the wristline.

4 Remove the original sleeve **pattern. Draw in the bicep line** on the pattern paper from the center fold of the paper at the bicep level of the drawn-in sleeve.

5 Draw in a new bicep line 1 inch above the original bicep line on the pattern paper of the new sleeve pattern draft.

6 Draw in the quarter fold position of the sleeve (see illustration) of the new sleeve pattern draft.

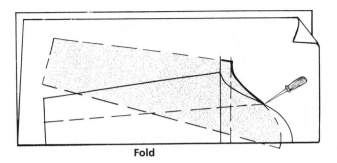

Fold

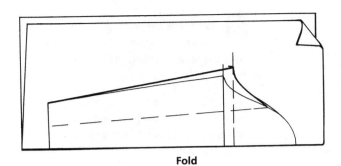

Fold

7 **Place the original sleeve on top of the paper sleeve draft.** Match the center of the sleeve to the paper fold and the original bicep lines.

8 **Pivot the sleeve up to the new bicep line.** Using an awl at the quarter fold/cap area, pivot the sleeve underarm up until the side seam/bicep corner touches the "new bicep line."

9 **Draw in a new cap line.** Using the pattern as a guide, draw from the quarter fold cap area down to the new bicep corner.

10 **Draw a new underarm sleeve seam line.** Using a straight ruler, connect the new underarm/bicep corner down to the original wristline.

11 **Blend the new cap line.** Using a curved ruler, blend a new capline. Reshape the underarm seams.

12 **Cut out the sleeve pattern.**

NOTE: These changes alter the length of the sleeve cap. Therefore, it is important to walk the sleeve into the armhole to determine if the sleeve cap length is too long or too short and whether the sleeve cap has sufficient ease. Step 14 offers directions for adding or subtracting cap distance.

13 **Walk the sleeve cap** into the desired garment armhole. (See basic sleeve pivoting instructions, pages 125–126.)

a. Place the underarm of the sleeve to the underarm of the bodice, matching the stitchlines and the side seams.

NOTE: The armhole notches for the bodice have already been established.

b. Pivot the sleeve around the armhole. Use a pencil or an awl at the stitchline of the sleeve to hold the sleeve in place. Starting at the underarm side seam corner, pivot the sleeve around the armhole until the edges of the sleeve and bodice meet.

While walking the sleeve, match and pencil in the front and back armhole notches (one on the front and two on the back).

c. Continue walking the sleeve the remainder of the armhole area. Move the awl to where the sleeve and the bodice armhole meet. Continue to pivot the sleeve around the bodice armhole, until the edges of the sleeve and bodice meet once again.

Repeat this pivoting procedure until the sleeve cap meets at the shoulder/armhole corner.

d. Crossmark the shoulder positions. While walking the sleeve, crossmark on the sleeve cap the front and back bodice shoulder position of the front and back bodice. Note the amount of ease in the sleeve cap.

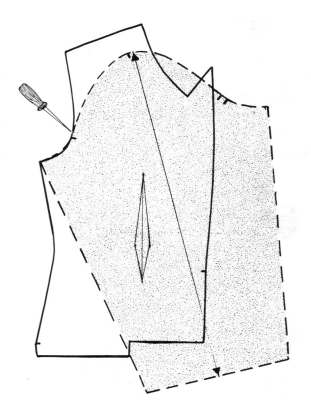

14 If the sleeve cap proves to be too long or too short, do the following.

a. Too short: Slash the center of the sleeve and the quarter folds from the top of the sleeve to the wrist level. Open and add the desired amount of cap distance. Divide the other half in half again. Add this amount to both side seam/bicep corners. Blend all new lines.

b. Too long: Slash the center of the sleeve and the quarter folds from the top of the sleeve to the wrist level. Close and subtract the desired amount. Divide the other half in half again. Subtract this amount from both side seam/bicep corners. Blend all new lines.

NOTE: A fitted sleeve could require 1 to 1 1/2 inches of ease in the sleeve cap. The fabric, style, and manufacturer are factors in determining the amount of ease required.

15 Repeat fitting steps as shown earlier in this unit (Fitting the Basic Sleeve, page 128). Also, complete the fitting on a live model to ensure proper arm movement.

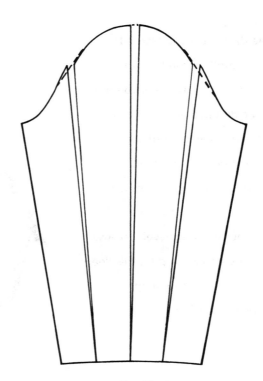

Too Short

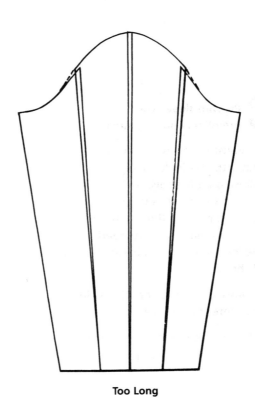

Too Long

Shirt Sleeve

The shirt sleeve is a tailored wrist-length sleeve that sets smoothly into an extended shoulder and a dropped armhole with only a minimum amount of ease. To accommodate the extended shoulders, the shirt sleeve has a shallow cap height with a higher than normal bicep level. Because of its generous bicep fit, this sleeve design allows freedom of movement as well as comfort.

1 **Prepare sleeve cap, grainline, and crossgrain.**

a. Adjust the sleeve cap by using either the basic sleeve or the adjusted basic sleeve. Extend the sleeve cap amount out and down to accommodate the amount the sleeve armhole was extended for the longer armhole measurement of the shirt.

b. Draw a straight of grainline in the center of the sleeve.

c. Draw a new bicep line on the sleeve at the new bicep level.

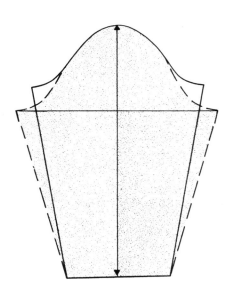

2 **Cut a piece of pattern paper** 32 inches long by 30 inches wide. Fold the paper in half lengthwise.

3 **Place the newly adjusted sleeve on top of the pattern paper,** matching the center of the sleeve (straight of grain) to the paper pattern fold.

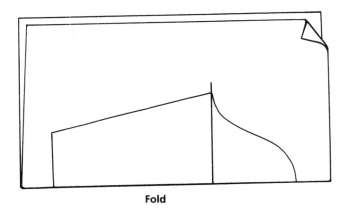

Fold

4 **Draw in the entire sleeve lightly** from the center of the sleeve cap (fold of paper) around and down to the wristline.

5 **Remove the original sleeve** pattern from the new sleeve draft.

6 **Draw in a bicep line on the pattern paper** from the center fold of the paper at the bicep level of the drawn-in sleeve.

7 **Draw in a new bicep line on the new sleeve draft.** Measure down 3 1/2 inches from the traced sleeve cap. At this position, draw in a new bicep line.

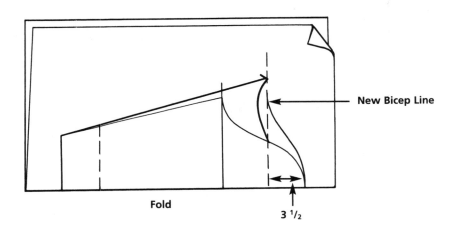

Fold

New Bicep Line

3 1/2

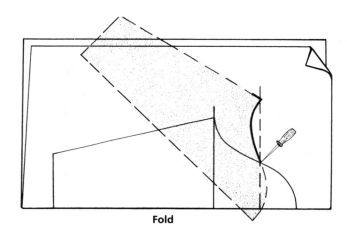
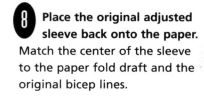

Fold

8 Place the original adjusted sleeve back onto the paper. Match the center of the sleeve to the paper fold draft and the original bicep lines.

9 Pivot the sleeve up to the new bicep line. Using an awl at the quarter fold/cap, pivot the sleeve underarm up until the side seam/bicep corner touches the new bicep line.

10 Draw in a new cap line. Using the pattern as a guide, draw from the quarter fold cap area down to the new bicep corner. Remove the original sleeve from the draft.

11 Draw a new underarm sleeve seam line. Using a straight ruler, connect the new underarm/bicep corner down to the original wristline.

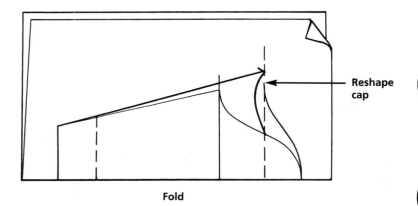

Reshape cap

Fold

12 Blend the new cap line. Using a curved ruler, blend a new sleeve cap stitchline. The sleeve cap should be a clean, smooth "lazy S shape."

13 Cut the sleeve pattern out.

NOTE:

a. These changes alter the length of the sleeve cap. Therefore, it is important to walk the sleeve into the armhole to determine if the sleeve cap length is long enough or too short and whether the sleeve cap has sufficient ease. Step 15 offers directions for adding or subtracting cap distance.

b. Most shirt sleeves require only **1/2 inch of ease** in the sleeve cap.

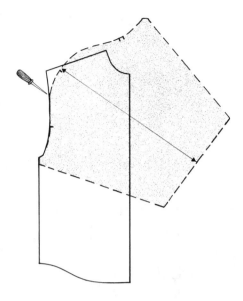

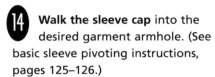 **Walk the sleeve cap** into the desired garment armhole. (See basic sleeve pivoting instructions, pages 125–126.)

a. Place the underarm of the sleeve to the underarm of the bodice, matching the stitchlines and the side seams.

NOTE: The armhole notches for the bodice have already been established.

b. Pivot the sleeve around the armhole. Use a pencil or an awl at the stitchline of the sleeve to hold the sleeve in place. Starting at the underarm side seam corner, pivot the sleeve around the armhole until the edges of the sleeve and bodice meet.

While walking the sleeve, match and pencil in the front and back armhole notches (one on the front and two on the back).

c. Continue walking the sleeve the remainder of the armhole area. Move the awl to where the sleeve and the bodice armhole meet. Continue to pivot the sleeve around the bodice armhole until the edges of the sleeve and bodice meet once again.

Repeat this pivoting procedure until the sleeve cap meets at the shoulder/armhole corner.

d. Crossmark the shoulder positions. While walking the sleeve, crossmark on the sleeve cap the front and back bodice shoulder position of the front and back bodice.

NOTE: A shirt sleeve usually requires 1/2 inch of ease, whereas a fitted sleeve could require 1 1/2 inches of ease. The fabric, style, and manufacturer are factors in determining the amount of ease required.

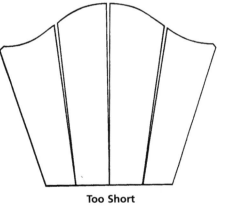

Too Short

15 **If the sleeve cap proves to be too long or too short,** do the following.

a. Too short: Slash the center of the sleeve and the quarter folds open from the top of the sleeve to the wrist level. Open and add the desired amount of cap distance. Add this amount to both side seam/bicep corners. Blend all new lines.

b. Too long: Slash the center of the sleeve and the quarter folds from the top of the sleeve to the wrist level. Close and subtract the desired amount. Blend all new lines.

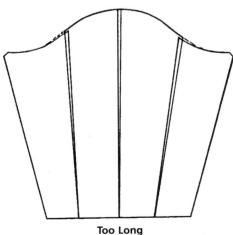

Too Long

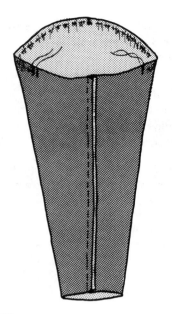

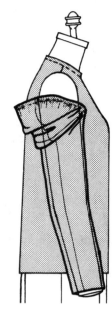

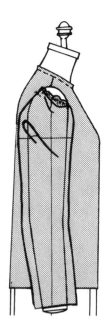

16 **Prepare the sleeve pattern for a fitting.** Cut shirt sleeve out of fabric. Sew the underarm seams together. Crimp the sleeve cap from the front notch to the back notches.

17 **Lift the arm to expose the underarm seams and pin the underarm seam** of the sleeve to the underarm seam of the bodice armhole. Place the pins on the stitchline, from the front notches down and around to the back notches.

18 **Pin the sleeve cap** to the remaining portion of the armhole, matching the shoulder notch to the shoulder seam of the bodice and all remaining stitchlines.

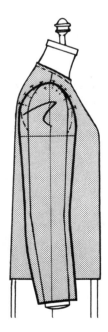

19 **Check the sleeve for accurate fit and hang.** See Fitting the Basic Sleeve, page 128, to check the sleeve for proper fit and any notes on adjustments.

Lowered or Exaggerated Armhole Sleeve

The important feature of the lowered or exaggerated armhole sleeve is that the bicep level and cap height are wider than normal. This allows the sleeve to fit into a lowered armhole on the bodice. The more the bodice armhole is lowered, the more the bicep level should be lifted and extended. This will create greater freedom of movement after the sleeve cap has been enlarged to accommodate the larger armhole.

This type of armhole may be used with a basic sleeve or a shirt sleeve look. For instance, a designer may want a sportswear styling with a sportive and active look. Or the designer may want an enlarged coat sleeve styling with a higher cap and shoulder padding. The style of garment and the desired cap height will influence the sleeve shape designed.

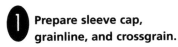

1 **Prepare sleeve cap, grainline, and crossgrain.**

a. Adjust the sleeve cap by using the basic sleeve. Extend the cap to accommodate the longer armhole measurement and additional side seam ease.

b. Draw a straight of grainline in the center of the sleeve.

c. Draw a new bicep line on the sleeve at the new bicep level.

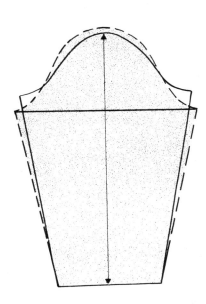

2 Cut a piece of pattern paper 32 inches long by 30 inches wide. Fold the paper in half lengthwise.

3 Place the newly adjusted sleeve on top of the pattern paper, matching the center of the sleeve (straight of grain) to the paper pattern fold.

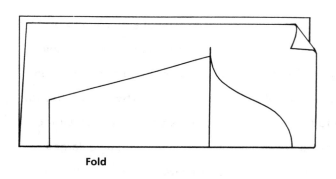

Fold

4 Draw in the entire sleeve lightly from the center of the sleeve cap (fold of paper) around and down to the wristline.

5 Remove the original sleeve pattern from the new sleeve draft.

6 Draw in a bicep line on the pattern paper from the center fold of the paper at the bicep level of the drawn-in sleeve.

7 Draw in a new bicep line on the new sleeve draft 1 1/2 to 2 inches above the original bicep line on the pattern paper.

8 Draw in the quarter fold position of the sleeve (see illustration).

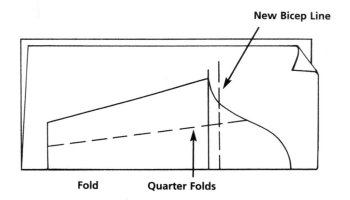

New Bicep Line

Fold   Quarter Folds

9 **Place the newly adjusted sleeve on top of the paper sleeve draft.** Match the center of the sleeve to the paper fold and the original bicep lines.

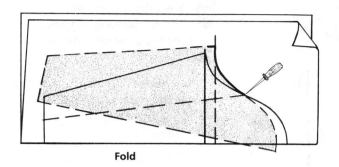

Fold

10 **Pivot the sleeve up to the new bicep line.** Using an awl at the quarter fold/cap area, pivot the sleeve underarm up until the side seam/bicep corner touches the new bicep line.

11 **Draw in a new cap line.** Using the pattern as a guide, draw from the quarter fold cap area down to the new bicep corner.

12 **Draw a new underarm sleeve seam line.** Using a straight ruler, connect the new underarm/bicep corner down to the original wristline.

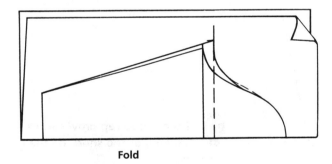

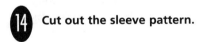

Fold

13 **Blend the new cap line.** Using a curved ruler, blend a new capline. Reshape the underarm seams.

14 **Cut out the sleeve pattern.**

NOTE: These changes alter the length of the sleeve cap. Therefore, it is important to walk the sleeve into the armhole to determine if the sleeve cap length is too long or too short and whether the sleeve cap has sufficient ease. Step 16 offers directions for adding or subtracting cap distance.

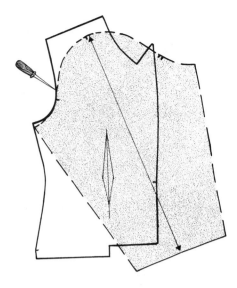

15 Walk the sleeve cap into the desired garment armhole. (See basic sleeve pivoting instructions, pages 125–126.)

a. Place the underarm of the sleeve to the underarm of the bodice, matching the stitchlines and the side seams.

NOTE: The armhole notches for the bodice have already been established.

b. Pivot the sleeve around the arm-hole. Use a pencil or an awl at the stitchline of the sleeve to hold the sleeve in place. Starting at the underarm side seam corner, pivot the sleeve around the armhole until the edges of the sleeve and bodice meet.

While walking the sleeve, match and pencil in the front and back armhole notches (one on the front and two on the back).

c. Continue walking the sleeve the remainder of the armhole area. Move the awl to where the sleeve and the bodice armhole meet. Continue to pivot the sleeve around the bodice armhole, until the edges of the sleeve and bodice meet once again.

Repeat this pivoting procedure until the sleeve cap meets at the shoulder/armhole corner.

d. Crossmark the shoulder positions. While walking the sleeve, crossmark on the sleeve cap the front and back bodice shoulder position of the front and back bodice. Note the amount of ease in the sleeve cap.

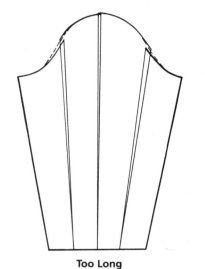

Too Long

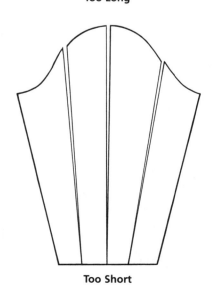

Too Short

16 If the sleeve cap proves to be too long or too short, do the following.

a. Too short: Slash the center of the sleeve and the quarter folds from the top of the sleeve to the wrist level. Open and add the desired amount of cap distance. Divide the other half in half again. Add this amount to both side seam/bicep corners. Blend all new lines.

b. Too long: Slash the center of the sleeve and the quarter folds from the top of the sleeve to the wrist level. Close and subtract the desired amount. Divide the other half in half again. Subtract this amount from both side seam/bicep corners. Blend all new lines.

NOTE: A fitted sleeve could require 1 1/4 inches to 2 inches of ease in the sleeve cap. The fabric, style, and manufacturer are factors in determining the amount of ease required.

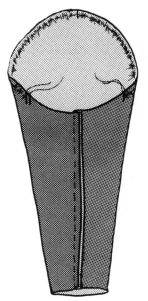

17 **Prepare the sleeve pattern for a fitting.** Cut the sleeve out of fabric. Sew the underarm seams together. Crimp the sleeve cap from the front notch to the back notches.

NOTE: If an elbow dart is required (usually in the fitted sleeve, but not in the shirt sleeve), draft an elbow dart at this time. Refer to Basic Sleeve, page 124.

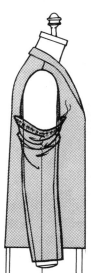

18 **Lift the arm to expose the underarm seams and pin the underarm seam** of the sleeve to the underarm seam of the bodice armhole. Place the pins on the stitchline, from the front notch down and around to the back notches.

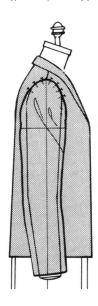

19 **Pin the sleeve cap to the remaining portion of the armhole,** matching the shoulder notch to the shoulder seam of the bodice and all remaining stitchlines. See Fitting the Basic Sleeve, page 128, to check the sleeve for proper fit and notes on adjustments.

Part Three

Design Variations

In Parts One and Two, the designer learned to mold and shape fabric on the dress form and to create basic patterns. In Part Three, the designer will learn to use these basic foundation skills to create bodices, skirts, and sleeves. In addition, the design of basic collars and pants, as well as more fashionable variations, is introduced.

Part Three enhances the designer's skills in handling a variety of fabrics. The designs are kept simple and natural, while the fabric is draped with the correct amount of ease proportion and is not overworked. Projects explore how to define the style and silhouette over the bust, hip, and waist by emphasizing the use of folds, darts, pleats, and fullness.

Many ideas develop after making a slash to release the excess fabric beyond the normal seam position. Projects illustrating this principle explain the manipulation of draped design. Working with a greater understanding of each method helps the designer recognize the qualities of a well-designed garment.

Chapter Nine

Bodice Variations and Asymmetric and Halter Designs

Objectives

By studying the various draping steps in this chapter, the designer should be able to:

- Develop creativity and stimulate a variety of bodice designs.

- Mold the fabric and a basic bodice pattern to fit the curves of the body over the bust.

- Manipulate the fabric to create folds, darts, pleats, and fullness radiating from the highest point of the bust.

- Manipulate the fabric to fit the curves of the body and over the bust and to shape it into a fitted waistline seam of the asymmetric or halter design.

- Drape soft fabric cut on the bias into fitted asymmetric halter or cowl designs.

- Understand how the crossgrain changes when darts are manipulated into different locations.

- Visualize and true up the bodice patterns with shirring and pleats in relationship to the figure, with the correct amount of ease allowance, armhole size, waistline shape, measurement, and balance.

- Visualize the front and back asymmetric designs in relation to the figure.

- Check the results of the draping process with regard to fit, hang, balance, proportion, and the true up.

Relocating the Basic Shoulder and Waist Darts

When draping a flat piece of fabric over the curves of the human body, the folds of the fabric radiate from the highest point of the bust. These folds, however, may be arranged in any position radiating from the bust. With a larger body and/or a fuller bust, the fabric excess will be wider, thereby creating wider darts. In contrast, a flat-busted figure has less fullness radiating from the apex, thereby resulting in narrower dart excess.

The shoulder and waist darts may be changed from their original locations to anywhere the designer chooses, because they were created by the excess fabric folds radiating from the bust. Thus, these two darts, or the excess fabric, can be combined into one large dart; divided into multiple darts, pleats, or tucks next to one another; or converted into gathers, anywhere on the bodice. These various dart manipulations will create different design details.

Examples of draping techniques that can change the bust fullness into a single dart, gathered fullness, and multiple pleats are given on the following pages. These examples will help a designer learn to value the number of choices available when draping the fabric excess on the body.

Prepare Fabric for Bodice Designs:
Side Bust Dart, Center Front Waistline Dart, French Dart, Shoulder Gathers, and Bustline Shirring

The bodice designs shown on the following pages use the same fabric preparation. The repetition of practicing these various bodice designs will help develop and stimulate skills in changing dart locations and creating a variety of bodice designs.

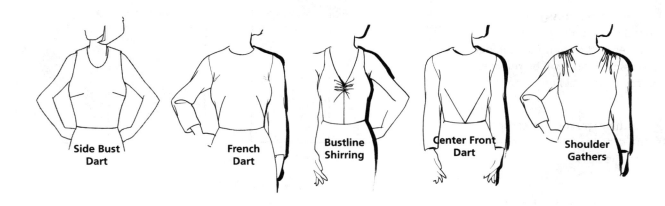

Side Bust Dart

French Dart

Bustline Shirring

Center Front Dart

Shoulder Gathers

1 **Length:** Measure the length for the front and back bodice along the straight of grain from the neckband to the waist and add 5 inches.

2 **Width:** Measure the width for the front and back bodice along the crossgrain from the center front of the dress form to the side seam of the bust level and add 5 inches.

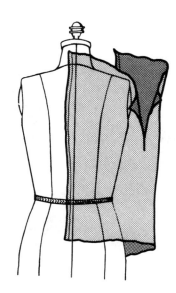
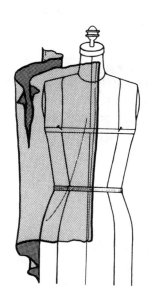

3 **ainline:** Draw the center front and center back grainline 1 inch from the torn edge. Press under this 1 inch.

4 **Crossgrain:** Using an L-square ruler, draw a crossgrain line perpendicular to the grainline in the center of the front fabric panel. This crossgrain line will be referred to as the bust level line.

5 On the dress form, measure the distance from the center front to the apex.

6 On the front piece, measure and crossmark the apex distance on the bust level line of the fabric. Also, crossmark the side seam and the center of the princess panel.

7 On the back fabric piece, measure and draw in the neckline crossmark, the shoulder blade crossgrain, and the plate crossmark.

Back

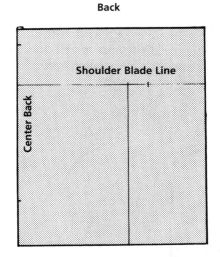

Front

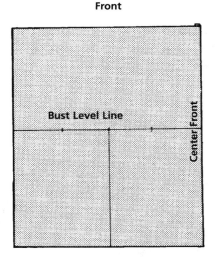

Side Bust Dart: *Draping Steps*

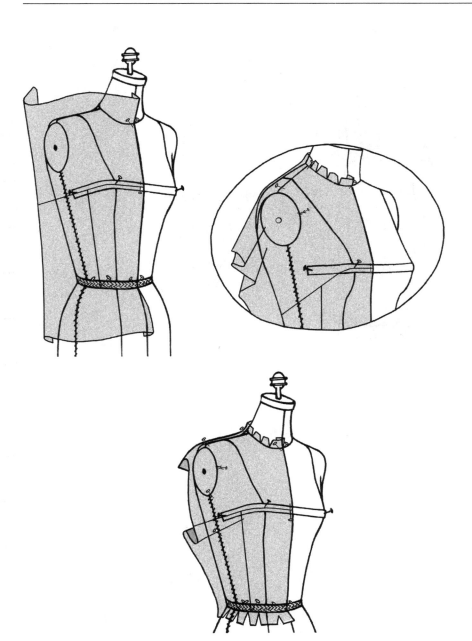

1 Pin the apex mark on the fabric to the apex position of the dress form.

2 Pin the center front grainline fold of the fabric to the center front position of the dress form.

Anchor pins at center front neck and center front waist. An additional pin may be needed at the bust level tape.

3 Drape the neckline by trimming the excess fabric around the neck area and clipping at intervals. Smooth the neckline in place.

4 Drape and pin the shoulder by smoothing the excess fabric across the upper chest area and over the shoulder.

5 Smooth and drape the fabric around the armhole plate, creating a 1/4-inch–1/4-inch pinch at the screw level at the armhole ridge. This is to ensure that the armhole does not get too tight.

6 Smooth and drape the fabric into the side seam. Allow all excess fabric to fall into the side seam. Lift the crossgrain until it is parallel to the floor. The center of the princess panel line will fall closer to the side seam, as all fullness is being transferred into the side bust area.

7 Clip, smooth, and drape the waistline fabric across the tape. Fold the side bust dart at the crossgrain with the excess fullness folding below the crossgrain.

Mark all key areas of the dress form to the fabric.

a. Neckline: Crossmark at center front neck and at the neckline/ shoulder ridge corner.

b. Shoulder seam: Lightly mark the shoulder seam and crossmark the shoulder ridge corner.

c. Armplate:
- Top at shoulder seam ridge
- Middle at screw level
- Crossmark bottom at the side seam.

d. Side seam: Lightly mark.

e. Waistline and waist dart: Crossmark at center front waist, side seam waist, and both sides of the dart.

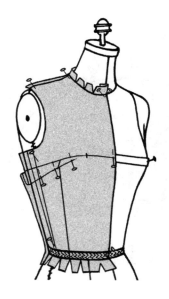
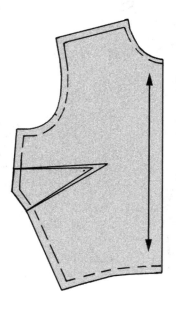

True Up

 Remove the fabric drape from the dress form. True up all seams. Add seam allowances and trim excess fabric.

2 Return the finished drape to the dress form and check for accuracy, fit, and balance.

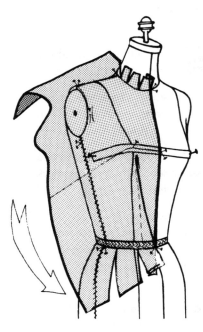

Center Front Waist Dart

1 Pin the apex mark on the fabric to the apex position of the dress form.

2 Pin the center front grainline fold of the fabric to the center front position of the dress form.

Anchor pins at center front neck and center front waist. An additional pin may be needed at the bust level tape.

3 Drape the neckline by trimming the excess fabric around the neck area and clipping at intervals. Smooth the neckline in place.

4 Drape and pin the shoulder by smoothing the excess fabric across the upper chest area and over the shoulder.

5 Smooth and drape the fabric around the armhole plate, creating a 1/4-inch–1/4-inch pinch at the screw level at the armhole ridge. This is to ensure that the armhole does not get too tight.

6 Smooth and drape the fabric past the side seam. The crossgrain will be angling downward (see illustration).

7 Allow all excess fabric to fall into the waistline area below the bust. Clip, smooth, and drape the waistline fabric across the waistline tape. Allow all excess fabric to be pinned at the center front/waist area of the dress form.

8 Mark all key areas of the dress form to the fabric.

a. Neckline: Crossmark at center front neck and at the neckline/shoulder ridge corner.

b. Shoulder seam: Lightly mark the shoulder seam and crossmark the shoulder ridge corner.

c. Armplate:
 • Top at shoulder seam ridge
 • Middle at screw level
 • Crossmark bottom at the side seam.

d. Side seam: Lightly mark.

e. Waistline and waist dart: Crossmark at center front waist, side seam waist, and both sides of the dart.

True Up

1 Remove the fabric drape from the dress form. True up all seams. Add seam allowances and trim excess fabric.

2 Return the finished drape to the dress form and check for accuracy, fit, and balance.

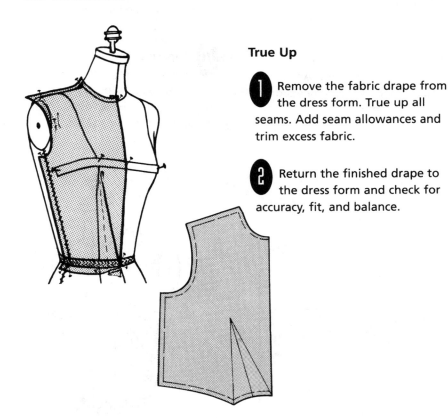

French Dart: Draping Steps

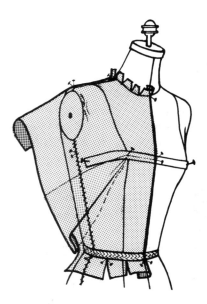

1 **Pin the apex** mark on the fabric to the apex position of the dress form.

2 **Pin the center front grainline** fold of the fabric to the center front position of the dress form.

Anchor pins at center front neck and center front waist. An additional pin may be needed at the bust level tape.

3 **Drape the neckline** by trimming the excess fabric around the neck area and clipping at intervals. Smooth the neckline in place.

4 **Drape and pin the shoulder** by smoothing the excess fabric across the upper chest area and over the shoulder.

5 **Smooth and drape the fabric around the armhole plate,** creating a 1/4-inch–1/4-inch pinch at the screw level at the armhole ridge. This is to ensure that the armhole does not get too tight.

6 **Smooth and drape the fabric to 2 inches above the waistline at the side seam.** The crossgrain will be angling downward (see illustration).

7 **Clip, smooth, and drape the waistline** fabric across the waistline tape. Allow all excess fabric to fall 2 inches above the waistline at the side seam.

8 **For a French dart,** allow all excess fabric to be pinned 2 inches above the waistline at the side seam.

9 **Mark all key areas** of the dress form to the fabric.

a. Neckline: Crossmark at center front neck and at the neckline/ shoulder ridge corner.

b. Shoulder seam: Lightly mark the shoulder seam and crossmark the shoulder ridge corner.

c. Armplate:
 • Top at shoulder seam ridge
 • Middle at screw level
 • Crossmark bottom at the side seam.

d. Side seam and French dart: Lightly mark the side seam and crossmark both sides of the French dart.

e. Waistline: Crossmark at center front waist and at the side seam waist.

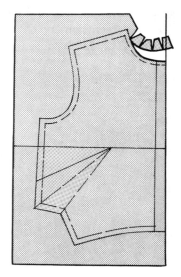

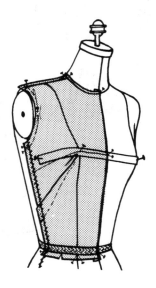

True Up

1 **Remove the fabric drape from the dress form.** True up all seams, add seam allowances, and trim excess fabric.

2 **Return the finished drape to the dress form** and check for accuracy, fit, and balance.

Converting Dart Excess into Shoulder Gathers: Draping Steps

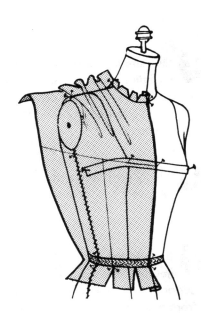

1 Pin the apex mark on the fabric to the apex position of the dress form.

2 Pin the center front grainline fold of the fabric to the center front position of the dress form.

Anchor pins at center front neck and center front waist. An additional pin may be needed at the bust level tape.

3 Drape the neckline by trimming the excess fabric around the neck area and clipping at intervals. Smooth the neckline in place.

4 Clip, smooth, and drape the waistline fabric across the waistline tape. Allow all excess fabric to be moved toward the side seam.

5 Smooth and drape the fabric past the side seam and up and around the armhole plate. Smooth the fabric flat over the armhole plate. Create a 1/4-inch–1/4-inch pinch at the screw level at the armhole ridge. This is to ensure that the armhole does not become too tight.

6 Allow the excess fabric to fall into the shoulder area.

7 Drape and pin the shoulder fullness. Divide the excess fabric, creating a gathered effect at the shoulder seam. Pin the fullness at the shoulder.

NOTE: This same process is followed if draping into a shoulder yoke.

8 Mark all key areas of the dress form to the fabric.

a. Neckline: Draw in the desired neckline.

b. Shoulder seam: Lightly mark shoulder seam and shoulder gathers and crossmark shoulder ridge.

c. Armplate:
   • Top at shoulder seam ridge
   • Middle at screw level
   • Crossmark bottom at the side seam.

d. Side seam: Lightly mark.

e. Waistline and waistline pleats: Crossmark at center front waist and side seam waist. Lightly mark the remainder of the waistline.

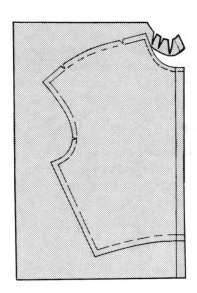

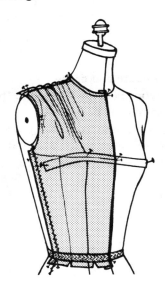

True Up

1 Remove the fabric drape from the dress form. True up all seams. Add seam allowances and trim excess fabric.

2 Return the finished drape to the dress form and check for accuracy, fit, and balance.

Bodice Variations and Asymmetric and Halter Designs

Converting Dart Excess into Center Front Bustline Shirring: *Draping Steps*

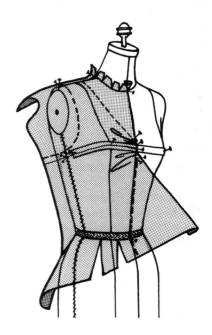

1 Pin the apex mark on the fabric to the apex position of the dress form.

2 Pin the center front grainline fold of the fabric to the center front position of the dress form.

Anchor pins at center front neck and center front waist. An additional pin may be needed at the bust level tape.

3 Drape the neckline by trimming the excess fabric around the neck area and clipping at intervals. Smooth the neckline in place.

4 Drape and pin the shoulder by smoothing the excess fabric across the upper chest area and over the shoulder.

5 Smooth and drape the fabric around the armhole plate, creating a 1/4-inch–1/4-inch pinch at the screw level at the armhole ridge. This is to ensure that the armhole does not become too tight.

6 Smooth and drape the fabric past the side seam. The crossgrain will be angling downward (see illustration). Allow all excess fabric to fall into the waistline area below the bust.

7 Clip, smooth, and drape the waistline fabric across the waistline tape. Allow all excess fabric to be moved to center front bustline area.

8 Evenly distribute and pin all excess fabric at the bustline area.

9 Draw in the desired neckline. Usually when a design has shirring at the center front bust, the neckline is lowered (see example).

10 Mark all key areas of the dress form to the fabric.

a. Center front and center front bust: Lightly mark the center front line of the dress form and where the gathered fullness is at center front.

b. Neckline: Draw in the desired neckline.

c. Shoulder seam: Lightly mark shoulder seam and crossmark shoulder ridge.

d. Armplate:
- Top at shoulder seam ridge
- Middle at screw level
- Crossmark bottom at the side seam.

e. Side seam: Lightly mark.

f. Waistline: Crossmark at center front waist and side seam waist and lightly mark the entire waistline.

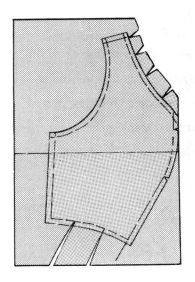
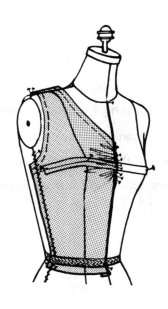

True Up

1 **Remove the fabric drape from the dress form.** True up all seams. Add seam allowances and trim excess fabric.

2 **Return the finished drape to the dress form** and check for accuracy, fit, and balance.

Notes

Asymmetric Bodice

The asymmetrical bodice design has an informal balance, with each side offering a different silhouette rather than the traditional balance. Generally, the larger front piece crosses center front with a smaller piece that lies underneath. The asymmetric design may be draped to one side with pleats, darts, or gathers. Many such designs have a side closing or cover only one shoulder.

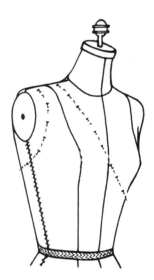

Prepare the Dress Form

Remove the bra tape on the dress form. Pin or use style tape indicating the desired neckline and/or armhole shapes.

NOTE: These steps are required for all designs.

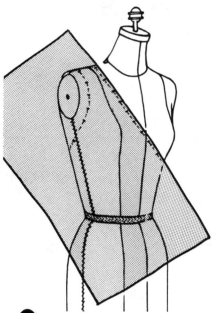

1 **Measure the length for the front bodice** along the desired neckline from the shoulder to the length of the bodice and add 10 inches.

2 **Measure the width for the front bodice** along the crossgrain from the center front of the dress form to the side seam at the bust level and add 10 inches.

Snip and tear the fabric at this width. Block and press the fabric at this time.

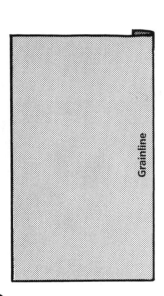

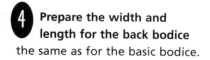

3 **Draw a grainline** 2 inches from the torn edge. Press under. This grainline will be the neckline edge of the garment design.

4 **Prepare the width and length for the back bodice** the same as for the basic bodice.

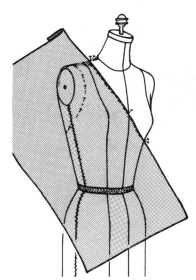

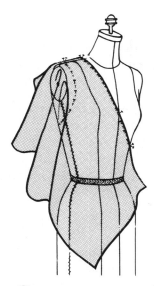

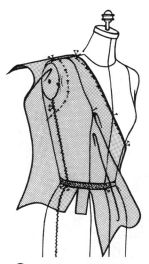

1 Pin the grainline fold of the fabric along the desired neckline. Allow several inches of the fabric to extend beyond the shoulder and several inches past the lowest point of the design. Place pins at the shoulder and the lowest point of the neckline.

2 Drape and pin the shoulder by smoothing the excess fabric across the upper chest area.

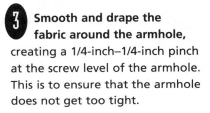

3 Smooth and drape the fabric around the armhole, creating a 1/4-inch–1/4-inch pinch at the screw level of the armhole. This is to ensure that the armhole does not get too tight.

4 Smooth and drape the fabric flat over the side seam. All excess fabric will now fall into the waistline area below the bust.

5 Clip, smooth, and drape the waistline fabric across the waist tape. Allow all excess fabric to drape into the styled area of the asymmetric design. Pin excess fabric at this location.

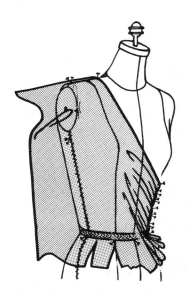

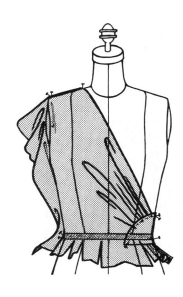

6 Fold, tuck, pleat, or gather in the fullness at the area where the asymmetric design requires the fullness. Add design features if desired.

Asymmetric Bodice: *Left Side Draping Steps*

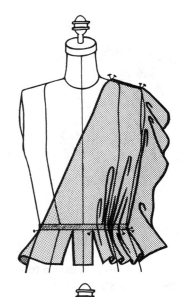

NOTE: These steps apply only if the left side of the design is different from that of the right side.

1 Pin the grainline fold of the fabric along the desired neckline of the left side.

2 Drape and pin the shoulder.

3 Smooth and drape the fabric around the armhole, creating a 1/4-inch–1/4-inch pinch at the screw level of the armhole.

4 Smooth and drape the fabric flat over the side seam. All excess fabric will now fall into the waistline area below the bust.

5 Fold, tuck, pleat, or gather in the fullness at the waistline below the bust. Pin excess fabric at this location.

6 Mark all key areas of the dress form on the fabric:

a. **Center front:** Place a crossmark at center front neck and center front waist. Mark the entire center front line of the dress form.

b. **Shoulder seam:** Lightly mark the shoulder seam and crossmark the shoulder ridge corner.

c. **Armplate:**
- Top at shoulder seam ridge
- Middle at screw level
- Crossmark bottom at side seam.

d. **Side seam:** Lightly crossmark.

e. **Waistline:** Lightly crossmark the entire waist area of the drape.

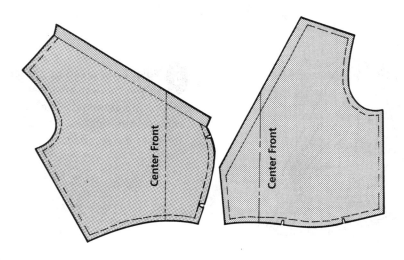

7 True up. Remove the fabric drape from the dress form. True up all seams, add seam allowances, and trim excess fabric. Pin the front drape to the back drape.

8 Return the finished drape to the dress form and check for accuracy, fit, and balance.

9 Drape the back bodice the same as the basic bodice.

Bias Halter

The bias halter is a front-fitted sleeveless bodice with a flat or rolled neckline strip extending to the back of the neckline. Generally, the side seam area of the lower bodice extends to the back, which may be tied, attached to a midriff, or sewn to the waist of a skirt.

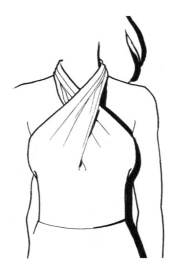

Halter Variation

Bias Halter: Preparing the Fabric

1 **Measure and cut a perfect 34-inch square** of fabric, which is wide enough for an entire front.

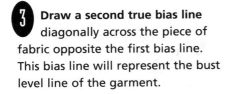

2 **Draw a true bias line** diagonally across the piece of fabric. This bias line will be the center front line of the garment.

3 **Draw a second true bias line** diagonally across the piece of fabric opposite the first bias line. This bias line will represent the bust level line of the garment.

4 For the back design, measure the width and length of the back style and add 3 inches. Snip and tear the fabric at this width and length.

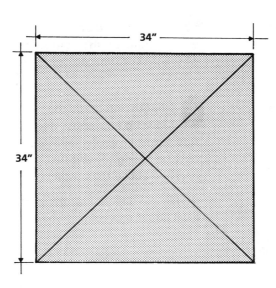

34"

34"

5 Draw in a grainline for the center back panel 1 inch from the torn edge and press under.

Bias Halter: *Draping Steps*

Prepare the Dress Form

Remove the bra tape on the dress form. Pin or use style tape indicating the desired neckline and/or armhole shapes.

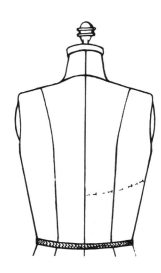
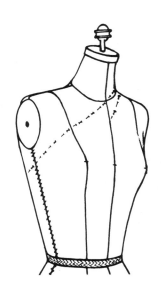

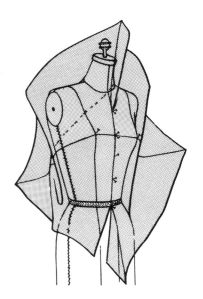
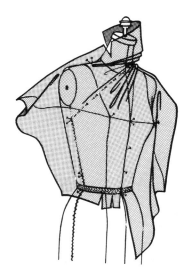
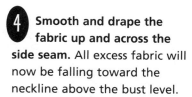
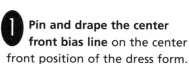
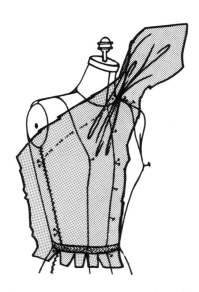

1 **Pin and drape the center front bias line** on the center front position of the dress form.

2 **Align the bias crossgrain** on the bust level of the dress form.

3 **Trim, clip, and drape the waistline on the right side of the dress form.**

4 **Smooth and drape the fabric up and across the side seam.** All excess fabric will now be falling toward the neckline above the bust level.

NOTE: The direction of the bust level line is now angled upward.

5 **Trim away the fabric** at the side seam, around the premarked bare armhole, and around the neck area, leaving a 2-inch excess.

6 **Smooth and drape the fabric around the trimmed armhole.**

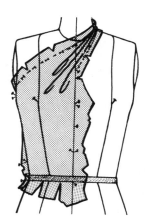

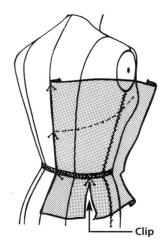

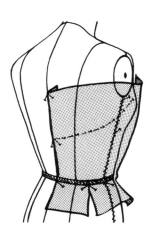

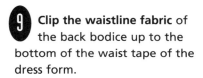

7 Fold, tuck, pleat, or gather in the fullness around the neckline, finishing at the center back neck area.

8 Pin the center back grainline fold of the fabric to the center back position of the dress form.

The center back panel should drape at least 2 inches above the chosen style line.

9 Clip the waistline fabric of the back bodice up to the bottom of the waist tape of the dress form.

10 Drape and smooth the waistline from center back, across the waist tape, toward the side seam.

11 Drape and smooth the back side seam flat. Match the side seam of the back bodice to the front side seam of the halter top.

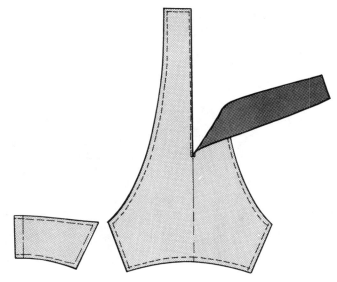

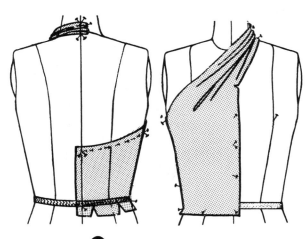

12 Mark all key areas of the dress form to the fabric.

a. Armhole/neckline: Follow the bare shoulder style line up and around the front and back neckline.

b. Side seam: Lightly crossmark.

c. Waistline: Lightly crossmark the entire waist area of the drape.

13 True up. Remove the fabric drape from the dress. True up all seams, add seam allowances, and trim excess fabric. Pin the front drape to the back drape.

Return the finished drape to the dress form and check for accuracy, fit, and balance.

Chapter Ten

Shirt and Kimono Designs:
Dartless Shapes

By studying the various draping steps in this chapter, the designer should be able to:

• Develop creativity and stimulate a variety of dartless shapes.

• Recognize grain and crossgrain of fabric in relation to the bust level on the front, shoulder blade level on the back, and side seams for a dartless shape.

• Drape a dartless shape with straight side seams and the correct amount of ease allowance, armhole size, and side seam balance.

• Visualize the front and back dartless shape in relation to the figure.

• Have the dartless shape hang straight from the bust level line in the front and shoulder blade level in the back to the hem.

• Visualize and true up the dartless patterns with the correct amount of ease allowance, armhole size, waistline shape, measurement, and balance.

• Check the results of the draping process for a dartless shape with regard to fit, hang, balance, proportion, and the true up.

The Dartless Blouse and Shirt Blocks:
Definition, Theory, & Principles

Definition

The **dartless blouse** block is a torso-length bodice without darts or a fitted waist seam. This block is used in designing blouses, vests, or dresses that require no fitted dart area and a traditional fitted armhole. The sleeve for this block requires a slightly capped sleeve with a lifted biceps line. This varies slightly from the traditional fitted sleeve.

The **dartless shirt** is also a torso-length bodice without darts of a fitted waist seam. This block/sloper is used in designing shirts or dresses that require no fitted dart area and a dropped shoulder with a lowered side seam to accommodate a shirt sleeve. Many manufacturers prefer to use a shirt sleeve rather than a kimono variation because the sleeve allows greater movement for the customer.

Variations of the Dartless Shirt or Blouse Blocks

- **Slightly fitted silhouette:** Within the silhouette, the waist area may be slightly fitted by using smaller fisheye waistline darts.

- **Boxy fitted silhouette:** The silhouette has a boxy shape without a waist-fitting seam or darts. The side seams hang away from the body and are parallel to center front or center back. The waist area may be belted or drawn in by using elastic.

Theory

The **dartless blouse** block and its variation may be used when:

- The design does not include any darting.

- Stylelines or gathers are created by simply slashing and opening within the design.

- The design has a basic armhole for a set-in sleeve.

- The design has *no* waist-fitting seam and usually hangs away from the body. You may, however, wish to give it fisheye darts or simply belt it.

   The **dartless shirt** block and its variations may be used when:

- The design does not include any darting.

- Stylelines or gathers are created by simply slashing and opening within the design.

- The design has a dropped shoulder armhole for a shirt sleeve.

- The design has *no* waist-fitting seam and usually hangs away from the body. You may, however, wish to give it fisheye darts or simply belt it.

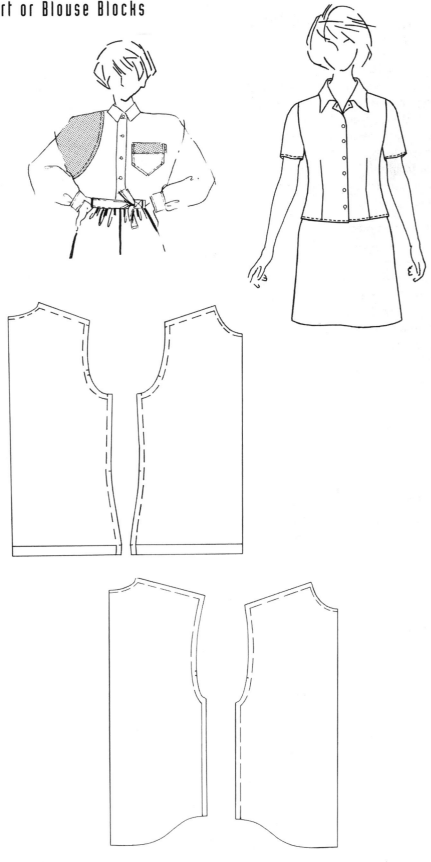

Principles: Analyzing the Dartless Blocks

The dartless blocks are used to create new designs for blouses, dresses, and vests (refer to theory, above). It is important to analyze the block to ensure that the following items are correct. If one of these items is wrong, the designs made from this block will not fit properly, and they will twist, drag, or pull.

- All pattern pieces have a definite relationship with the figure that enables them to hang straight up and down and be parallel to the floor. This grainline and crossgrain alignment, in addition to the side seam angle, allows the designer to maintain the correct balance between the front and the back of the garment.

- The center front and center back are on perfect grain.

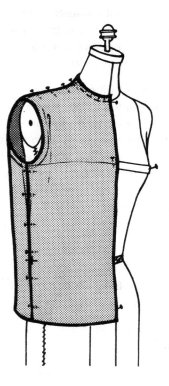

- The bust level line of the front bodice is on perfect crossgrain, allowing the area below the bust level line to hang straight up and down.

- The shoulder blade level line of the back bodice is on perfect crossgrain, allowing the area below the shoulder blade level line to hang straight up and down.

- On the front bodice, the center of the princess panel line (centered distance from the apex to the side seam) is on perfect grain and is parallel to the center front. This ensures that the side seam maintains the same angle as the back.

Notes

Dartless Shirt/Blouse: *Preparing the Fabric*

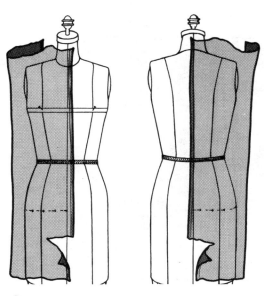

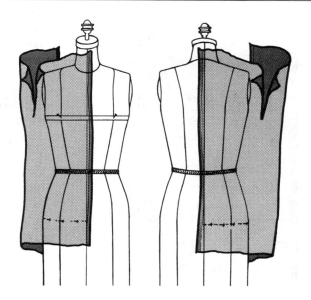

1 **Measure the length** (along the straight of grain) for both the front and back from the neckband to the hip level and add 5 inches.

Snip and tear the fabric at this length.

2 **Measure the width** (along the crossgrain) for both the front and back from the center of the dress form to the side seam and add 4 inches.

Snip and tear the fabric at this width.

Back   **Front**

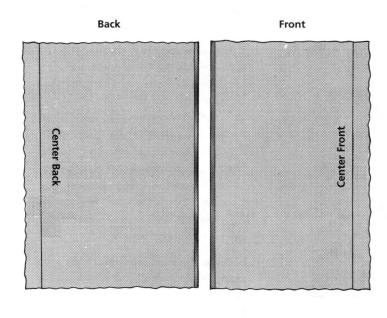

Center Back

Center Front

3 **Draw the center front and center back grainlines** 1 inch from the torn edge and press under.

Press under at center front and center back.

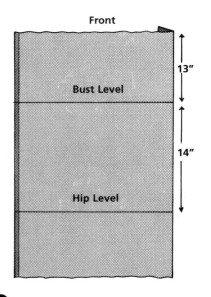

Front

13"

Bust Level

14"

Hip Level

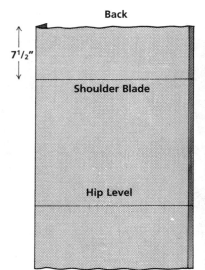

Back

7½"

Shoulder Blade

Hip Level

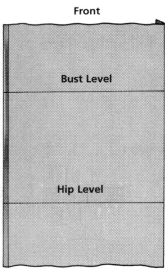

Front

Bust Level

Hip Level

4 **On the front fabric piece, draw in two crossgrains.**

a. Draw the bust level line. Draw the first crossgrain line **13 inches** from the top edge of the front fabric piece.

b. Draw in the hipline. Draw the second crossgrain line **14 inches** from the first crossgrain line. This indicates the hip level line. On some dress forms this measurement may change slightly.

5 **On the back fabric piece, draw in two crossgrains.**

a. Draw in the shoulder blade level line. Draw the first crossgrain line 7 1/2 inches from the top edge of the back fabric piece.

b. Draw in the hip level line. Place the front and back fabric pieces side by side. Draw in a crossgrain line on the back piece to match the crossgrain on the front piece at the hip level.

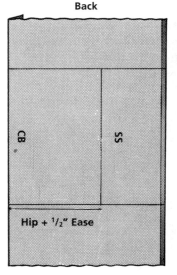

Back

CB

SS

Hip + ½" Ease

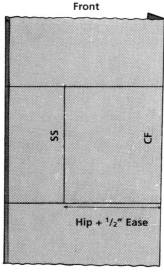

Front

SS

CF

Hip + ½" Ease

6 **Draw in the side seams for the front and back fabric pieces.**

a. Measure the dress form at the hip level for the front and back.

• Measure from center front to the side seam on the dress form and add 1/2 inch for ease. Transfer this measurement to the front fabric piece and crossmark.

• Measure from center back to the side seam on the dress form and add 1/2 inch for ease. Transfer this measurement to the back fabric piece and crossmark.

b. Draw the front and back side seam. From the side seam crossmarks, draw a side seam perfectly parallel to the center grainline.

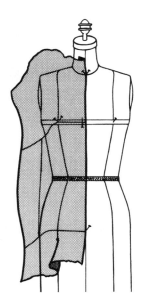

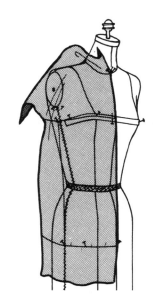

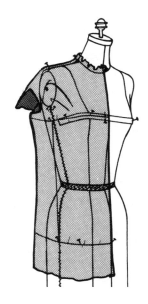

1 **Pin the center front grainline** fold of the fabric on the center front position of the dress form. Be sure to align the crossgrain on the bust level of the dress form.

Anchor pins at center front neck and center front hip. An additional pin may be needed at the bust level tape.

2 **Smooth and pin the crossgrain** of the fabric across the dress form to the side seam. Distribute the 1/2 inch ease evenly across the dress form.

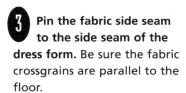

3 **Pin the fabric side seam to the side seam of the dress form.** Be sure the fabric crossgrains are parallel to the floor.

4 **Pin the shoulder/neck area.** Trim and clip the excess fabric around the neck area. Smooth the fabric flat over the shoulder/neck area.

5 **Drape and smooth the fabric over the shoulder/armhole** area of the dress form and pin in place.

All excess fabric will fall over the armplate area at this time.

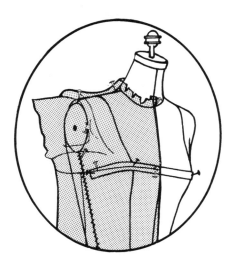

6 **Distribute armhole fullness.**

a. **Divide in half** all excess fabric over the armhole at the middle of the armhole ridge area.

b. **Gently push a slight amount of fabric** toward the body in the middle of the armhole ridge area.

c. **Pin the armhole ridge** area, keeping the excess fabric evenly distributed.

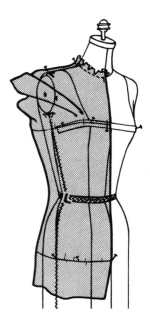

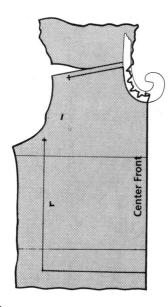

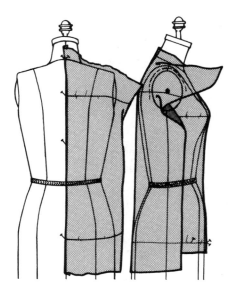

7 **Mark key areas** of dress form on the fabric.

a. Neckline: Lightly crossmark.

b. Shoulder seam: Lightly crossmark.

c. Armplate:
- Top at shoulder ridge
- Middle of the armhole: Crossmark middle of armhole ridge fullness.
- Bottom at side seam

d. Side seam: Crossmark at the waistline.

8 **True up the neckline and shoulder seams.** Add seam allowances to the front fabric drape, the neckline, and the shoulder. Trim the excess fabric.

Extend the lower edge of the drape to the desired length of the design.

Place the front drape back on the dress form.

9 **Pin the center back grainline** fold of the fabric to the center back position of the dress form.

10 **Match the back hip level crossgrain** to the front hip level crossgrain at the side seams.

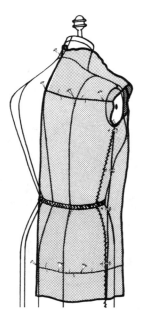

11 **Pin the back crossgrain** to the dress form, evenly distributing the 1/2 inch ease.

12 **Match and pin the back side seam to the front side seam.** Be sure the hip level crossgrains are still matching and the fabric is not distorted. The front and back fabric pieces should be hanging plumb.

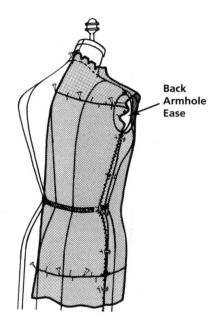

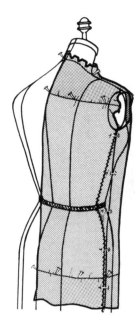

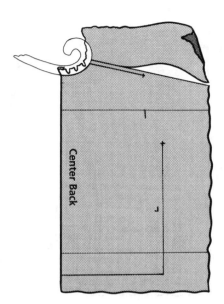

Back Armhole Ease

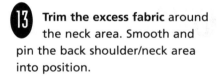

Center Back

13 **Trim the excess fabric** around the neck area. Smooth and pin the back shoulder/neck area into position.

NOTE: The back armhole area will show a definite amount of ease about halfway from the shoulder seam to the shoulder blade level crossgrain. Leave this ease in the armhole.

14 **Mark all key areas** of the dress form on the back drape.

a. **Neckline**

b. **Shoulder**

c. **Armplate:**
   • Top at shoulder ridge
   • Middle at screw level
   • Bottom at side seam

d. **Side seam:** Crossmark at the waistline.

15 **True up the back necklines and shoulder seams.** Remove the back drape from the dress form. Add seam allowances to the back neckline and shoulders. Trim excess fabric.

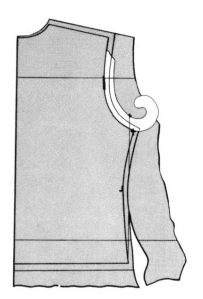

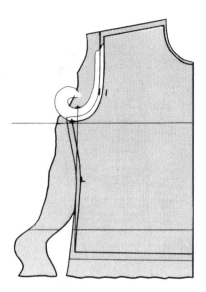

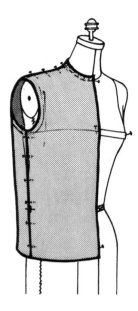

 True up the front and back side seams and armholes.

a. Drop the armhole/side seam position 2 inches from the side seam plate mark.

b. Add 5/8 inch body ease to the side seam. Connect these new crossmarks and draw in a new side seam with a skirt curved ruler.

c. Draw the armhole, using a French curve. Shape as illustrated. Remember, when the side seams are pinned together, the armhole should be in the shape of a horseshoe.

17 Check and complete the front and back armhole distance.

a. Measure the front and back armholes. The back armhole should measure 1/2 inch more than the front armhole (correct armhole balance).

b. If the armholes do not measure correctly, scoop out the back armhole a bit (1/4 inch) and straighten or fill in the front armhole (1/4 inch).

c. Add seam allowances to all remaining areas and trim excess fabric.

NOTE: Refer to Sleeves, pages 134–143, for an appropriate sleeve design.

18 Pin the front and back drapes together. Return the drape to the dress form. Check for balance and fit. If necessary, make corrections.

NOTE: The fabric at the front armhole area will appear slightly folded (for all dartless drapes).

Dartless Shirt Look

Many times a man's shirt look is desired. Therefore, a few changes in the shoulder and armhole/side seam areas are necessary to create the more enlarged armhole fit and casual look.

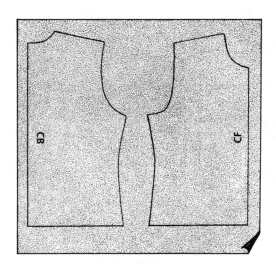

1 Trace the dartless shirt/blouse pattern onto pattern paper.

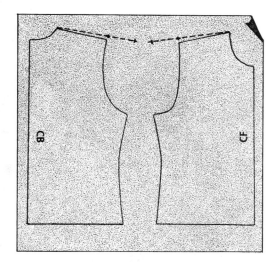

2 Raise the shoulder 3/4 inch at the original armhole/shoulder corner.

3 Reshape the shoulder by drawing a straight line from the shoulder/neck corner to the 3/4-inch mark.

4 Extend the new shoulder line 3 1/2 inches from the original armhole/shoulder corner.

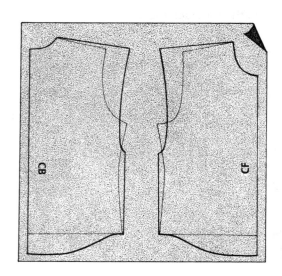

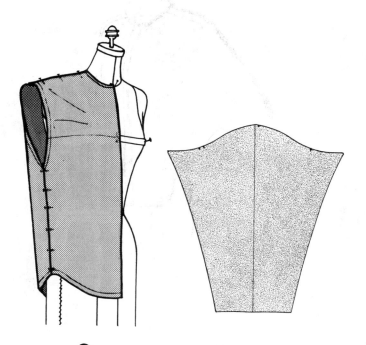

5 Reshape the armhole/side seam and hem areas.

a. Lower the armhole/side seam corner 4 inches from the original armhole/side seam corner.

b. Add 1/2-inch ease to the side seam.

c. Draw in a new shirt sleeve armhole. Connect the new shoulder corner to the new side seam corner to create an enlarged armhole. Use a hip curve ruler.

NOTE: The lowered armhole shape no longer has the characteristic horseshoe appearance.

If desired, reshape the hem into a "shirttail" look.

6 Develop the shirt sleeve. Refer to Shirt Sleeves, pages 134–138, to create a correctly lifted sleeve to fit into this newly shaped armhole.

The Classic Shirt with One-Piece Yoke

The **one-piece classic yoke shirt** is a traditional, conservative shirt with a one-piece yoke. The yoke extends across the shoulder blade level on the back and drapes over the front shoulder, down to the front yoke style line. The all-in-one yoke eliminates the need for a shoulder seam.

The body of the classic shirt has a pleated or gathered back and a shirt armhole with a shirt sleeve. The design features of a collar, cuff, plackets, and pockets are finishing details that are determined by the design.

Illustrated here are the steps for draping the traditional all-in-one yoke and then draping a shirt with shirring radiating from the yoke. For a completely dartless shirt design draped into this yoke, simply follow the "dartless shirt" steps previously illustrated in this chapter.

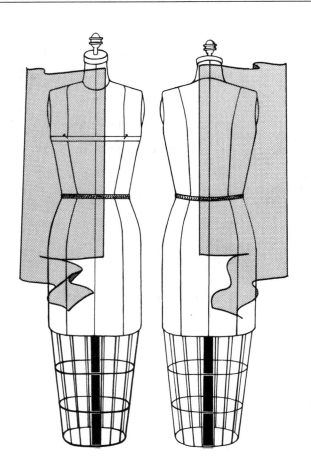

1 Measure the length and width desired for a front and back bodice piece. Add a few inches. Snip and tear the fabric at this desired length and width.

2 Draw the grainline on the front and back bodice piece 1 inch from the torn edge.

3 Draw the crossgrain for the front at the bustline level. Draw the crossgrain for the back at the shoulder blade level.

4 Mark the apex and side seam. Draw the center of the princess panel line on the front fabric piece. For more detailed instruction on preparing the bodice fabric pieces, refer to Basic Bodice, pages 47–49.

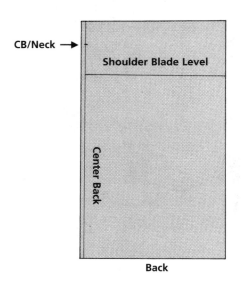

CB/Neck →

Shoulder Blade Level

Center Back

Back

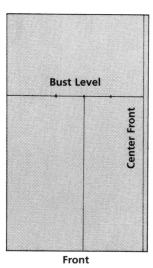

Bust Level

Center Front

Front

Preparing the Yoke Fabric

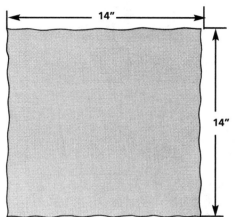

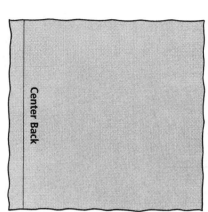

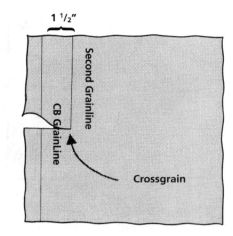

❶ Measure the desired length and width of the yoke. Cut a perfect square approximately 14 inches.

❷ Draw the center back grainline 1 inch along the torn edge and parallel to the grain of the fabric.

❸ Prepare the back neck opening.

a. Measure up from the lower edge half the measurement of the fabric piece. Draw a perfect crossgrain 1 1/2 inches long.

b. Draw a second grainline parallel and 1 1/2 inches from the center back grainline.

c. Cut the fabric on the crossgrain line and on the second grainline and remove this rectangular piece of fabric.

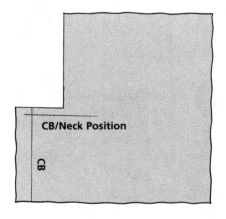

❹ Draw a short crossgrain line 1/2 inch below the cut crossgrain. This indicates the center back/neck position.

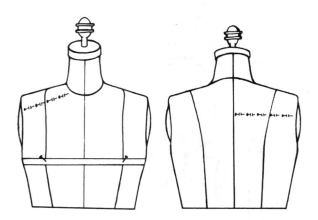

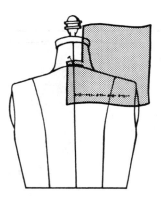

1 **Prepare the dress form.**
Pin the desired yoke style line on the dress form.

2 **Pin the center back grainline of the yoke** fabric at the center back position of the dress form.

3 **Align the neckline position mark** on the fabric to the neckline seam on the dress form.

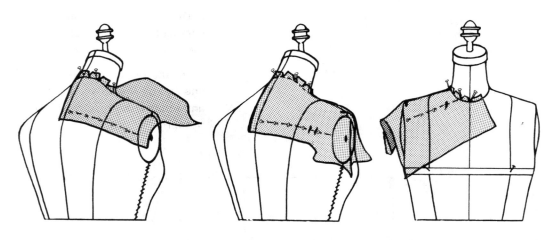

4 **Clip, smooth, and pin the neckline** until the fabric lies smoothly over the shoulder of the dress form. Continue to clip, smooth, and pin the front neckline until the fabric touches the front style line.

5 Mark all key areas of the dress form to the fabric.

a. Draw the style line and the style line notches: Single on front; double on back.

b. Mark the armhole ridge: Crossmark the ridge on the front and back yoke.

c. Neckline.

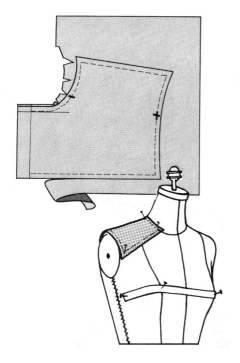

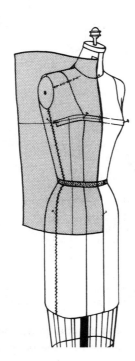

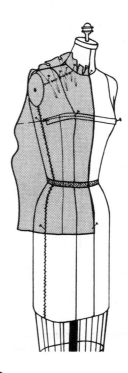

6 **True up all seams.** Remove the yoke drape from the dress form, true up all seams, add seam allowances, and trim excess fabric. Return the finished yoke to the dress form and check for accuracy, fit, and balance.

7 **Drape the front bodice grainline.** Pin the center front grainline fold of the fabric on the center of the dress form.

8 **Drape the crossgrain,** matching the apex, side seam, and center of the princess panel.

9 **Smooth the fabric up from the crossgrain.** Evenly distribute all excess fabric into the yoke style line. Clip, trim, and smooth in the neckline.

10 **Mark all key areas** of the dress form to the fabric.

a. Neckline: Lightly mark the remainder of the neckline.

b. Yoke style line.

c. Matching notches: Match to the yoke notches.

d. Armplate:
  • Shoulder ridge
  • Plate at screw level
  • Plate at side seam

e. Side seam: Mark and trim excess fabric, leaving enough for trueing and seam allowances.

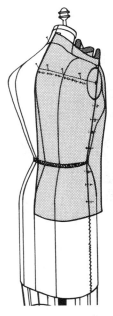

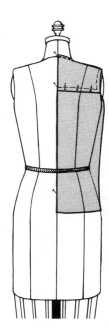

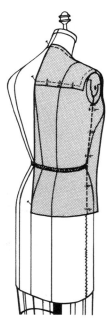

11 Place the back straight of grainline to the center back of the dress form.

12 Align the crossgrain at the shoulder blade level. Pin in place. Allow the fabric to hang smoothly and freely from the shoulder blade level.

13 Pin the front side seam to the back side seam.

14 Drape and pin the back style line seam up into the back yoke seam. Pin the yoke to the bodice drape.

15 Mark all key areas from the dress form to the fabric.

a. Back yoke style line.

b. Matching notches: Match to the yoke notches.

c. Bottom of armplate at the side seam.

d. Side seam.

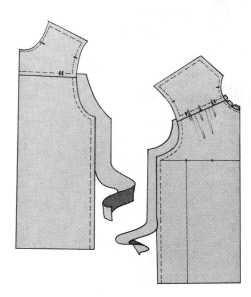

16 True up all seams. Remove the fabric drape (front, back, and yoke) from the dress form. True up all seams, add seam allowances, and trim excess fabric.

a. When trueing the front armhole: Pin the front bodice style line to the front yoke style line. Then, true up the armhole.

b. When trueing the back armhole: Pin the back bodice style line to the back yoke style line. Then, true up the armhole.

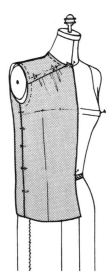

17 Return the finished drape to the dress form and check for accuracy, fit, and balance.

Various Front Yoke Designs

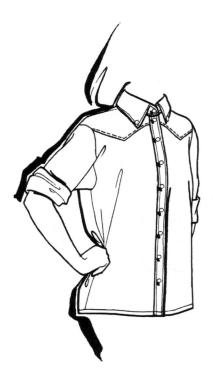

A bodice yoke is a portion of a garment fitted at the shoulders. Yokes are used to support the lower section of the garment, which may be designed in a variety of lengths and styles.

There are many shapes used to enhance or create a particular design. Choose them with the principles of line and learn the tricks that help create a most flattering silhouette.

Shown here are three different yoke style lines. All three yokes are draped following the same instructions. A shirt or dress design may be draped into these various yoke styles. Refer to shirt drape previously illustrated in this chapter.

If a dress design is desired, follow the yoke dress designs in the dress chapter.

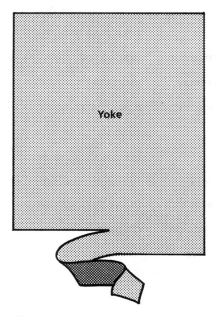

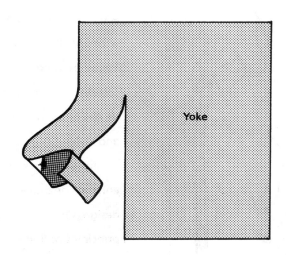

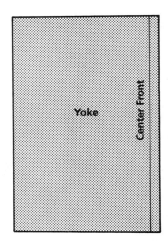

1 **Measure the length for the yoke** (along the straight of grain) from the neckband to the yoke style line and add 3 inches. Snip and tear the fabric at this length.

2 **Measure the width for the yoke** (along the crossgrain) from the center front to the armhole and add 3 inches. Snip and tear the fabric at this width.

3 **Draw a center front grainline** 1 inch from the torn edge on the prepared yoke piece. Press under.

4 **Measure down on the grainline** 4 inches. Crossmark at this measurement on the prepared yoke piece.

Front Bodice Yoke: Draping Steps

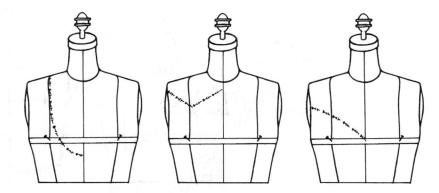

1 **Prepare the dress form.** Referring to the design sketch, pin the desired yoke style line on the dress form.

2 **Drape a bodice to match the desired yoke design.** Follow the bodice instructions for either the pleated bodice (pages 376–378), circular bodice (pages 379–382), or the all-in-one bodice yoke (pages 180–182).

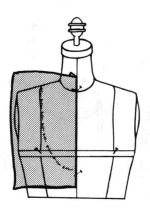

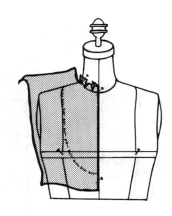

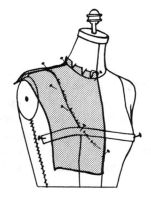

3 **Place the center front yoke grainline** to the center front position of the dress form. Align the center front neckline position crossmark of the yoke to the center front neckline position of the dress form.

4 **Clip, smooth, and pin the neckline** of the yoke.

5 **Smooth the fabric over and past the shoulder seam** of the dress form. Pin in place.

6 **Smooth the fabric past the desired yoke style line.** Pin in place.

7 Mark all key areas of the dress form to the fabric of the yoke.

a. Neckline.

b. Shoulder seam and shoulder ridge.

c. Yoke style line.

d. Yoke style line notch.

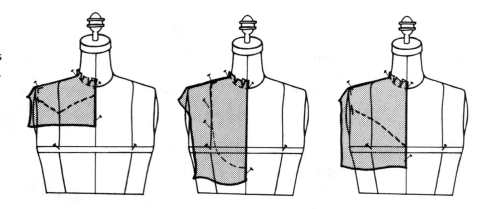

8 True up all seams. Remove the yoke drape from the dress form. True up all seams, add seam allowances, and trim excess fabric. Return the yoke to the dress form and check for accuracy, fit, and balance.

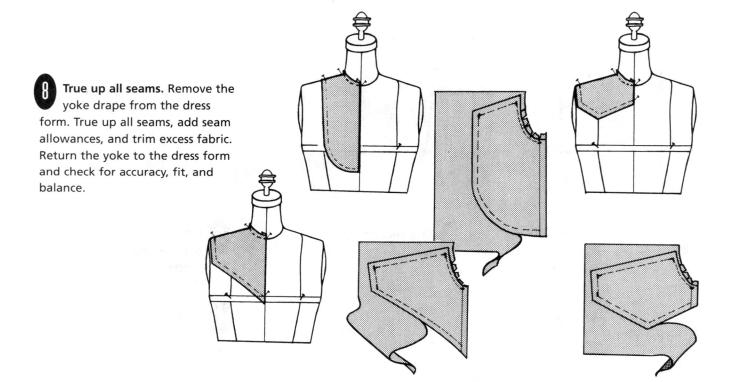

The Dartless Kimono Blocks:
Definition, Theory, & Principles

Definition

The **dartless kimono** is an all-in-one bodice/sleeve. The sleeve styling does not require a traditional armhole but is cut in one piece with the front and back of the garment. The underarm depth of the kimono may vary, as can the length of the sleeve. The shoulder seam is draped to follow the slope of the shoulder, and the side seam hangs parallel to center front. The kimono blocks are used to create a variety of designs for dresses and blouses.

Variations of the Kimono Block

The **waist-fitted kimono** is an all-in-one bodice with the sleeve. This eliminates the traditional armhole. There is a fitted waistline seam with a waistline dart.

The **waist-fitted version** of this style is draped with a waistline seam. A waistline dart is necessary to have a fitted waistline.

Theory

The **dartless kimono block** and its variations may be used when:

- The design does not include any darting.

- Stylelines or gathers are created by simply slashing and opening within the design.

- The design has *no* waist-fitting seam and usually hangs away from the body. You may, however, wish to give it fisheye darts or simply belt it.

- This sleeve does not require a traditional armhole and is cut in one piece with the front and back of the garment.

   The **waist-fitted kimono** sleeve block may be used when:

- The design has a fitted waist seam.

- The waist dart amount could be converted into tucks, stylelines, or gathers or simply kept as a dart somewhere within the design.

- This sleeve does not require a traditional armhole and is cut in one piece with the front and back of the garment.

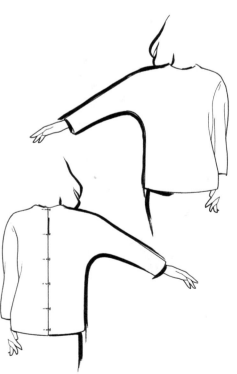

Principles: Analyzing the Kimono Block

It is important to analyze the block to insure that the following items are correct. If one of these items is wrong, the designs made from this block will not fit properly, and they will twist, drag, or pull.

- All pattern pieces have a definite relationship with the figure that enables them to hang straight up and down and be parallel to the floor. The grainline and crossgrain alignment, in addition to the side seam angle, allows the designer to maintain the correct balance between the front and back of the garment.

- Grainline should be straight and in the middle of the sleeve.

- The bust level line of the front bodice is on perfect crossgrain, allowing the area below the bust level line to hang straight up and down

- The shoulder blade level line of the back bodice is on perfect crossgrain, allowing the area below the shoulder blade level line to hang straight up and down.

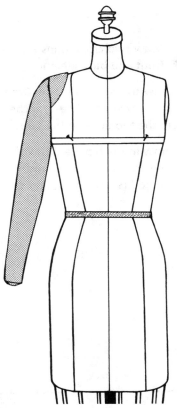

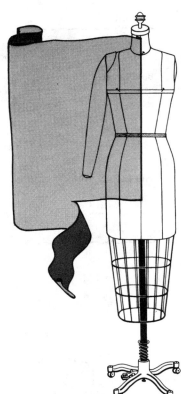

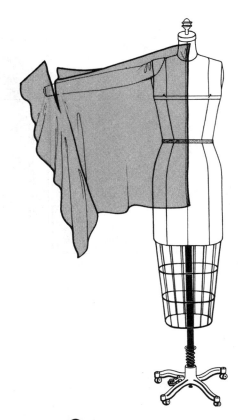

1 **Prepare arm for dress form.** For best results in measuring, draping, and fitting a kimono dartless block, prepare and attach the arm to the dress form. Refer to pages 14–15 to prepare this arm for the dress form.

2 **Measure the length for the front and back drape** along the straight of grain. Measure from the neckband to the hip level and add 5 inches. Snip and tear the fabric at this length.

3 **Measure the width for the front and back drape** along the crossgrain. Measure from the center of the dress form to the wrist level of the arm. Snip and tear the fabric at this width.

Back

Front

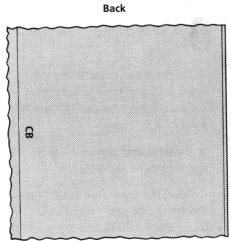

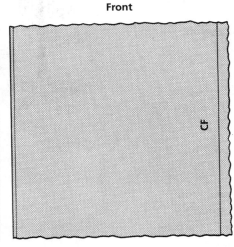

4 **Draw the grainlines for the front and back kimono** 1 inch from the torn edge and press under.

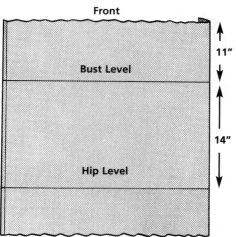

Back

Front

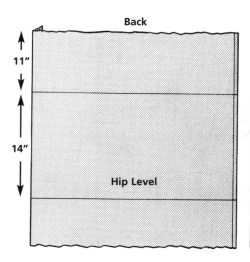

11"

14"

Hip Level

Bust Level

11"

14"

Hip Level

5 **Draw two crossgrains for the front and back kimono.**

a. Draw the bust level line. Draw the first crossgrain line 11 inches from the top edge of the fabric.

b. Draw in the hipline. Draw the second crossgrain line 14 inches from the first crossgrain line.

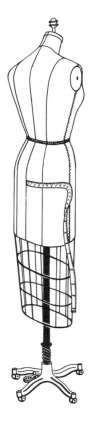

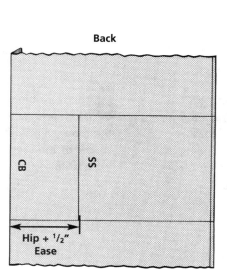

Back

CB

SS

Hip + ¹/₂"
Ease

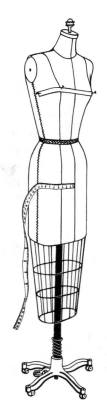

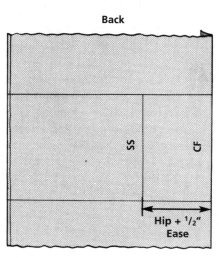

Back

SS

CF

Hip + ¹/₂"
Ease

6 **Draw the back side seam.**

a. Measure the dress form at the hip level from the center back to the side seam, and **add 1/2 inch** for ease.

b. Transfer and crossmark this measurement to the fabric.

c. Draw a back side seam. From the back side seam crossmark, draw a side seam perfectly parallel to the center back grainline.

7 **Draw in the front side seam.**

a. On the dress form at the hip level, measure from center front to the side seam and **add 1/2 inch** for ease.

b. Transfer and crossmark this measurement to the fabric.

c. Draw the front side seam. From the front side seam crossmark, draw a side seam perfectly parallel to the center front grainline.

Dartless Kimono: Draping Steps

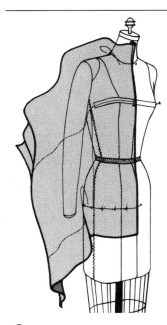
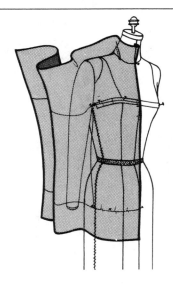
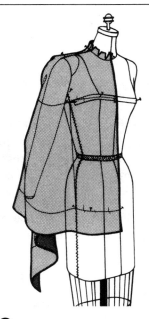

1 Pin the center front grainline fold of the fabric on the center front position of the dress form. Be sure to align the crossgrain at the bust level of the dress form.

Anchor pins at center front neck and center front hip. An additional pin may be needed at the bust level.

2 Smooth and pin the crossgrain of the fabric across the dress form to the side seam. Distribute the 1/2-inch ease evenly across the dress form.

3 Pin the fabric side seam to the side seam of the dress form. Be sure the fabric crossgrains are parallel to the floor.

4 Pin the shoulder/neck area. Trim and clip the excess fabric around the neck area and smooth the fabric flat over the shoulder/neck area.

Mark shoulder

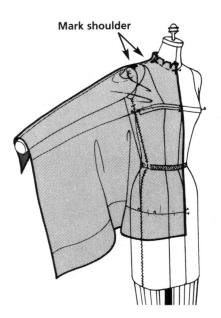

5 Mark the key areas of the dress form on the fabric.

a. **Neckline:** Lightly mark.

b. **Shoulder neck corner:** Crossmark.

c. **Shoulder seam to the ridge:** Lightly mark.

d. **Side seam:** Mark 2 inches below the armplate.

e. **Waistline:** Crossmark at the side seam.

Remove the fabric drape from the dress form.

6 True up the neckline and side seam and draw in the kimono sleeve.

a. Raise the shoulder line 1/2 inch at the shoulder ridge.

b. Extend the shoulder line 23 inches from the raised shoulder ridge corner. This raised shoulder line creates a sleeve seam with a higher shoulder slant.

c. Draw a line 8 inches long perpendicular from the shoulder seam, using an L-square ruler.

d. Square the underarm line from the wristline back to the side seam, using an L-square ruler.

e. Measure 1/2 inch toward the center front at the side seam/waistline position. Place a crossmark.

f. Draw in the desired underarm kimono shape from the elbow level to the side seam crossmark.

g. Shape the hip area at the side seam. Blend following the 1/2-inch waistline crossmark back to the original side seam.

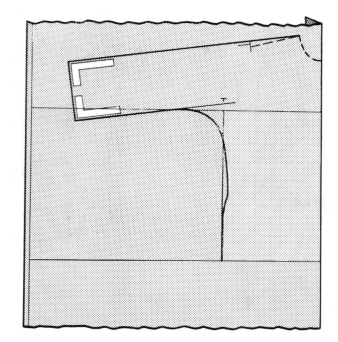

7 Add seam allowances to the front trued up drape. Cut the front drape out.

8 Draft the back kimono drape.

a. Place the front kimono drape on top of the prepared fabric for the back drape, matching crossgrains.

b. Extend the back center fold grainline 1/2 inch past the front center front fold grainline. Be sure both center grainlines remain parallel.

c. Pin both layers of fabric together, following the front outline drape.

Design Variations

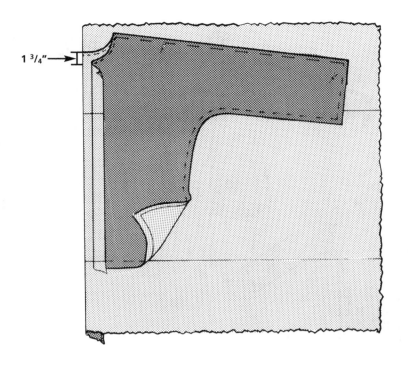

1 ³/₄"→

Transfer and draw the back shoulder and back neckline.

a. Mark the back shoulder line. Follow the stitch line of the front shoulder line.

b. Shape the back neckline. Using a French curve, blend from the back shoulder neckline corner to the center back grainline. Referring to the illustration, notice that the back neckline is about 1 3/4 inches higher than the front neckline.

c. Draw in the beginning of the wrist line.

d. Draw in all seam allowances to these lines.

Slide front drape down ¹/₂" from the original back shoulder

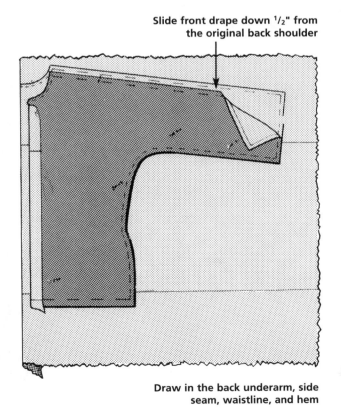

Draw in the back underarm, side seam, waistline, and hem

Finish transferring the front seams to the back.

a. Remove all pins and slide the front drape down 1/2 inch from the shoulder. Keep the center back and center front parallel with the back remaining extended out 1/2 inch past center back.

b. Repin the front trued up lines— underarm/side seam, wrist, and hem.

c. Draw in the back underarm/side seam line, wrist line, and hem, following the stitch line of the front.

NOTE: This allows the back shoulder line to extend 1/2 inch more than the front, maintaining body balance.

True all seams, add seam allowances, and trim excess fabric.

12 Check the fit of the kimono drape.

a. Pin the front and back kimono together. Return the drape to the dress form. Place anchor pins along the center front and center back seams. Recheck and mark if necessary. Retrue when off the dress form.

b. Check the hang of this drape.
- The front and back drapes are plumb (no twists).
- Side seams align with the dress form side seams.
- Shoulder seams lie on the shoulder seam of the dress form.

NOTE: If the drape hangs incorrectly, this usually indicates that the shoulder and the back neck area need to be adjusted. This may result in a slightly larger back sleeve width.

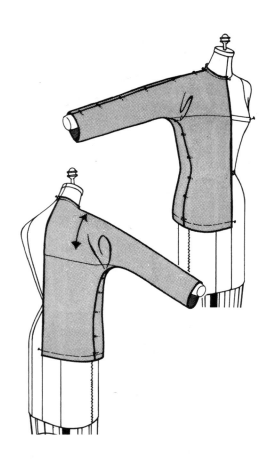

Variation to Achieve Extra Lift

Slash the underarm area of the sleeve up to the shoulder-ridge position. Pivot the sleeve up and blend in new shoulder and underarm lines.

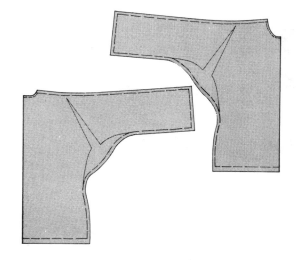

Chapter Eleven

Princess Shapes

By studying the various draping steps in this chapter, the designer should be able to:

- Develop creativity and stimulate a variety of princess shapes.

- Recognize grain and crossgrain of fabric in relation to the bust level on the front, shoulder blade level on the back, and side seams for a princess shape.

- Drape a flat piece of fabric to fit the curves of the body over the bust.

- Shape the contour of the princess panels into a fitted waist seam or into a seam that is not fitted at the waist but has the correct amount of ease allowance.

- Add flare to the princess panels for a princess slip dress.

- Visualize the front and back princess panels in relation to the figure.

- True up the front and back princess panels with the correct amount of ease allowance, armhole size, waistline shape, measurement, and balance.

- Check the results of the draping process for a princess shape with regard to fit, hang, balance, proportion, and the true up.

Princess Bodice

A fitted waist bodice with vertical seams, rather than darts, is known as the princess bodice. These vertical seams divide the bodice into separate panels. When these seams are sewn together, they take on the same shape as the basic bodice, but with vertical seams.

Typically, a princess bodice has a close-fitting waist with an unbroken style line that usually extends from the shoulder or armhole to the waistline. This style line almost always crosses over the midpoint of the bustline (apex) and replaces the need for darts. A princess bodice

back should always be designed similarly to the chosen front princess bodice.

There are many variations to a princess style. Illustrated here are examples of some typically fashioned princess bodices.

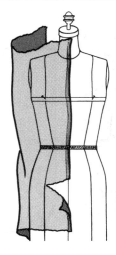

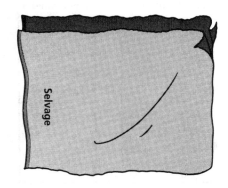

1 **Measure the length** for the front and back panels (along the straight of grain) from the neckband to the waist and add 5 inches.

Snip and tear the fabric at this length.

2 **Divide the fabric piece in half.** Fold the fabric from selvage to selvage. Snip and tear the fabric piece in half lengthwise.

Use one piece for the front panels and the other piece for the back panels.

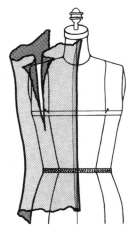

3 **Measure the width for the center front panel** (along the crossgrain) from the center front of the dress form to 4 inches past the apex. Using one of the fabric pieces prepared in step 2, snip and tear the fabric at this width.

Use the remaining front fabric piece for the side front panel.

Side Front Panel   **Front Panel**

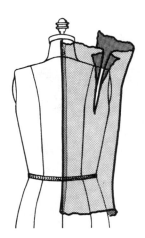

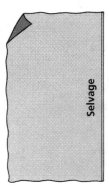

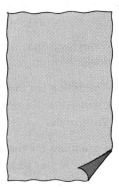

4 **Measure the width for the center back panel.** Measure from the center back of the dress form to the back princess seam at the shoulder blade level and add 4 inches.

Using the other fabric piece prepared in step 2, snip and tear the fabric this width.

Use the remaining back fabric piece for the side back panel.

Back Panel   **Side Back Panel**

Side Front Panel   **Front Panel**

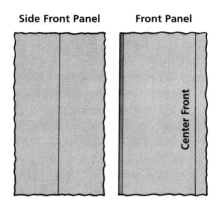

Side Front Panel   **Front Panel**

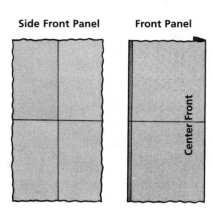

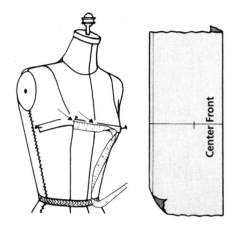

5 Draw in the grainlines on the front panels.

a. **Draw the grainline for the center front panel** 1 inch from the torn edge and press under.

b. **Draw the grainline for the side front panel** at the center of the fabric piece.

6 Draw the crossgrain lines for the front and side front panels in the center of both panels (crosswise).

7 Crossmark the apex.

a. **Measure the dress form** from center front to the apex.

b. **Crossmark the apex** this distance on the center front panel on the crossgrain line.

Back Panel   **Side Back Panel**

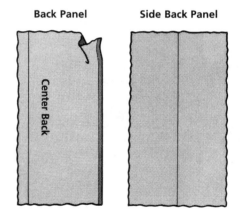

Back Panel   **Side Back Panel**

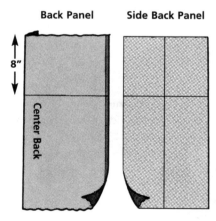

8 Draw in the grainlines on the back panels.

a. **Draw the grainline for the center back panel** 1 inch from the torn edge. Press under.

b. **Draw the grainline for the side back panel** in the center of the fabric piece (lengthwise).

9 Draw the crossgrain line for both back panels 8 inches from the top of the fabric edge.

Center Front Princess Panel: *Draping Steps*

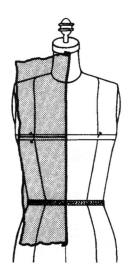

1 **Pin the apex** crossmark on the fabric to the apex position on the dress form.

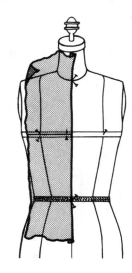

2 **Pin the center front grainline** fold of the fabric to the center position of the dress form.

Anchor pins at center front neck and center front waist. An additional pin may be needed at the bust level tape.

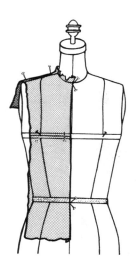

3 **Drape the neckline** by trimming the excess fabric around the neck area and clipping at intervals. Smooth the neckline in place.

4 **Drape and smooth the fabric over the shoulder seam** of the dress form to just past the princess seam. Pin in place.

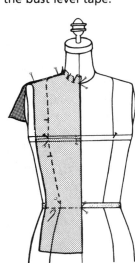

5 **Drape and smooth the waistline** across the waistline tape from center front to just past the princess seam. Pin in place.

6 **Mark all key areas** of the dress form on the center front panel:

a. Neckline: Lightly mark.

b. Shoulder seam: Lightly mark.

c. Waistline: Lightly mark.

d. Princess seam and style line: Crossmark 2 inches above and below apex.

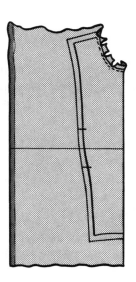

7 **True up center front panel.** Add seam allowances and trim all excess fabric. Place panel back on the dress form.

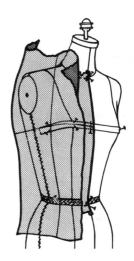

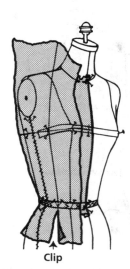

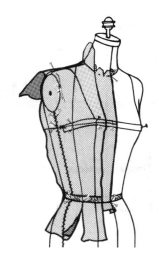

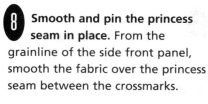
Clip

1 **Pin the grainline of the side front panel** to the center of the front princess panel on the dress form.

2 **Match the crossgrain of the side front panel to the crossgrain of the center front panel.** Anchor pins on the crossgrain at the bust level. Place another anchor pin on the straight of grain at the waistline.

3 **Clip the waistline** at the center of the front princess panel up to the bottom of the waist seam tape.

4 **Drape and pin the waistline in place.** From the grainline of the front panel, smooth the fabric across the waist seam tape toward the side seam. Also, drape toward the princess seam. Pin.

5 **Smooth and pin the side seam in place.** From the grainline of the side front panel, smooth the fabric past the side seam of the dress form. Do not allow the grainline to slip out of position. Pin the side seam in place.

6 **Continue to smooth the fabric flat over the armplate.** Create a 1/4-inch–1/4-inch pinch at the mid-armhole area ridge.

7 **Drape the shoulder** by carefully smoothing the excess fabric above the bust level up and over the shoulder of the dress form.

NOTE: The grainline will angle toward the neckline above the bust level.

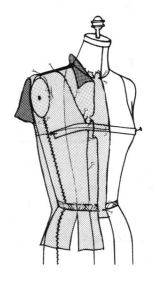

8 **Smooth and pin the princess seam in place.** From the grainline of the side front panel, smooth the fabric over the princess seam between the crossmarks.

NOTE: Excess fabric will drape over the bust level area, creating ease at the princess seam between the crossmarks.

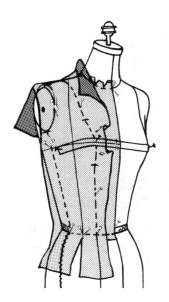

9 **Mark all key areas** of the dress form on the side front panel:

a. Princess seam and style line crossmarks: Match to center front panel crossmarks.

b. Armplate:
  - Shoulder seam at ridge
  - Middle of plate at screw level (1/4-inch–1/4-inch pinch)
  - Bottom of plate at side seam

c. Shoulder seam.

d. Side seam.

e. Waistline.

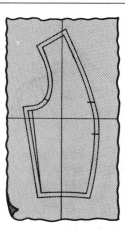

10 **True up all the lines.** Remove the side front panel from the dress form and true up all the lines. Add seam allowances and the front armhole notch.

Trim excess fabric. Pin to front panel. Place the drape on the dress form to check seams, crossmarks, fit, and balance.

Center Back Princess Panel: *Draping Steps*

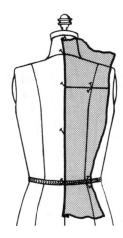

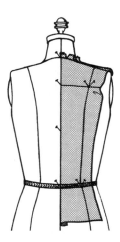

1 **Pin the center back grainline** fold of the fabric to the center back position of the dress form.

2 **Align and pin the crossgrain** of the fabric to the shoulder blade level of the dress form.

3 **Drape and smooth the back waistline** from center back to just past the princess seam. Pin the waistline in place.

4 **Drape and smooth the back neckline.** Carefully trim the excess fabric around the neck area and clip at intervals. Smooth the fabric around the neckline.

5 **Smooth the fabric over the shoulder** of the dress form and pin in place.

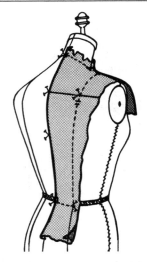

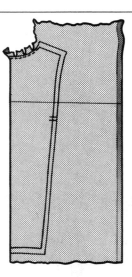

6 **Mark all key areas** of the dress form on the center back panel:

a. Neckline.

b. Waistline.

c. Shoulder seam.

d. Back princess seam and style line crossmarks: Double crossmarks are used in the back.

7 **True up all lines.** Remove the center back panel drape from the dress form. True up all lines, add seam allowances, and trim all excess fabric. Place this center back panel drape on the dress form.

Side Back Princess Panel: Draping Steps

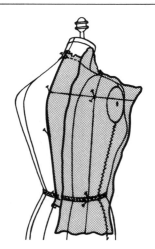

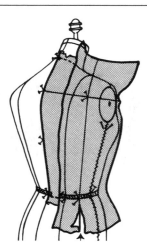

1 **Pin the grainline of the side back panel** to the center of the back princess panel on the dress form.

2 **Match all crossgrains** at the shoulder blade level.

3 **Clip the waistline at the side back panel** up to the bottom of the waist seam tape.

4 **Drape and pin the waistline in place.** From the grainline of the back panel, smooth the fabric across the waist seam tape toward the side seam. Also, drape toward the princess seam.

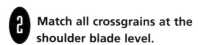

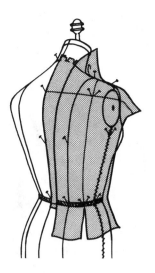

5 **Drape the shoulder** by smoothing the excess fabric from above the shoulder blade level up and over the shoulder seam of the dress form.

NOTE: The grainline will be angled toward the neckline (over the crossgrain).

6 **Smooth and pin the side seam in place.** From the grainline of the side back panel, smooth the fabric past the side seam of the dress form. Do not allow the grainline to slip out of position. Pin the side seam in place.

7 **Drape and pin the princess seam in place.** From the grainline of the side back panel, smooth the fabric past the princess seam of dress form. Do not allow the grainline to slip out of position. Pin the princess seam.

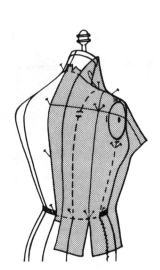

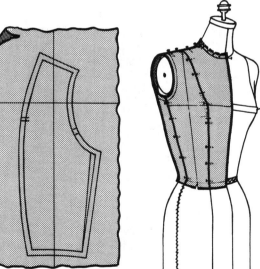

8 **Mark all key areas** of the dress form on the side back panel:

a. Princess seam and style line crossmarks: Match to center back panel double crossmarks.

b. Armplate:
- Shoulder seam at ridge
- Middle of plate at screw level
- Bottom of plate at side seam

c. Shoulder seam.

d. Side seam.

e. Waistline.

9 **True up all lines.** Remove the drape from the dress form. True up all lines, add seam allowances and back armhole notches, and trim all excess fabric. Pin the entire garment together and place the drape on the dress form. Check for accuracy, fit, and hang.

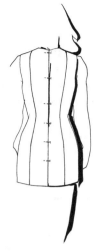  

A torso princess bodice is styled with vertical seams rather than darts. This divides the bodice front and back into two panels. It also has no waist fitting seam, allowing for long vertical slimming lines. Once sewn, the princess bodice represents the same shape as the basic torso bodice, or dress, but with vertical seams.

The torso princess drape offers versatility to an important classic and creates a crisp, longer, and slimmer look. Fashionable tops for suits, dresses, or sportswear separates may be designed in this length and shape. Many designers use this classic pattern to create a sensational body fit and look.

Torso Princess Bodice: Preparing the Fabric

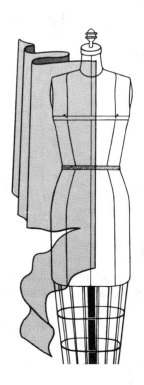 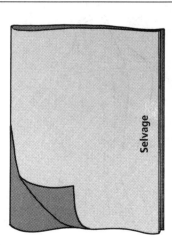

1 **Measure the length for the front and back panels** (along the straight of grain) from the neckband to the hip area and add 5 inches. Snip and tear the fabric at this length.

2 **Divide the fabric piece in half.** Fold the fabric from selvage to selvage. Snip and tear the fabric piece in half lengthwise.

Use one piece for the front panels and the other piece for the back panels.

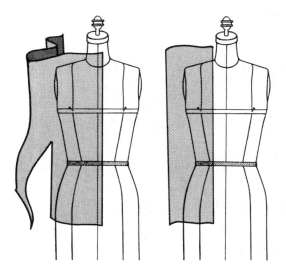 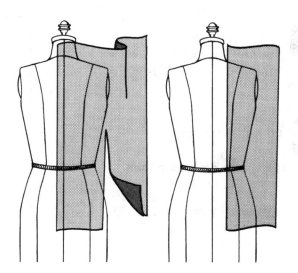

3 Measure the width for the center front panel (along the crossgrain) from the center front of the dress form to 5 inches past the apex. Using one of the fabric pieces prepared in Step 2, snip and tear the fabric at this width.

Use the remaining fabric piece for the side front panel.

4 Measure the width for the center back panel from the center back of the dress form to the back princess seam at the shoulder blade level and add 5 inches. Using the other fabric piece, snip and tear the fabric at this width.

Use the remaining back panel piece for the side back panel.

Side Front Panel   Front Panel

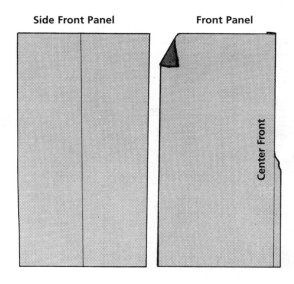

5 Draw the grainline for the center front panel 1 inch from the torn edge and press under.

6 Draw the grainline for the side front panel in the center of the fabric piece.

Side Front Panel **Front Panel**

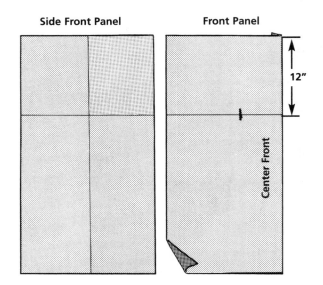

7 Draw the crossgrain lines for the front and side front panels 12 inches from the top edge of the fabric.

8 Crossmark the apex.

a. Measure the dress form from center front to the apex.

b. Crossmark the apex this distance on the center front panel on the crossgrain line.

Back Panel **Side Back Panel**

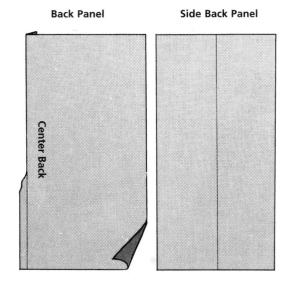

9 Draw the grainline for the center back panel 1 inch from the torn edge and press under.

10 Draw the grainline for the side back panel in the center of the fabric piece.

Back Panel **Side Back Panel**

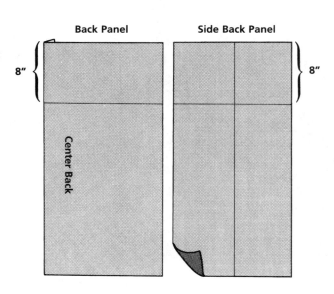

11 Draw the crossgrain lines for both back panels 8 inches from the top edge of the fabric.

Center Front Princess Panel: *Draping Steps*

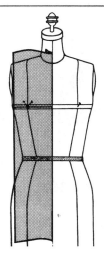

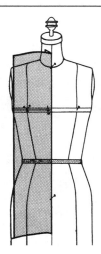

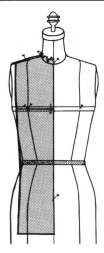

1 **Pin the apex** crossmark on the fabric to the apex position on the dress form.

2 **Pin the center front grainline** fold of the fabric on the center position of the dress form.

Anchor pins at center front neck and center front hip. An additional pin may be needed at the bust level tape.

3 **Drape the front neckline** by trimming the excess fabric around the neck area and clipping at intervals. Smooth the neckline in place.

4 **Drape and smooth the fabric over the shoulder seam** of the dress form to just past the princess seam. Pin in place.

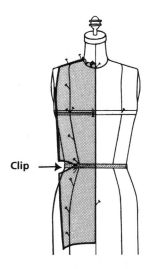

Clip ←

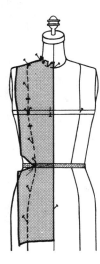

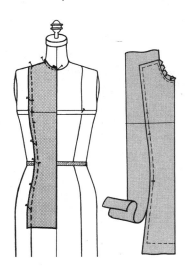

5 **Clip the waistline at the princess seam.**

6 **Drape the princess seam.** Smooth the fabric from center front to just past the princess seam. Pin the princess seam.

NOTE: The fabric at the waistline will be smooth, but not snug.

7 **Mark all key areas** of the dress form on the center front panel.

a. **Neckline.**

b. **Shoulder seam.**

c. **Princess seam.**

d. **Style line crossmarks:** Crossmark 2 inches above and below apex.

e. **Hem.**

8 **True up the center front panel.** Add seam allowances and trim all excess fabric. Place panel back on the dress form.

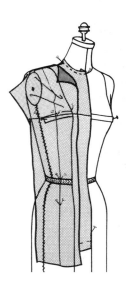

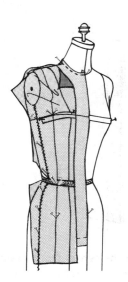

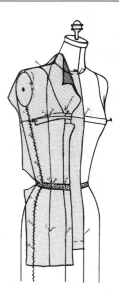

1 Pin the grainline of the side front panel to the center of the princess panel on the dress form.

2 Match the crossgrain of the side front panel to the crossgrain of the center front panel. Anchor pins on the crossgrain at the bust level. Place another pin on the straight of grain at the waistline and the hipline.

3 Clip the waistline at the side seam.

4 Smooth and pin the side seam in place. From the grainline of the side front panel, smooth the fabric past the side seam of dress form. Pin the side seam in place.

5 Continue to smooth the fabric flat over the armplate. Leave the 1/4-inch–1/4-inch pinch at the mid-armhole area ridge.

6 Drape the shoulder by carefully smoothing the excess fabric above the bust level up and over the shoulder of the dress form.

NOTE: The grainline will angle toward the neckline above the bust level.

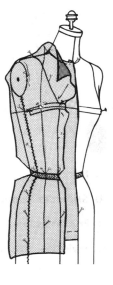

7 Clip the waistline at the princess seam.

8 Smooth and pin the princess seam in place. From the grainline of the side front panel, smooth the fabric past the princess seam of the dress form. Pin in place.

NOTE: Excess fabric will drape over the bust level area, creating ease at the princess seam between the crossmarks.

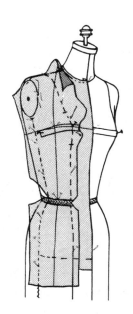

9 **Mark key areas** of the dress form on the side front panel:

a. Princess seam.

b. Style line crossmarks: Match to center front panel crossmarks.

c. Armplate:
   • Shoulder seam at ridge
   • Middle of plate at screw level (1/4-inch–1/4-inch pinch)
   • Bottom of plate at side seam

d. Shoulder seam.

e. Side seam.

f. Hem.

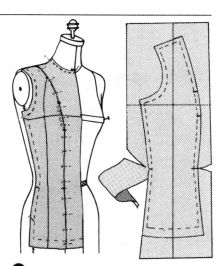

10 **True up all the lines.** Remove the side front panel from the dress form. True up all the lines and add seam allowances.

Trim all excess fabric. Pin the front panel to the side front panel. Place the drape on the dress form to check seams, crossmarks, fit, and balance.

Center Back Princess Panel: *Draping Steps*

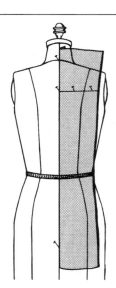

1 **Pin the center back grainline** fold of the fabric to the center back position of the dress form.

2 **Align and pin the crossgrain** of the fabric to the shoulder blade level of the dress form.

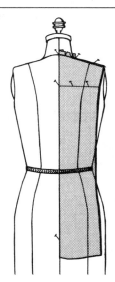

3 **Drape and smooth the back neckline** by carefully trimming the excess fabric around the neck area and clipping at intervals.

4 **Continue to drape and smooth the shoulder** over the shoulder of the dress form. Pin in place.

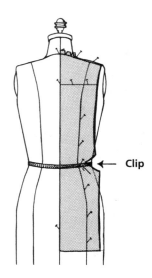

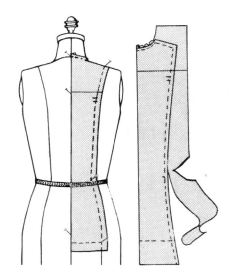

← Clip

5 Clip the waistline at the princess seam.

6 Drape the princess seam. Smooth the fabric across the dress form from center back to just past the princess seam. Pin in place.

NOTE: The waist area will drape smoothly, but will not be snug.

7 Mark all key areas of the dress form on the center back panel:

a. Neckline.

b. Shoulder seam.

c. Back princess seam.

d. Style line notches: A double notch is used in the back.

e. Hem.

8 True up all lines. Remove the center back panel drape from the dress form. True up all lines, add seam allowances, and trim all excess fabric. Place the drape back on the dress form.

Side Back Princess Panel: Draping Steps

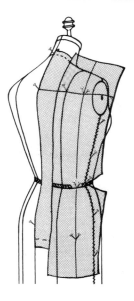

1 Pin the grainline of the side back panel to the center of the back princess panel on the dress form.

2 Match all crossgrains at the shoulder blade level.

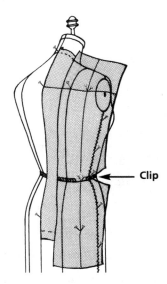

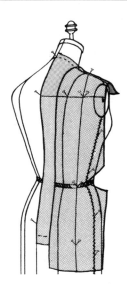

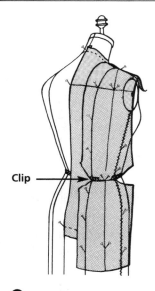

3 Clip the waistline at the side seam.

4 Smooth and pin the side seam in place. From the grainline of the side back panel, smooth the fabric past the side seam of the dress form. Pin the side seam in place.

5 Drape the shoulder by smoothing the excess fabric from above the shoulder blade level up and over the shoulder seam of the dress form.

NOTE: The grainline will be angled toward the neckline (above the crossgrain).

6 Clip the waistline at the princess seam of the side back panel.

7 Smooth and pin the back princess seam in place. From the grainline of the side back panel, smooth the fabric past the princess seam of the dress form. Do not allow the grainline to slip out of position. Pin the princess seam in place.

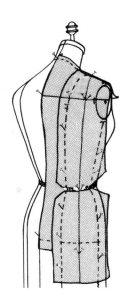

8 Mark all key areas of the dress form on the side back panel:

a. **Princess seam and style line crossmarks:** Match to center back panel double crossmarks.

b. **Armplate:**
  • Shoulder seam at ridge
  • Middle of plate at screw level
  • Bottom of plate at side seam

c. **Shoulder seam.**

d. **Side seam.**

e. **Hem.**

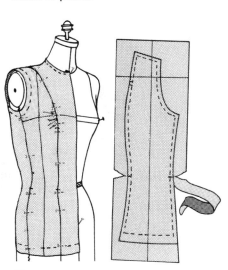

9 True up all lines. Remove the drape from the dress form. True up all lines, add seam allowances, and trim all excess fabric.

Pin the entire garment together and place the drape on the dress form. Check for accuracy, fit, and hang.

Princess Slip Dress

The princess slip dress is sleeveless, with a neckline beginning above the bust. It is held in place with thin spaghetti straps. The slip dress is styled with vertical seams that divide the dress front and back into two panels. The princess slip dress has no waist fitting seam, allowing for long vertical slimming lines. An additional "flare" amount is draped into the dress panels from the waist area to the hemline. The slip dress is usually made of soft fabric that gives the dress a feathery, flowing appearance.

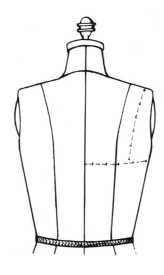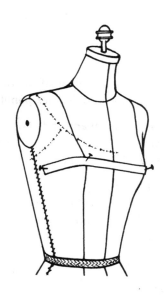

Prepare the Dress Form

Place pins on the dress form at the desired bustline.

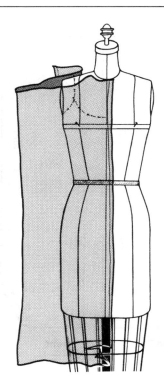

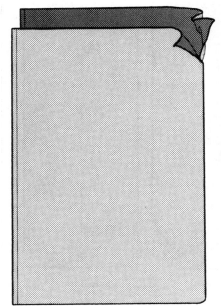

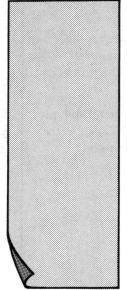

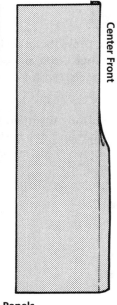

Front Panels

Center Front

1 Measure the length for the front and back panels (along the straight of grain) from the neckband to the desired length and add 5 inches. Snip and tear the fabric at this length.

2 Divide the fabric piece in half. Fold the fabric from selvage to selvage and snip and tear the fabric piece in half lengthwise.

Use one piece for the front panels and the other piece for the back panels.

3 Measure the width for the center front panel (along the crossgrain) from the center front of the dress form to the front princess seam at the apex and add 5 inches. Snip and tear the fabric this width.

Use the remaining fabric piece for the side front panel.

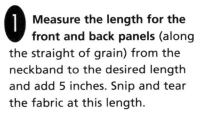

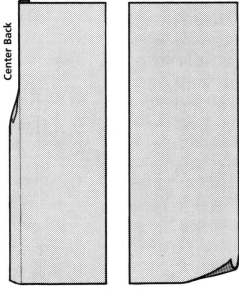

Center Back

4 Measure the width for the center back panel from the center back of the dress form to the back princess seam at the shoulder blade level and add 5 inches. Using the other fabric piece, snip and tear the fabric this width.

Use the remaining back panel piece for the side back panel.

Back Panels

5 Draw in the fabric grainlines.

a. Draw the grainline for the center front and center back panels 1 inch from the torn edge. Press under.

b. Draw the grainline for the side front and side back panels in the center of the fabric pieces.

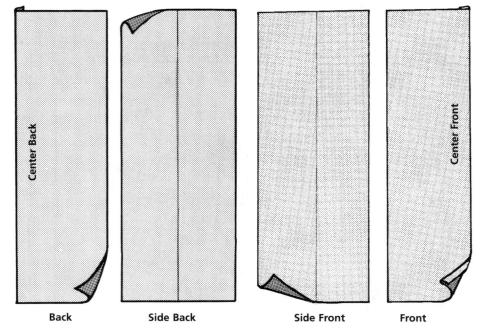

Back **Side Back** **Side Front** **Front**

Notes

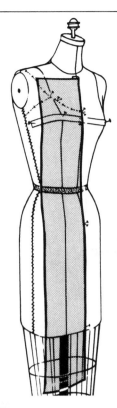

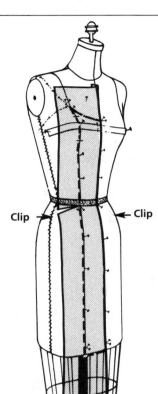

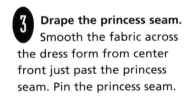

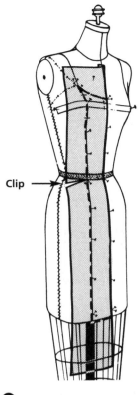

1 **Pin the center front grainline** fold of the fabric to the center position of the dress form. The fabric piece should extend at least 3 inches above the front styled neckline.

2 **Clip the waistline at the princess seam.**

3 **Drape the princess seam.** Smooth the fabric across the dress form from center front just past the princess seam. Pin the princess seam.

NOTE: The fabric at the waistline will be smooth, but not snug.

4 **Mark all key areas** of the dress form on the center front panel:

a. Bustline styled neckline.

b. Princess seam.

c. Style line notches: Crossmark 2 inches above and below apex.

d. Hem: Follow the bottom of the dress form or a rung.

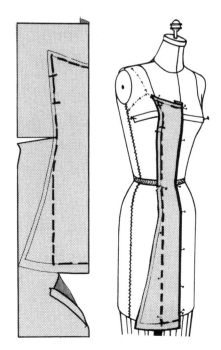

5 **True up the center front panel.**

Add the amount of flare desired at the hemline of the princess seam. Blend this flare into the waistline at the princess seam.

Add seam allowances and trim all excess fabric. Place panel back on the dress form.

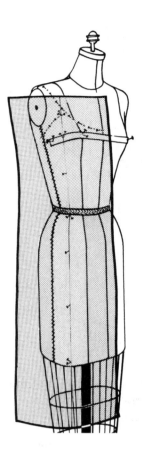

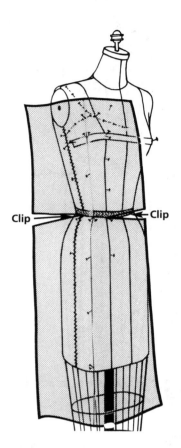

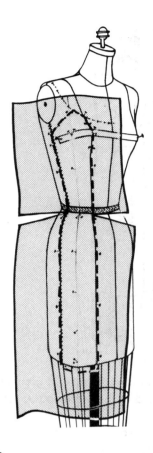

1 **Pin the grainline of the side front panel** to the center of the princess panel on the dress form. The fabric piece should extend at least 3 inches above the styled neckline.

2 **Clip the waistline at the side seam.**

3 **Smooth and pin the side seam in place.** From the grainline of the side front panel, smooth the fabric past the side seam of the dress form. Pin the side seam in place.

4 **Clip the waistline at the princess seam.**

5 **Smooth and pin the princess seam in place.** From the grainline of the side front panel, smooth the fabric past the princess seam of the dress form. Pin in place.

NOTE: The excess fabric will drape over the bust level area, creating ease at the princess seam between the notches.

6 **Mark all key areas of the dress form on the side front panel:**

a. **Princess seam.**

b. **Style line notches:** Match to center front panel notches.

c. **Bustline styled neckline.**

d. **Side seam.**

e. **Hem.**

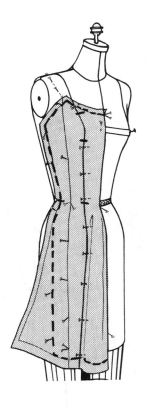

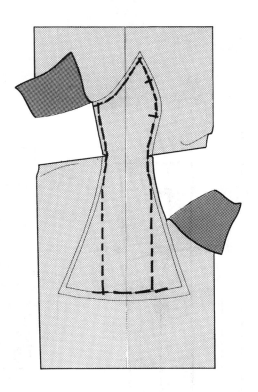

7 **True up all lines.** Remove the side front panel from the dress form and true up all the lines. Add the amount of flare desired at the hemline of the princess seam and the side seam. Blend this flare into the waistline.

Add seam allowances and trim all excess fabric. Pin the front panel to the side front panel. Place the drape on the dress form to check seams, notches, and balance.

Center Back Princess Slip Dress Panel: *Draping Steps*

1 **Pin the center back grainline** fold of the fabric to the center back position of the dress form. The back panel should extend at least 3 inches above the back styled neckline.

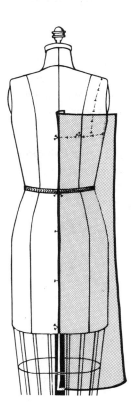

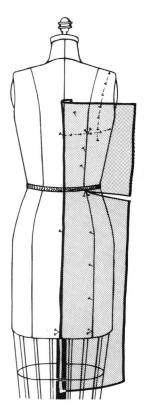

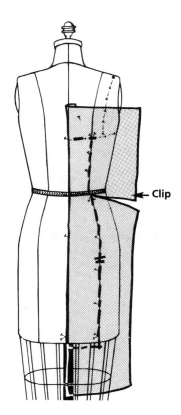

Clip

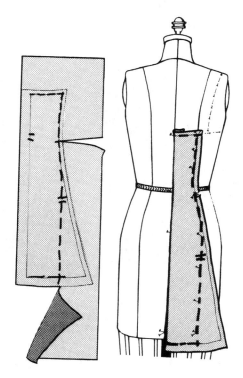

2 Clip the waistline at the princess seam.

3 Drape the princess seam. Smooth the fabric across the dress form from center back to just past the princess seam. Pin in place.

NOTE: The waist area will drape smoothly, but will not be snug.

4 Mark all key areas of the dress form on the center back panel:

a. Bustline styled neckline.

b. Back princess seam.

c. Style line notches: A double notch is used in the back.

d. Hem.

5 True up all lines. Remove the center back panel drape from the dress form and true up all lines. Add the amount of flare desired at the hemline of the princess seam. Blend this flare into the waistline at the princess seam.

Add seam allowances and trim all excess fabric. Place the drape back on the dress form.

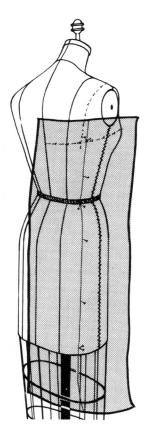

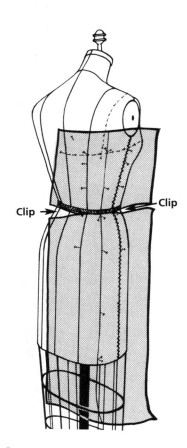

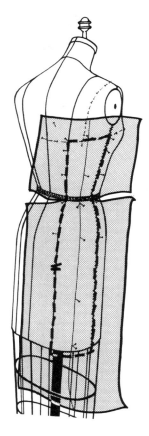

1 **Pin the grainline of the side back panel** to the center of the back princess panel on the dress form.

2 **Clip the waistline at the side seam.**

3 **Smooth and pin the side seam in place.** From the grainline of the side back panel, smooth the fabric past the side seam of the dress form. Pin the side seam in place.

4 **Clip the waistline at the princess seam.**

5 **Smooth and pin the back princess seam in place.** From the grainline of the side back panel, smooth the fabric past the princess seam of the dress form. Do not allow the grainline to slip out of position. Pin the princess seam in place.

6 **Mark all key areas** of the dress form on the side back panel:

a. Princess seam.

b. Styleline notches: Match to center back panel double notches.

c. Bustline styled neckline.

d. Side seam.

e. Hem.

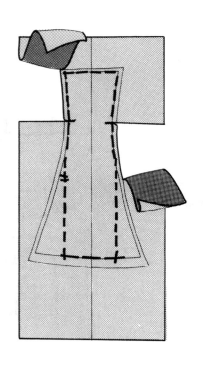

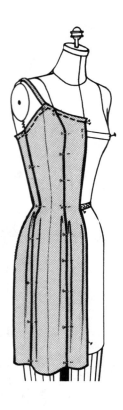

7 **True up all lines.** Remove the drape from the dress form and true up all lines. Add the amount of flare desired at the hemline of the princess seam and the side seam. Blend this flare into the waistline.

Add seam allowances and trim all excess fabric. Pin the entire garment together and place the drape on the dress form. Check for accuracy, fit, and hang.

Notes

Chapter Twelve

Skirts

Objectives

By studying the various draping steps in this chapter, the designer should be able to:

• Recognize grain and crossgrain of fabric in relation to the hip level line of front and back skirt variations.

• Design and drape variations for flared, dirndl, peg, and circular skirt styles.

• Drape a flat piece of fabric into a fitted waistline without darts and create flares falling from the upper hip of the body.

• Drape a flat piece of fabric and draw in fullness into a waistline with pleats and fullness.

• Drape a flat piece of fabric and shape multiple flares that fall from the fitted dartless waistline into multiple flares at the lower edge of the hemline.

• Check and balance the front and back side seams on all skirt variations.

• True up and visualize the front and back skirt pieces in relation to the figure.

• Check the results of the draping process for the skirt back and make necessary changes.

Flared Skirt

The flared skirt is fitted in at the waist and hip area with flares falling from the bottom of the hip. The waistline seam has a distinctive semicircular curve. When the waistline curve is sewn into a straight waistband or waistline, the lower section flows evenly and smoothly over the hip.

The traditional flared skirt does not have a center front seam. However, it does have side seams and a center back seam. This skirt is also called an A-line skirt.

Manufacturers use the flared (A-line) skirt as a block or sloper. The designs created from the flared skirt have a definite A-line or circular silhouette. Style lines, waistbands, a variety of pockets, and different hem lengths can easily be adapted to create a combination of designs. The length of the skirt is dictated by the season and, of course, the occasion and purpose of the design.

It is important to drape a flared skirt in the same fabric quality required by the finished design.

Flared Skirt: Preparing the Fabric

1 **Measure the length** (along the straight of grain) for both the front and back skirt from 5 inches above the waist tape to the desired length of the design.

Snip and tear the fabric at this length.

2 **Divide the fabric piece in half.** Fold the fabric from selvage to selvage. Snip and tear the piece in half lengthwise.

One piece will be used for the skirt front, and the other piece will be used for the skirt back.

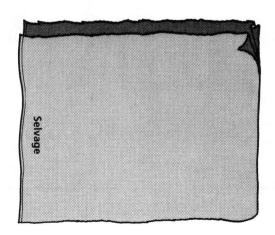

Selvage

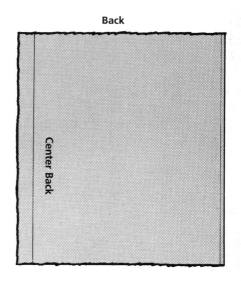

Back

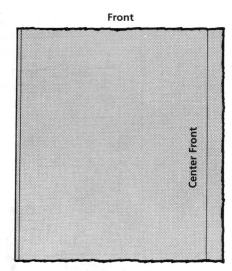

Front

3 Draw the center front and center back grainlines on the fabric 1 inch from the torn edge and press under.

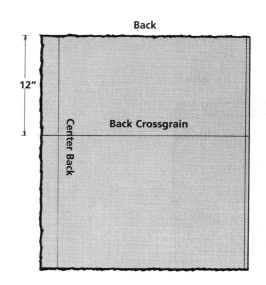

Back

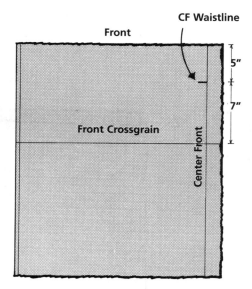

Front

CF Waistline

12"

5"

7"

4 **Crossmark the waistline.** Measure down 5 inches from the top of the fabric (on the grainline). Pencil in a waistline mark.

5 **Draw a perfect crossgrain at the hip level on both the front and back skirts.**

a. On the skirt front, measure down **7 inches** from the waistline mark. Draw a perfect front crossgrain at this level.

b. On the skirt back, measure down **12 inches** (on the grainline) from the top edge of the fabric. Draw a perfect back crossgrain at this level.

Flared Skirt: Draping Steps

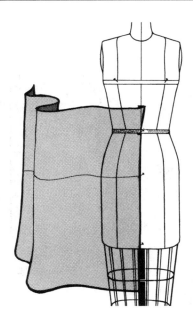

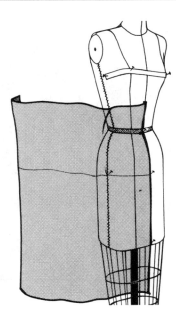

1 **Prepare the dress form.**

Pin, or use style tape, at the front and back hip level line.

2 **Pin the center front grainline fold** of the fabric to the center front position of the dress form.

3 **Smooth and pin the crossgrain of the fabric at the hip level** of the dress form to the side seam. Anchor a pin at the side seam/hip level.

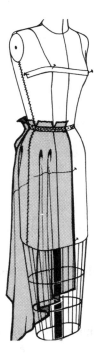

4 **Drape the waistline of the front panel.** Clip the fabric from the top edge down to the waistline and trim excess fabric. Smooth the fabric over the dress form at the waistline from the center front over to the side seam. Pin at the side seam/waist corner.

5 **Remove the pin at the side seam/hip** and allow the drape to fall freely.

NOTE: Two skirt flares will fall from the hip level.

6 **Mark all key areas:**

a. **Waistline front.**

b. **Side seam.**

c. **Hem: Follow the bottom of the dress form or rung.**

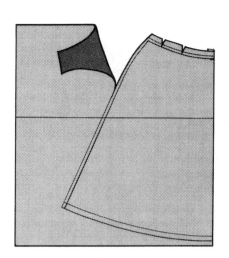

Front

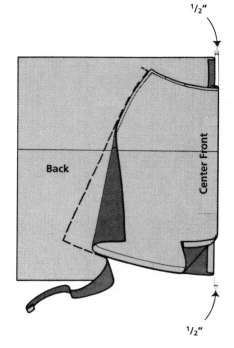

½"

Back

Center Front

½"

b. Extend the front grainline fold 1/2 inch past the back grainline fold. Be sure both center grainlines remain parallel. This distance allows for the difference between the back waistline amount and the front waistline amount.

c. Pin the two layers of fabric together.

d. Draw the back skirt stitchlines. Follow the same markings as the skirt front (side seam, hem, and temporary waistline).

NOTE: The back waistline will be redone when a final fit is checked. This is because the front and back waistline shapes are slightly different.

7 **True up the front drape.** Remove the fabric drape from the dress form. True up the front drape, add seam allowances, and trim all excess fabric.

8 **Draft back skirt drape.**

a. Place the skirt front drape on top of the back fabric prepared for the skirt back drape, matching crossgrains.

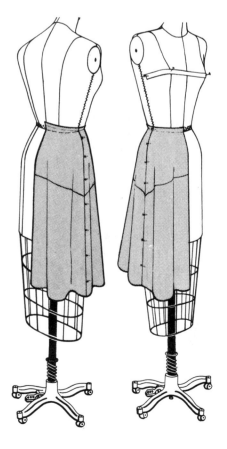

9 **Check the fit and balance** of the flared skirt drape.

a. Pin together the front and back side seams. Place this drape on the dress form.

b. Double check the hang of this drape. Pin center front and center back waists. Adjust the back waistline until the skirt hangs properly.
  • Side seams of drape fall on side seams of dress form.

  • The front and back drapes hang correctly (no twists or sags from the waistline).
  • Center back waistline is lower than the trued up waistline of the back drape.

NOTE: If the drape does not hang correctly, this usually indicates that the center back at the waistline should be dropped (approximately 1/4 to 1/2 inch).

c. Pencil in a new back waist shape.

Flared Six-Gore Skirt

The flared six-gore skirt has vertical seams that divide the basic straight skirt into equal or nonequal panels. This added seam divides the skirt into six gores that are fitted at the waistline and flare out at the hemline. These seams provide the designer with a place to add additional flare, pleats, or decorative stitching.

This classic can be made in a variety of fabrics with a variety of waistbands and pocket details. Its length varies with the season.

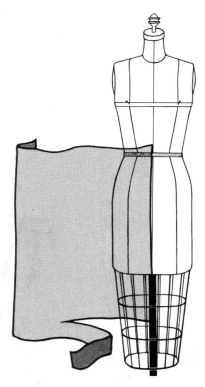

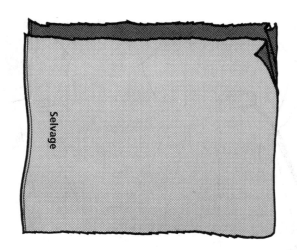

1 **Measure the length** (along the straight of grain) 2 inches above the waist to the desired length of the skirt. Snip and tear the fabric at this length.

2 **Divide the fabric piece in half lengthwise.** Fold fabric from selvage to selvage. Snip and tear fabric piece in half lengthwise.

One piece will be used for the front panels, and the other piece will be used for the back panels.

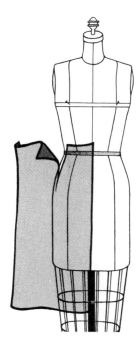

3 **Measure the width for center front panel** (along the crossgrain) from the center front of the dress form to the widest part of the princess seam. Add 4 inches to this width. Snip and tear the fabric at this width.

Use remaining fabric piece for the side front panel.

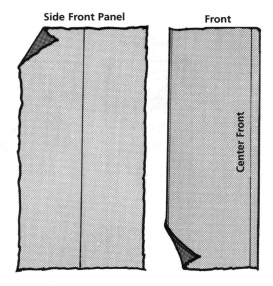

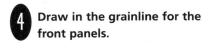

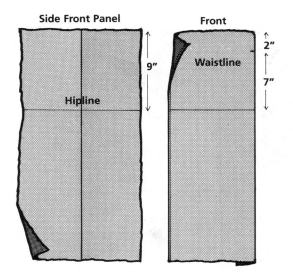

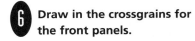

4 Draw in the grainline for the front panels.

a. Draw the grainline for the center front panel 1 inch from the torn edge. Press under.

b. Draw the grainline for the side front panel at the center of the fabric piece.

5 Draw a waistline mark. On the center front panel, measure down 2 inches from top edge of the fabric and draw a waistline mark.

6 Draw in the crossgrains for the front panels.

a. From the waistline mark, measure down another **7 inches** and draw a perfect crossgrain line at this level.

b. On the side front panel, measure down **9 inches** and draw a perfect crossgrain line.

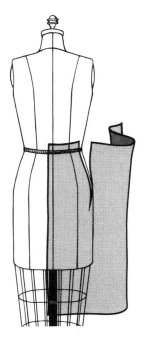

7 Measure the width for the center back panel (along the crossgrain). Measure from center back of the dress form to the widest part of the back princess seam. Add 4 inches to this width. Snip and tear the fabric at this width.

Use remaining fabric piece for the side back panel.

Back Panel   **Side Back Panel**

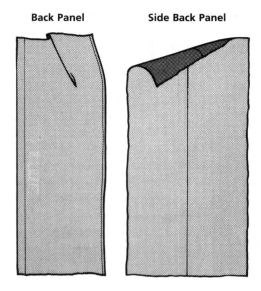

Back Panel   **Side Back Panel**

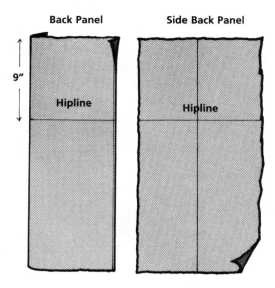

8 Draw the grainline for the center back panel 1 inch from the torn edge and press under.

9 Draw the grainline for the side back panel at the center of the fabric piece.

10 Draw the crossgrain lines of the back panels 9 inches from the top edge of both back panels.

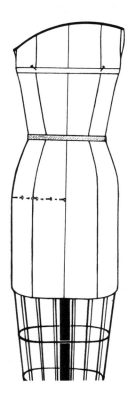

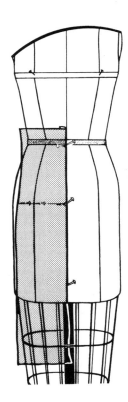

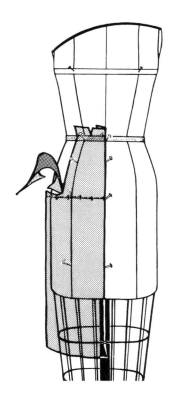

1 **Prepare the dress form.**

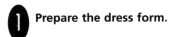

Pin, or use style tape, at the front and back hip level line.

2 **Pin the center front grainline** fold of the fabric on the center front position of the dress form.

3 **Align the fabric crossgrain to the hip level line** on the dress form. Pin both the center front and the crossgrain.

4 **Drape the waistline and the princess seam of the center front panel.**

a. Carefully trim and clip the fabric from the top edge down to the waistline. Smooth the fabric over the dress form waist tape just past the princess seam. Pin in place.

b. Drape the front princess seam. Smooth the fabric over the entire princess seam of the dress form from the waistline down to the bottom of the dress form. Trim the fabric at the princess seam down to the hip level.

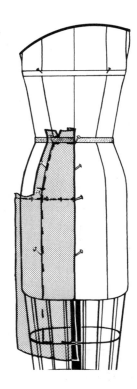

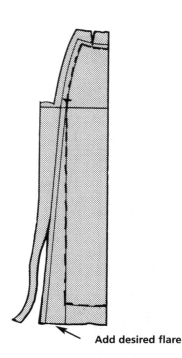

Add desired flare

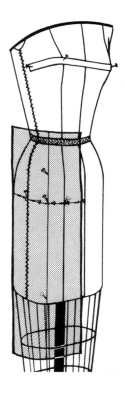

5 **Mark key areas** of the center front panel:

a. Waistline: Lightly mark center front to the princess seam.

b. Princess seam: Lightly mark waistline to bottom.

c. Style line notch: Mark just above crossgrain.

d. Hem.

6 **True up all lines:**

a. Remove the center front panel drape from the dress form. True up all lines.

b. Add desired flare at hemline. This amount is usually 1 to 2 inches, depending on the length and style of skirt. Blend this additional flare into the princess seamline just above or just below the crossgrain.

c. Add seam allowances and trim all excess fabric.

7 **Pin the grainline of the side front panel** to the center of the princess panel on the dress form.

8 **Match the crossgrain of the side front panel** to the hip level line. Pin the crossgrain at this level.

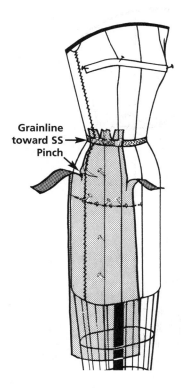

Grainline toward SS Pinch

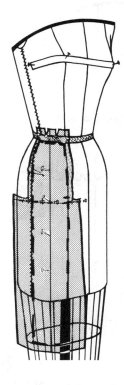

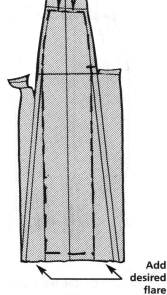

Add desired flare

⑨ Drape the waistline, princess seam, and side seam of the side front panel.

a. Clip the fabric from the top edge down to the waistline. Smooth the waistline from the grainline toward the seam.

b. Smooth the princess seam from the grainline to past the princess seam of the dress form from the waistline down to the bottom of the dress form. Trim the fabric at the princess seam down to the hipline.

c. Smooth the side seam from the grainline to past the side seam over the hip. Trim excess fabric from the waistline down to the hipline.

NOTE: It may be necessary to allow the grainline, at the waistline, to fall about 1/2 inch toward the side seam. This will allow the side panel to be smooth over the princess seam and creates a pinch at the side seam. (See illustration.)

⑩ Mark key areas of the side front panel:

a. Waistline: Lightly mark from princess seam to side seam.

b. Princess seam: Lightly mark from the waistline to the bottom.

c. Style line notch: Mark just above crossgrain to match front notch.

d. Hem.

⑪ True up all lines:

a. Remove the side front panel drape from the dress form. True up all lines.

b. Add desired flare at the hemline. This amount will match the amount used for the center front panel. Blend this additional flare into the princess seamline and the side seamline. Be sure to blend this amount smoothly just above or just below the crossgrain.

c. Add seam allowances and trim excess fabric.

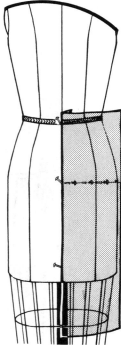
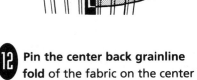
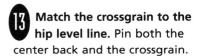
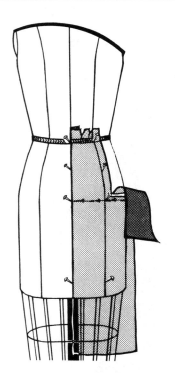
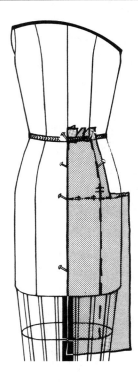

12 Pin the center back grainline fold of the fabric on the center back position of the dress form.

13 Match the crossgrain to the hip level line. Pin both the center back and the crossgrain.

14 Drape the waistline of the center back panel. Carefully trim and clip the fabric from the top edge down to the waistline. Smooth the fabric over the dress form waist tape just past the princess seam. Pin waistline in place.

15 Drape the back princess seam. Smooth the fabric over the entire princess seam of the dress form from the waistline down to the bottom of the dress form. Trim the fabric at the princess seam down to the hipline.

16 Mark key areas of the center back panel:

a. **Waistline:** Lightly mark from center back to the princess seam.

b. **Princess seam:** Lightly mark from the waist down to bottom.

c. **Style line notches:** Mark double notch just above hipline.

d. **Hem.**

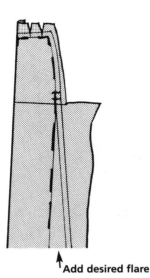

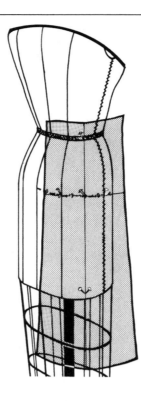

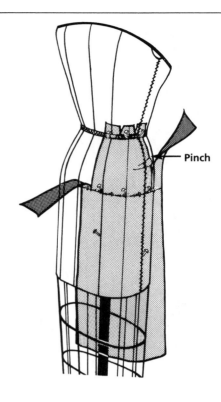

Pinch

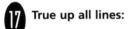

Add desired flare

17 **True up all lines:**

a. Remove the center back panel drape from the dress form. True up all lines.

b. Add desired flare at the hemline. This amount is usually a bit less than the amount of flare added on the front panels. Smooth and blend this additional flare into the princess seam just above or just below the crossgrain.

c. Add seam allowances and trim excess fabric.

18 **Pin the grainline of the side back panel** to the center of the back princess panel on the dress form.

19 **Match the crossgrain of the side back panel** to the hip level line. Pin the crossgrain at this level.

20 **Drape the waistline.** Clip the fabric from the top edge down to the waistline. Smooth the waistline from the grainline toward the seam.

21 **Smooth and drape the princess seam** from the grainline to past the princess seam of the dress form from the waistline down to the bottom of the dress form. Trim the fabric at the princess seam down to the hipline.

22 **Drape and smooth the side seam** from the grainline to past the side seam over the hip. Trim excess fabric from the waistline down to the hipline.

NOTE: It may be necessary to allow the grainline, at the waistline, to fall about 1/2 inch toward the side seam. This will allow the side panel to be smooth over the princess seam and creates a pinch at the side seam. (See illustration.)

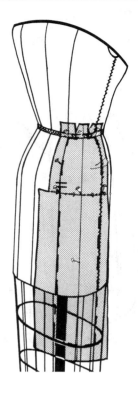

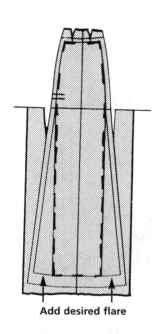

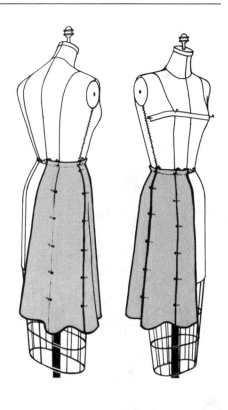

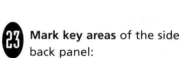

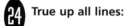

Add desired flare

23 **Mark key areas** of the side back panel:

a. Waistline: Lightly mark from side seam to princess seam.

b. Princess seam: Lightly mark from waistline to bottom.

c. Side seam: Lightly mark entire side seam.

d. Style line notch: Mark double notch to match back panel.

e. Hem.

24 **True up all lines:**

a. Remove the side back panel from the dress form. True up all lines.

b. Add desired flare at the hemline. This amount will match the amount used for the center back panel. Blend this additional flare into the princess seamline and the side seam. Be sure to blend this amount smoothly just above or just below the crossgrain, whichever creates the smoother line.

c. Add seam allowances and trim excess fabric.

NOTE: A perfectly balanced skirt has 1/2 inch less flare in the back hemline to balance to the 1/2 inch less in the waistline.

25 Pin and place the entire drape on the dress form. Check for accuracy.

Gored Skirt with Kick Pleats and Box Pleats

These pleated skirts maintain the same vertical seams as the six-gore skirts, which are fitted at the waistline and flare out at the hemline.

Kick Pleat

The gored skirt with kick pleats, however, has vertical seams with an added underpleat extension in the gore. The length and width of a kick pleat depend on the design. A typical pleat is narrower at the top and wider at the hemline.

Box Pleat

The box pleat has the same vertical seams as the kick pleat and the same underpleat extension. However, it has an additional underpiece that is sewn into the pleat extension areas of the skirt.

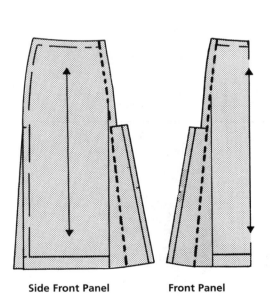

Side Front Panel   **Front Panel**

NOTE for knife pleat: Illustrated is an added pleat placed on the seamline of the gore. The pleat is drawn in from the hip level to the hemline.

When pinning to check for fit and proportion, place the correct sides of the gore panel together. Pin the gore from the top of the waistline, across the top of the pleat, and down to the hemline. After the skirt

is pinned, the pleat extension may be pressed to one side. The upper portion of the pleat will then be held in place with decorative topstitching.

Side Front Panel **Underpleat** **Front Panel**

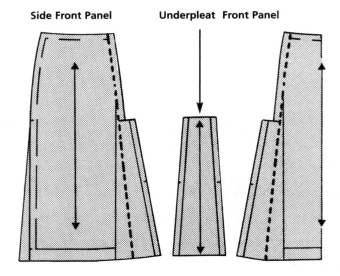

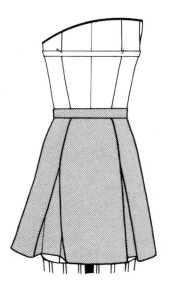

When pinning to check for fit and proportion, pin the additional underpiece to each side of the pleat extension. Then, pin the gore from the top of the waistline down to the pleat. Press each pleat extension back toward the panel and to the center of the underpiece.

These classic pleated skirts can be made in a variety of fabrics with different waistbands and pocket details. Their length varies with the season.

Notes

Dirndl Skirt

The dirndl (or gathered) skirt is a rectangular fabric piece gathered and sewn into a fitted waistline or yoke. The amount of fullness and the lengths may vary.

This is a good lesson in drawing in fullness and maintaining grainlines.

This skirt offers a fresh and carefree look for many design concepts. The variety of fabrics, pockets, flounces, and trims available can update, accentuate, and enhance the design.

Dirndl Skirt: *Preparing the Fabric*

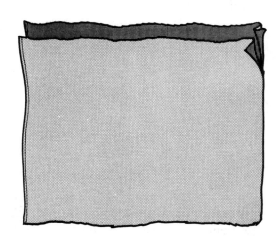

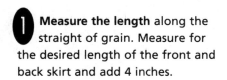

1 **Measure the length** along the straight of grain. Measure for the desired length of the front and back skirt and add 4 inches.

Snip and tear the fabric at this length.

2 **Divide the fabric piece in half.** Fold the fabric from selvage to selvage in half. Snip and tear the fabric at this width.

3 Draw the grainlines for the front and back skirts 1 inch from the torn edge. Press under.

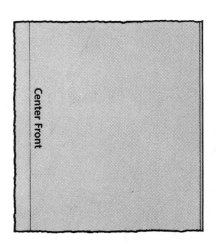

4 Draw in the front and back hipline:

a. **Measure down 11 inches** from the top edge of the fabric.

b. **Draw in a perfect crossgrain at this position.** This should be done for the front and back skirts.

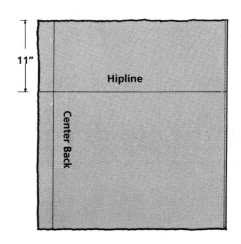
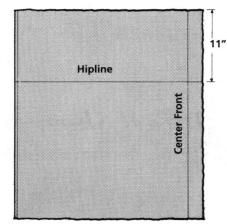

5 Draw a side seam 2 inches from the selvage side of the fabric parallel to the center grainline.

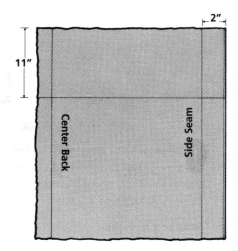
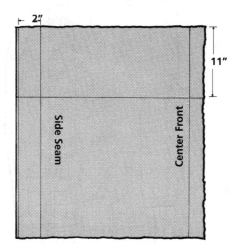

Dirndl Skirt: *Draping Steps*

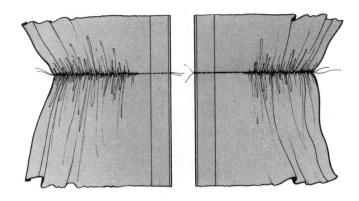

1 **Prepare the dress form.**

Measure down 7 inches on the center front of the dress form. Place a tape parallel to the floor at this hip level from center front to center back. Place pins on the dress form at this level and remove the tape.

2 **Gather the fabric on the crossgrain line** for both the front and back. Bring in the fullness to the amount of the hip measurement.

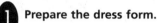

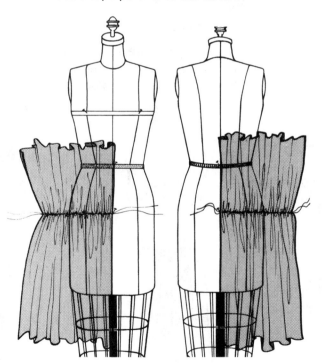

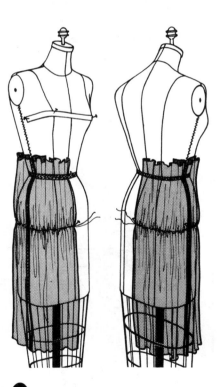

3 **Pin the center front and back grainline folds** of the fabric pieces on the center positions of the dress form.

4 **Align the crossgrain at the hip level.**

5 **Pin the crossgrains to the hip level of the dress form.** Evenly distribute the gathered fabric across the dress form to the side seam at the hip level. Be sure the fabric crossgrains are parallel to the floor and the side seams match.

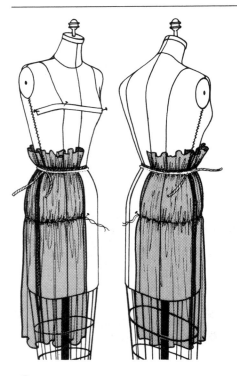

6 **Gather the fullness at the waistline.** Draw in the fullness at the waistline with a piece of twill tape. Evenly distribute the gathers.

7 **Mark key areas:**

a. Waistline.

b. Hem: Lightly mark the bottom of the dress form or a rung. The hem should be parallel to the floor.

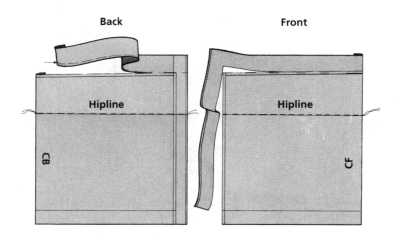

Back   Front

Hipline   Hipline

CB   CF

8 **True up the drape.** Remove the fabric from the dress form, true up the drape, and add seam allowances.

9 Pin the front and back pieces together and place on the dress form to check for accuracy. Make all necessary corrections.

The peg skirt is easily recognized by its billowing fullness over the hip area. This fullness is formed by draping deep folds, which are drawn into the waistline. At the same time, the lower edge is drawn back into the body allowing enough movement with ease and freedom. This skirt is also known as the hobble skirt.

A beautifully draped peg skirt depends largely on the skill of the designer, because the waistline details have to be skillfully placed into position to create the hip fullness. This skirt, which is flattering and quite feminine, is usually draped out of soft, pliable fabrics.

Peg Skirt: Preparing the Fabric

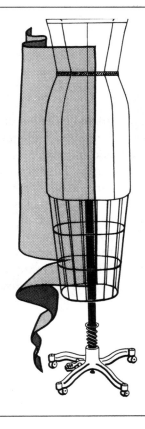

1 **Measure the length** along the straight of grain of the desired skirt and add 6 inches. Snip and tear the fabric at this length.

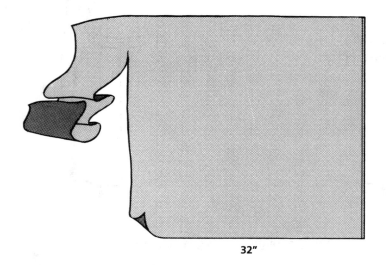

32"

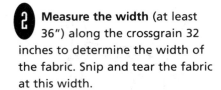
Measure the width (at least 36") along the crossgrain 32 inches to determine the width of the fabric. Snip and tear the fabric at this width.

NOTE: When the drape is completed, there will be a seam at the center front and a seam at center back. However, there will be no side seam.

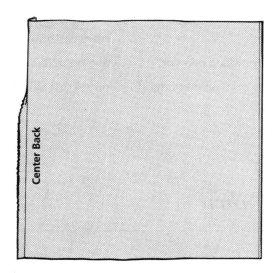

Center Back

3 **Draw the center back grainline** parallel to the grainline on the left side of the fabric and press under.

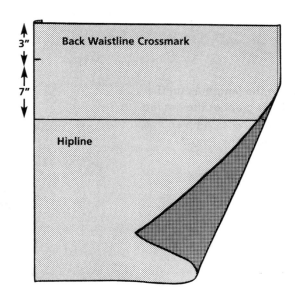

3"

Back Waistline Crossmark

7"

Hipline

4 **Mark the center back waist position.** From the top edge of the fabric, measure down 3 inches on the center back grainline. Draw a waistline mark.

5 **Draw in the hipline.** On the center back grainline, measure down 7 inches from the waistline mark. Draw a perfect crossgrain.

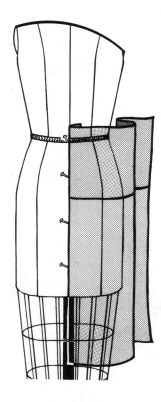  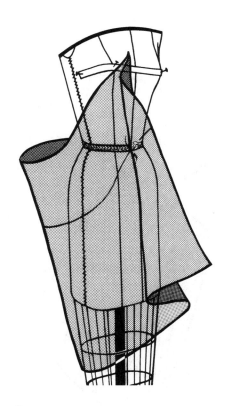

1 **Pin the center back grainline** fold of the fabric to the center back position of the dress form.

2 **Drape the back waistline** and back waist dart. Smooth the fabric across the back waist seam tape to the princess seam. Drape a 1-inch-deep back waist dart.

3 **Drape the crossgrain to center front.** Using the hipline on the fabric as a guide, lift and hold the fabric. Draw it into the center front/waist position. Pin the hipline at the center front waistline of the dress form. The grainline will angle in a bias direction.

NOTE: This lifting process will maintain greater fullness at the waist level and minimum fullness at the hem level. However, enough fullness must be allowed at the hem level for walking ease.

If the skirt front is draped on a true bias, maximum waistline fullness is achieved. However, if the center front is draped on a partial bias line, less fullness is created at the waistline.

Both methods are acceptable draping procedures.

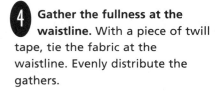
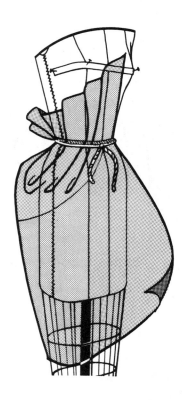

4 **Gather the fullness at the waistline.** With a piece of twill tape, tie the fabric at the waistline. Evenly distribute the gathers.

5 **Pleat the desired number of pleats at the waistline.** At the same time, push down slightly on each pleat to help billow the fabric at the hip level. Also, slightly pull up the center front bias waist position.

NOTE: Pushing down and maintaining gathers (instead of pleats) will give a style variation to this very dramatic skirt. The number of pleats or darts and the amount of fullness desired is up to the individual designer.

 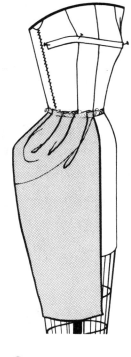 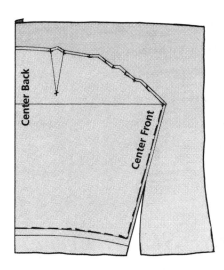

6 **Mark all key areas:**

a. Waistline.

b. Pleats.

c. Hem.

Pin the pleats in place and remove the twill tape.

7 **True up the drape.** Remove the fabric from the dress form. True up the drape, add seam allowances, and trim excess fabric. Pin in the pleats and place drape back on the dress form. Check for accuracy, making all necessary corrections.

Circular Skirt

The circular skirt has a fitted waist seam with an exaggerated circular curve in the waistline. When this waistline is sewn into a straight waistband, multiple flares of fullness fall into the hemline, thereby creating a multiple flared skirt silhouette. The lower edge may have any amount of sweep desired, depending on the amount of fullness draped into the waist. It may also be designed in any length.

For example, a short circular skirt may be used to design a skating or ballet costume, whereas a longer softer design may be more suitable for an evening dress.

Circular Skirt: *Preparing the Fabric*

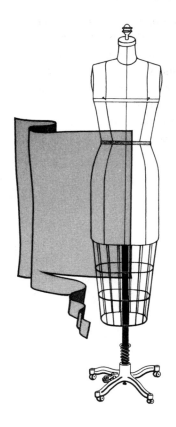

❶ **Measure the length along the straight of grain.** Measure for the front and back skirt 5 inches above the waist tape to the desired length of the design.

Snip and tear the fabric at this length.

Front

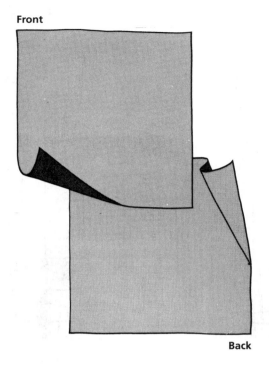

Back

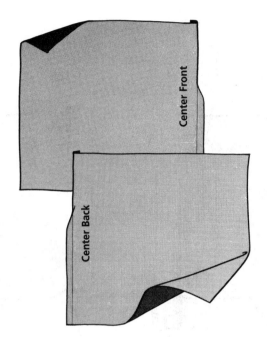

2 **Measure the width** at least 36 inches along the crossgrain. Measure the same measurement as the desired length for the front and back skirt. This makes a perfect square.

3 **Draw grainlines for the center front and center back** skirt 1 inch from the torn edge and press under.

Front

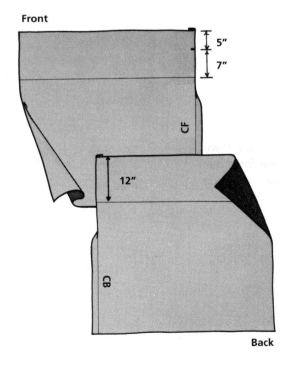

Back

4 **Mark the center front/waist position.** Measure down 5 inches from the top edge of the fabric on the grainline. Draw a waistline mark.

5 **Draw the front and back crossgrains.**

a. On the front fabric piece, measure down **7 inches** from the waistline mark. Draw a perfect front crossgrain at this hip level.

b. On the back fabric piece, measure down **12 inches** on the grainline from the top edge of the fabric. Draw a perfect back crossgrain at this hip level.

Circular Skirt: Draping Steps

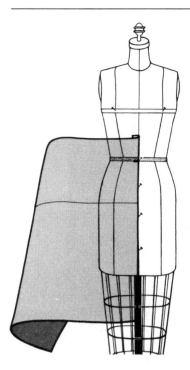

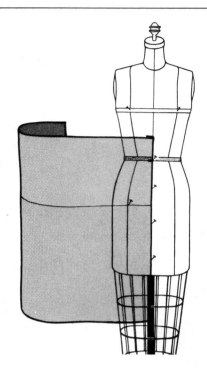

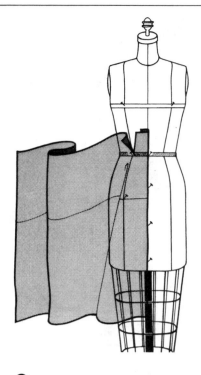

1 **Pin the center front grainline fold** of the fabric at the center front position of the dress form.

2 **Align the waistline mark** on the fabric to the center front waistline position of the dress form.

3 **Drape the crossgrain to the princess seam.** Following the hip level of the dress form, smooth and drape the crossgrain to the princess seam. Anchor a pin at this position.

4 **Drape the front waistline to the princess seam.**

a. Clip the fabric from the top edge down to the waistline.

b. Smooth and drape the fabric at the waistline to the princess seam.

c. Anchor a pin on the waistline at the princess seam.

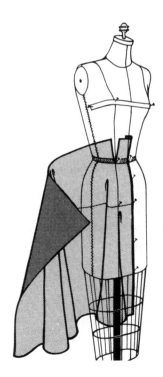

5 **Drape the first skirt flare.** Pivot the fabric downward from the waistline at the princess area, forming a nice flowing flare.

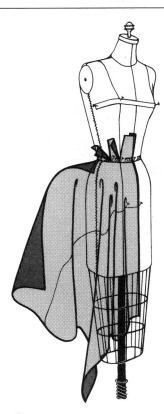

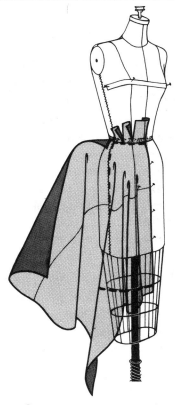

6 **Clip, pivot, pin, and drape the second flare** about 1 inch from the first flare, at the waistline. Smooth the fabric downward and toward the side seam.

7 **Continue to clip, pivot, and pin the waistline** where each flare is desired.

8 **Mark key areas:**

a. **Waistline.**

b. **Side seam.**

c. **Hem:** Follow the bottom of the dress form cage.

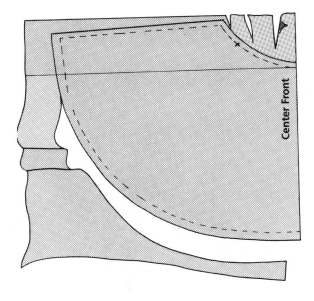

9 **True up the front drape.** Remove the fabric drape from the dress form. True up the front drape, add seam allowances, and trim the excess fabric.

10 Place the front skirt drape on top of the prepared fabric for the back drape.

a. Match the crossgrains of the front and back skirt. At the same time, place the center fold grainlines parallel, allowing the front to extend 1/2 inch over the back grainline. Keep the grainlines parallel. This distance allows for the difference between the back waistline amount and the front waistline amount.

b. Draw the skirt back stitch lines. Follow the same markings as the skirt front (temporary waistline, side seam, and hem).

NOTE: The back waistline will be redone when the final fit is checked. This is because the front and back waistline shapes are slightly different.

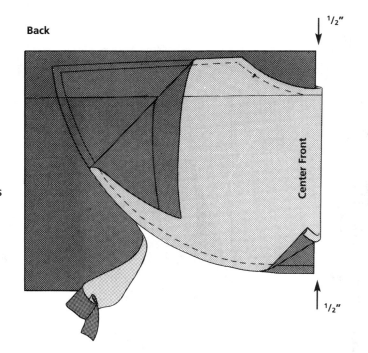

Back

½"

Center Front

½"

11 Check the fit and balance of the circular skirt. Pin the fabric pieces together at the front and back side seams. Place this drape back on the dress form. Adjust the back waistline until the skirt hangs properly and the side seams are in alignment with the side seams on the dress form. Pin center front and center back waists.

Bias Circular Skirt

As one drapes a bias fabric into a circular skirt, the bias quality of the fabric provides inherent stretchability. The features of a bias fabric into a circular skirt design include:

• The designer creates the amount of fullness.

• Each flare must be draped with the same amount of fullness. This allows for the same degree of stretch in the hemline.

• The front and back drapes do not need the same amount of fullness, but often they are the same.

• The shape of the waistline is controlled by the amount of fullness; the front and back waistlines will not always be symmetrical.

• The waistlines will definitely be a different shape; the back will be deeper and more rounded.

• The natural balance, side seam to side seam, is still achieved.

• Center front and center back will not always be on perfect bias. This depends on the amount of fullness draped into the skirt.

• The hemlines will show a minimum of fall out, or even no fall out, when draped and sewn.

1 **Measure the length** desired for a front and back skirt. Measure the length along the straight of grain from the waistline to the desired length and add 12 inches. Snip and tear the fabric at this length.

2 **Use the entire width of the fabric pieces for the front and back circular skirt drape.**

3 **Draw the grainline** from the front and back skirt fabric pieces 1 inch from the selvage.

4 **Draw the crossgrain** for the front and back skirt fabric pieces 10 inches from the top of the fabric edge. Draw the crossgrain halfway across the fabric piece.

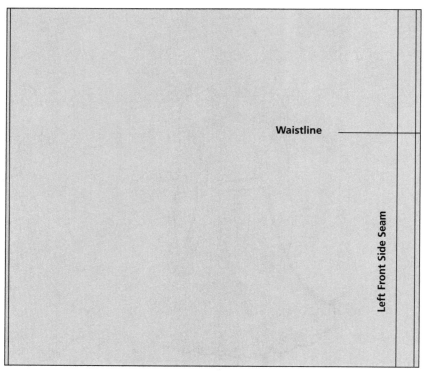

Front Skirt

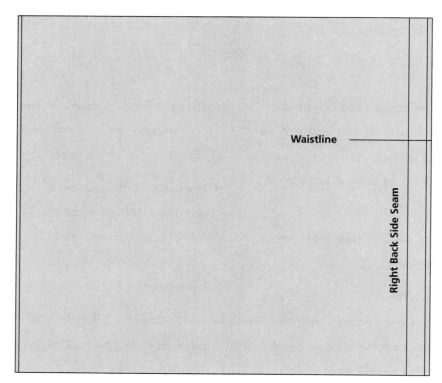

Back Skirt

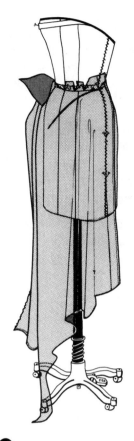

1 **Pin the grainline** to the side seam of the left front side seam of the dress form.

2 **Align and drape the crossgrain** on the waistline of the left side seam of the dress form. Pin at the side seam.

3 Allow the fabric to hang smoothly and evenly across the front of the dress form.

4 **Trim, smooth, pin, and clip the waistline for the first flare.**

a. Approximately 2 inches from the side seam, trim the fabric from the top edge down to the waistline.

b. **Smooth and drape** the fabric at the waistline to approximately 2 inches from the side seam.

c. **Clip the fabric** from the top edge down to the waistline.

5 **Drape the first skirt flare.** Pivot the fabric downward from the waistline pin, forming a nice flowing flare. Place another pin on the bottom of the flare to hold it in place.

NOTE: Each flare must have the same amount of fullness to maintain a balanced hemline.

6 **Trim, smooth, pin, and clip the waistline for the second flare.**

a. **Smooth and drape** the front waistline about 1 1/2 inches from the first flare. Anchor another pin at this waistline position.

b. **Trim, pin, and clip** the fabric at the new waistline location.

c. **Pivot the drape** of the second flare downward from the waistline at the second waistline pin.

Form the same amount of flare as was in the first flare.

7 Continue to smooth, trim, pin, clip, and pivot the waistline where each flare is desired until the entire front skirt is draped.

8 Mark key areas from the dress form to the fabric:

a. Waistline.

b. Side seam.

c. Hem: Follow the bottom of the dress form as a guide.

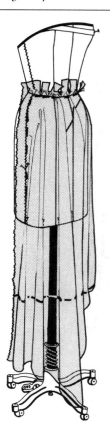

Bias Circular Back Skirt: *Draping Steps*

1 Pin the grainline to the side seam of the right back side seam of the dress form.

2 Align and drape the crossgrain on the waistline of the right side seam of the dress form. Pin at the side seam.

3 Allow the fabric to hang smoothly and evenly across the back of the dress form.

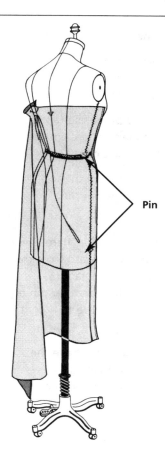

Pin

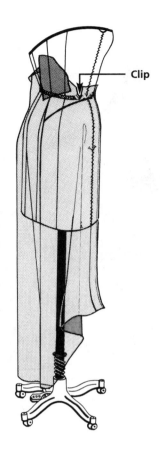 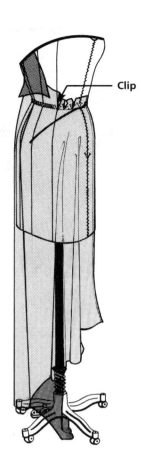 

4 **Trim, smooth, pin, and clip the waistline.**

a. Approximately 2 inches from the side seam, trim the fabric from the top edge down to the waistline.

b. Smooth and drape the fabric at the waistline to approximately 2 inches from the side seam.

c. Clip the fabric from the top edge down to the waistline.

5 **Drape the first skirt flare.** Pivot the fabric downward from the waistline pin, forming a nice flowing flare. Place another pin on the bottom of the flare to hold it in place.

NOTE: Each flare must have the same amount of fullness to maintain a balanced hemline.

6 **Trim, smooth, pin, and clip** the waistline for the second flare.

a. Smooth and drape the back waistline approximately 1 inch from the first flare. Anchor another pin at this waistline position.

b. Trim, pin, and clip the fabric at the new waistline location.

c. Pivot the drape of the second flare downward from the waistline at the second waistline pin.

Form the same amount of flare as was in the first flare.

7 **Continue to smooth, trim, pin, clip, and pivot** the waistline where each flare is desired until entire back skirt is draped.

8 **Mark key areas** from the dress form to the fabric.

a. Waistline.

b. Side seam.

c. Hem: Follow the bottom of the dress form as a guide.

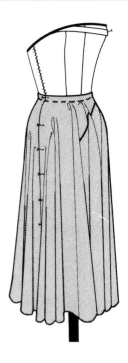

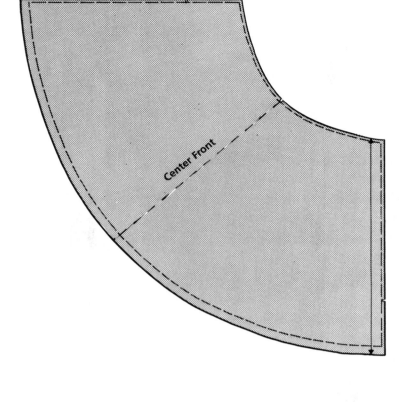

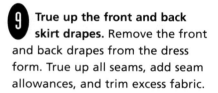

9 **True up the front and back skirt drapes.** Remove the front and back drapes from the dress form. True up all seams, add seam allowances, and trim excess fabric.

Check the fit and balance. If necessary, make corrections.

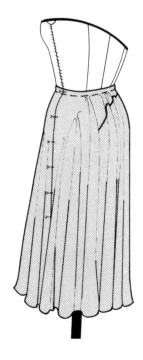

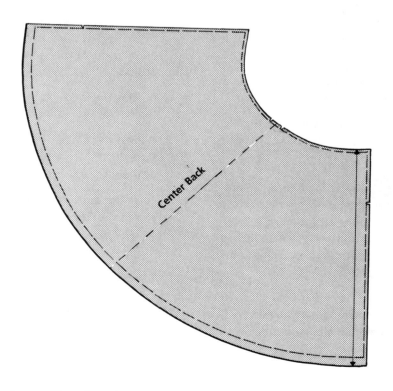

A skirt hip yoke is a fitted top portion of a skirt without the use of darts. A horizontal seam in the hip area divides the skirt into two sections. The yoke seam may be designed parallel to the waistline or shaped into any pointed or curved shape desired. The lower portion of the yoke may be connected to a skirt by means of shirring, gores, or pleats, without the use of darts. The hip yoke controls a waistline fit and supports the remainder of the skirt design, whether it is gathered, straight, or circular.

The hip yoke with a gathered skirt section can create many different looks. The yoke may be shaped in a variety of styles and widths. The amount of fullness in the skirt section depends on the particular style. The gathered skirt that falls from a styled yoke enables a designer to complete a style in which the fullness in the skirt hangs straight up and down (hanging plumb). At the same time, the designer can control the amount of fullness desired. The gathered skirt is a classic design, allowing the designer to use border prints.

Hip Yoke: *Preparing the Fabric*

① **Prepare the dress form.**

Pin or use style tape for the desired yoke design.

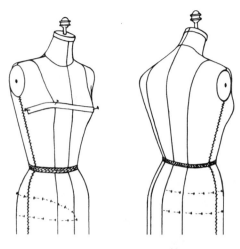

Shaped Yoke **Straight Yoke**

② **Measure the length** (along the straight of grain) for both the front and back yokes and add 5 inches. Snip and tear the fabric at this length.

③ **Measure the width** of the widest part of the desired front and back yoke area (hip) and add 5 inches. Snip and tear the fabric at this width.

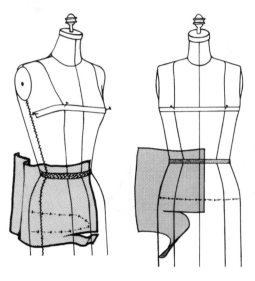

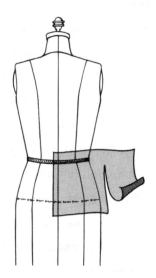

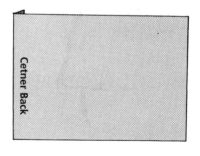

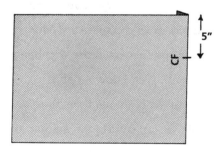

④ **Draw the grainlines** for the front and back yokes 1 inch from the torn edge and press under.

⑤ **Crossmark a waistline position.** From the top edge of the fabric (on the front grainline) measure down 5 inches and crossmark.

Hip Yoke: *Draping Steps*

1 **Establish the center front/center back yoke grainline.**

a. Place the center front grainline fold of the yoke piece on the center front position of the dress form. Extend the yoke piece 2 inches above the waistline.

b. Place the center back grainline fold of the back yoke piece to the center back position of the dress form. Extend the yoke piece 2 inches above the waistline.

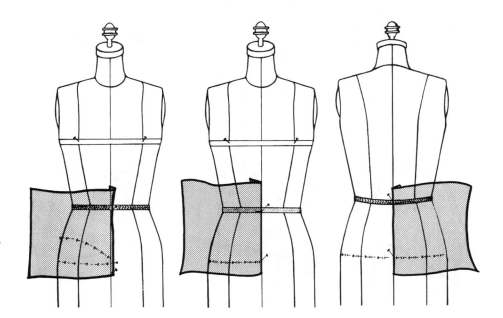

2 **Drape the front and back yoke waistline.** Trim and clip the fabric from the top of the fabric down to the waistline. (Be careful not to clip past the waistline position.) Drape and smooth the fabric at the waistline from the center of the dress form over to the side seam. Anchor a pin at the side seam/waist corner.

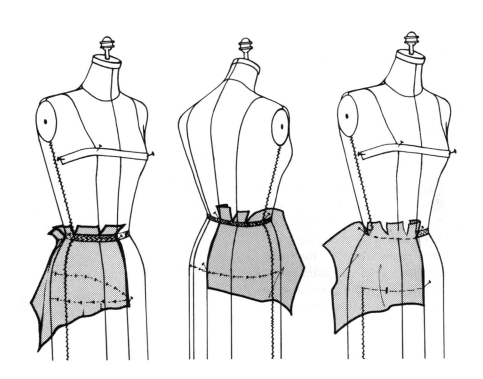

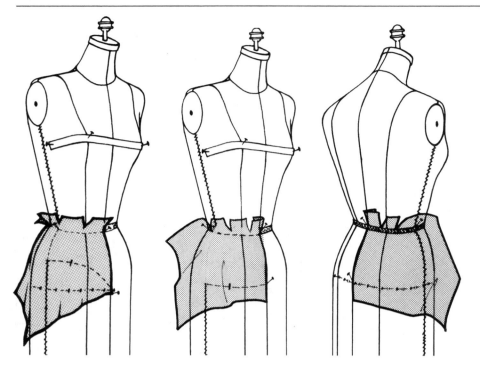

3 Mark all key areas of the dress form to the front yoke fabric:

a. Waistline front and back.

b. Side seam front and back.

c. Front and back yoke style lines.

d. Yoke style line notches: One for the front and two for the back.

4 True up all lines. Remove the front and back yoke drape from the dress form. True up all lines, add seam allowances, and trim excess fabric. Pin the front and back yoke side seam to each other. Return the yoke drape to the dress form to drape the skirt section.

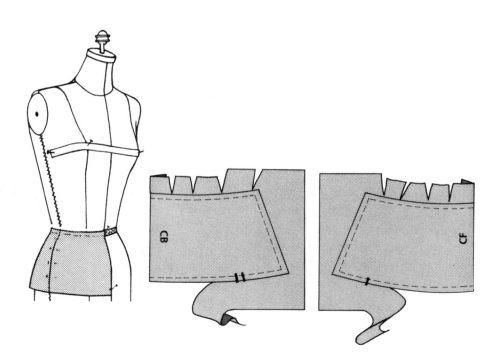

Circular Skirt with Hip Yoke: *Preparing the Skirt Fabric*

1 **Measure the length** (along the straight of grain) for the front and back skirt.

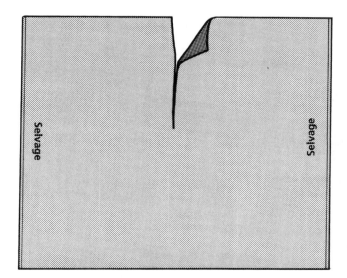

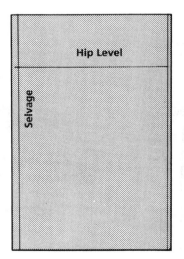

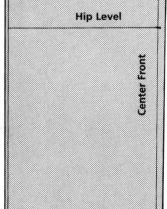

2 **Fold the fabric from selvage to selvage.** Snip and tear the fabric in half. One piece will be used for the front skirt, and the other piece will be used for the back skirt.

3 **Draw the straight of grainlines and crossgrains** for the front and back skirt.

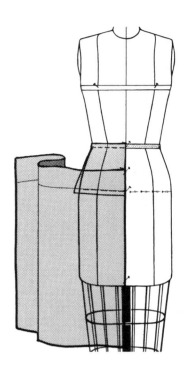

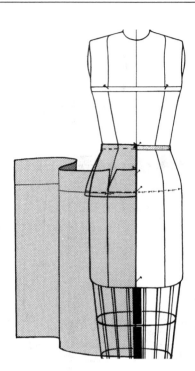

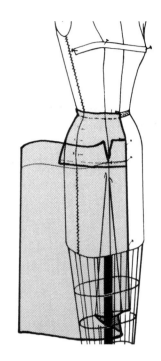

1 **Pin the center front grainline fold of the skirt** on the center front position of the dress form.

2 **Align the crossgrain at the hip level.** Pin the crossgrains at the hip level and not at the yoke style seam. In this sketch, however, both the yoke style seam and the hip level are the same.

3 **Smooth, clip, and pin the skirt style line.**

Approximately 3 inches from center front, smooth, trim, and clip the fabric from the top edge down to the yoke style seam.

Pin the skirt style seam to the yoke style seam and not to the dress form.

4 **Pivot the fabric down** from the style seam at the princess area, forming a nice flowing flare. Pin the skirt style seam to the yoke style seam, maintaining this flare.

5 **Smooth, clip, pin, and pivot approximately 1 inch from the first flare.** At the skirt style seam, smooth the fabric toward the side seam. Pin, clip, and pivot the skirt style seam at this position, forming a second flare.

6 **Continue to smooth, pin, clip, and pivot** the front skirt style seam where each flare is desired.

7 **Mark all key areas** of the dress form to the fabric:

a. **Skirt style seam and matching notches.**

b. **Side seam.**

c. **Hem:** Follow a rung on the dress form.

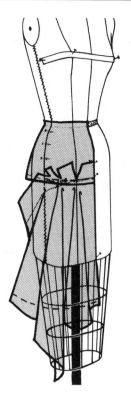

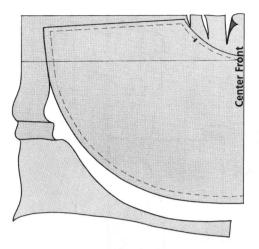

8 **True up the front skirt drape.** Remove the front skirt drape from the dress form. True up the front skirt drape, add seam allowances, and trim excess fabric.

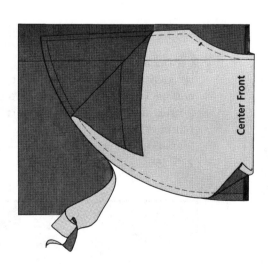

9 **True up the back skirt.**

a. **Place the skirt front drape on top of the prepared fabric for the back drape, matching the crossgrains of the front and back skirt.**

b. **Place the center fold grainlines parallel,** allowing the front to extend 1/2 inch over the back grainline, while still parallel. This distance allows for the difference between the back style seam amount and the front style seam amount.

c. **Draw in the skirt back stitchlines,** following the same markings as the skirt front (style seam, side seam, and hem).

10 Pin the yoke and skirt fabric piece together and return to the dress form. Check the fit and balance. Make any necessary corrections.

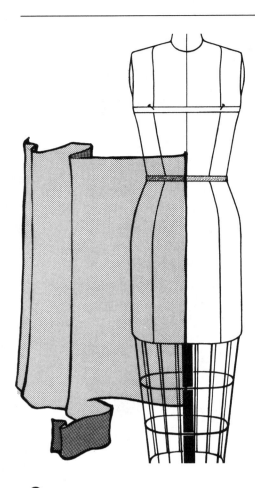

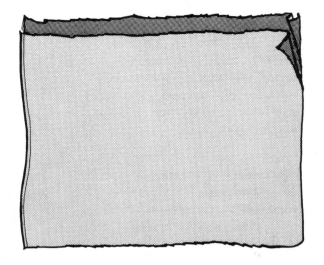

2 **Divide the fabric piece in half.** Fold the fabric from selvage to selvage. Snip and tear the piece in half lengthwise.

One piece will be used for the skirt front, and the other piece will be used for the skirt back.

1 **Measure the length** along the straight of grain for both the front and back skirts.

3 Draw all the grainlines and crossgrain lines for the front and back skirt. For more detailed instructions in preparing the skirt fabric, refer to Dirndl Skirt: Preparing the Fabric, pages 239–240.

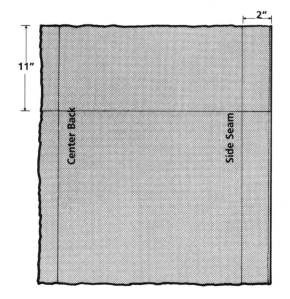

Gathered Skirt with Hip Yoke: Draping Steps

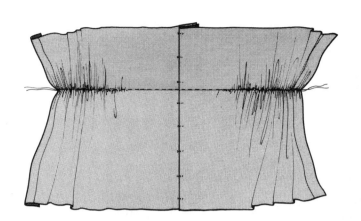

1 **Gather the fabric on the crossgrain line** on both front and back. Pin the side seams together.

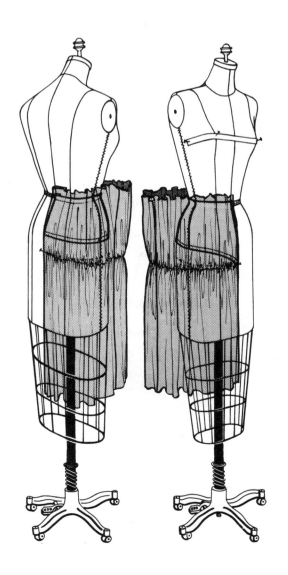

2 **Pin the center front and center back grainline** folds of the fabric on the center positions of the dress form.

3 **Align front and back crossgrains** at the hip level. Pin the crossgrains in place.

NOTE: Be sure to pin the crossgrains at the hip level and not at the yoke line.

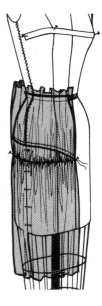

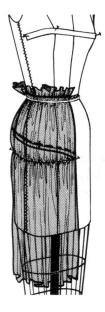

4 **Pin the side seams** of the fabric on the side seams of the dress form. Evenly distribute the gathered fabric across the dress form.

NOTE: Be sure the fabric crossgrains are parallel to the floor and that the side seams match the side seams of the dress form.

5 **Gather up the fabric at the waistline** with a piece of twill tape. Evenly distribute the gathers.

NOTE: The skirt is draped over the desired yoke.

6 **Mark key areas:**

a. Yoke style line: Mark through the gathers.

b. Style line notches.

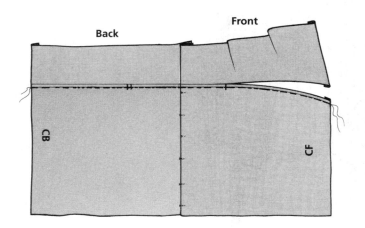

7 **True up the drape.** Remove the fabric from the dress form and true up the drape. Add seam allowances and trim excess fabric.

8 **Pin the gathered skirt to the styled yoke** and place on the dress form to check for accuracy, making all necessary corrections.

Pleated Skirt with Hip Yoke: *Preparing the Fabric*

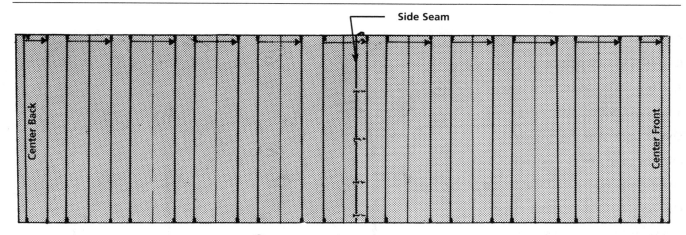

Side Seam

Center Back

Center Front

1 **Prepare the hip yoke drape** (see pages 260–262). Prepare the dress form.

2 **Measure the length** along the straight of grain for both the front and back skirts. Use the entire width of the fabric for the front and another piece for the back.

3 **Pin the side seams** together, allowing for the necessary seam allowances.

4 **Starting from the side seam,** mark two times the width of each pleat on both sides of the side seam.

5 **Mark the distance of the space between the pleats.** Continue these measurements for the entire width of the fabric.

6 **Pleat the fabric** for both the front and back until the entire width of the fabric is used.

7 **Draw in a crossgrain** 9 inches down from the top of the fabric.

Pleated Skirt with Hip Yoke: *Draping Steps*

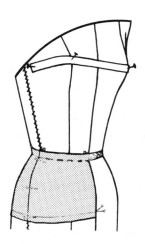

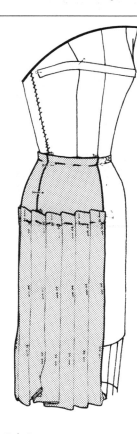

1 **Drape the yoke** and draw in the desired style line.

2 **Pin the center front and center back grainline** folds of the fabric on the center positions of the dress form.

3 **Align front and back crossgrains at the hip level.** Pin the crossgrains in place.

NOTE: Be sure to pin the crossgrains at the hip level and not at the yoke line.

4 **Trim the excess fabric at the yoke seam,** leaving enough for seam allowances.

Asymmetric Skirt

A wrap skirt adds a large extension (usually 3 inches) past center front. Two front skirts are draped to give a top layer with some styling detail and an underskirt that usually remains basic. The top extension "wrap" may have additional styling elements, including various shapes, pleats, ruffles, or fringes.

Asymmetric Skirt: *Preparing the Fabric*

Fold fabric in half—snip and tear

1 **Measure the length** (along the straight of grain) for the front and back skirt from 2 inches above the waist to the bottom of the dress form and add 4 inches. Snip and tear the fabric at this length.

2 **Measure the width for the right and left front panels.** Fold the front fabric piece in half from selvage to selvage. Snip and tear the fabric piece in half lengthwise. Use one piece for the right front panel and use the other piece for the left front panel.

3 **Measure the width for the back skirt.** Measure, along the crossgrain, from center back to the side seam at the hip level, and add 3 inches. Snip and tear the fabric at this width.

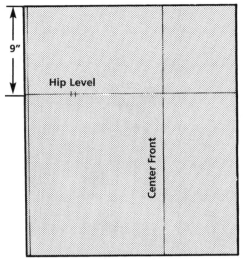

Right Front Skirt

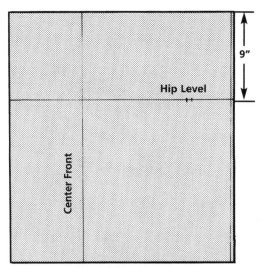

Left Front Skirt

4 Draw the center front grainline on the right and left skirt panels. On the fabric, measure 7 inches from the torn edge.

5 Draw a crossgrain on the right and left skirt panels. Measure down 9 inches from the top edge of the panel. Using an L-square ruler, draw in the crossgrain on both panels.

6 Draw the side seam for the right and left skirt panels. Measure from center front to the side seam (at the hip level) and add 1/2 inch for ease. Transfer this measurement to the fabric on the hip line. Using this mark, draw a side seam perfectly parallel to the center front grainline from the hip line down.

7 Draw the back grainline, crossgrain, and side seam the same as for the basic back skirt.

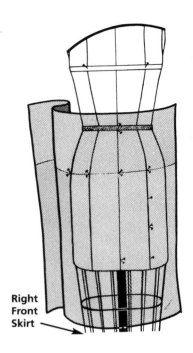

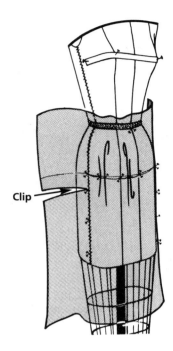

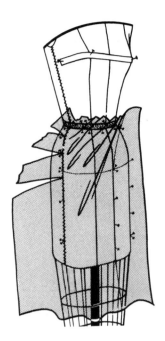

Right Front Skirt

1 **Pin the right center front grainline of the fabric** on the center front position of the dress form, matching the crossgrain of the fabric to the hip level line on the dress form.

2 **Smooth and pin the crossgrain** of the fabric (evenly distributing the ease) across the dress form to the side seam.

3 **Pin the side seam,** from below the hip level, to the dress form.

4 **Clip the fabric** from the outer edge of the fabric into the side seam at the point from which the lowest pleat will radiate. Place a pin on the side seam at this clip.

Clip

5 **Fold the first pleat at the waistline.** The first pleat should start at the waistline between center front and the opposite princess panel. It should drape from the waistline to nothing at the pinned side seam.

6 **Continue to clip, pin, fold, and drape the remaining of the desired number of waistline pleats.**

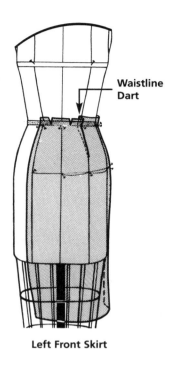

Left Front Skirt

1. **Pin the left center front grainline of the fabric** on the center front position of the dress form, matching the crossgrain of the fabric to the hip level line on the dress form.

2. **Smooth and pin the crossgrain** of the fabric (evenly distributing the ease) across the dress form to the side seam.

3. **Pin the side seam,** from below the hip level, to the dress form.

4. **Drape in one or two waistline darts** and the remainder of the side seam down to the hip level. Smooth the fabric from center front to the princess seam. Crossmark the waistline at the princess seam. Drape in one or two waistline darts.

Entire Back Skirt

5. **Drape the back skirt the same** as the basic back skirt. Match side seam to side seam and crossgrain to crossgrain.

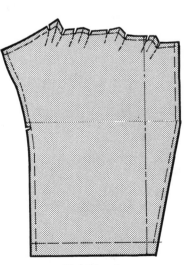

Right Front

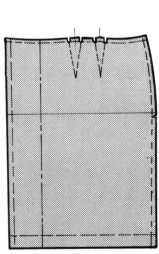

Left Front

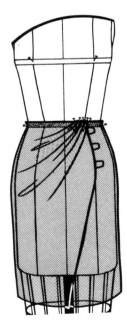

6. Mark all key areas:

a. **Waistline:** Front and back

b. **Darts:** Left front and back

c. **Pleats:** Right front

7. **True up.** Remove the fabric drape from the dress form. True up all seams, add seam allowances, and trim excess fabric.

Return the finished drape to the dress form and check for accuracy, fit, and balance.

Objectives

By studying the various draping steps in this chapter, the designer should be able to:

- Recognize grain and crossgrain of fabric in relation to the hip level and crotch line of pants.

- Drape a flat piece of fabric and shape the front and back crotch seams, allowing for the desired amount of crotch ease.

- Drape a flat piece of fabric and shape the leggings with the desired amount of fullness.

- True up and visualize the front and back pant panels in relation to the figure.

- Check and balance the front and back side seams on all pants variations.

Pants

Pants will always be an important part of the fashion scene. The waist area can be flat and plain, pleated slightly, or full. The pants can be finished with a waistband, elastic, or a drawstring or faced. Pants are seen in many lengths, from very short to just below the ankle. The leg shapes vary from slightly flared to straight or tapered. Careful draping on a pant form will enable the designer to create a wonderful appearance regardless of style or fabric.

Design Variations

Pants: *Preparing the Fabric*

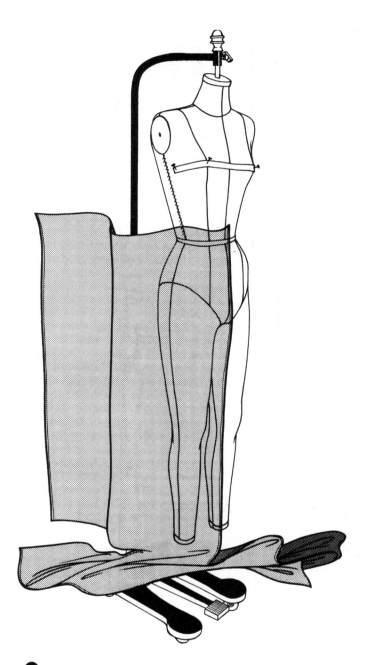

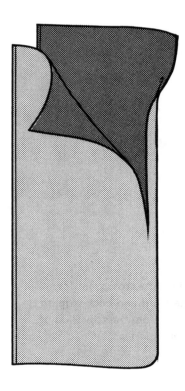

1 **Measure the length** along the straight of grain. Measure from 2 inches above the waist to the desired length (ankle) of the pants.

Snip and tear the fabric at this length.

2 **Fold the fabric piece in half from selvage to selvage.** Snip and tear this piece in half lengthwise.

One piece will be used for the front legging, and the other piece will be used for the back legging.

Back   **Front**

3 Draw the grainline for the **front and back legging** in the middle of the fabric pieces.

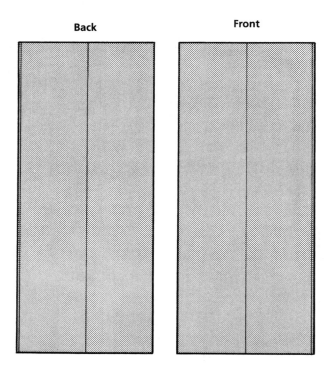

Back   **Front**

4 Draw the crossgrain for the **front and back legging** 10 inches from the top edge of the fabric pieces.

10″   10″

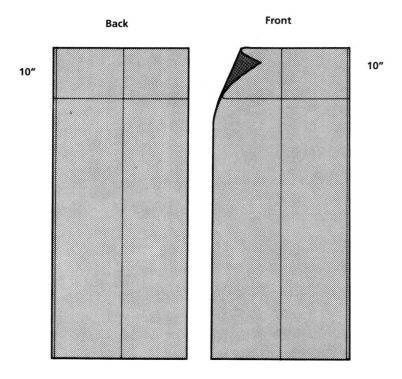

Pants: *Draping Steps*

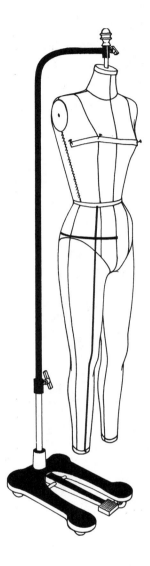
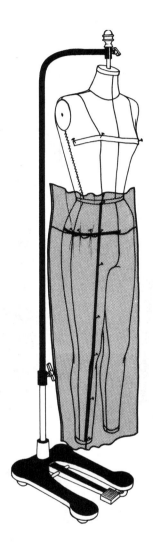

1 Prepare the pant form:

a. Pin style tape on the pant form at the hip level. This style tape should extend from center front to center back of the form. This hip level tape will represent the crossgrain position of the fabric.

b. Pin another style tape in the center of the front and back leg of the pant form. This style tape will represent the straight of grain position of the fabric.

2 **Align and pin the center front grainline and crossgrain** of the fabric on the front hip level tape and grainline tape of the dress form. Be sure to allow for ease on the crossgrain.

3 **Align and pin the center back grainline and crossgrain** of the fabric on the back hip level tape and grainline tape of the dress form. Be sure to allow for ease on the crossgrain. Refer to step 4 for more information about proper amount of ease.

4 Smooth the fabric up toward the waistline from the hip level.

5 Drape in the desired styling of the waistline area (darts, pleats, release tucks, gathers, and so on).

NOTE: For a fuller waistline area, such as gathers or pleats, much more ease would need to be added on the crossgrain.

6 Trim, clip, and drape the front and back crotch areas, allowing for the appropriate crotch ease for the desired pant.

7 Pin and drape the center front and center back seam. Smooth the fabric up from the crotch to the center waistline area. Keep in mind the desired waistline styling.

8 Pin the front and back inseams together. Style the inseam legging and shape the desired width.

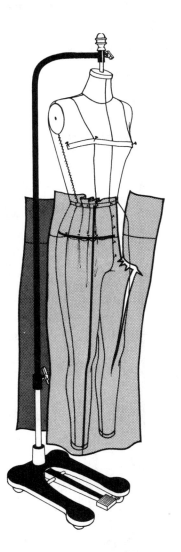

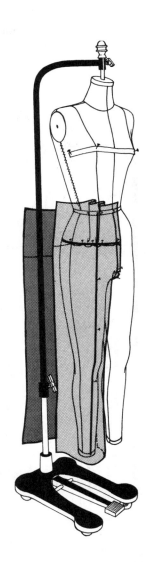

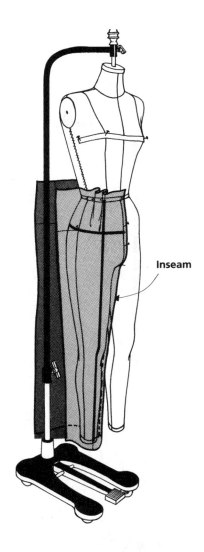

Inseam

9 **Pin the front and back side seams together** from the hip level up. Complete the desired shaping of the front and back waistline at the side seam.

10 **Pin the front and back side seams** together from the hip level down. Style the side seam legging shape desired from the hip level down.

NOTE: The legging shape should be equal from both sides of the legging grainline.

11 Mark key areas:

a. Waistline: Crossmark any darts, tucks, or pleats.

b. Center front and center back crotch.

c. Front and back inseams.

d. Front and back side seams.

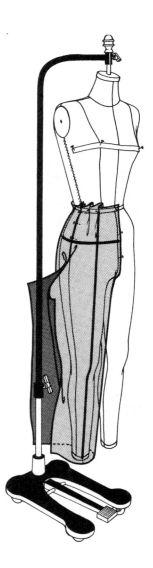

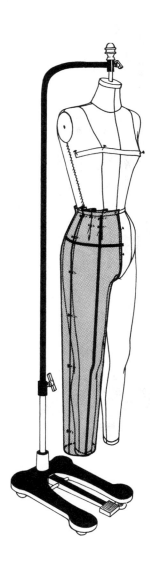

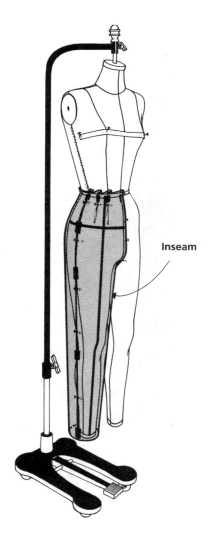

Inseam

12 **True up all lines.** Remove the front and back pant drape from the pant form. True up all lines, add seam allowances, and trim excess fabric.

13 **Pin the front and back pant at the side seam and inseams.** Return the fabric drape to the pant form and check for accuracy.

Back   Front

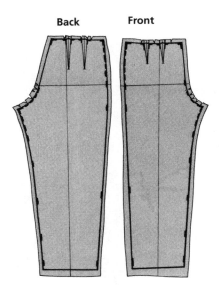

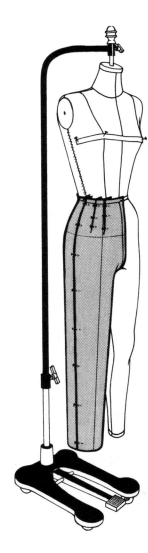

Pants: Variation

Straight-Legged Pants

Drape the legging straight down.

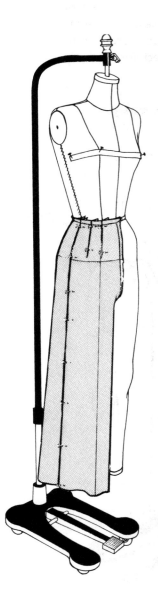

Chapter 14

Raglan Sleeve

By studying the various draping steps in this chapter, the designer should be able to:

- Recognize grain and crossgrain of fabric in relation to the sleeve.

- Combine and attach the raglan sleeve to a bodice yoke and achieve an easy sleeve movement.

- Drape a desired raglan style line and shape for a blouse.

- Check the fit and hang of the raglan style line.

- Make sleeve or style line adjustments if necessary.

Raglan Sleeve

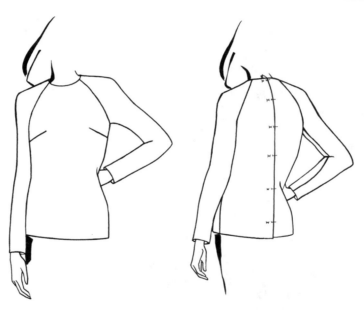

The raglan sleeve has a traditional underarm side seam that extends up to the front and back neckline. The design of the raglan creates a yoke area on the bodice, retaining its original underarm armhole curve in both the bodice and the sleeve. The depth of the armhole is the same as the normal armhole and falls in the same manner as any set-in sleeve. The sleeve is usually cut in two pieces with a shoulder seam.

The sleeve, however, needs a wider bicep line and a longer underarm seam so that the arm can be raised comfortably. Therefore, use Adjusted Sleeve with More Arm Movement (pages 130–133) to drape this raglan style.

If the lower portion of the armhole is deeper than the normal armhole, then use the Lowered or Exaggerated Armhole Sleeve (pages 139–143) to drape this raglan style.

Raglan Sleeve: Preparing the Fabric

 Prepare the dress form.

Pin the desired yoke (raglan) seam on the front and back. The yoke line should start at the armplate, just below the screw level, and finish 1 inch below the shoulder at the neckline.

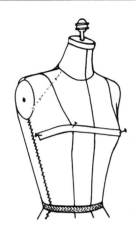

Preparing the Sleeve Fabric

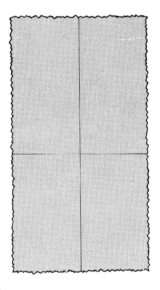

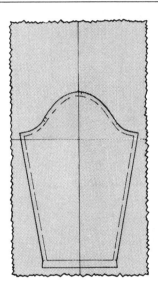

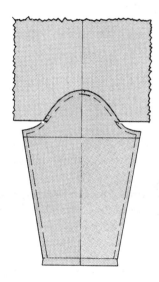

1 **Measure the length of the Adjusted Sleeve with More Arm Movement** (pages 130–131).

2 **Cut a piece of muslin 34 inches long by 30 inches wide.**

a. Draw in a grainline in the center of the muslin piece.

b. Draw in a crossgrain (bicep line) on a piece of muslin 16 inches from the top of the muslin piece.

3 **Place the Adjusted Sleeve with More Arm Movement, without the elbow dart, on the muslin** matching center of the sleeve (straight of grain) to the grainline on the muslin. Align the biceps level line of the sleeve to the crossgrain line.

4 **Draw in the entire sleeve lightly.**

5 **Remove the original sleeve pattern.**

6 **Add seam allowances to the entire sleeve.**

7 **Cut out the sleeve from the wrist level up to 3 inches of the underarm of the sleeve.** Leave the remaining muslin on the cap area of the sleeve.

1 **Measure the length** (along the straight of grain) for both the front and back from the neckband to the hip level and add 5 inches.

Snip and tear the fabric this length.

2 **Measure the width** (along the crossgrain) for both the front and back from the center of the dress form to the side seam and add 4 inches.

Snip and tear the fabric this width.

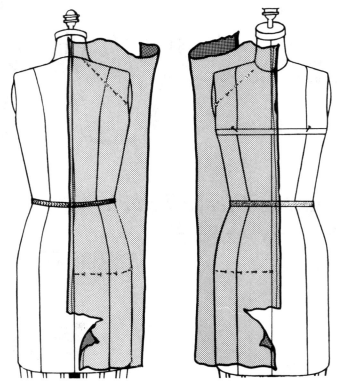

3 **Draw the center front and center back grainlines** 1 inch from the torn edge. Press under.

4 **On the front and back fabric piece, draw in the crossgrains.**

5 **Draw in the side seams for the front and back fabric pieces.** (Refer to Basic Shift, page 102, for more detailed instructions.)

Bodice Draping Steps

 Pin the following areas:

a. Center front bodice.

b. Crossgrains.

c. Fabric side seam to the side seam of the dress form.

d. Shoulder neck area.

 Drape and smooth the fabric over the yoke style line area of the dress form. Pin in place.

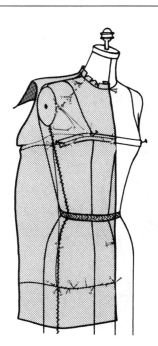

 Drape the armhole and the side bust dart.

a. Smooth the fabric over the dress form armplate. Create a 1/4-inch pinch at the screw level (middle at ridge) of the armhole. Allow all excess fabric to fall over the bust level area at this time.

b. Drape the side bust dart. Allow the excess fabric to fall onto the crossgrain and fold in the side bust dart at the bustline level. Fold and pin a side bust dart using the excess fabric on the crossgrain bust level line.

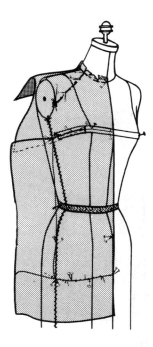

4 **Mark key areas** of the front dress form on the fabric:

a. Neckline: Lightly crossmark.

b. Front yoke style line: Lightly crossmark.

c. Side seam at the waistline.

d. Armplate:
- Middle of the armhole
- Bottom at side seam

5 True up the front bodice, add seam allowances, and place the drape on the dress form.

NOTE: To blend raglan style line: If a smooth continuous line is desired from the mid-armhole area into the yoke style line, it will be necessary to blend these two points.

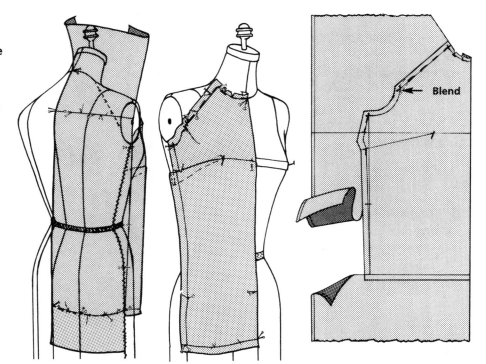

Blend

6 Fold the back side seam under and pin the back side seam to the front side seam. The seam allowance of the front will be toward the back.

7 Match the back hip level crossgrain to the front hip level crossgrain at the side seams.

8 Pin the center back grainline fold of the fabric to the center back position of the dress form. Be sure the hip level crossgrains are still matching and the fabric is not distorted. The front and back fabric pieces should be hanging plumb.

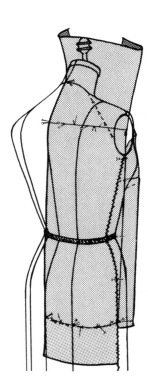

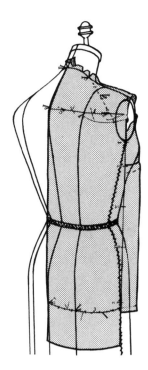
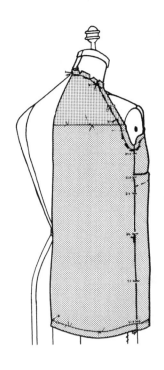
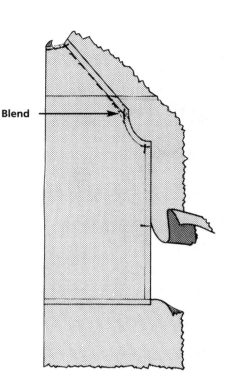

Blend

9 Smooth and pin the back shoulder/neck area into position.

NOTE: The back armhole area will show a definite amount of ease about halfway from the shoulder seam to the shoulder blade level crossgrain. Leave this ease in the armhole.

10 Drape and smooth the fabric over the yoke style line area of the dress form. Pin in place.

11 Mark key areas of the back dress form on the fabric:

a. Neckline: Lightly crossmark.

b. Back yoke style line: Lightly crossmark

c. Side seam at the waistline.

d. Armplate:
- Middle of the armhole: Crossmark the middle of armhole ridge fullness.
- Mark the bottom at the side seam.

12 True up all seams. Remove the front and back drape from the dress form and true up all seams. Add seam allowances: 1/4 inch at the back neckline and 1/2 inch to all other seams.

NOTE: To blend raglan style line: If a smooth continuous line is desired from the mid-armhole area into the yoke style line, it will be necessary to blend these two points.

13 Return the drape to the dress form and check for accuracy, fit, and balance. The drape should fit smoothly around the neckline without gaping or stretching. Also, the entire bodice drape should fit all areas of the dress form correctly.

Sleeve Draping Steps

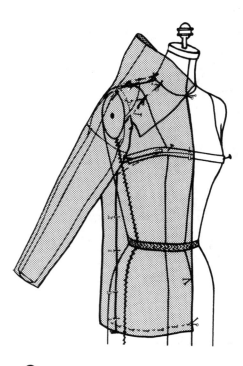

1 **Prepare the dress form.**

Attach the arm to the dress form.

2 **Pin the underarm seam of the sleeve together.**

3 **Place the sleeve over the arm on the dress form.** Align the sleeve grainline in the center of the arm and toward the shoulder seam of the dress form.

4 **Hold the arm out from the dress form and pin** the underarm section of the sleeve cap into the lower armhole of the bodice.

5 **Drape the sleeve into the front and back style lines** of the garment desired.

a. Smooth the front cap area of the sleeve toward the neckline and pin along all style line seams.

b. Smooth the back cap area of the sleeve toward the neckline and pin along all style line seams.

6 **Smooth the front and back shoulder seams together.** From the yoke style line, smooth the fabric up to the shoulder seam of the dress form. Excess fabric will be created above the shoulder seam.

NOTE: Attaching the arm to the dress form will add about a 3/8-inch shoulder excess at the shoulder/ridge intersection.

7 **Mark key areas** of the sleeve on the fabric:

a. Neckline: Lightly crossmark.

b. Front yoke style line: Lightly crossmark.

c. Back yoke style line: Lightly crossmark.

d. Shoulder seam to ridge.

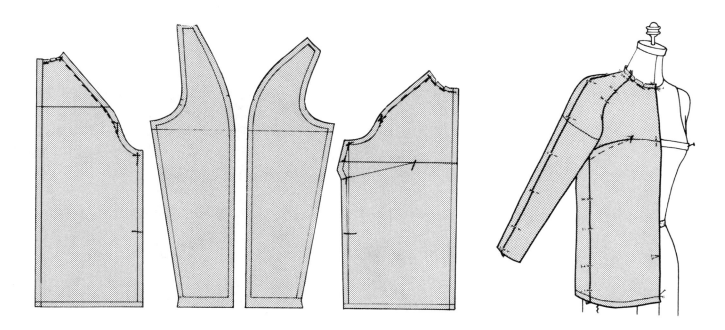

8 **True up all seams.** Remove the sleeve and the front and back drape from the dress form and true up all seams.

a. Separate the front and back sleeve. Cut the sleeve at the grainline. This will make a full shoulder seam, a separate front sleeve, and a back sleeve.

b. Add seam allowances: 1/4 inch at the front and back neckline of the sleeve and 1/2 inch to all other seams.

c. Add a 1-inch hem allowance at the bottom of the sleeve.

NOTE: To blend raglan style line: If a smooth continuous line is desired from the armhole into the yoke style line, it will be necessary to blend these two points.

Chapter Fifteen

Collars

Collars

The focal point of a garment is the neckline. Collars frame the face and, in most cases, are noticed before other details of the garment. It is important, therefore, that a collar is flattering and that effort is spent in carefully draping and trueing the desired collar design.

This chapter describes a variety of collars that encircle the neck edge. Some collars lie flat on the shoulders, some collars rise up from the neckline and then fold over onto the shoulders, and some collars stand up from the neck edge. By using correct and skillful draping methods, a designer can create multiple styles from a traditional collar. By changing the shape of the neckline, the designer can control the amount of stand desired for a particular design, thereby creating a flat collar rather than a traditional stand collar, or vice versa. Also, the designer can see the exact width and outside shape necessary to create a perfectly balanced design.

Design Variations

Convertible Collar

The convertible collar is a rollover collar without a separate stand. The collar can be designed in a variety of shapes, usually pointed, and may be worn open or closed against the front neckline. The neck edge of this collar is relatively straight and produces a high-standing collar that rolls back onto itself. The neck edge of a collar that has a slight curve gives a less pronounced stand when sewn into a garment. A convertible collar works well on almost any neckline, from V-necklines to jewel necklines.

Convertible Collar: *Preparing the Fabric*

1 **Measure the width** of the desired collar design (along the straight of grain) and add 4 inches.

Illustrated: approximately **6 inches.**

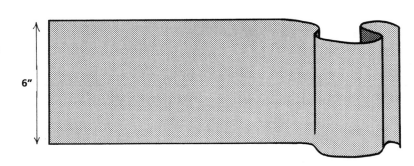

2 **Measure the length** of the desired collar design (along the crossgrain) from center back to center front and add 4 inches. Snip and tear the fabric at this crossgrain length.

Illustrated: approximately **12 inches.**

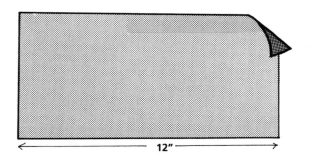

3 **Draw the center back grainline** 1 inch along the torn edge and parallel to the grain of the fabric. Press under.

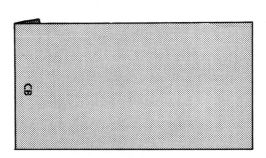

4 **Draw a perfect crossgrain line** 1 inch from the lower edge of the fabric. Use an L-square ruler.

5 **Draw a shorter second crossgrain line** 1/2 inch above the first crossgrain line, starting about 3 inches from the grainline fold (see illustration).

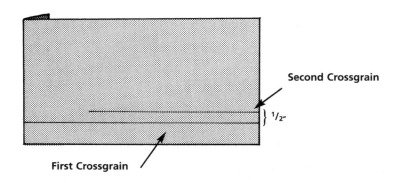

Second Crossgrain

First Crossgrain

1/2"

Notes

Convertible Collar: *Draping Steps*

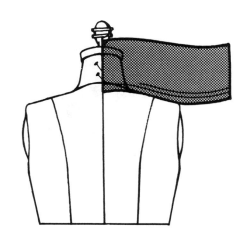  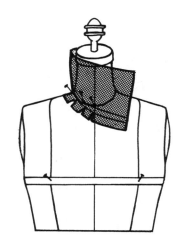

1 **Drape convertible collar** into the designed neckline of the garment.

2 **Pin the center back grainline** fold of the fabric on the center back neckline position of the dress form.

3 **Align the crossgrain of the fabric** on the neckline of the dress form.

4 **Drape the back neckline.** Clip, smooth, and pin the crossgrain along the neckline from the center back to the shoulder of the dress form.

5 **Drape the front neckline.** Clip, smooth, and pin the crossgrain line from the shoulder to the front neckline of the dress form.

6 **At the same time, allow the second crossgrain to drop** and shape onto the neckline at the center front position of the dress form.

If desired, draw in the neckline at this time.

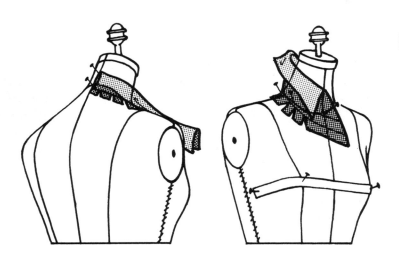

7 **Drape the collar stand.** Anchor a pin on the center back upper fold. This is to ensure that the collar stand does not fall off of the center back and stays perpendicular to the grain. Fold the fabric over on itself (the desired width) at center back. The fold will continue around to the front of the drape, gradually disappearing at center front.

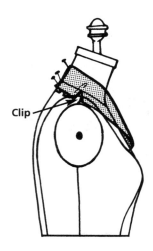

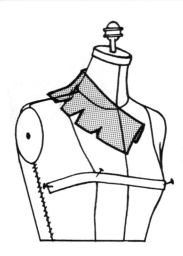

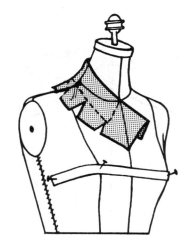

Clip

8 **Clip the collar at the shoulder.** To allow the collar to lie down easily, clip from the outer raw edge up to the desired width of the collar. After clipping, place another pin at the center back, just below the neckline.

9 **Trim and clip the fabric up to the desired collar width and shape.** The collar will automatically lie over the shoulder and drape flat at center front point.

10 **Draw the desired outer edge styling.** Starting at center front neck, continue to draw the desired width, finishing at center back.

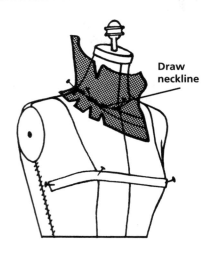

Draw neckline

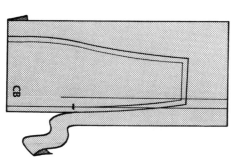

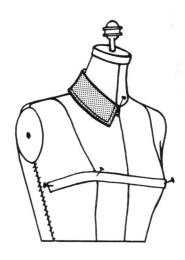

11 **Draw the neckline.** Flip the collar up and draw the front neckline from the shoulder to center front.

12 **Crossmark a shoulder position notch.**

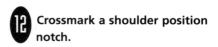

13 **True up all seams:**

a. Remove the collar from the dress form and true up all lines. Add 1/4 inch.

b. Transfer the collar shape to the other side of muslin.

c. Add a 1/4-inch seam allowance around the collar edges and trim excess fabric.

14 **Check the collar fit and outside shape.** Return the trued collar to the dress form and check for accuracy, fit, shape, and balance. The drape should fit smoothly around the neckline without gapping or stretching.

The mandarin collar is generally a narrow, standing collar that curves around the neck smoothly. Variations in the width of the collar and how closely it is draped to the neckline will create many different designs. It can be stiff and close to the neck for a military effect; it can be a soft, loose band for a more casual look; or it can be made with its opening in the back, creating a narrow standing band collar. Also, a tie collar can be developed by adding long tie strips at the center front ends.

Mandarin Collar: Preparing the Fabric

1 **Measure the width** of the desired collar and add 2 inches. Snip and tear the fabric at this width.

Illustrated: approximately **4 inches.**

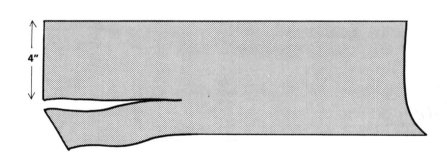

4"

2 **Measure the neck area** from center back to center front and add 4 inches. Snip and tear the fabric (along the crossgrain) at this length.

Illustrated: approximately **12 inches.**

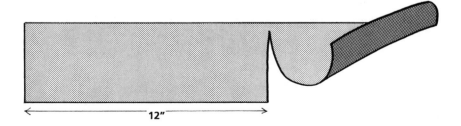

12"

3 0 2

3 **Draw the center back grainline**
1 inch along the torn edge and
parallel to the grain of the fabric.
Press under.

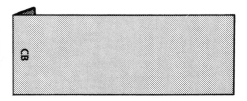

4 **Draw a perfect crossgrain line**
1 inch from the lower edge of
the fabric.

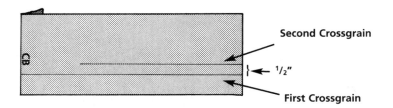

Second Crossgrain

¹/₂"

First Crossgrain

5 **Draw a second crossgrain
line** 1/2 inch above the first
crossgrain line, starting about
3 inches from the grainline fold
(see illustration).

Notes

Mandarin Collar: Draping Steps

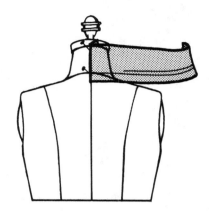

1 **Drape the mandarin collar** into the designed neckline of the garment.

2 **Pin the center back grainline** fold of the fabric on the center back position of the dress form neckline.

3 **Align the crossgrain** of the fabric on the neckline of the dress form.

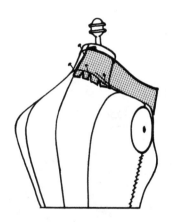

4 **Drape the crossgrain.** Clip, smooth, pin, and drape the crossgrain along the back neckline seam of the dress form from the center back to the shoulder seam.

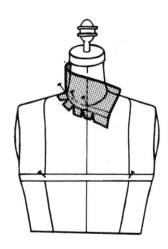

5 **Drape the crossgrain on the neckline** of the dress form to center front. From the shoulder, continue to clip, smooth, pin, and drape the crossgrain on the front neckline of the dress form. Allow the second crossgrain to drop and shape onto the neckline at the center front position of the dress form.

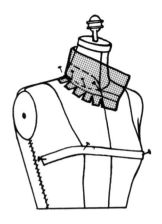

6 Draw the new front neckline from the shoulder to center front.

7 Crossmark a shoulder position notch.

8 Draw the desired outer edge styling from center front neck to center back in the desired width and parallel to the neckline.

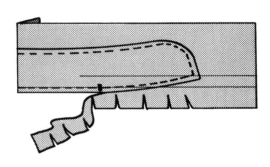

9 True up all seams.

a. Remove the collar from the dress form and true up all seams.

b. Add a 1/4-inch seam allowance around the outer edges and trim excess fabric. The center back grainline will be placed on the fold of the fabric.

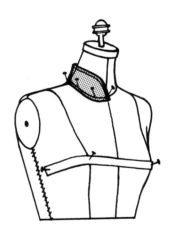

10 Check the collar fit and outside shape. Return the trued collar to the dress form and check for accuracy, fit, shape, and balance. The drape should fit smoothly around the neckline without gapping or stretching.

Variation

For a band collar, prepare the fabric drape in the same manner, draping the collar from center front to center back.

Peter Pan Collar

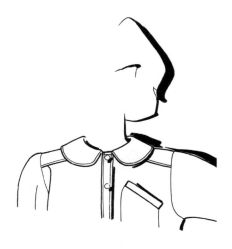

A traditional peter pan collar is a lie-down collar that has very little roll because the neck edge is curved similarly to the garment neckline. The round shape and flat drape are recognizable characteristics in a traditional peter pan collar. However, the collar width may vary from very narrow to exceptionally wide, and the outside edge may be shaped in various designs.

The peter pan collar can provide appealing design qualities in such fabrics as fine cottons, laces, openwork weaves, or silks.

Peter Pan Collar: *Preparing the Fabric*

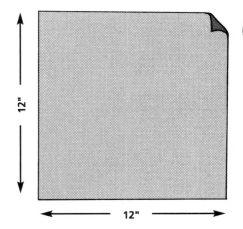

12"

12"

1 **For the length and width of this collar,** measure the desired area and add 9 inches. Cut a perfect square this measurement.

Illustrated: approximately **12-inch square.**

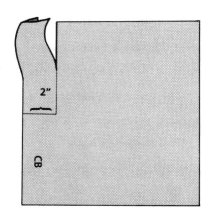

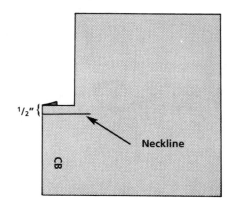

2 Draw the center back grainline 1 inch along the torn edge and parallel to the grain of the fabric. Press under.

3 Prepare back neck opening.

a. **Draw a perfect crossgrain 2 inches long** half the distance from the lower edge of the fabric piece. Draw a perfect crossgrain 2 inches long at this position.

b. **Draw a second grainline** parallel to and 2 inches from the center back grainline.

c. **Cut along the crossgrain line and the second grainline** and then remove this rectangular piece of fabric.

4 Draw a short crossgrain **1/2 inch below** the cut edge crossgrain. This indicates the center back/neck position.

Notes

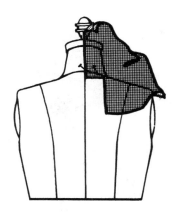

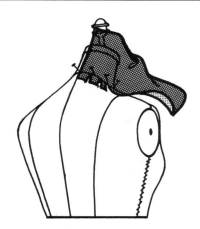

1 Drape the peter pan collar into the designed neckline of the garment.

2 Pin the center back grainline of the fabric to the center back position of the dress form neckline.

3 Align the center back neckline position (1/2-inch short crossgrain mark) of the fabric on the center back position of the dress form.

4 Clip, smooth, and pin the crossgrain along the back neckline seam of the dress form from the center back to the shoulder seam.

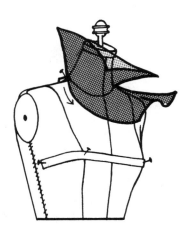

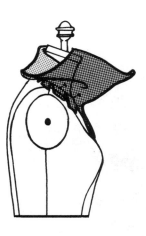

5 Clip, smooth, and pin the front neckline.

a. Pivot the lower edge of the fabric piece around the front neckline of the dress form from the shoulder seam of the garment. Keep the fabric flipped up.

b. Clip, smooth, drape, and pin the fabric around the front dress form neckline, finishing at center front position.

6 Flip the fabric piece down over the neckline so the fabric is lying down over the body and shoulder areas.

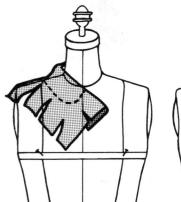
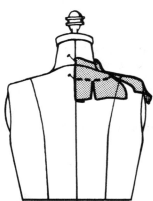
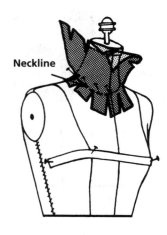

Neckline

7 **Clip the outer edge of the fabric** up to where the outer edge of the collar may be drawn. This will allow the collar to lie smoothly.

8 **Draw the desired collar style,** starting at the center front neck area of the dress form.

NOTE: It is vital that the center back grainline should remain on the center back of the dress form.

9 **Draw the desired neckline** from the center back to the center front.

10 **Draw a crossmark at the shoulder seam** of the dress form.

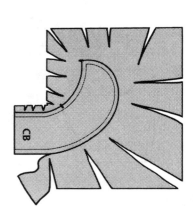
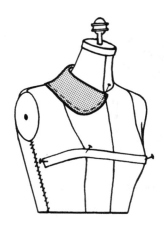

CB

11 **True up all seams.**

a. Remove the collar from the dress form and true up all seams.

b. Add a 1/4-inch seam allowance around the outer edges and trim excess fabric.

c. To make a complete collar, place the center back grainline on the fold of the fabric.

12 **Return the trued collar to the dress form** and check for accuracy, fit, and balance. The drape should fit smoothly around the neckline without gapping or stretching.

Turtleneck Collar

The turtleneck collar is a one-piece standing bias collar rolled over to cover the neckline. This bias turnover effect makes a smooth roll possible and allows the collar to be draped into a high neckline to give a close-to-the-body effect or into a wide lowered neckline to give a cowl-draped effect. The turtleneck collar serves two design functions: It provides extra warmth for its wearer and adds a decorative and flattering design to the neck edge.

Turtleneck Collar: *Preparing the Fabric*

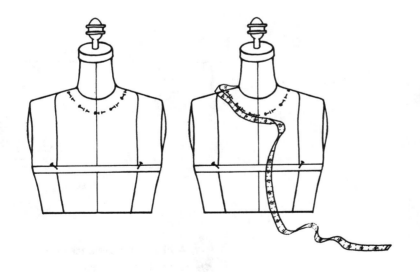

1 **Prepare the dress form.**

a. Place pins at the desired neckline on the dress form.

b. Measure the total desired neckline. Remember, the wider and/or lower the neckline, the more exaggerated the turtleneck collar.

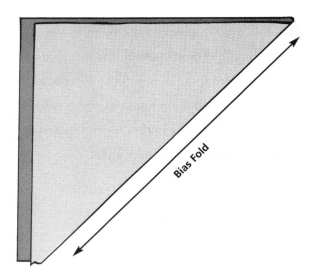

2 **Fold a large piece of fabric** on the bias (30 inches to 40 inches square).

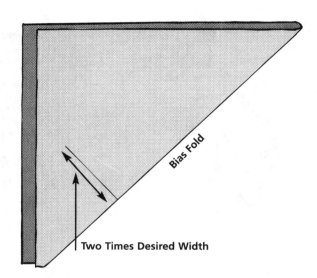

3 **Square a line from the fold** twice the desired width of the collar. Add 1/2 inch. This line should be placed as close to the left end of the fabric as possible.

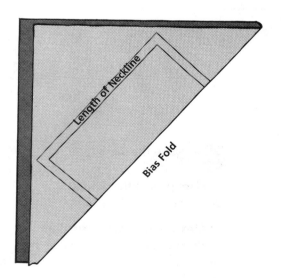

4 **Draw a line parallel to the bias fold** that is the length of the neckline. Start at the line squared from the fold.

5 **Square another line down to the bias fold** at the end of the neckline length.

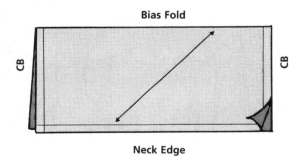

6 **Add seam allowances on all outer lines.** Cut along these lines and remove the excess fabric.

Turtleneck Collar: Draping Steps

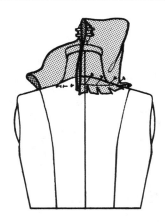

1 **Pin and clip both layers of the fabric along the desired neckline** guideline. Pin the center back guideline to the center back position of the dress form. Keep the fabric folded.

2 **Align the neckline edge** of the fabric on the desired neckline guideline of the dress form.

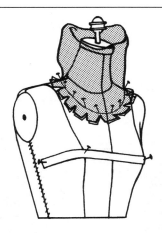

3 **Pin and clip both layers of the fabric until the entire desired neckline is encircled.** Follow the desired neckline guideline on dress form.

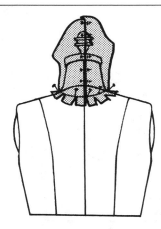

4 **Match and pin the right and left center back guidelines** from the neck edge up to the fold of the fabric.

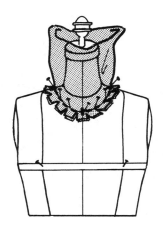

5 Draw the entire neckline.

6 Crossmark the shoulder position notches.

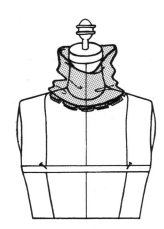

7 **Fold the bias fold edge of the fabric back over on itself,** covering the neckline.

NOTE: This drape enables the designer to check the proportion of width and amount of fullness. Lowering and/or raising the neckline will lengthen and/or shorten the amount of fullness. At the same time, adding or shortening the width of the drape will create less or more collar stand.

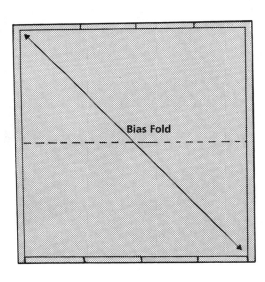

Bias Fold

8 **True up all seams.** Remove the collar from the dress form and true up all seams.

NOTE: The collar will remain on the bias.

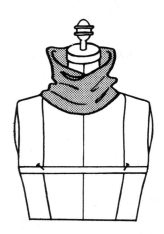

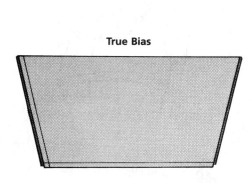

True Bias

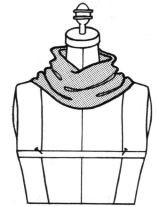

9 **Return the trued collar to the dress form.** Check for accuracy, fit, and balance. The drape should roll and fit smoothly around the neckline.

Variation

For a more draped or cowl effect, prepare the fabric wider at the folded edge. Taper the collar back onto the desired neckline.

Notes

Asymmetric Collar

There are many varieties of asymmetrical collar designs and many neckline shapes in which this collar may be draped. This collar typically crosses over the center front. The collar may have a slight roll or a high stand at the neck edge, depending on the design desired. The best results of this collar design are achieved when it is draped, because of the crossover effect. The asymmetrical collar puts pizzazz back into an otherwise simple collar and may turn any neckline into instant fashion.

Asymmetric Collar: Preparing the Fabric

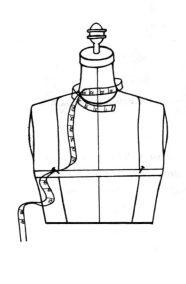

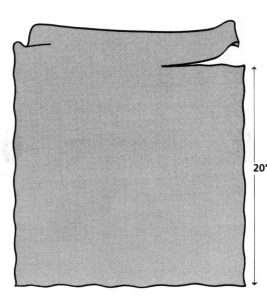

1 **Measure the desired neckline distance** (along the crossgrain) of both right and left sides of the dress form for the length of this collar. Snip and tear the fabric at this length.

Illustrated: approximately **20 inches.**

20"

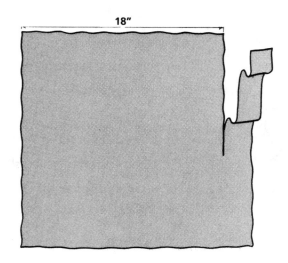

2 Measure the desired width of the collar (along the grainline) and double this measurement.

Illustrated: approximately **18 inches.**

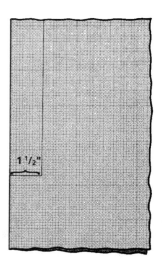

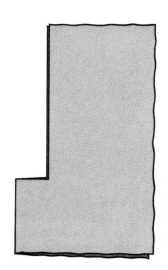

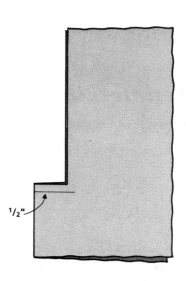

3 Prepare the back neck opening.

a. Fold the fabric in half lengthwise, parallel to the grainline.

b. Measure up from the lower edge one-third of the measurement of the fabric piece. Measure along the foldline.

c. Draw a perfect crossgrain line 1 1/2 inches long.

d. Draw a grainline 1 1/2 inches from and parallel to the fold of the fabric.

4 Cut along the crossgrain line and the grainline and remove the excess fabric.

5 Draw a short crossgrain line 1/2 inch below the cut crossgrain. This indicates the center back/neck position.

Asymmetric Collar: *Draping Steps*

1 **Pin the center back grainline** of the fabric to the center back position of the dress form neckline. Keep the fabric open and flipped up.

2 **Align the center back neckline crossmark** on the fabric to the center back neckline on the dress form.

3 **Clip, smooth, and pin the entire back neckline** from shoulder seam to shoulder seam. Keep the fabric flipped up.

4 **Fold the fabric down onto the body** and over the back draped neckline. The fabric should be lying smooth and clean.

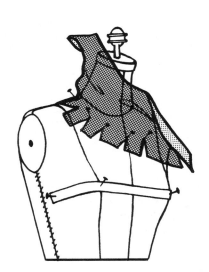

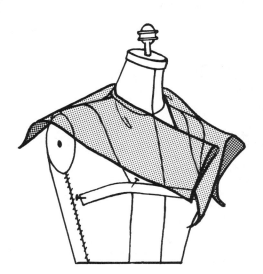

5 **Drape the right front neckline.** From the shoulder position, flip the fabric up onto the front neck of the dress form. Drape the desired right front neckline of the collar, passing the center front position and finishing the desired asymmetrical position.

NOTE: The straighter this front neckline, the more stand the collar will have. Therefore, for less stand, drape the front neckline with a definite curving seam.

6 Flip the fabric of the right front collar so it is lying down over the shoulder and body.

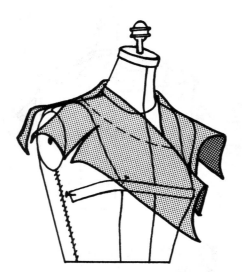

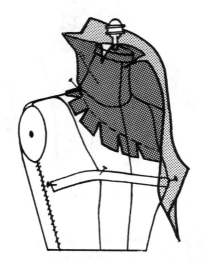

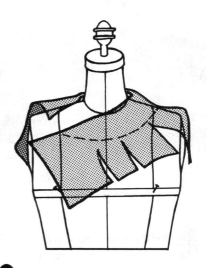

7 Clip the outer edge of the fabric up to the desired collar style to allow the collar to lie smoothly. Draw the desired collar style.

8 Draw the right front collar neckline. With the collar flipped up, draw the right front collar neckline to the center back position.

9 Crossmark the shoulder seam position and the center front position of the dress form.

10 Drape the left front collar, following the same draping procedures as the right front collar (Steps 4, 5, and 6). Continue to clip, smooth, and pin the left front neckline from the shoulder seam to past the center front.

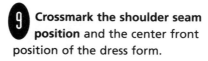

11 Draw the entire left neckline. Flip the collar up and draw the entire left neckline.

12 Crossmark the shoulder seam position and the center front position of the dress form.

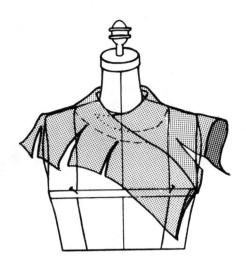

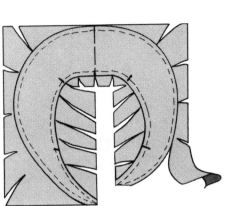

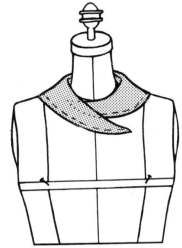

13 **Flip the fabric of the left front collar so it is lying down** over the shoulder and body.

14 **Clip the outer edge of the fabric** up to the desired collar style. This allows the collar to lie down smoothly.

15 **Draw the desired style.**

NOTE: The back collar width should be exactly the same from shoulder seam to shoulder seam.

16 **True up all seams.** Remove the collar from the dress form and true up all seams. Add a 1/4-inch seam allowance around the outer edge and trim excess fabric. Label the center back grainline on the fold of the fabric.

17 **Check for accuracy, fit, and balance** by returning the trued collar to the dress form. The drape should fit smoothly around the neckline without gapping or stretching.

Chapter 16

Jacket Designs

Jacket Designs

Jacket and coat designs are based on principles similar to those of the shift designs. This is because the silhouette hangs straight from the hip to the hem. Also, the waist area could be fitted by using fisheye darts or princess seams.

Since jackets are worn over other clothing, they are draped with a slightly larger neckline. Also, a larger armhole is developed using a shoulder pad and a lower armhole. Some companies use a dress form for jackets that is one size larger than their dress-size form to easily maintain the fit and be larger than the dress size.

The chapter on sleeves illustrates the one-piece jacket sleeve. The two-piece jacket sleeve is drafted, using the completed one-piece jacket sleeve. (Refer to the sleeve chapter for the jacket sleeve.)

The sewing steps for a tailored suit are covered in *A Guide to Fashion Sewing,* 3rd edition, published by Fairchild Books.

Design Variations

Notched Collar

The notched-collar garment has a single- or double-breasted lapel and always has a front opening. The design has an indentation, or "notch," cut out where the collar joins the lapel. The collar is cut separately from the lapel, which makes it similar to a convertible collar. The lapels and collars vary in many shapes, lengths, and widths.

The notched collar drapes and finishes into a carefully styled lapel, which is cut in one piece with the front of the garment. The collar, cut separately, can be made with either a high back neck stand, by draping in a straight back neckline, or a shallow back neck stand, by draping a curved back neckline. The notched collar is great for suits, jackets, coats, dresses, or blouses. It provides a tailored, flattering, and custom touch to traditional garments. The notched collar may provide crisp and sharp or soft and rounded shapes to a neckline.

Notched Collar: *Preparing the Fabric*

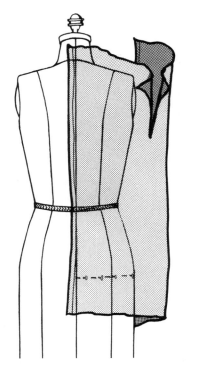
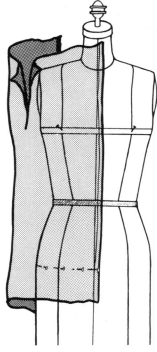

1 **Measure the length** for the front and back bodice (along the straight of grain) from the neckband to the length of the desired garment and add 4 inches. Snip and tear the fabric at this length.

2 **Measure the width for the front bodice** (along the crossgrain) from the center front to the side seam and add **9 inches.** Snip and tear the fabric at this width.

3 **Measure the width for the back bodice** (along the crossgrain) from the center back to the side seam and **add 4 inches.** Snip and tear the fabric at this width.

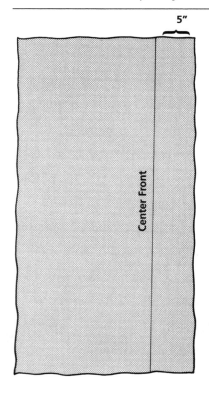

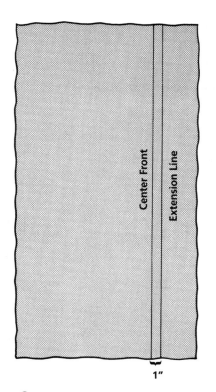

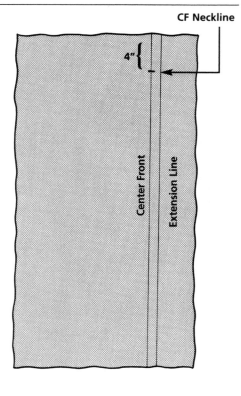

4 Draw the center front grainline 5 inches from the torn edge of the fabric. Do not press under.

5 Draw the desired extension line toward the torn edge and parallel to the center front grainline.

Illustrated: **1 inch.**

If a double-breasted design is desired, add a 2- to 2 1/2-inch extension amount.

6 Crossmark a center front neckline position. Measure down 4 inches from the top edge of the fabric on the center front grainline and crossmark.

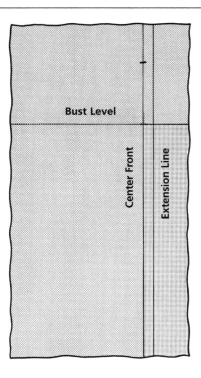

Neckline to Bust Level

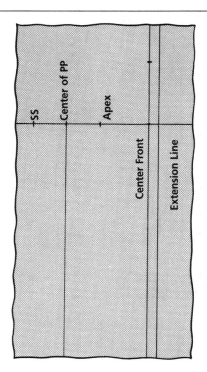

7 **Determine the position of the crossgrain line.**

a. Measure the distance from the center front neck to the bustline level on the dress form.

b. Measure and crossmark this neckline to bust level distance on the center front line of the fabric.

c. Draw a perfect crossgrain line at the bust level line crossmark, using an L-square ruler.

8 **Crossmark the apex, the side seam, and the center of the princess panel line on the crossgrain line.** If necessary, refer to Basic Bodice, page 48.

9 **For a straight jacket,** draw in the hip level line, the center front to side seam distance plus 1/2 inch of ease, and the side seam.

Notched Collar: Preparing the Collar

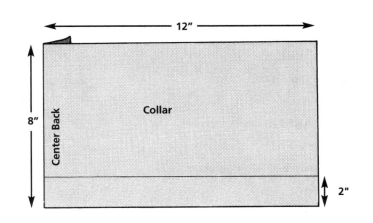

1 **Measure the length** of the desired collar. This should be approximately 12 inches (crossgrain).

2 **Measure the width** of the desired collar and add 4 inches. This should be approximately 8 inches (lengthwise grain).

3 **Draw a straight of grain** 1 inch from the torn edge and parallel to the grain of the fabric and press under.

4 **Draw a crossgrain** 2 inches from the lower edge of the fabric piece (see illustration).

Notched Collar: Back Bodice Draping Steps

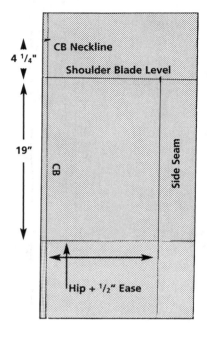

CB Neckline

4 ¼"

Shoulder Blade Level

19"

CB

Side Seam

Hip + ½" Ease

Preparing the Back Fabric Piece

1 **Draw in the center back grainline,** the back neckline crossmark, the shoulder blade level, the side seam, and the hipline on the fabric piece as illustrated.

Refer to The Basic Shift for more detailed fabric preparation (pages 101–102).

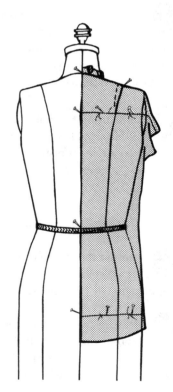

Back Drape

2 Referring to the design sketch, **completely drape the back** to match the desired design of the front. Refer to The Basic Shift (page 105) for more detailed draping steps.

NOTE: The back neck area should be draped to the natural back neckline to accommodate the notched collar. Also, if the jacket has shoulder pads, place a shoulder pad on the dress form before draping.

3 **Mark all key areas** of the back drape:

a. Neckline.

b. Shoulder.

c. Shoulder dart.

d. Armhole ridge.

e. Armplate at the screw level.

f. Side seam.

g. Armhole at the side seam.

h. Hem.

4 **True up the back,** add seam allowances, and return the drape to the dress form to check the fit.

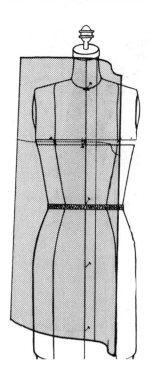

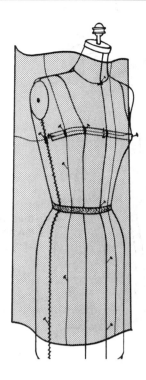

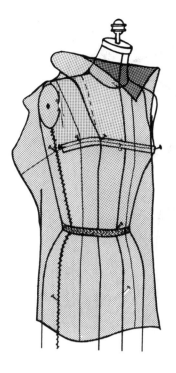

1 Pin the apex crossmark on the fabric to the apex position of the dress form.

2 Smooth and drape the fabric from the apex over to the center front of the dress form.

a. Pin the neckline crossmark to the center front neck of the dress form.

b. Pin the remainder of the center front grainline to the center front of the dress form, from the neckline down.

3 Align and pin the side seam and the center of the princess panel lines to the dress form. Anchor pins at the center of princess panel and on the side seam at the hipline.

4 Align and pin the crossgrain at the bust level and at the hip level, making sure not to distort or pull the fabric.

5 Pin the side seam and waist area. Remove the pin at the center of the princess panel at the waistline and allow the fabric to hang loosely to the hip (plumb).

NOTE: If a fitted waist seam is desired, clip and smooth in a fitted waistline and waistline dart. Pin the remaining side seam.

6 Smooth the fabric up and over the dress form armplate to the shoulder. Create a 1/4-inch–1/4-inch pinch at the screw level (middle at ridge) of the armhole. This is to ensure the armhole does not become too tight. Pin in place.

7 Drape a shoulder dart by keeping the side seam area smooth and flat. Allow all excess fabric to fall on the shoulder princess seam. (This amount varies from one bust size to another.) Fold and pin this excess fabric on the shoulder princess seam of the dress form. The excess fabric is folded toward the center front neck.

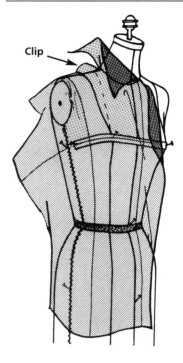

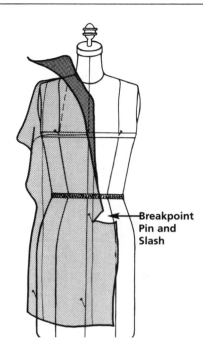

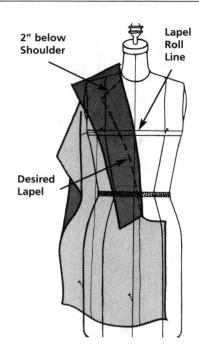

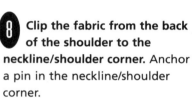

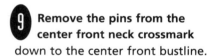

8 Clip the fabric from the back of the shoulder to the neckline/shoulder corner. Anchor a pin in the neckline/shoulder corner.

9 Remove the pins from the center front neck crossmark down to the center front bustline.

10 Place a pin at the desired breakpoint position (depth of the finished neckline) on the extension line.

11 Pin the grainline and the extension line to the dress form. Pin from the breakpoint position down to the bottom of the drape.

12 Remove center front line pins from the dress form above the breakpoint pin.

13 Slash the fabric at the breakpoint from the outer edge of the fabric into the breakpoint pin.

14 Fold in a lapel roll line by folding back the fabric in the front of the garment. Start at the extension breakpoint pin and finish at the neckline/shoulder pin.

15 Draw the desired lapel shape. Start at the neckline fold about 2 inches below the shoulder (refer to sketch). Finish drawing at the breakpoint on the extension line.

NOTE: The neckline fold above the lapel line is the new front neckline of the jacket.

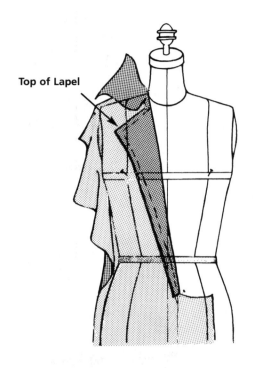

Top of Lapel

 Trim the excess fabric at the top portion of the front neckline and the entire lapel, leaving 1 inch of excess fabric. Clip the fabric where the lapel meets the neckline. Also trim the lapel down to the breakpoint, leaving 1 inch of excess fabric.

17 **Mark all key areas** of the front drape:

a. **Neckline** down to the top of the lapel.

b. **Shoulder.**

c. **Darts.**

d. **Armhole.**

e. **Side Seam.**

f. **Hem.**

Notes

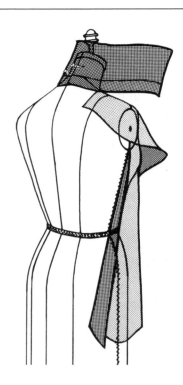

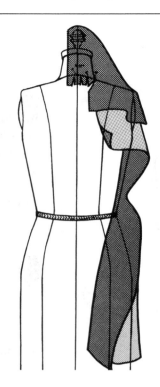

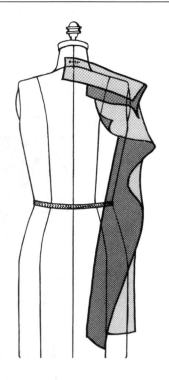

1 **Pin the center back collar grainline** of the fabric on the center back position of the dress form neckline.

2 **Align the collar crossgrain** on the neckline of the dress form.

3 **Clip, smooth, and pin the collar crossgrain** along the back neckline seam of the dress form to the shoulder seam of the dress form. Clip and pin at the neckline/shoulder corner.

4 **Fold the fabric over onto itself to create a collar stand.**
Anchor a pin on the center back upper fold at center back neck. (This is to ensure that the collar stand does not fall off the center back and remains perpendicular to the grain.)

Fold the fabric over onto itself at this upper fold pin.

5 **Trim and clip the back collar outer edge** of the fabric up to the desired width and shape of the collar. By being clipped, the collar will lie smoothly over the back shoulder area.

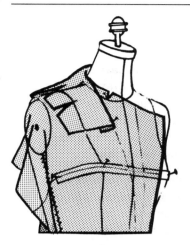

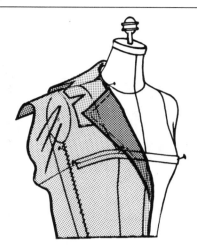

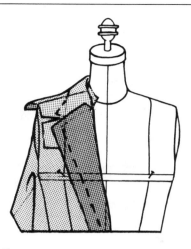

6 Drape the front collar into the roll line of the bodice lapel.

7 Place the lapel out past center front, from the shoulder/lapel neckline clip.

Allow the front of the collar to fold into the same angle as the underneath side of the roll line of the lapel. Adjust the collar until the desired amount of stand is reached.

8 Lay the lapel on top of the collar. From the neckline clip, allow the lapel to lie on top of the draped collar.

The roll line will flip back onto the garment to make the front of the collar.

9 Draw in the desired collar style. Start drawing at center back and angling it into the top of the lapel about 1 1/2 inches from the lapel outer edge. Crossmark this position on the lapel with a lapel neckline notch (refer to illustration).

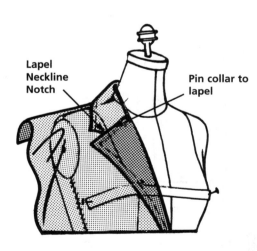

Lapel Neckline Notch

Pin collar to lapel

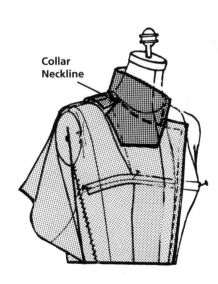

Collar Neckline

11 Draw in the collar neckline.

a. Turn the collar and lapel up and out.

b. Draw in the back collar neckline from center back of the dress form to the shoulder of the dress form. Mark the shoulder position notch.

c. Using the jacket neckline as the guide, continue to mark the collar front neckline to the lapel neckline notch.

d. Transfer the lapel neckline notch to the collar where the lapel and the collar meet.

10 Pin the lapel and the collar together where the collar and the lapel meet.

Check for desired lapel shape. Reshape if necessary.

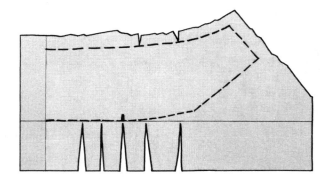

12 **True up all collar seams.** Remove the collar from the dress form and true up all collar seams. Add a 1/4-inch seam allowance around the collar outer edges and trim excess fabric.

NOTE: Usually the center back of the finished top collar is placed on the fold. For an under collar, a center back seam is often used, and this collar piece is placed on the bias for an easier roll.

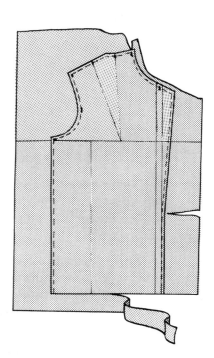

13 **True up all bodice seams.** Remove the bodice drape from the dress form and true up all bodice seams. Add seam allowances and trim excess fabric.

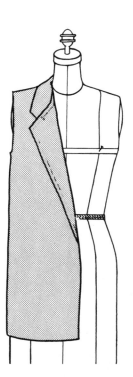

14 **Check the garment fit and collar shape.** Return the trued collar and garment to the dress form and check for accuracy, fit, and balance. The drape should fit smoothly around the neckline without gapping or stretching.

Shawl Collar

The main characteristic of a shawl collar is that the lapel and upper collar are cut in one piece with the garment. The collar has a center back seam to allow the front of the jacket to stay on the straight of grain. The length and width of the collar vary greatly depending upon the intended effect of the styled jacket. The outer shape of the collar may have a curved, scalloped, or notched edge.

The back neck area may be straight for a higher stand or have a slight curve for a little less stand. The back neck shaping allows the collar to roll the amount the designer wants.

The shawl collar works successfully in every sort of neckline from high neck to dramatically low-cut lines. It is important to take great care in draping and styling the selected shape to give a polished and put-together look.

Shawl Collar: *Preparing the Fabric*

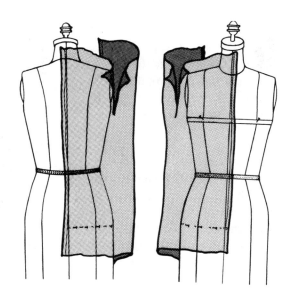

1 **Measure the length** for the front and back drape (along the straight of grain) from the neckband to the length of the desired garment. **Add 10 inches.** Snip and tear the fabric at this length.

2 **Measure the width** for the front and back drape (along the crossgrain) from center front to the side seam. Add 10 inches for the front. **Add 4 inches** for the back. Snip and tear the fabric at this width.

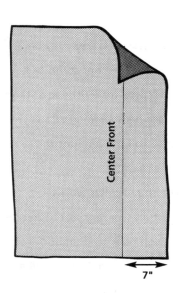

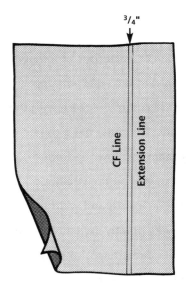

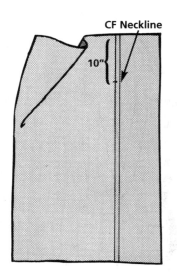

3 **Draw the center front grainline** 7 inches from the torn edge of the fabric. Do not press under.

4 **Draw in the desired extension** line toward the torn edge and parallel to the center front grainline.

Illustrated: **3/4 inch.**

5 **Crossmark the center front neckline position.** Measure down 10 inches from the top edge of the fabric on the center front grainline and crossmark.

6 **Determine the position of the crossgrain line.**

a. Measure the distance from the center front neck to the bustline level on the dress form. This is the neckline to bust level distance.

b. Measure and crossmark the neckline to bust level distance on the center front line of the fabric.

c. Draw a perfect crossgrain line at the bust level line crossmark, using an L-square ruler.

7 **Crossmark the apex, the side seam, and the center of the princess panel line on the crossgrain line.** If necessary, refer to Basic Bodice, page 48.

8 **For a straight jacket,** draw in the hipline 14 inches from the bust level line. Draw in a side seam the distance from center front to the side seam and add 1/2 inch for ease. Refer to The Basic Shift, page 102.

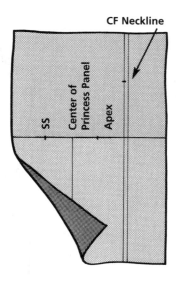

Shawl Collar: Back Bodice Draping Steps

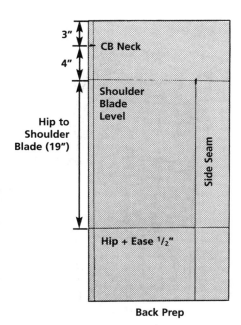

Back Prep

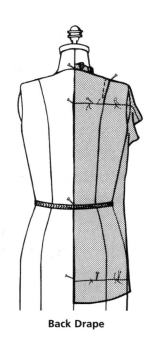

Back Drape

Preparing the Back Fabric Piece

 **Draw in the center back grainline,** the back neckline crossmark, the shoulder blade level, the side seam, and the hipline on the fabric piece as illustrated.

2 Referring to the design sketch, **completely drape the back** to match the desired design of the front. Refer to The Basic Shift, page 105, for more detailed draping steps.

NOTE: The back neck area should be draped to the natural back neckline to accommodate the notched collar. Also, if the jacket has shoulder pads, place a shoulder pad on the dress form before draping.

3 **True up the back,** add seam allowances, and return the drape to the dress form.

4 **Mark all key areas** of the back drape:

a. Neckline.

b. Shoulder.

c. Shoulder dart.

d. Armhole ridge.

e. Armplate at screw level.

f. Armplate at side seam.

g. Side seam.

h. Hem.

Shawl Collar: Front Bodice Draping Steps

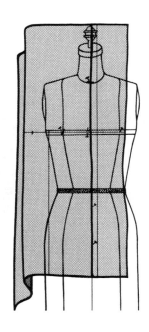

1 **Pin the apex crossmark** on the fabric to the apex position of the dress form.

2 **Smooth and drape the fabric from the apex** over to the center front of the dress form.

a. Pin the neckline crossmark to the center front neck of the dress form.

b. Pin the remainder of the center front grainline to the center front of the dress form, from the neckline down.

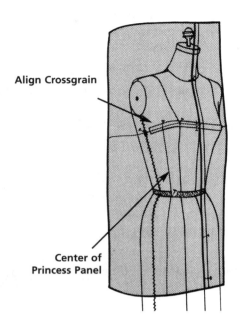

Align Crossgrain

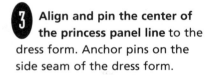

**Center of
Princess Panel**

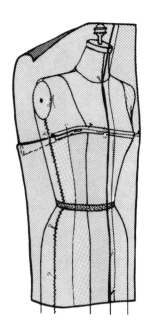

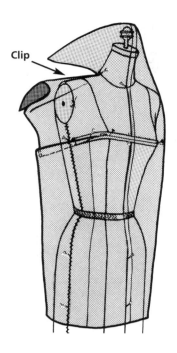

Clip

3 **Align and pin the center of the princess panel line** to the dress form. Anchor pins on the side seam of the dress form.

4 **Align and pin the crossgrain** at the bust level and the hip level. Make sure not to distort or pull the fabric.

NOTE: The side seam should be perfectly parallel to the center of the princess panel line.

5 **Drape the side bust dart and shoulder area.**

a. Drape the shoulder area by laying the fabric smooth and flat over the shoulder ridge.

b. Smooth the fabric over the dress form armplate. Create a 1/4-inch–1/4-inch pinch at the screw level (middle at ridge) of the armhole. This is to ensure the armhole does not become too tight. Pin in place.

c. Unpin the bust level line and allow the excess fabric to fall below the crossgrain line. Fold the excess fabric up and into the bustline level line. This creates a side bust dart, using the excess fabric that is falling below the bust level line.

d. Allow all fabric below the dart and the bustline to hang loosely to the hip (plumb).

6 **Clip the fabric,** starting at the back princess area into the neckline/shoulder corner. Anchor a pin in the neckline/shoulder corner.

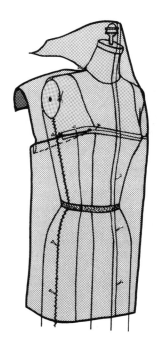

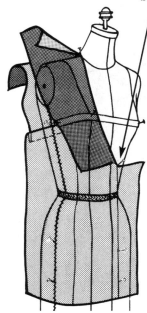

**Slash to
breakpoint pin**

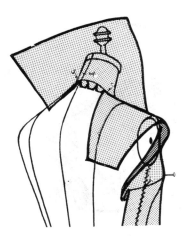

7 Pin the breakpoint, grainline, and extension lines.

a. Place a pin at the desired breakpoint position (depth of the finished neckline) on the extension line.

b. Pin the grainline and the extension line to the dress form from this breakpoint position down to the bottom of the drape.

c. Remove the pins above the breakpoint pin.

8 Slash the fabric at the breakpoint from the outer edge of the fabric into the breakpoint pin.

9 Trim the excess fabric from the breakpoint pin down to the bottom of the fabric.

10 Fold in a lapel/collar roll line by turning back the fabric in the front of the garment. Start at the extension breakpoint pin and finish at the neckline/ shoulder pin.

11 Clip, pin, smooth, and drape the fabric around the back neckline.

a. Lift the lapel area up, starting from the shoulder/neckline pin.

b. Clip pin and drape the back lapel area around the back neckline of the dress form.

c. Mark the finished neckline.

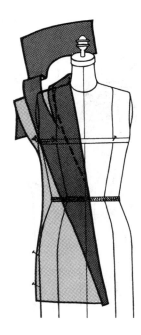

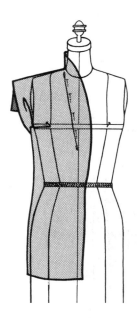

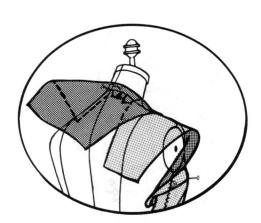

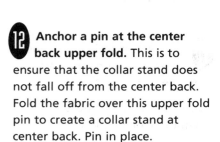

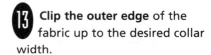

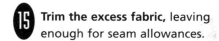

12 Anchor a pin at the center back upper fold. This is to ensure that the collar stand does not fall off from the center back. Fold the fabric over this upper fold pin to create a collar stand at center back. Pin in place.

13 Clip the outer edge of the fabric up to the desired collar width.

14 Draw the desired outer edge of the collar, starting at the breakpoint pin. Finish drawing at the center back of the collar.

15 Trim the excess fabric, leaving enough for seam allowances.

16 Drape a fisheye dart. Flip the collar up and drape a fisheye dart on the roll line of the collar. The dart should start at the neckline/shoulder corner and drape to the center front of the jacket.

NOTE: The fisheye dart creates a slight roll.

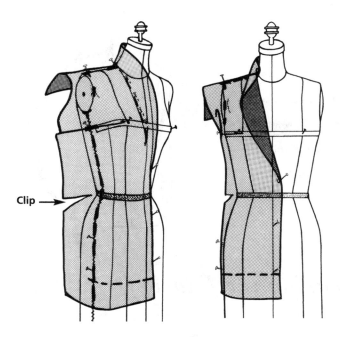

Clip →

17 **Mark all key areas** of the dress form on the front and back drape:

a. Shoulders.

b. Fisheye dart.

c. Armplate:
• Shoulder seam at ridge
• Plate at screw level
• Plate at underarm/side seam

d. Side seam and dart.

e. Bottom of desired design or waistline.

NOTE: For a more fitted side seam, clip the waist area of the side seam. Drape the side seam closer to the dress form.

18 **True up all seams.** Remove the front and back drape from the dress form and true up all seams. Add 1/4-inch seam allowances at the back neckline and the outer edges of the collar. Add a 1/2-inch seam allowance to all other seams.

19 **Check the drape.** Pin the front and back to each other. Return the drape and collar to the dress form and check for accuracy, fit, and balance. The collar should fit smoothly around the neckline without gapping or stretching. Also, the entire bodice drape should fit all areas of the dress form correctly.

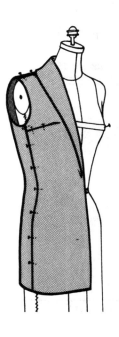

Jacket Designs: *Demi-Princess Jacket with Revere Collar*

The demi-princess jacket is a classic design featuring vertical slimming lines that divide the bodice front and back into two panels. The underarm/side princess panel starts just below mid-armhole and creates a princess seam closer to the side seam area. Because the princess seam does not cross over the bust point, a small side bust dart is draped in place, radiating from the princess seam.

The demi-princess jacket drape offers versatility to an important classic jacket and creates a crisp, longer, and slimmer look. Many fashionable suits or sportswear separates may be designed in this length and shape.

Demi-Princess Jacket: *Preparing the Fabric*

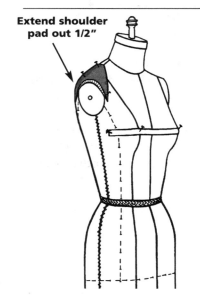

Extend shoulder pad out 1/2"

1 **Prepare the dress form.**

a. Place pins or use style tape on the dress form at the desired princess seam location.

b. Select the size of the shoulder pad that you would like for your design. (Shoulder pad thicknesses vary from season to season, depending upon the styles at that time.) Place the pad over the shoulder of the dress form, extending it out 1/2 inch beyond the shoulder tip of the dress form. Pin in place.

2 **Measure the length** for the front, back and side panels of the jacket (along the straight of grain) from the neckband to the hem area and add 4 inches. Snip and tear the fabric at this length.

3 **Divide this fabric piece into three equal widths** for the front, side/underarm, and back panels of the jacket along the crossgrain.

Desired Length, Plus 4"

Approximately 15"

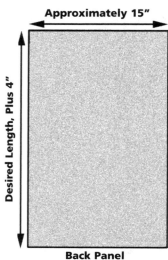

Back Panel

Approximately 15"

Under Side Seam Panel

Approximately 15"

Front Panel

Prepare grainlines and crossgrains for all three panels:

a. Front panel:
- Using one of the panel pieces, draw a center front grainline 5 inches from the torn edge of the fabric. Do not press under.
- Draw the desired extension line toward the torn edge and parallel to the center front grainline.

Illustrated: **1 inch.**

- Crossmark a center front neckline position 4 inches from the top edge of the fabric on the center front grainline.
- Measure the distance from the center front neck to the bustline level on the dress form. Transfer this neckline to bust level distance and draw a perfect crossgrain line, using an L-square ruler.

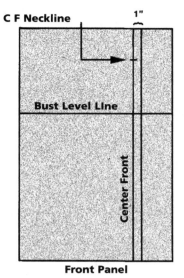

Front Panel

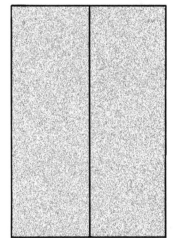

Underarm Side Seam Panel

b. Underarm side seam panel:
- Using the middle piece, draw a grainline in the center of the fabric piece.

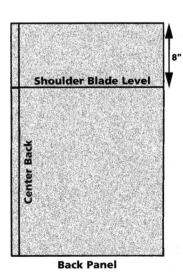

Back Panel

c. Back panel:
- Using the last panel, draw a center back grainline 1 inch from the torn edge of the fabric. Press under.
- Draw a perfect crossgrain line 8 inches from the top edge of the fabric. This line represents the shoulder blade level line.

Front Jacket Panel

1 **Pin the center front grainline** of the fabric on the center position of the dress form. Align and pin the crossgrain at the bust level, making sure the fabric is hanging plumb.

2 **Anchor pins at center front neck and center front hip.** An additional pin may be needed at the bust level tape.

3 **Drape and smooth the fabric** over the shoulder seam of the dress form.

4 **Continue to smooth the fabric flat** over the armplate. Leave the 1/4-inch–1/4-inch pinch at the mid-armhole area ridge (just above the demi-princess styleline). Continue to drape just past the demi-princess styleline. Pin in place.

5 **Clip the waistline** at the princess seam.

NOTE: The fabric at the waistline will be smooth but not snug.

6 **Drape in a bustline dart** by folding in the excess fabric that is created over the bustline area. Fold the dart excess toward the waistline.

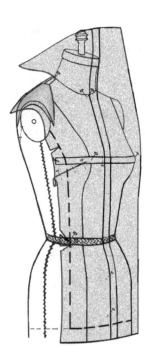

7 Drape the revere collar:

a. Place a pin at the desired breakpoint position (depth of the finished neckline) on the extension line. Slash the fabric at the breakpoint on the outer edge of the fabric into the breakpoint pin.

b. Pin the grainline and the extension line to the dress form from the breakpoint position down to the bottom of the drape.

c. Remove center front line pins from the dress form above the breakpoint pin.

d. Fold in a revere lapel by folding back the fabric in the front of the garment. Start at the extension breakpoint pin and finish at the neckline/shoulder pin.

e. Draw in the desired outer edge of the revere shape, starting at the neckline/shoulder. Finish drawing at the breakpoint on the extension line. Trim all excess fabric away from the extension line and around the collar.

f. Drape a fisheye dart. Flip the revere collar up and drape a fisheye dart on the roll line of the collar. The dart should start at the neckline/shoulder corner and drape to the center front of the jacket.

NOTE: The fisheye dart allows for a slight roll on the roll line of the revere.

8 **Mark all key areas** of the dress form on the front panel.

9 **Remove the front panel from the dress form and true up all the lines.** Add seam allowances and the front armhole notch. Place the drape on the dress form to check seams and fit.

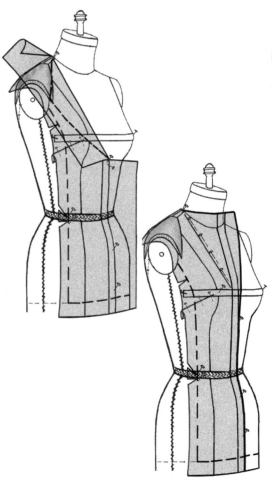

The Center Back Panel

1 **Pin the center back grainline** fold of the fabric to the center back position of the dress form.

2 **Align and pin the crossgrain** of the fabric to the shoulder blade level of the dress form.

3 **Drape and smooth the back neckline** by carefully trimming the excess fabric around the neck area and clipping at intervals.

4 **Continue to drape and smooth** the shoulder over the shoulder of the dress form. Pin in place.

5 **Continue to smooth the fabric flat** over the armplate to just past the demi-princess style line. Pin in place. Continue to smooth the fabric across the dress form from center back to just past the demi-princess seam. Pin in place.

6 **Clip the waistline** at the princess seam.

NOTE: The fabric at the waistline will be smooth but not snug.

7 **Mark all key areas** of the dress form on the center back panel:

a. Neckline.

b. Shoulder seam.

c. Back princess seam.

d. Style line notches: A double notch is used in the back.

e. Hem.

8 **True up all lines.** Remove the center back panel drape from the dress form and true up all lines. Add seam allowances. Trim all excess fabric. Place the drape back on the dress form.

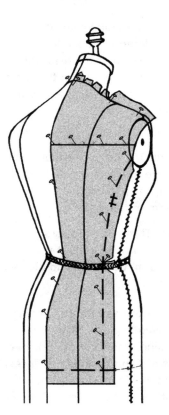

The Underarm/Side Seam Panel

1 **Pin the grainline** of the underarm/side seam panel to the side seam of the dress form. Anchor another pin on the straight of grain at the waistline and the hipline.

2 **Pin 1/4 inch of ease** on each side of the grainline from the top of the panel down to the bottom of the panel.

NOTE: This ease is necessary to build in enough ease at the underarm, waistline, and hipline.

3 **Smooth and pin the princess seam in place.** From the grainline, smooth the fabric past the front and back demi-princess seams. Pin in place. Clip the waistline at the princess seam.

NOTE: The fabric at the waistline will be smooth but not snug.

4 **Mark all key areas** of the dress form on the underarm/side seam panel princess seam:

a. Styleline crossmarks: Match to center front panel crossmarks.

b. Armplate: Mark at the bottom of plate at side seam and place notch here.

c. Hem.

5 **True up** underarm/side seam panel and check drape:

a. Remove the drape from the dress form and true up all lines. Add seam allowances. Trim all excess fabric.

b. Pin the front and back panels to the underarm/side seam panel. Place the drape on the dress form to check seams, crossmarks, fit, and hang.

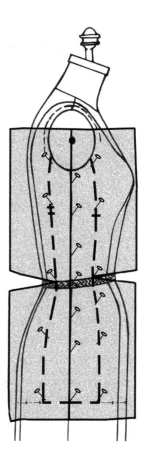

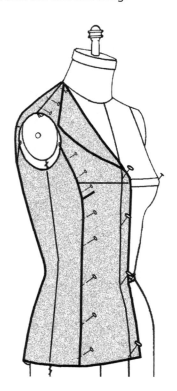

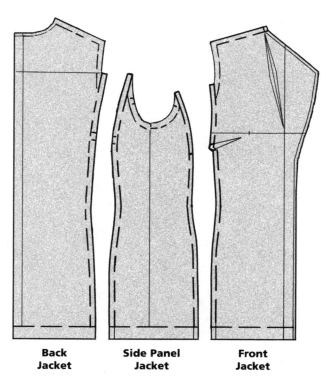

Back Jacket   **Side Panel Jacket**   **Front Jacket**

Part Four

Advanced Design Variations

After mastering the principles and techniques of draping, the designer will be able to apply this information to designing and creating more unusual and complicated cuts. Those approaching the challenging designs in this section must have experience in the application of basic and intermediate draping styles and sewing skills. Much pleasure and satisfaction can be derived from creating original styles.

These projects show how to emphasize a figure's most pleasing attributes through subtle illusion. Thus, designers learn to achieve a total effect, while still paying attention to the most minute details.

This part discusses bias dresses, sculptured dresses, yoke-styled garments, and knit and halter designs. It explores how fabric, with its various fibers and weaves, reacts differently to each design.

Other considerations are draping the cloth against the body on the bias weave and with knit fabric. Although there are step-by-step guidelines for these designs, a great deal of finesse and technique is required to accurately drape these styles.

Bias-Cut Slip Dress

Because of the inherent stretchability of bias fabric, designers such as Donna Karan used it to create new dress styles for the 1990s. The bias-cut slip dress has won approval in the retail market at all levels. It can be slipped on over the head, which makes it easy to get into and out of, and it is comfortable to wear. As designers, you should understand that if bias-cut garments are draped improperly, they will hug the body and every imperfection will be emphasized.

The bias-cut slip dress is sleeveless, with a neckline beginning above the bust. It is held in place with thin spaghetti straps. This dress is cut on the bias of a soft fabric, which results in a closer fit that stretches and conforms to the movements of the body.

The slip dress is an alternative to the bodysuit. It may be worn alone or with a soft cardigan, a tailored blazer, or leggings.

Bias-Cut Slip Dress: Preparing the Fabric

1 **For the length and width of the dress,** measure and cut two perfect 45-inch squares.

2 **Draw a true bias line** diagonally across the pieces of fabric.

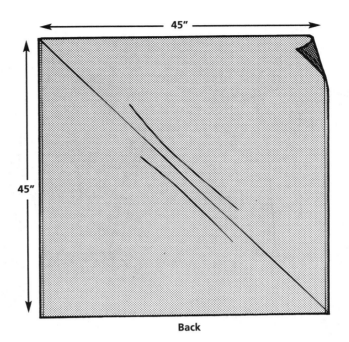

Back

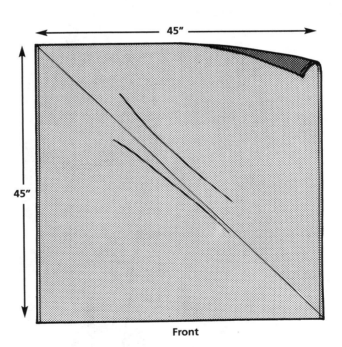

Front

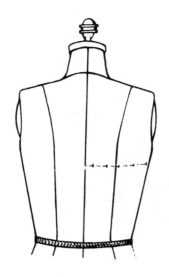
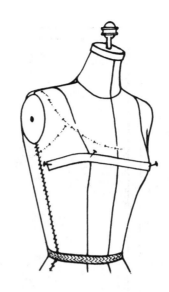
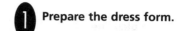

1 Prepare the dress form.

Place pins on the dress form at the desired bustline. Remove the bust level tape (bra) from the dress form.

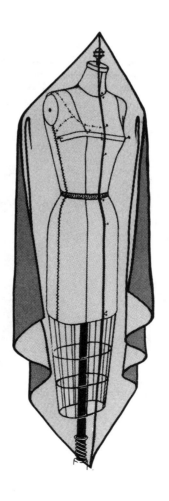

2 Pin the bias line of the fabric to the center front position of the dress form. The fabric piece should extend at least 3 inches above the styled bustline.

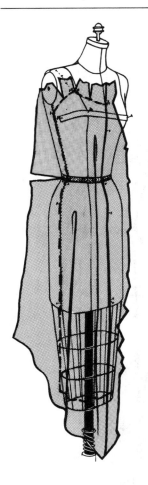

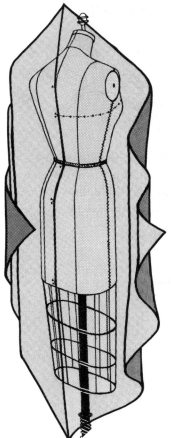

3 Smooth, clip, and pin the fabric across the neckline style line. Approximately 2 inches from center front, clip the fabric from the top edge down to the neckline style line. Pin the neckline style line seam at the clip.

4 Create a slight flowing flare below the bust. Because the fabric is on the bias and is soft, the bust area can be molded into a close-to-body fit. As this bias drape is molded over the bustline, a slight flare will be created below the bust that extends to the hemline.

5 Smooth, clip, and pin approximately 2 inches from the first clip of the neckline style line. Mold and smooth the remainder of the bust area. Continue to smooth the fabric across the neckline style line seam, over the bust, and toward the side seam.

6 Clip, smooth, and fit the side seam down to the waistline. As the side seam is being fitted, a second slight flare will be created from the hipline in the middle of the princess panel. Drape in the remainder of the side seam below the waistline.

7 Mark all key areas of the dress form on the center front panel:

a. Front bustline style line seam.

b. Waistline at side seam: Place a waistline notch.

c. Side seam: Lightly mark.

d. Hem: Follow the bottom of the dress form or a rung.

Do not remove the drape from the dress form.

8 Pin the bias line of the fabric to the center back position of the dress form. The fabric piece should extend at least 3 inches above the styled bustline.

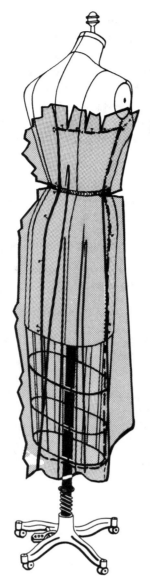

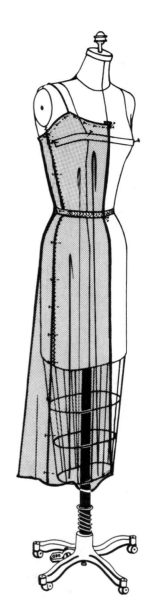

11 Smooth, clip, and pin approximately 2 inches from the first clip of the back neckline style line. Mold and smooth the remainder of the back neckline area. Continue to smooth the fabric across the neckline style line seam toward the side seam.

12 Clip, smooth, and fit the side seam down to the waistline. As the back side seam is being draped, pin it to the front side seam. As the side seam is being fitted, a second slight flare will be created from the hipline in the middle of the princess panel. Drape in the remaining of the side seam below the waistline.

13 Match the back side seam to the front side seam, pinning and fitting the dress until the desired side seam shape is achieved.

14 Mark all key areas of the dress form on the center front panel:

a. Back bustline style line seam.

b. Waistline at side seam: Place a waistline notch.

c. Side seam: Lightly mark.

d. Hem: Follow the bottom of the dress form or a rung.

9 Smooth, clip, and pin the fabric across the back neckline style line. Approximately 2 inches from center back, clip the fabric from the top edge down to the back neckline style line. Pin the neckline style line seam at the clip.

10 Create a slight flowing flare below the back neckline style line. As this bias drape is being molded over the back neckline style line, a slight flare will be created at the princess seam that extends to the hemline.

15 Drape and measure the amount of spaghetti strapping needed for this design. Add an inch for seam allowance.

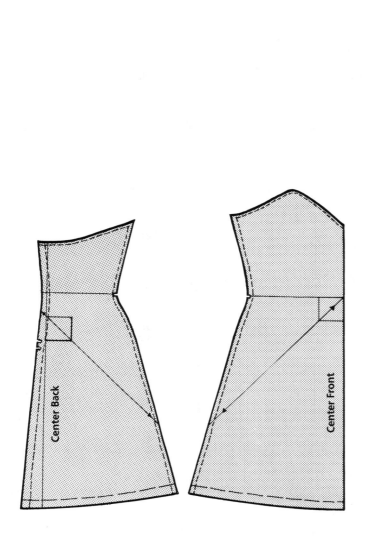

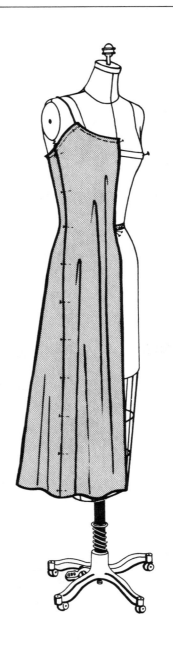

16 **True up the front and back dress.** Remove the fabric drape from the dress form. True up all seams, add seam allowances, and trim excess fabric. Pin the front drape to the back drape.

Return the finished drape to the dress form and check for accuracy, fit, and balance.

"Sculptured" Dress

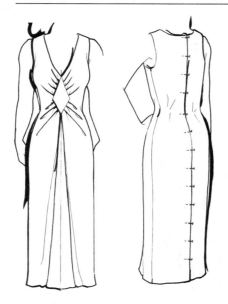

A "sculptured" dress has excess fabric tucks or pleats around the bust area that radiate from a shaped motif and blend to nothing at the side seam. The tucks or pleats distribute and shape the fabric around the bust and create a smooth molded effect in the waist area of the dress. These multiple folds will hug, wrap, and drape the body to produce a sultry, sexy, and provocative dress.

"Sculptured" Dress: Preparing the Fabric

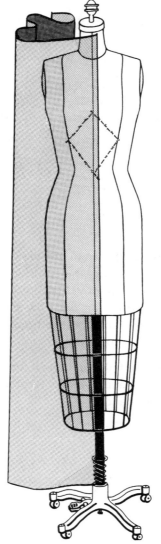

1 Measure, along the straight of grain, 60 inches to 88 inches, which is the length for the front and back. Snip and tear the fabric at this length.

2 Measure, along the crossgrain, the width for the front and back.

a. For the front drape, it will be necessary to use the full width of the fabric goods.

b. For the back drape, measure from the center back to the side seam and add 8 inches. Snip and tear the fabric at this width. The measurement will be at least 18 inches.

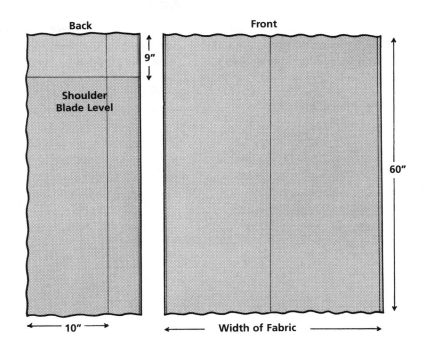

3 Draw the grainline for the front in the middle of the fabric piece.

4 Draw the grainline for the back panel 10 inches from the torn edge.

5 Draw the crossgrain for the back panel 9 inches from the top edge of the fabric.

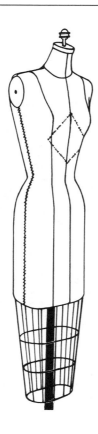

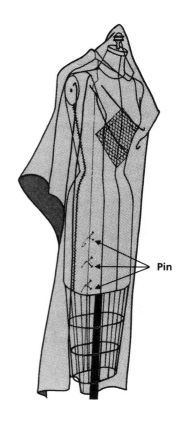

Pin

1 **Prepare the dress form.**

Refer to the garment design and note on the dress form the area of emphasis from which the drapes will radiate.

2 **Design and drape in the desired motif** (with all necessary seam allowances). Place this motif on the dress form. (This area was previously noted.)

3 **Place the grainline for the front dress.**

a. Position the grainline on the center of the princess panel on the dress form. Pin this grainline from the bottom of the dress form up to the hipline with at least three pins.

b. Allow all excess fabric to fall over the shoulder and the top of the dress form while draping the lower area of the design.

c. Drape and pin the fabric across center front of the dress form. Keep the grain of the fabric parallel to center front. Secure pins on the center front position with a couple more pins.

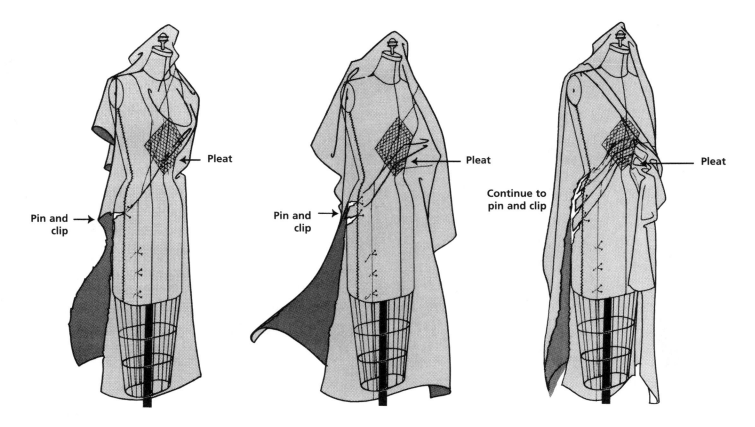

4 **Trim, clip, and then create first pleat.**

a. Clip the fabric approximately 2 inches from the side seam of the dress form. Clip fabric up from the bottom edge to where the lowest pleat will radiate.

b. Place a pin on the side seam at the point from where the lowest pleat will radiate.

c. Clip into the side seam to this pin.

d. Fold the first drape from the design motif to nothing at the pinned side seam.

NOTE: The grainline will start to angle toward the center front and become more exaggerated in this direction as the pleats are continued. Also, this first pleat is the most difficult of the pleating process. Be patient.

5 **Create the second pleat.**

a. Smooth the fabric up on the side seam at the point from which the second pleat will radiate.

b. Place a pin on the side seam at this point.

c. Clip into the side seam to this pin.

d. Fold the second drape from the design motif to nothing at the second pin on the side seam.

6 **Continue to pin, clip, and place the remainder of the pleats.** Pin and clip the side seam about every inch or so. At each pinning and clipping, fold a new drape, each radiating from the design motif. Also, continue to clip and trim the side seam past the waistline.

Trim parallel to
the grainline
into the motif

7 Smooth the fabric upward in a clockwise direction, flat over the armplate and shoulder, after the side seam area has been draped. Be careful not to stretch the fabric.

8 Trim away the excess fabric that is falling toward the back of the dress form, leaving approximately a 4-inch excess. Recheck the shoulder draped area.

9 Clip the fabric to the center of the design motif from the edge of the fabric near the grainline.

10 Trim the fabric around the design motif area that has been draped. Leave enough fabric for seam allowances and the upper bodice drape.

11 Create pleats at the design motif.

a. Use the excess fabric that falls below the bustline. Working left to right, pin and place pleats at the design motif stitchline. Allow each pleat to fall over the bust area and radiate to nothing over the bust.

b. Trim excess fabric at the design motif (one pleat at a time) as pleats are pinned and draped in place.

12 Trim the neckline area. Leave at least 2 inches of excess fabric for possible neckline shape changes and seam allowances.

13 Pin and drape in the desired neckline. Trim excess fabric at the neckline, shoulder, and side seam.

14 Mark key areas of the dress form to the fabric:

a. Shoulder.

b. Desired front armhole shape.

c. Desired front neckline shape.

d. Side seam.

e. Motif (stitchline) and pleats.

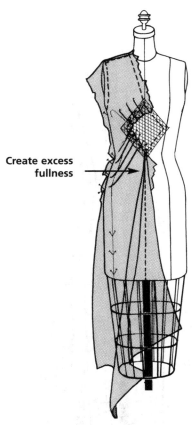

Create excess fullness →

15 **Create more fullness in the center front.** Clip, pin, and allow excess fabric to fall from nothing at the lowest section of the design motif and to flow as extra fullness to the hem/center front area. Transfer and draw in a new center front position of the dress form to the fabric drape.

NOTE: The skirt area will cascade more easily if the fabric is pulled up slightly at the design motif.

"Sculptured" Dress: Back Draping Steps

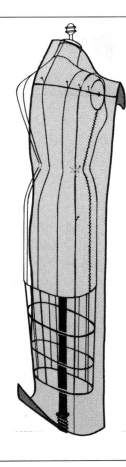

1 **Place the back crossgrain at the shoulder blade level.** Pin in place.

2 **Place the back straight grainline in the center of the back princess panel.** Pin in place. Pin the center back near the hem on the dress form rung.

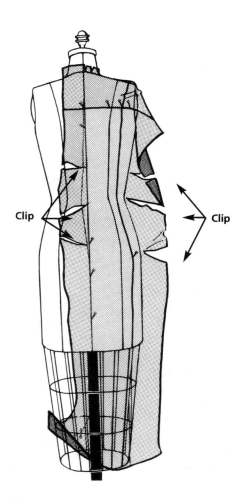

Clip

Clip

3 Trim, clip, and drape in the back neckline.

4 Drape the back shoulder area. Smooth the fabric over and past the shoulder seam and drape in the shoulder area.

5 Clip the waistline area at center back and the side seam. Also, clip once above and once below the waist area at the side seam and center back.

6 Smooth, shape, and pin a fitted center back seam. Approximately 3/4 of an inch will be smoothed out at the center back/waist area. The waist area will extend up and drape to nothing at the crossgrain line and down to nothing at the hipline.

7 Smooth, shape, and pin a fitted side seam. Finish draping the side seam by pinning the front side seam to the back side seam.

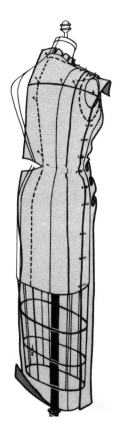

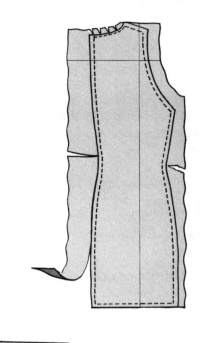

8 **Mark all key areas** of the dress form to the fabric:

a. Desired back neckline shape.

b. Shoulder seam: Match front shoulder seam.

c. Desired armhole shape.

d. Side seam.

9 **True up** motif, front, and back dress. Remove the fabric drape from the dress form. True up all seams, add seam allowances, and trim excess fabric. Pin the front drape to the back drape.

Return the finished drape to the dress form and check for accuracy, fit, and balance.

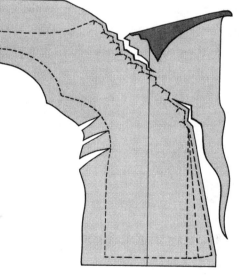

Bustier Designs

Designing the Bustier

The bustier is a form-fitting strapless bodice that fits snugly around the rib cage. A traditional bustier foundation garment has princess seams with a low-cut front and back neckline. Front princess seams are always used to create and support an extra tight fit at the princess seams and side seam. The back design is usually one piece allowing for either a center back zipper or an elasticized back area.

Many design variations for a bustier are possible, but there are three basic styles in which a bustier is designed:

• The **basic princess bodice** that finishes at the waistline with a skirt design.

• The **torso-length princess bodice** that finishes below the waistline at the high hip.

• The **empire princess bodice** that has a defined bust cup.

Draping the Bustier Foundation

Special boning and sewing techniques help support the foundation garment section of this classic strapless dress. This is referred to as a bustier foundation, which is sewn between the actual bustier design (layered between the outside of the garment and the lining). This foundation garment is always a princess seam bodice.

 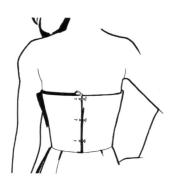

Bustier Designs: *Preparing the Fabric*

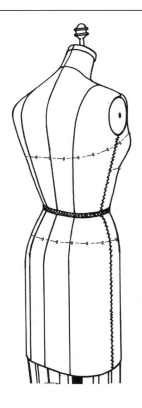

 Prepare the dress form.

Place pins or style tape on the dress form at the desired bustline. Remove the bust level (bra) tape from the dress form.

NOTE: If the bustier design includes a bra design or a torso-length design, the pins or style tape should be placed on the dress form to indicate these designs.

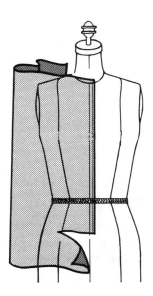

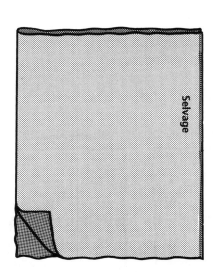

2 **Measure the length** (along the straight of grain) from the neckline to the waist and add 4 inches.

3 **Divide the fabric piece in half.** Fold the fabric from selvage to selvage and snip and tear the fabric piece in half lengthwise.

One piece will be used for the front panels, and the other piece will be used for the back panels.

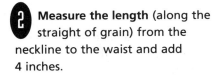

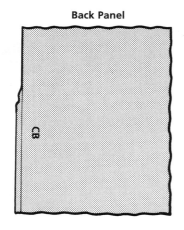
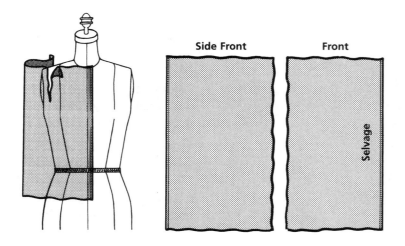
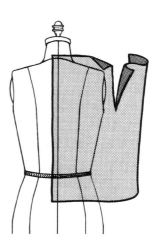

Side Front

Front

Selvage

4 **Measure the width** for the center front panel (along the crossgrain) from the center front of the dress form to the princess seam at the apex and add 4 inches.

Use the remaining front fabric piece for the side front panel.

5 **Measure the width for the back panel,** using the fabric piece prepared in Step 3. Measure from the center back of the dress form to the side seam and add 4 inches. Snip and tear the fabric at this width.

Back Panel

Side Front Panel

Front Panel

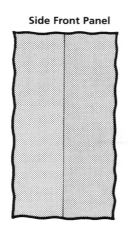
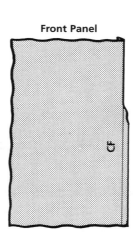

CB

CF

6 **Draw the grainlines for the fabric pieces.**

a. Draw the grainline for the center front panel 1 inch from the torn edge and press under.

b. Draw the grainline for the side front panel at the center of the fabric piece.

c. Draw the grainline for the back panel 1 inch from the torn edge and press under.

Bustier Designs: *Draping Steps*

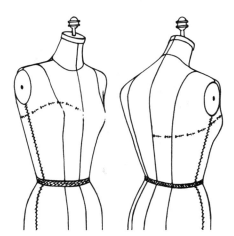

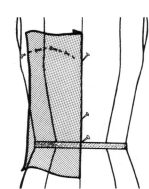

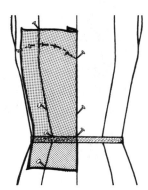

 Prepare the dress form.

Place pins on the dress form at the desired bustline. Remove the bust level (bra) tape from the dress form.

2 **Pin the center front grainline fold** of the fabric to the center front position of the dress form. The fabric piece should extend at least 3 inches above the styled bustline and at least 3 inches below the waistline seam.

3 **Drape to the princess seam.** Smooth the fabric across the dress form from center front to just past the princess seam, and pin.

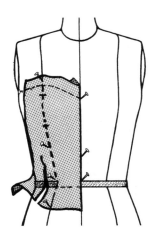

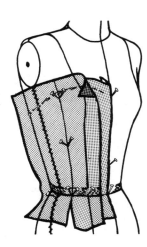

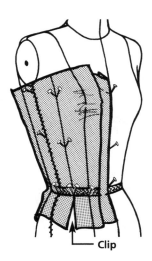

Clip

4 **Mark all key areas** of the dress form on the center front panel:

a. Bustline styled area.

b. Princess seam and style line notches: 1 1/2 inches above and below apex.

c. Waistline.

Trim excess fabric, allowing for seam allowances.

5 **Pin the grainline of the side front panel** to the center of the princess panel on the dress form. The side front panel should extend at least 3 inches above the styled bustline and at least 3 inches below the waistline seam.

6 **Clip and drape the waistline.**

a. Clip the waistline fabric at the center of the front princess panel up to the bottom of the waist seam tape.

b. Drape and smooth the waistline in place. Smooth the fabric across the waistline from the grainline to the side seam. Also, smooth the waistline from the grainline to the princess seam.

Dresses

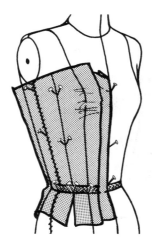

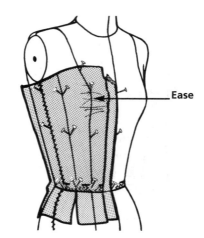

Ease

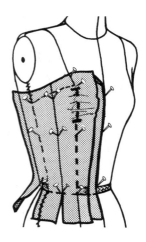

7 Smooth and pin the side seam in place. From the grainline of the side front panel, smooth the fabric past the side seam of the dress form. Do not allow the grainline to slip out of position. Pin the side seam in place.

8 Smooth and pin the princess seam in place. From the grainline of the side front panel, smooth the fabric past the princess seam of the dress form. Do not allow the grainline to slip out of position. Pin the princess seam in place.

9 Mark all key areas of the dress form to the side front panel:

a. Bustline styled area.

b. Princess seam and style line notches: Match to center front panel notches.

c. Waistline.

d. Side seam.

Trim excess fabric, allowing for seam allowances.

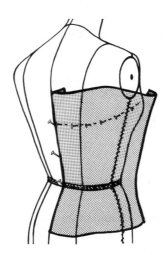

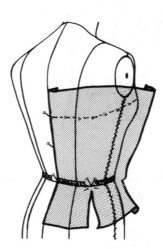

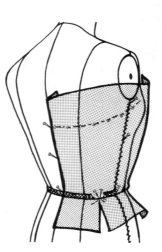

10 Pin the center back grainline fold of the fabric to the center back position of the dress form. The center back panel should extend at least 3 inches above the styled bustline and at least 3 inches below the waistline seam.

11 Clip the fabric at the center of the back princess panel up to the bottom of the waist tape. Smooth the fabric across the waistline tape and pin at the side seam/waist.

12 Pin the side seam in place. Smooth the fabric past the side seam. Be careful not to distort the grain of the fabric.

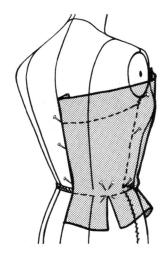

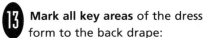

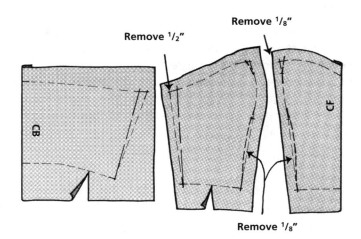

Remove ¹/₂″

Remove ¹/₈″

Remove ¹/₈″

13 **Mark all key areas** of the dress form to the back drape:

a. **Styled bustline.**

b. **Waistline.**

c. **Side seam.**

14 **True up all seams.** Remove the entire drape from the dress form and true up all seams.

a. To ensure a well-fitted bustline, readjust the princess seam by eliminating 1/8 inch above and below the notches. Blend in a new princess seam.

b. To ensure a secure underarm fit, eliminate 1/2 inch at both the front and back side seam bustline area. Blend this new side down to the waistline.

Draping Variation for Torso Length and/or Bra Design

Follow the same princess drape as illustrated on the previous pages.

• **For the torso-length design:** You will need to clip the waistline of the seam allowance at the princess seams and the side seams.

• **For the bra design:** You will need to shape a lower and upper cup as illustrated, leaving a seam at the bustline level. This seam will be shaped to conform to the bust cup fit of the design.

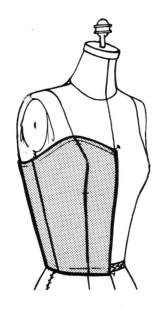

15 **Add seam allowances and trim excess fabric.** Match the notches and pin the fabric pieces together. Return the fabric drape to the dress form and check for accuracy, fit, and balance.

NOTE: It is advisable to collapse the shoulders of the dress form to check this final drape.

This drape should be transferred to pattern paper. The pattern will be used as a guide for the foundation garment and the lining. In future references, this princess bodice will be referred to as the **bustier pattern.**

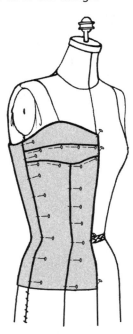

Dresses

Bustier Designs: Draping the Outside Garment Design

The outside bustier design must be draped separately from the foundation garment *if the outside design does not include a princess seam.* The outside bustier design could be darted, ruffled, pleated, layered, or gathered to create a sculptured bustier design that does not include a princess seam. Depending upon the fabric and the style of the outside design, the bustier may be featured in a shapely seamed cocktail dress, a sportive day dress, or a slim luxurious evening gown.

Illustrated here are design variations of bustier fashions finished over a bustier foundation. Note the unique and sumptuous quality that a finished bustier design offers.

1 **Drape the outside garment design.** Refer to the desired bustier design (samples illustrated here) as the guide for creating the outside garment design.

NOTE: The neckline bustline shape must be the same shape as the foundation bustier pattern neckline. However, within this shape, the bustier may be pleated, tucked, ruffled, or gathered. Also, the princess seams are not mandatory, but the side seams are necessary.

2 **Mark key areas** and remove the fabric from the dress form.

3 **True up,** add seam allowances, and trim excess fabric.

4 **Sew the garment design together,** leaving an opening at the center back (this is usually for a zipper).

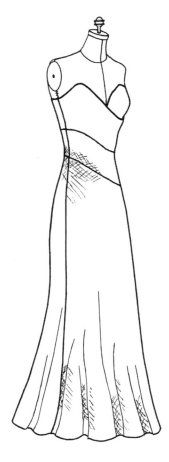

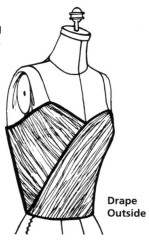

Drape Outside

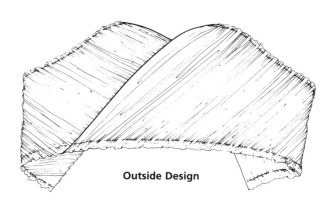

Outside Design

In addition to draping the bustier design, bustier-styled dresses need special attention for the sewing techniques. A bustier foundation is necessary to correctly add boning.

Boning is added in the princess and side seams to help keep the bodice on the body and ensure the fit and wearability of the garment. The boned foundation is sewn between the outside design of the garment and a prepared lining. Cut a copy of the bustier pattern out of strong, woven fabric, such as kettle cloth or pocketing fabric.

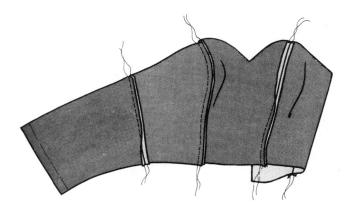

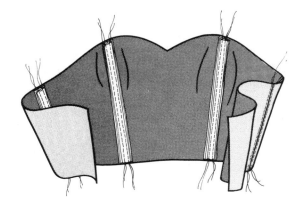

1 **Sew the bustier foundation pieces together.** This includes the princess seams and the side seams, leaving an opening at the center back seam. Press all seam allowances open.

2 **Pin strips of boning to each princess seam and side seam.** The strips of boning should lie on the wrong side of the garment, covering the seams.

NOTE: The boned ends of each strip should be trimmed (approximately 1/2 inch) and the excess fabric at each end should be turned over the boned edges.

3 **Stitch the boning to the princess seams and side seams,** using a zipper foot.

Variations

As more strength or support is needed, boning may be placed and attached in a variety of areas, for example, across the side bust panel from top to bottom.

Boning Variation for Torso Length and/or Bra Design

The design variations will require one of the following versions of the bustier foundation shape:

- **For the torso-length design:** Stitch the boning to the princess seams and side seams, using a zipper foot or cording foot.

- **For additional waistline support:** Place and stitch an inside belting at the waistline. This will secure the waist and give extra support within the garment. You will need to clip the waistline of the seam allowance at the princess seams and the side seams.

- **For the bra design:**
  1. Trace the bra section of the pattern onto pattern paper. Do not add any seam allowances. Cut the bra pattern pieces out of desired padding fabric.
  2. Zig-zag stitch the bra pieces together. Place the bra on the inside of the garment 1 inch from the top neckline shape. Contour the bra into the existing foundation garment and stitch close to the edge of the bra.

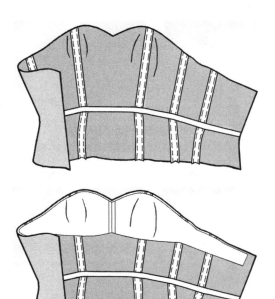

Bustier Designs: *Lining*

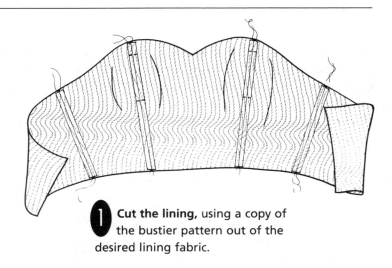

Lining the bustier is necessary to cleanly finish all outer edges of the bustier bodice. It also adds strength to the overall bodice and hides the foundation garment. The lining is the same as the foundation garment but has no boning and is made out of a fabric of your choice—usually a lighter-weight fabric than the garment.

1 **Cut the lining,** using a copy of the bustier pattern out of the desired lining fabric.

2 **Sew all lining pieces together,** leaving an opening at the center back. Press all seam allowances open.

Bustier Designs: *Sewing Steps*

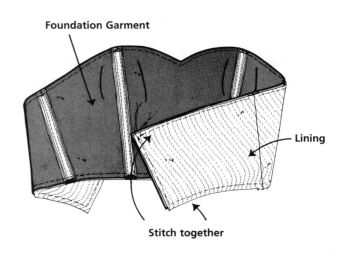

Foundation Garment

Lining

Stitch together

1 **Pin the foundation garment to the wrong side of the lining.** Stitch all outer edges together so that the lining and the foundation garment will act as one.

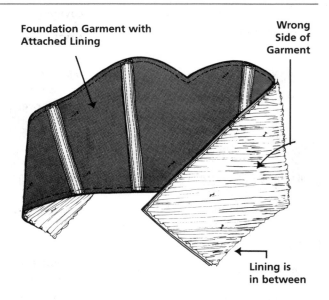

Foundation Garment with Attached Lining

Wrong Side of Garment

Lining is in between

2 **Place the lining,** with the attached foundation garment, to the outside garment design, matching correct sides.

3 **Sew the neckline seams together,** using a 1/4-inch seam allowance.

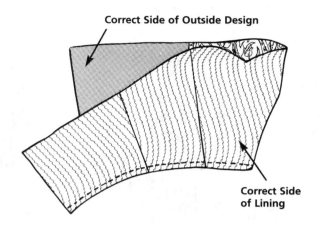

Correct Side of Outside Design

Correct Side of Lining

4 **Understitch all the layers of the seam allowance to the lining.** Understitching is accomplished by first placing the lining (with the attached foundation garment) flat. Then fold the entire neckline seam allowance to the lining side and stitch close to the seam edge.

5 **Turn the garment pieces** so the correct side of the lining and the garment design are facing out.

NOTE: Raw edges will remain at the center back seams and the waistline seams.

6 **Attach the skirt to the waistline seam and set in the zipper.** The bustier garment is now ready to be attached to the desired skirt design. Sew the skirt waist seam to the bustier waist seam.

Pin and sew in a zipper that will extend at least 7 inches into the skirt seam and the center back seam.

**Front and Back Bodice Yoke
with Circular Bodice**

**Front and Back Bodice Yoke
with Pleated Bodice**

A separate front and back bodice yoke crosses the shoulders in the front and the back. The front and back yokes are attached by a shoulder seam, which allows the front and back yoke pieces to maintain a straight of grain at both the front and back seams.

Often the lower section of the garment will be designed with gores, gathers, pleats, or circular shapes sewn to the yoke.

Instructions are provided in these projects for sewing separate front and back bodice yokes into a circular and a pleated bodice. To create gathers rather than pleats, follow the same draping steps for pleats, but drape in fullness rather than pleats.

Separate Front and Back Bodice Yokes:
Preparing the Fabric

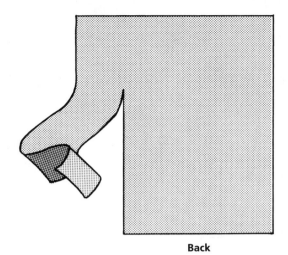

Back

Front

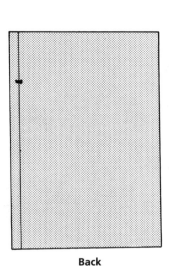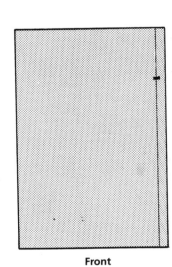

Back

Front

1 Measure the length for the front and back yokes (along the straight of grain) from the neckband to the yoke style line. Add 3 inches. Snip and tear the fabric at this length.

2 Measure the width for the front and back yokes (along the crossgrain) from the center front to the armhole. Add 3 inches. Snip and tear the fabric at this width.

3 Draw a center front and center back grainline 1 inch from the torn edge on the prepared yoke piece and press under.

4 Measure down on the grainline 4 inches. Crossmark this measurement on the prepared front and back yoke pieces.

Separate Front and Back Bodice Yokes:
Draping Steps

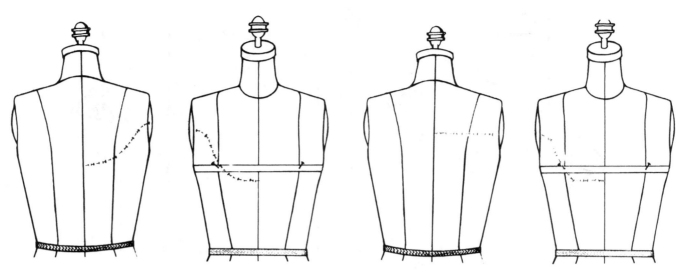

 Prepare the dress form.

Referring to the design sketch, pin the desired yoke style line on the dress form front and back.

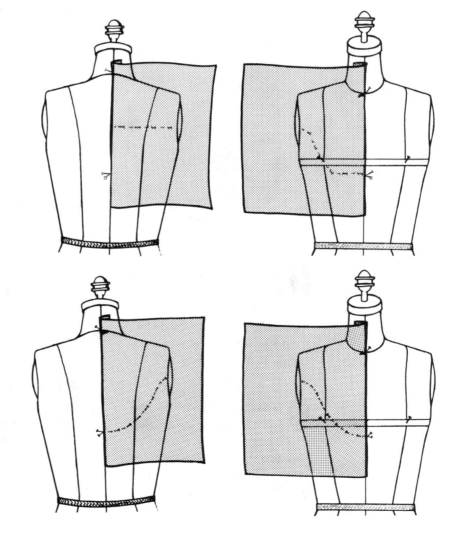

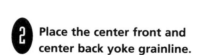 **Place the center front and center back yoke grainline.**

a. Place the center front grainline fold of the front yoke piece to the center front position of the dress form. Align the center front neckline crossmark of the yoke to the center front neckline position of the dress form.

b. Place the center back grainline fold of the back yoke piece to the center back position of the dress form. Align the center back neckline crossmark of the yoke to the center back neckline position of the dress form.

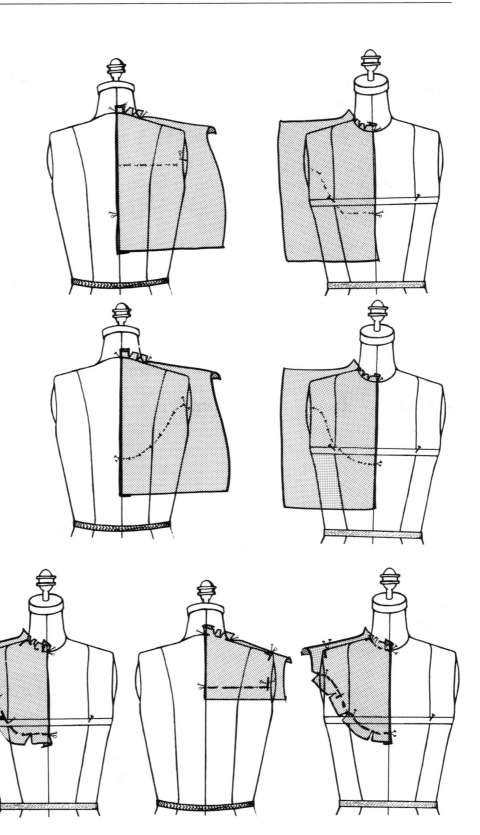

3 Clip, smooth, and pin the front and back neckline of the yoke pieces.

4 Smooth the yoke fabric over and past the shoulder seam of the dress form. Match the front shoulder seam to the back shoulder seam.

5 Smooth the yoke fabric past the desired yoke style line for both the front and back. Clip at the style line if necessary. Pin in place.

6 Mark all key areas of the dress form to the front and back yoke fabric pieces:

a. Neckline: Lightly mark.

b. Shoulder seam and shoulder ridge.

c. Yoke style line: Lightly mark.

d. Yoke style line notches: Make one for the front and two for the back.

7 **True up all seams.** Remove the yoke drape from the dress form, true up all seams, add seam allowances, and trim excess fabric. Return the yoke to the dress form and check for accuracy, fit, and balance. The chosen bodice style should be draped with the trued-up yoke on the dress form.

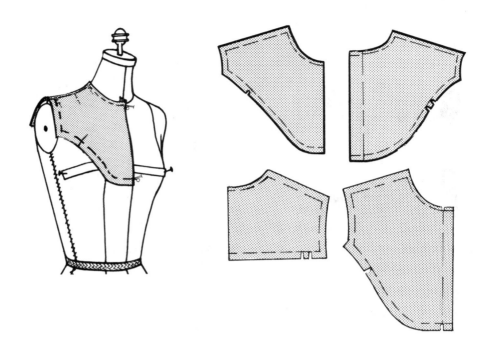

Pleated Bodice: *Preparing the Fabric*

1 **Measure the length desired for a front and back blouse.** Measure the length (along the straight of grain) from the neckband to the desired length and add a few inches. Snip and tear the fabric at this desired length.

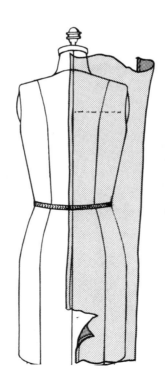
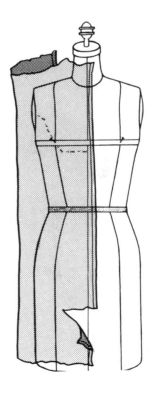

2 **Divide the fabric piece in half.** Fold the fabric from selvage to selvage. Snip and tear the piece in half lengthwise.

One piece will be used for the bodice front, and the other piece will be used for the bodice back.

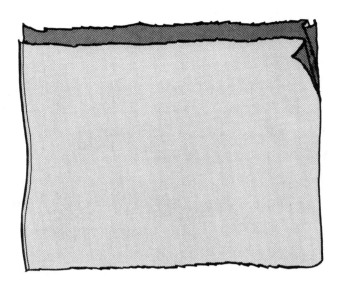

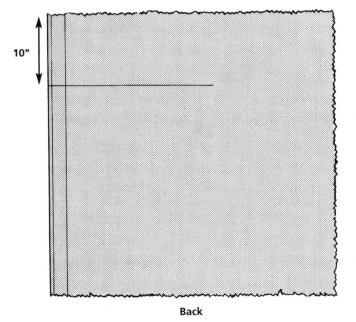

Back

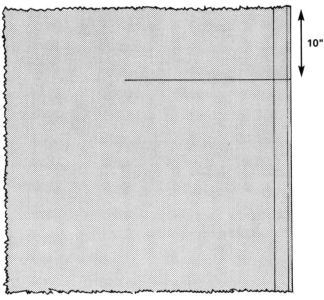

Front

3 **Draw the center front and center back grainlines** on the fabric 1 inch from the torn edge and press under.

4 **Draw the crossgrain for the front and back bodice fabric pieces** 10 inches from the top of the fabric edge. Draw the crossgrain across the fabric piece for the front bustline level and the back at the shoulder blade level.

Pleated Bodice: Draping Steps

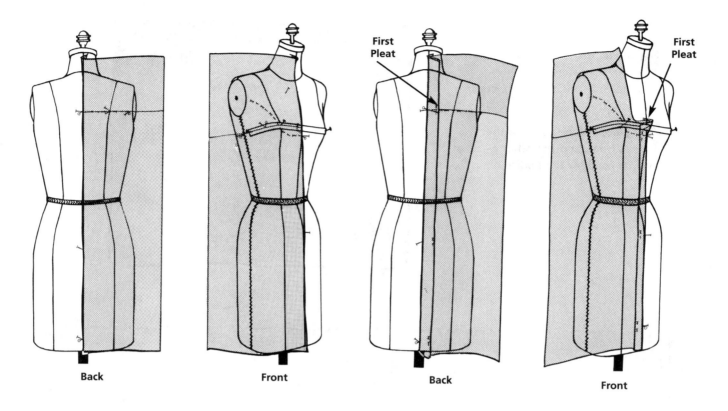

Back

Front

First
Pleat

Back

First
Pleat

Front

❶ Pin the grainlines to the dress form.

a. Pin the center front grainline fold of the bodice to the center front position of the dress form.

b. Pin the center back grainline fold of the bodice to the center back position of the dress form.

❷ Align and drape the crossgrain.

a. For the front drape, align the crossgrain at the bustline level. Allow the fabric to hang smoothly and evenly from the bust level. Pin at the side seam.

b. For the back drape, align the crossgrain at the shoulder blade level. Allow the fabric to hang smoothly and evenly from the shoulder blade level. Pin at the side seam.

❸ Drape the front bodice pleats.

a. Drape the desired number of pleats at the bust level of the bodice. Be sure to leave approximately a 3/4-inch space from each pleat.

b. Pin each pleat straight up and down and parallel from center front.

NOTE: The width of the pleat should be two times the desired final width of the pleat. Example: 1 1/2 inches will yield a 3/4-inch pleat.

❹ Drape the back bodice pleats.

a. Drape the desired number of pleats at the back shoulder blade level of the blouse. Be sure to leave about a 3/4-inch space from each pleat.

b. Pin each pleat straight up and down and parallel to center back.

NOTE: The width of the pleat should be two times the desired final width of the pleat. Example: 1 1/2 inches will yield a 3/4-inch pleat.

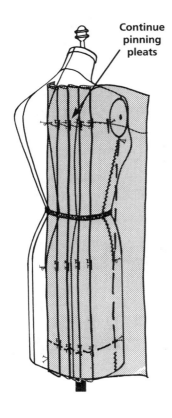

Continue
pinning
pleats

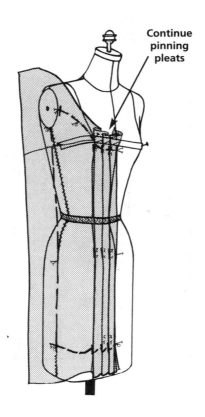

Continue
pinning
pleats

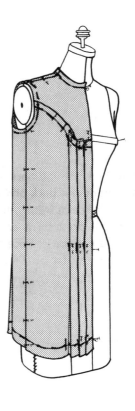

5 **Drape the remainder of the front bodice.**

a. Pin the pleats at the front style line.

b. Pin the remainder of the front and back yoke. Keeping the crossgrain in place at the bust level, continue to drape the remainder of the front yoke style. The blouse should remain parallel to center front. The side seam should remain parallel to center front.

c. Trim away the excess fabric around the front yoke.

6 **Drape the remainder of the back bodice.**

a. Pin the pleats at the back style line.

b. Pin the remainder of the back yoke. Keeping the crossgrain in

place at the shoulder blade level, continue to drape the remainder of the back yoke style. The bodice should remain parallel to center back. The side seam should remain parallel to center back.

c. Trim away the excess fabric around the back yoke.

7 **Mark all key areas** from the dress form to the fabric:

a. Bodice style seam: This will match the yoke style line seam.

b. Matching notches: Match to the yoke notches.

c. Bottom of armplate at the side seam.

d. Side seam.

e. Hem: Follow the bottom of the dress form as a guide.

8 **True up the front and back bodice drape.** Remove the front and back bodice drape from the dress form. True up all seams, add seam allowances, and trim excess fabric.

a. When trueing the front armhole: Pin the front bodice style line to the front yoke style line. Then true up the armhole.

b. When trueing the back armhole: Pin the back bodice style line to the back yoke style line. Then true up the armhole.

9 **Pin the front and back yoke to the front and back bodices.** Pin the side seams, return the drape to the dress form, and check the fit and balance. If necessary, make corrections.

Notes

Circular Bodice: Preparing the Fabric

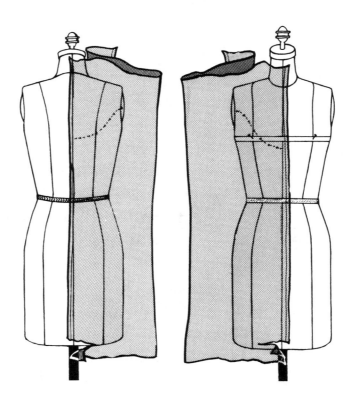

1 **Measure the length desired for a front and back bodice.** Measure the length (along the straight of grain) from the neckband to the desired length and add a few inches. Snip and tear the fabric at this desired length.

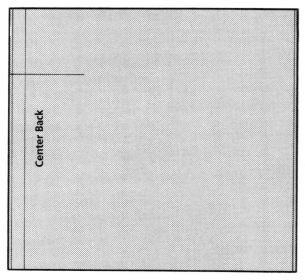

Back

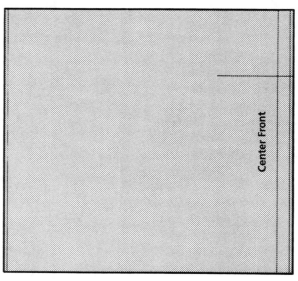

Front

2 **Use the entire width of the fabric pieces for the front and back circular bodice drape.**

3 **Draw the grainline for the front and back bodice fabric pieces** 1 inch from the selvage.

4 **Draw the crossgrain for the front and back bodice fabric pieces** 10 inches from the top of the fabric edge. Draw the crossgrain halfway across the fabric piece for the front bustline level and the back at the shoulder blade level.

Circular Bodice: Draping Steps

1 **Pin the center front/center back grainline fold** of the bodice on the center front/center back of the dress form.

2 **Align and drape the crossgrain.**

a. For the front drape, align the crossgrain at the bustline level. Allow the fabric to hang smoothly and evenly from the bust level. Pin at the side seam.

b. For the back drape, align the crossgrain at the shoulder blade level. Allow the fabric to hang smoothly and evenly from the shoulder blade level. Pin at the side seam.

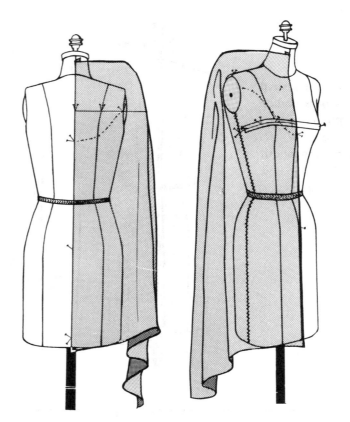

3 **Smooth, clip, and pin the front and back style line seam.** Approximately 2 inches from center front or center back, clip the fabric from the top edge down to the yoke style seam. Pin the bodice style seam to the yoke style line seam at the clip.

4 **Pivot the fabric down** from the style seam, forming a nice flowing flare. Place another pin on the bodice style seam to the yoke style seam, maintaining this flare.

5 **Smooth, clip, pin, and pivot about 1 inch from the first flare.** At the bodice style line seam, smooth the fabric toward the side seam. Clip, pin, and pivot the front and back style line seam at this position, forming a second flare.

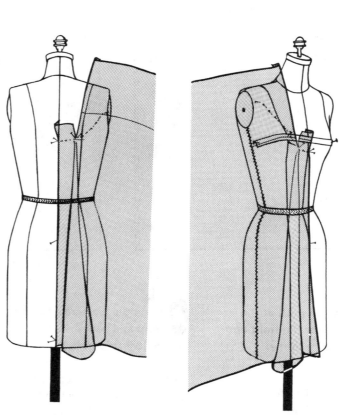

6 **Continue to smooth, clip, pin, and pivot** the front and back style line seam where each flare is desired.

7 **Mark all key areas** from the dress form to the fabric:

a. Bodice style seam: This will match the yoke style line seam.

b. Matching notches: Match to the yoke notches.

c. Bottom of armplate at the side seam.

d. Side seam.

e. Hem: Follow the bottom of the dress form as a guide.

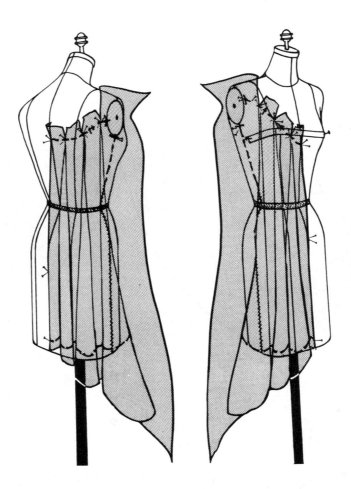

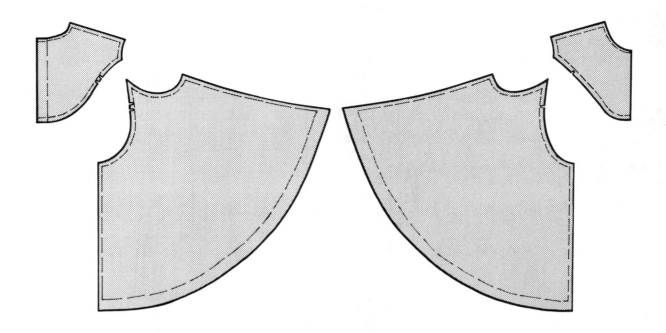

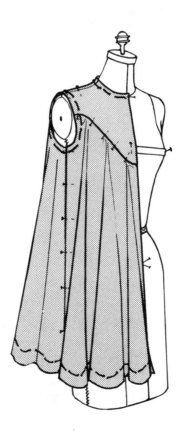

8 True up the front and back bodice drape. Remove the front and back bodice drape from the dress form. True up all seams, add seam allowances, and trim excess fabric.

a. When trueing the front armhole: Pin the front bodice style line to the front yoke style line. Then true up the armhole.

b. When trueing the back armhole: Pin the back bodice style line to the back yoke style line. Then true up the armhole.

9 Pin the front and back yoke to the front and back bodices. Pin the side seams. Return the drape to the dress form. Check the fit and balance. Make all necessary corrections.

Waist Midriff Dress

A waist midriff design has a horizontal seam between the bust and the waistline. A waist midriff traditionally fits snugly under the slope of the bust while maintaining the shape of the waistline and controlling the fit of the remainder of the bodice design. Usually, the midriff is simply styled parallel to the waistline or shaped into any pointed or curved shape desired.

Waist Midriff Dress: Preparing the Midriff Fabric

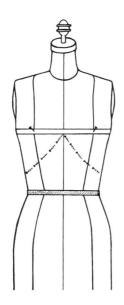
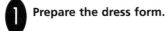

1 **Prepare the dress form.**

Pin the desired midriff style line on the dress form front and back.

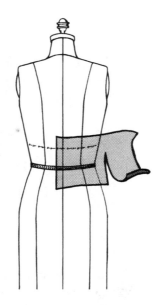

2 **Measure the length for the front and back midriff** (along the straight of grain) from the top of the midriff to the waistline and add 6 inches. Snip and tear the fabric at this length.

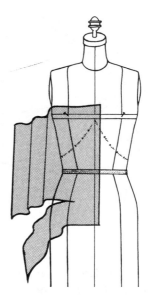

3 **Measure the width for the front and back midriff** (along the crossgrain) from the center front to the side seam and add 3 inches. Snip and tear the fabric at this width.

4 **Draw center front and center back grainlines** 1 inch from the torn edge on the prepared midriff pieces and press under.

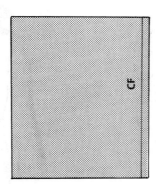

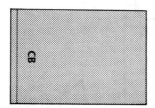

Waist Midriff Dress: Preparing the Bodice Fabric

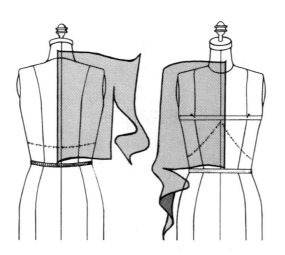

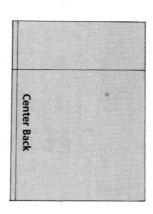

Center Back

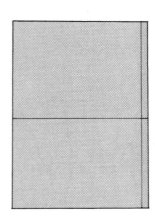

1 **Measure the length and width desired for the front and back bodice** and add a few inches. Snip and tear the fabric the desired length and width.

2 **Draw the straight of grainlines and crossgrains for the front and back bodice fabric pieces.**

a. Draw the grainline on the front and back bodice 1 inch from the torn edge and press under.

b. Draw the crossgrain for the front at the bustline level and the crossgrain for the back at the shoulder blade level.

For more detailed instructions, refer to Basic Bodice, pages 47–49.

Waist Midriff Dress: Midriff Draping Steps

1 Pin the center front grainline of the midriff to the center front position of the dress form. Align the fabric so it extends above and below the desired midriff section.

2 Pin the center back grainline of the midriff to the center back position of the dress form. Align the fabric so it extends above and below the desired midriff section.

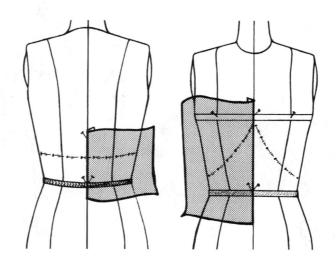

3 Drape the front and back midriff waistline. Clip the fabric at the front and back waistline. Smooth the fabric across the waistline tape toward the side seam.

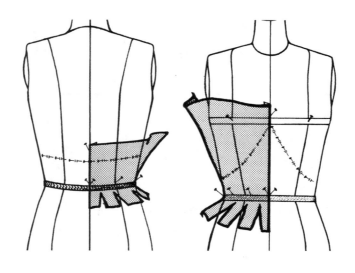

4 Drape the front and back midriff style line. Clip the fabric at the front and back style line. Smooth the fabric across the style line seam toward the side seam.

5 Mark all key areas of the dress form to the midriff fabric:

a. Midriff style line.

b. Side seam.

c. Waistline.

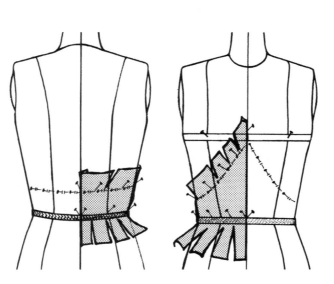

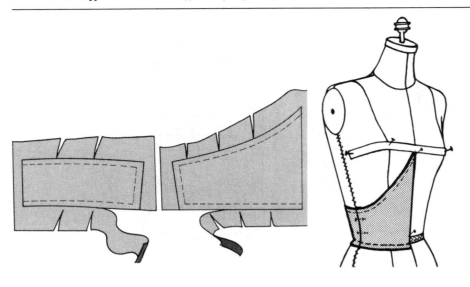

6 **True up all seams.** Remove the front and back midriff drape from the dress form. True up all seams, add seam allowances, and trim excess fabric. Pin the front side seam to the back side seam. Return the midriff to the dress form and check for accuracy.

Notes

Waist Midriff Dress: Bodice Draping Steps

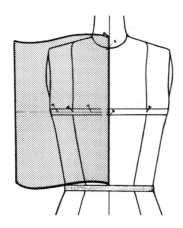

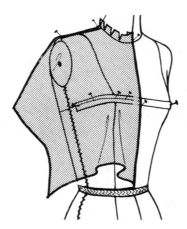

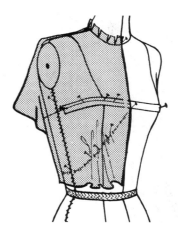

1 Pin the center front grainline of the bodice to the center front position of the dress form. Align the crossgrain at the bustline level. Pin in place.

2 Trim, clip, smooth, and pin the front bodice neckline.

3 Smooth and pin the fabric over the shoulder and side seam of the dress form. Drape in a counterclockwise direction, smoothing the fabric over shoulder and the side seam, allowing all fabric excess to fall below the bust. Pin the shoulder and the side seam.

4 Drape the front bodice into the midriff style line. With the excess fabric falling underneath the bust area, evenly distribute and pin all fullness at the midriff style line below the bust area. Drape the remainder of the bodice smoothly into the midriff.

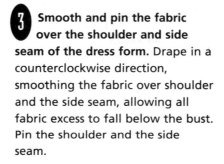

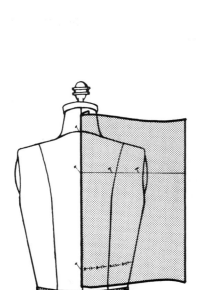

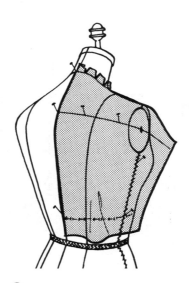

5 Drape the back bodice. Pin the center back grainline of the back bodice to the center back of the dress form.

6 Align and pin the crossgrain at the shoulder blade level of the dress form.

7 Trim, clip, smooth, and pin the back bodice neckline.

8 Smooth and pin the fabric over the shoulder and side seam of the dress form. Pin in place. Some excess fullness will fall at the midriff seam in the middle of the back. This excess fullness will be converted into gathers.

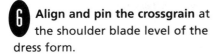

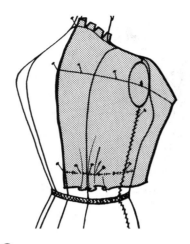

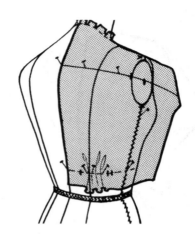

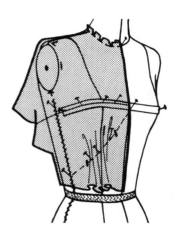

9 Drape the back bodice into the back midriff style line. Evenly distribute and pin all fullness at the midriff style line. Pin the entire midriff style line.

10 Mark all key areas of the dress form to the front and back drape:

a. Front and back neckline.

b. Shoulder seams.

c. Armplate:
 • Shoulder ridge
 • Center and screw level
 • Bottom and side seam

d. Side seams.

e. Midriff style line and style line notches.

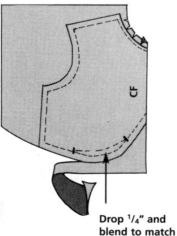

Drop ¹/₄" and blend to match

11 True up all seams. Remove the drape (front, back, and midriffs) from the dress form. True up all seams, add seam allowances, and trim excess fabric.

NOTE: The front bodice style line, between the midriff notches, may need to be dropped 1/4 inch. This allows the bodice drape to give the illusion of a fuller bust.

12 Pin the midriff and bodice fabric pieces together and return to the dress form. Check for accuracy, fit, and balance. Make any necessary corrections.

Select the desired skirt design from Chapter 12.

Chapter Eighteen

Knits

Objectives

By studying the various draping steps in this chapter, the designer should be able to:

• Mold and manipulate knit fabric on the dress form.

• Drape the knit fabric close to the body shape without the need for darts or complex seaming construction.

• Maintain the grain of knit fabric to create a smooth design without overworking the fabric.

• Explore the fit and shape of the finished pattern with regard to the different degrees of stretch in the knit fabric.

• Handle pliable fabrics to define a design and determine the most flattering style for the figure.

• True up and check the results of the draping process and its relationship to fit, hang, balance, and proportion.

Basic Knit Bodice/Dress

The basic knit bodice/dress is a tight-fitting garment that offers crisp, close-to-the-body comfort, without the need for darts or complex seaming construction. A wide variety of knit fabrics is available with different degrees of stretch. Therefore, the degree of stretch must be considered before designing and draping a knit garment. The newest double knits may be cut to look tailored for suits and dresses, casual for shirts and sportswear, or glamorous with added glitter for evening wear. The shoulders may become extreme, with the use of shoulder pads, or discreet, as the design demands. A knit garment may be fabricated, colored, and shaped to specifically suit a mood, occasion, or environment.

The fitted knit bodice sloper is a hip-length pattern that is developed by draping knit fabric of your choice into a fitted body shape. A variety of necklines, sleeve lengths, style lines, and hem lengths can easily be adapted to this foundation pattern.

NOTE: The stretch quality of the sample fabric should be the same as the stretch quality for the desired finished garment.

1 **Measure the length** for the front and back from the neckband on the dress form to the desired length of the garment. Add 2 inches. Cut the fabric at this length.

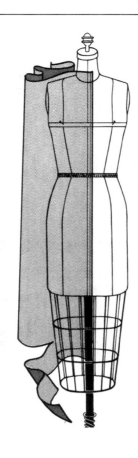

2 **Measure the width** for both the front and back from the center of the dress form to the side seam. Add 3 inches. Cut the fabric at this width.

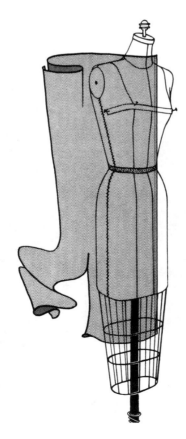

3 **Draw the center front and center back lines** for the front and back bodice 1 inch from the edge. Keep fabric pieces flat.

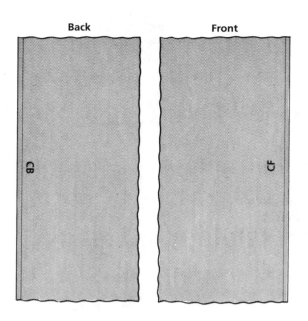

4 **Draw the front crossgrain** 12 inches from the top edge of the fabric.

5 **Draw the back crossgrain** 9 inches from the top edge of the fabric.

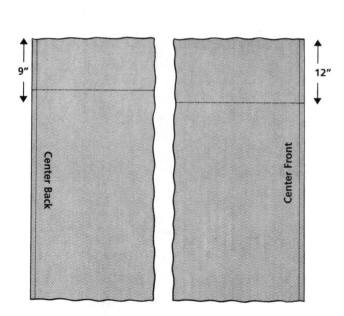

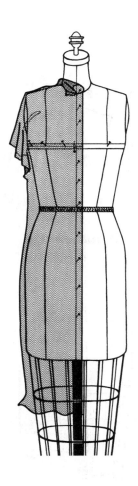

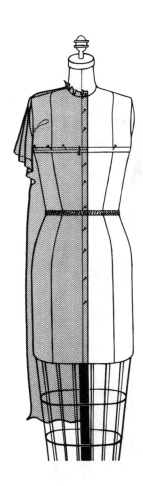

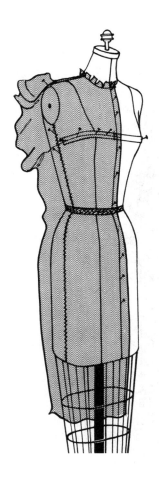

1 **Pin the center front line** of the fabric on the center front position of the dress form.

2 **Align the crossgrain** at the bust level. Pin at frequent intervals—approximately every 2 inches.

3 **Drape the front neckline.** Trim and clip the front neckline. Smooth the fabric around the neckline past the shoulder seam of the dress form.

4 **Drape the front shoulder seam and the front armhole areas.**

a. Smooth the fabric up and over the shoulder seam of the dress form.

b. Smooth all excess fabric over the armhole ridge and flat past the armplate.

NOTE: Be sure to drape out all excess ease.

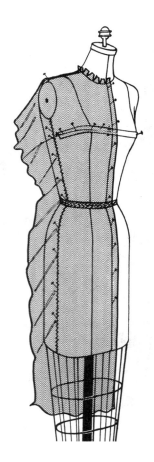 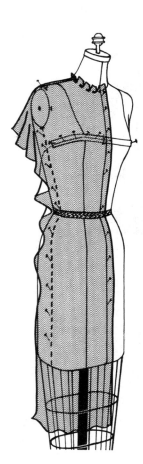 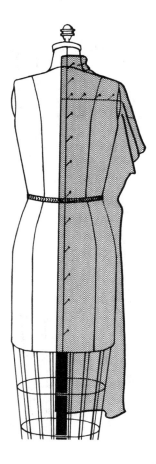

5 **Drape the front bodice side seam.** Smooth all excess fabric past the side seam at the crossgrain and underneath the armplate. Continue to smooth the side seam into the side seam shape desired.

6 **Mark all key areas** of the dress form to the fabric:

a. Front neckline.

b. Armplate:
  • Top at shoulder seam ridge
  • Middle at screw level
  • Crossmark bottom at side seam.

c. Front side seam.

d. Hem.

7 **Pin the center back line** of the fabric on the center back position of the dress form.

8 **Align the crossgrain at the shoulder blade level.** Pin at frequent intervals—approximately every 2 inches.

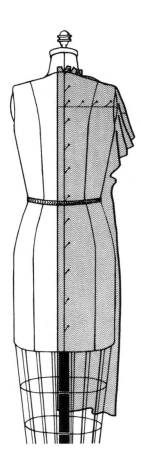

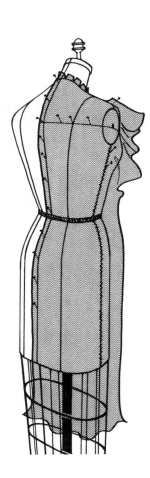

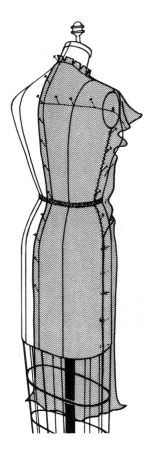

9 Drape the back neckline. Trim and clip the neckline. Smooth the fabric around the neckline past the shoulder seam of the dress form.

10 Drape the back shoulder seam and back armhole areas. Smooth the fabric up and over the shoulder seam of the dress form. Smooth all excess fabric past the side seam at the crossgrain and underneath the armplate.

11 Drape the back bodice side seam. Continue to smooth the side seam into the shape desired. Match and pin the front side seam to the back side seam.

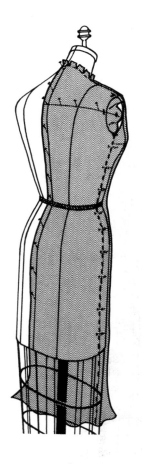
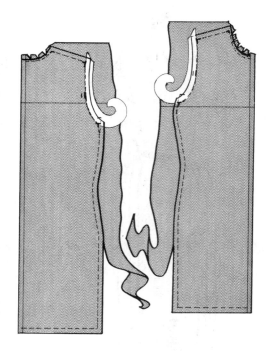
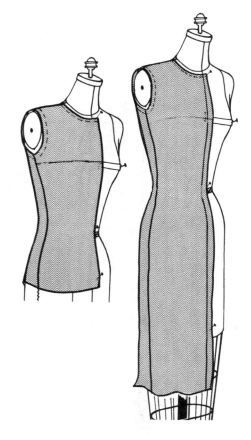

12 Mark all key areas of the dress form to the fabric:

a. Back neckline.

b. Shoulder seams.

c. Armplate:
- Top at shoulder seam ridge
- Middle at screw level
- Bottom at side seam

d. Back side seam.

e. Hem.

13 True up all lines. Remove the knit drape from the dress form and true up all lines. True up the armhole by dropping the side seam position 1 inch and removing 1/4 inch from the dropped side seam/armhole corner. Add seam allowances and trim the excess fabric.

NOTE: The technique of removing 1/4 inch at the side seam/armhole corner ensures that a smooth, nongapping armhole is created.

NOTE: For an armhole that is balanced front and back, measure the armhole distances. Either the armhole distances should be equal in length or the back should be slightly longer.

14 Sew together the front and back shoulder seams. Insert a piece of twill tape at the shoulder seam, using a ball needle.

15 Sew together the front and back side seams. Using a ball needle, sew the seam with a "stretch and sew" technique.

16 Place the knit drape on the dress form and check for accuracy, fit, and balance.

NOTE: For a knit top, choose the desired length and cut the drape at that length.

Basic Knit Sleeve

numbers (1/8- or 1/4-inch increments) in the direction with less stretch.

Knit sleeves, such as the muscle sleeve or the cap sleeve, can be developed from a basic knit sleeve pattern. The basic knit sleeve pattern can be developed from the basic sleeve pattern, steps 1 through 13, pages 120–123. However, use measurements provided in the chart. The front and back cap shapes will remain the same, because the armhole shapes are so similar. An elbow dart is not required in knit sleeves.

The basic knit sleeve is specially developed to fit into the smaller armhole created in a knit bodice. Traditional sportswear made from knit fabrics requires a knit sleeve, unless the design is sleeveless.

The measurements used for this sleeve are for maximum stretch for double- or single-knit fabrics and fit into a basic knitted bodice armhole. Therefore, when using a fabric with less stretch, use slightly larger

Basic Knit Sleeve Measurement Chart

Before you draft the basic knit sleeve, study the following four important measurements.

1. Overarm length (distance from the shoulder to the wrist)

Size	8	10
Overarm length	22 3/4"	23"

2. Cap height (remaining distance from the armpit to the shoulder)

Size	8	10
Cap height	5 1/4"	5 3/8"

3. Elbow circumference (measurement around the elbow plus 2 inches of ease)

Size	8	10
Elbow circumference	4 1/4"	4 3/8"

4. Bicep circumference (measurement around the upper arm plus 2 inches of ease)

Size	8	10
Bicep circumference	5 1/4"	5 3/8"

NOTE: Drafting a size 8 or 10 sleeve will provide a guide to create and drape a correct sleeve cap for knit fabrics. Refer to step 4, page 398, for detailed instructions.

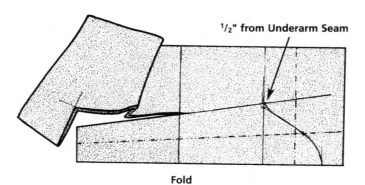

¹/₂" from Underarm Seam

Fold

The basic knit sleeve is developed from the basic sleeve, pages 120–124. However, refer to chart, page 397, for measurements.

1 When preparing the cap shape, **crossmark the bicep line** 1/2 inch in from the underarm seamline. An elbow dart is not required.

2 **Determine the sleeve cap notches** and sleeve cap distance. Pivot the stitchline of the sleeve cap into the stitchline of the desired armhole. Refer to the pivoting steps, pages 125–126, for a clear example of pivoting technique and notch placement. If the sleeve cap is too short, add measurements at the underarm seams.

3 **Sew together the underarm seams** and then sew the sleeve into the basic knit bodice.

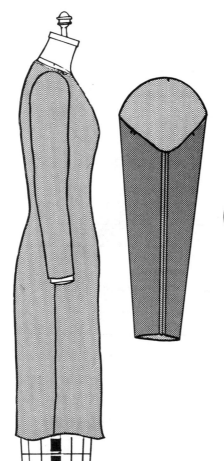

4 **Place the knit garment with the attached knit sleeve onto the dress form** and check for a clean, smooth fit and hang. The armhole area should not show any gapping or overstretching.

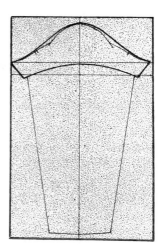

Sleeve Variations

A very common sleeve used in knit garments is the cap or muscle sleeve. **Illustrated here is the completed muscle sleeve.** Using the basic knit sleeve, raise the bicep level 2 inches and pivot the sleeve bicep level. Draw a new cap and underarm seam. For more details in pivoting a bicep line, refer to Sleeves, page 130.

Knit Halter

The description for a halter made with knit fabric is the same as the bias halter discussed on pages 161–163. The differences are the fabric, grainline, and measurements. Almost always the outer edges are finished with bias binding to give all edges extra strength and body with minimum expense.

Knit Halter: *Preparing the Fabric*

1 **Measure and cut a perfect 44-inch square** of knit fabric, which is wide enough for an entire front and back.

2 **Draw a center front grainline** in the middle of the piece of fabric. This line will be the center front line of the garment.

3 **Draw a crossgrain line** in the middle of the fabric piece opposite direction (crossgrain) from the grainline. This line will represent the bust level line of the garment.

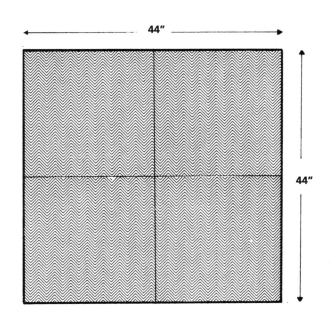

Knit Halter: *Draping Steps*

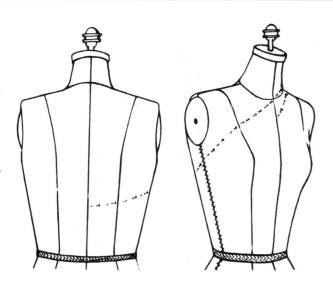

1 Prepare the dress form.
Remove the bra tape on the dress form. Pin or use style tape to indicate the desired neckline and/or armhole shapes.

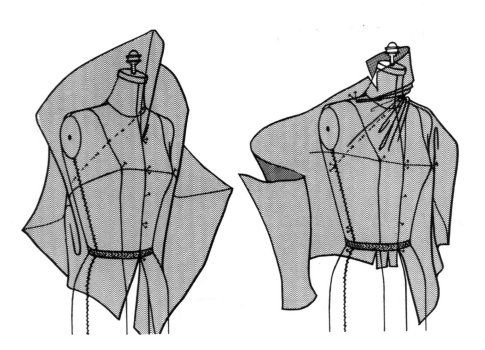

2 Pin and drape the center front grainline on the center front position of the dress form.

3 Align the crossgrain line on the bust level of the dress form.

4 Trim, clip, and drape the waistline. Drape the entire waistline from side seam to side seam. Pin in place.

5 Smooth and drape the fabric up and across the side seam. Excess fabric will now be falling toward the neckline above the bust level.

NOTE: The bust level line is now angled upward.

6 Trim away the fabric at the premarked bare armhole from center back to the front shoulder near the neck area, leaving a 2-inch excess.

7 Smooth and drape the fabric around the trimmed armhole.

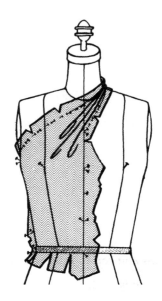

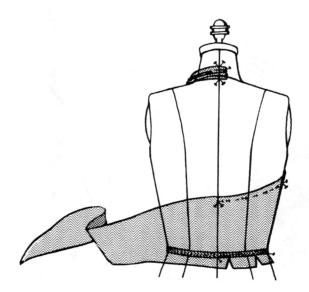

8 Fold, tuck, pleat, or gather in the fullness around the neckline, finishing at the center back neck area.

9 Drape and smooth across the side seam. Extend the excess fabric across the side seam to the desired length of the back halter waist tie.

10 Clip and shape the fabric around the back waistline to the desired styled shape of the garment.

11 Drape and smooth the back side seam flat. Match the side seam of the back bodice to the front side seam of the halter top.

12 Mark all key areas of the dress form to the fabric:

a. Armhole/neckline: Follow the bare shoulder style line up and around the front and back neckline.

b. Side seam: Lightly crossmark.

c. Waistline: Lightly crossmark the entire waist area of the drape.

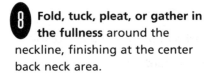

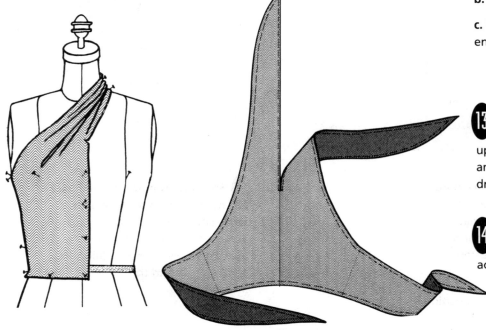

13 True up. Remove the fabric drape from the dress form. True up all seams, add seam allowances, and trim excess fabric. Pin the front drape to the back drape.

14 Return the finished drape to the dress form and check for accuracy, fit, and balance.

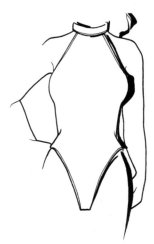

The knit leotard and/or bathing suit is a one-piece garment without legs although sometimes with sleeves. The knit leotard is the newest-looking style in exercise wear and bathing suits. This popular knit garment exposes the legs completely and allows the designer to use many different leg cuts. Knit fabrics, such as spandex or latex, are ideal fabrics for this clean-cut simple actionwear. The leotard is developed from the dartless knit top to achieve a close-to-the-body fit. It is then fitted and adjusted on the dress form. This method offers a fast and easy method for achieving an accurate knit leotard block.

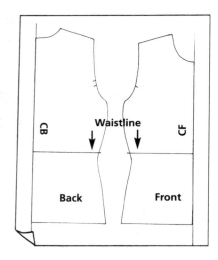

1 **Trace front and back onto pattern paper.** Using the fitted knit pattern, which is made of the same knit quality as your desired leotard, trace onto pattern paper.

2 **Draw the waistline position.**

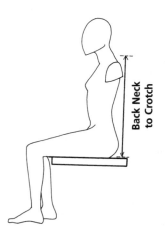

3 **Measure from the natural back neck position to the crotch,** while sitting straight on a chair. This measurement should be approximately 27 inches. Subtract 1 1/2 inches from this measurement.

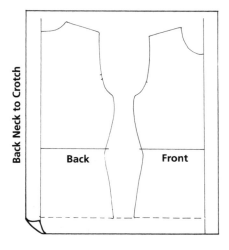

Back Neck to Crotch

Back   Front

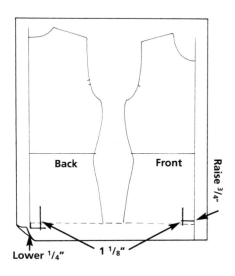

Back   Front

Raise ³/₄"

Lower ¹/₄"   1 ¹/₈"

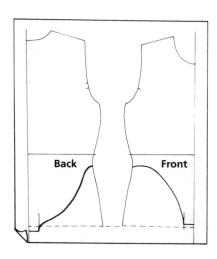

Back   Front

④ Transfer the back neck to crotch length onto the back pattern.

a. Measure down from the back neckline of the pattern the measurement determined in the previous step. Crossmark this measurement.

b. Square a line across the pattern for front and back at this crossmark.

⑤ Draw the front crotch. Raise the front crotch up 3/4 inch and measure in 1 1/8 inches toward the side seam at the crotch depth line. Crossmark and draw these positions.

⑥ Draw the back crotch depth. Lower the back crotch 1 1/4 inches from the original crotch level and measure in 1 1/8 inches toward the side seam at the crotch depth line. Crossmark and draw these positions.

⑦ Draw the desired legging—in this example, a French cut.
Using a curved ruler, this line should start at the crotch crossmark, extend into a 90-degree angle, and move up to or just below the waistline (see illustration).

NOTE: To ensure maximum coverage over the buttocks, the line drawn for the back will drop considerably (see illustration).

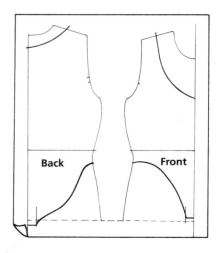 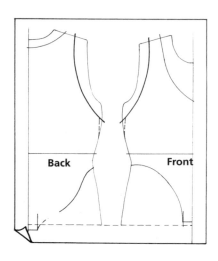 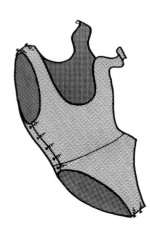

8 Draw the desired front and back neckline, using a curved ruler.

NOTE: If a low front neckline is desired, then a higher back neckline is necessary, and vice versa, because structurally the leotard will gap and fall off the shoulders.

9 Draw the desired front and back armholes, using a curved ruler. At this time, once again remove 1/4 inch at the new armhole/side seam corner. Blend in a new side seam/armhole corner.

NOTE: This is done to take out any excess ease that was created by dropping the armhole.

10 Cut out a full pattern (left to right) of a knit fabric. Pin together the shoulders, side seams, and crotch.

NOTE: The stretch quality of the sample fabric should be the same as the basic knit pattern and the same as the desired garment.

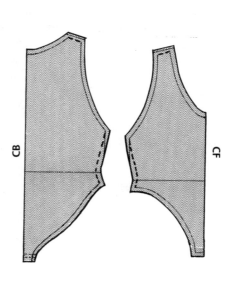 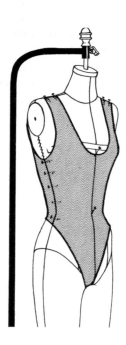

11 Place the leotard onto a pant form. Be very careful to pin the center positions.

12 Fit the shoulders, side seams, and crotch by repinning the desired changes. With a felt-tip pen, draw all corrections and adjustments.

13 Retrue all alterations. Remove the drape from the pant form. Retrue all seams and add a 3/8-inch seam allowance. Because of the changes when fitting, a new pattern may be necessary.

NOTE: Refer to page 411 for detail information on elastic for the legging.

Knit Bodysuit

The fitted knit bodysuit is a form-fitting, one-piece garment with legs and sometimes with sleeves. The legging may be short, three-quarter length, or long.

Style, practicality, and comfort are part of what makes the bodysuit so inviting. This one-piece knitted garment is worn by the fashion-minded, the sports-minded,

and also the serious competitive athlete. It can be made in a variety of knit fabrics such as mohair, jersey, or tricot to maintain complete freedom of body movement. However, this type of bodysuit cannot be styled or made in woven fabrics, which use a completely different pattern theory.

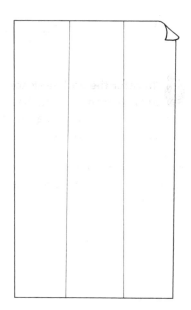

1 Cut a piece of pattern paper 60 inches long by 30 inches wide.

2 Draw two grainlines the length of the paper and 11 inches in from each end.

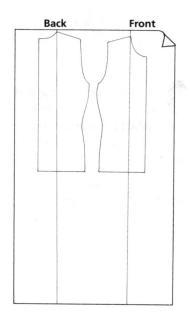

Back Front

3 Trace front and back bodice pattern onto pattern paper. Use a fitted knit bodice pattern that is made of the same knit quality as your desired bodysuit.

4 Align the grainlines at the shoulder/neck corners and parallel to center.

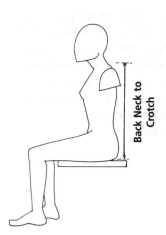

Back Neck to Crotch

5 Measure from the natural back neck position to the crotch while sitting straight on a chair. This measurement should be approximately 27 inches. Subtract 1 inch from this measurement.

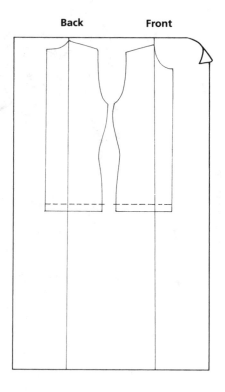

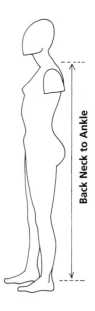

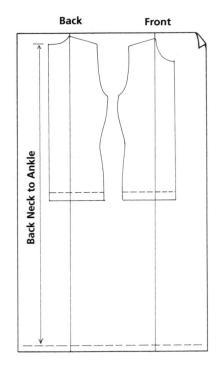

6 Transfer the back neck-to-crotch length onto the back pattern. With a ruler, measure down from the back neckline of the pattern. Mark this measurement and square a line across the pattern for the front and back.

7 Measure from the natural back neck position to the ankle while standing straight. Subtract 1 1/2 inches from this measurement.

NOTE: This measurement may change slightly, depending on the stretch quality of the desired knit fabric.

8 Transfer the back neck-to-ankle length onto the back pattern. With a ruler, measure the overall length down from the back neckline of the pattern. Mark this measurement and square a line across the pattern for both the front and back.

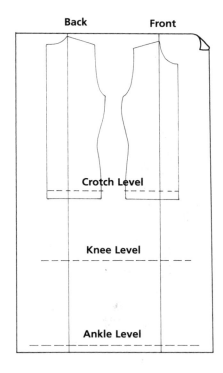

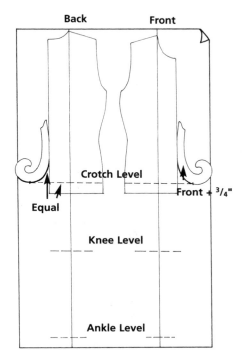

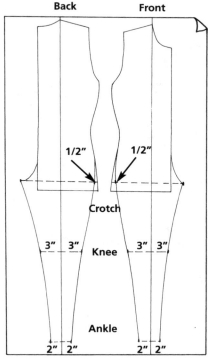

9 Locate the knee level line.

a. Measure from the crotch line to the ankle line and subtract 2 inches. Divide this measurement in half and add 3 inches to this measurement.

b. Measure up from the ankle line. Mark this measurement and square a line across the pattern for both the front and back.

10 Develop the crotch.

a. To develop the front crotch, measure from center front to the straight of grainline and subtract 3/4 inch. Extend this new measurement from the center front toward the edge of the paper.

b. To develop the back crotch, measure from the center back to the straight of grainline. Extend the measurement from the center back toward the edge of the paper.

c. Draw these new extended lines up into the center lines, using a French-curve ruler.

11 Develop the legging.

a. At the ankle line, measure 2 inches on both sides of the grainline. Crossmark this position.

b. Crossmark a new side seam position. At the crotch line from the side seam, remove 1/2 inch from the side seam.

c. Measure 3 inches on both sides of the grainline. Crossmark this position on the knee line.

d. Blend the crotch line to the knee level, using a long, curved ruler.

e. Blend a new side seam up to the waistline and down to the knee line, crossing the new side seam crossmark. Using a straight ruler, blend from the knee level to the ankle level.

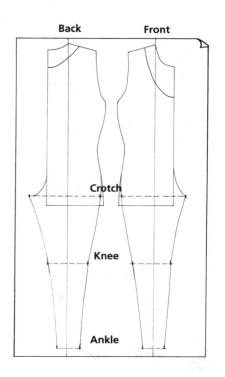

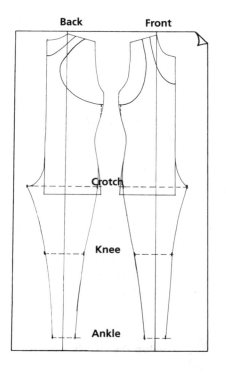

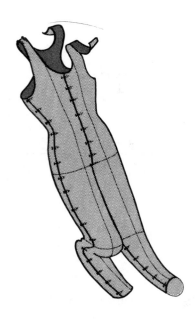

12 **Draw the desired front and back neckline,** using a curved ruler.

NOTE: If a low front neckline is desired, then a higher back neckline is necessary, and vice versa, because structurally the body suit will gap and fall off the shoulders.

13 **Draw the desired front and back armholes,** using a curved ruler. Remove 1/4 inch at the new armhole/side seam corners. Blend in a new side seam/armhole corner.

14 **Cut out a full pattern** (left and right) of a knit fabric. Pin together the shoulders, side seams, and inseams.

NOTE: The stretch quality of the sample fabric should be the same as the basic knit pattern and the same as the desired garment.

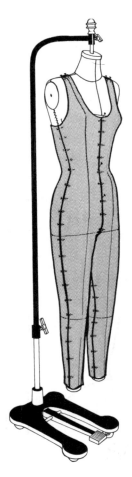

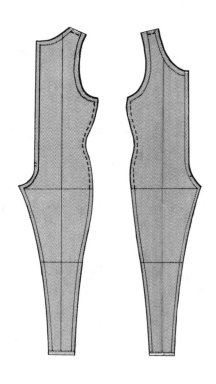

15 **Place the bodysuit onto a pants form,** being very careful to pin the center positions.

16 **Fit the shoulders, side seams, inseams, and crotch** by repinning the desired changes. With a felt-tip pen, draw all corrections and adjustments.

17 **Retrue all altered seams.** Remove the drape from the pant form. Retrue all seams and add 3/8-inch seam allowances. Because of the changes when fitting, a new pattern may be necessary.

Knit Panties

Knit fabrics are becoming increasingly important for their easy wear qualities. Lightweight knit fabrics provide gentle shaping and maximum elasticity for the hiphugger, bikini style briefs, or the soft stretch brief. Designing briefs can be a real joy if the basic drape and fit are well done.

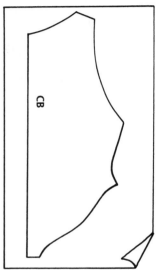
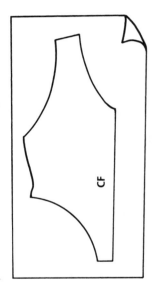

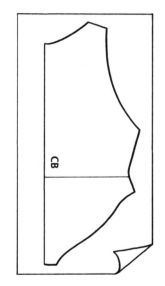
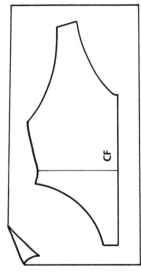

1 Trace the front and back leotard patterns onto a new piece of pattern paper.

2 Draw a front and back waistline or a front and back hipline for the panty brief.

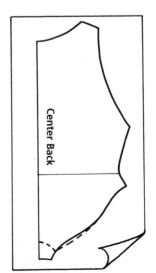
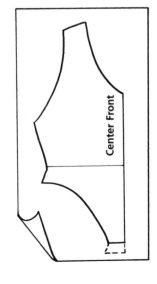

3 Reshape the front and back crotch seams.

a. For a body-fitting front crotch, extend and shape the front crotch seam approximately 2 inches (see illustration).

b. For a body-fitting back crotch, subtract approximately 2 inches and draw a concave line at the back crotch seam (see illustration).

c. Cut the crotch seams at the original front crotch.

d. Cut the back crotch at the new back-shaped crotch.

e. Connect the front to the back to make a separate crotch piece.

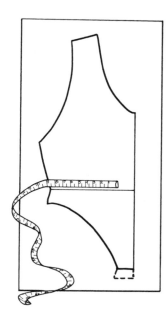

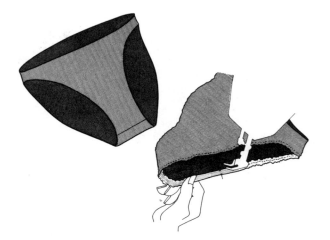

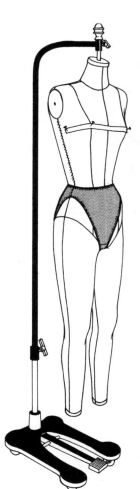

4 **Measure the waistline and legging elastic.**

a. The waistline or hipline elastic should measure approximately 2 inches smaller than the desired finished measurement.

b. When sewing the legging, elastic should measure approximately 22 inches per leg.

5 **Cut the entire panty out** of the same stretch quality fabric in which the finished panty will be produced.

6 **Sew the crotch and side seams together.** Using a stretch-and-sew method, single-needle serge the elastic into the waistline and the two legging areas. Sew less elastic into the lower back legging area to provide a more secure back fit.

7 **A final fit of a panty should be done on the human body.** Place the sewn panty onto the dress form and make any fitting corrections.

Chapter Nineteen

Cowls

Objectives

By studying the various draping steps in this chapter, the designer should be able to:

- Drape a fitted bodice cowl design using a soft fabric cut on the bias.

- Manipulate the bias fabric to fit the curves of the body over the bust and shape it over the contour of the body with a waistline seam.

- Visualize the front and back neckline cowl in relation to the figure.

- True up and check the results of the draping process with regard to fit, hang, balance, and proportion.

Basic Neckline Cowl

Cowls are draped on the bias, usually in lighter, finer fabrics to enhance a soft, harmonious look. A basic neckline cowl can be used subtly or to add imaginative zing to an otherwise low-key garment. The drape should be done in the same quality of fabric as the finished garment.

This section illustrates draping a front cowl. To drape a back cowl, follow the same draping as illustrated on the front cowl.

To drape a bias skirt, follow the draping steps on pages 255–258.

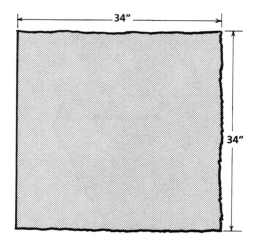

1 **Measure and cut a perfect square** of soft fabric wide enough for an entire front or entire back bodice (approximately 34 inches square).

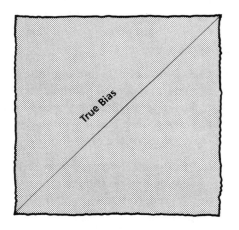

2 **Draw a true bias line** diagonally across the piece of fabric.

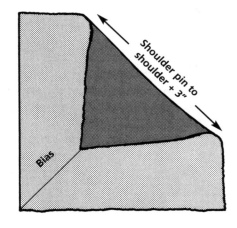

3 **Determine the neckline edge and facing area.** Turn a corner of the fabric deep enough to reach from one shoulder pin through the neckline pin and over to the other shoulder pin. Add 3 inches for ease and press in place.

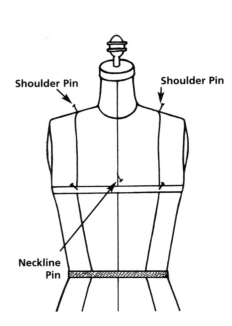

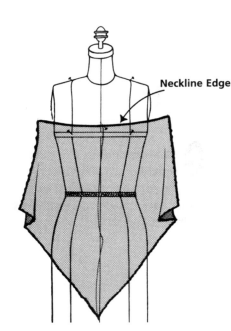

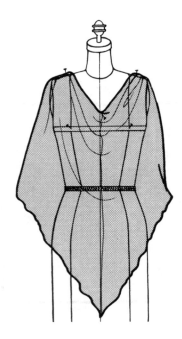

1 **Prepare the dress form.** Determine the desired neckline depth. Place a pin on the dress form at this neckline position. Also, place a pin on each shoulder seam the width of the

2 **Drape the center front neckline.** Place the folded edge of the fabric on the dress form.

3 Match the center front bias line of the fabric to the center front neckline pin on the dress form.

4 **Drape and pin the shoulders** into position by holding the fabric at each end of the foldline of the fabric edge.

Swing the fabric up and onto the shoulders. Allow the neckline cowl to fall in gently. Be sure to keep the center front bias line on the center front of the dress form.

NOTE: The pleating process in Step 5 is optional. If no shoulder pleats are desired, continue draping with Steps 6 and 7.

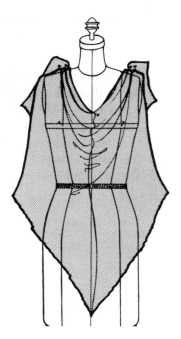

5 **Lift and pleat each shoulder** to form additional desired cowl drapes.

NOTE: Refer to the garment design to determine the number of cowl drapes desired.

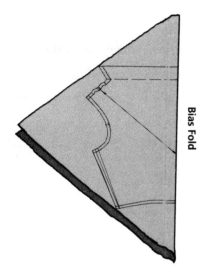

Bias Fold

6 **Clip the waistline fabric.** Pin and drape the waistline, side seam, and armhole areas.

7 **Mark all key areas** of the dress form on one side of the drape only:

a. **Shoulder seam.**

b. **Side seam.**

c. **Waistline.**

d. **Armhole area and desired armhole shape.**

8 **True up the front cowl drape.**

a. Fold the drape on the center front bias fold.

b. True up all seams and add seam allowances.

c. At the neckline fold, determine the width of the desired neckline facing. Keep the bodice drape folded. Trace all necessary markings from the trued side to the unmarked side. Trim excess fabric.

d. Place the drape back on the dress form. Check for accuracy and make all necessary corrections.

NOTE: Refer to The Basic Bodice, pages 57–60, for trueing the shoulder, side seam, and waistline areas.

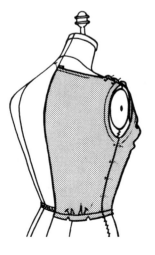

9 **Drape a back bodice design.** Refer to one of the basic back drapes to correctly drape the back bodice design.

NOTE: A low back neckline cannot be used because the drape will fall off the shoulders. Also, the neckline shoulder areas should match.

Yoke Cowl Design

A yoke cowl becomes quite effective when a cowl design requires the remainder of the garment to be dartless and free flowing. It also allows the grainline of this garment area to remain parallel to the center front position.

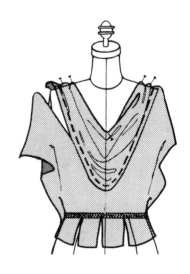

1 **Draw in the desired yoke style line,** after completing the cowl drape. Add seam allowances and trim excess fabric.

2 **Drape the desired garment style into the yoke cowl,** keeping the cowl yoke in place. The garment style grainline will remain parallel to the center front position of the dress form.

Underarm/Side Seam Cowl

The underarm/side seam cowl drape produces soft curved bias folds at the underarm seam. The fabric is placed on the true bias and is draped without a side seam. The underarm/side seam cowl is effective on a soft and sumptuous drape without looking overdone. It offers design inspiration for soft and fluid fabrics and creates a mood of easy elegance.

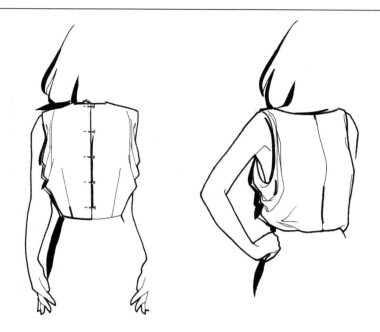

Underarm/Side Seam Cowl: *Preparing the Fabric*

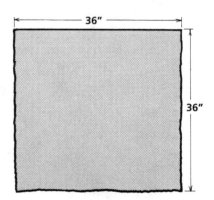

1 **Measure and cut a 36-inch square of soft fabric.** This will be enough fabric to drape a front and back waist seam design, forming an underarm cowl.

NOTE: The drape should be done in the same quality of fabric as the finished garment.

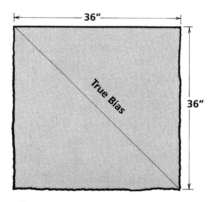

2 **Draw a true bias line** diagonally across the 36-inch piece of fabric.

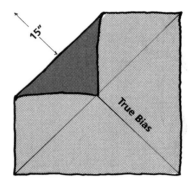 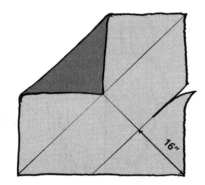

3 Measure down 15 inches from the top edge on the bias line.

5 Measure up 16 inches from the bottom edge on the bias line.

4 Draw a perfect cross bias line on the 15-inch position. Fold back the fabric on this line.

6 Draw a perfect cross bias line at the 16-inch position. Trim the fabric on this line.

Underarm/Side Seam Cowl: *Draping Steps*

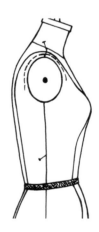 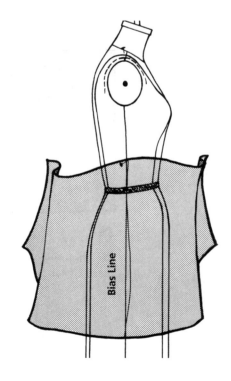

1 Prepare the dress form. Determine the depth of the underarm cowl desired. Place a pin on the dress form at this underarm/side seam position. Also, place a pin on the shoulder seam at the desired shoulder/armhole position.

2 Pin the fabric on the dress form at the underarm side seam pin.

3 Position and match the bias line at the foldline to the side seam pin of the dress form.

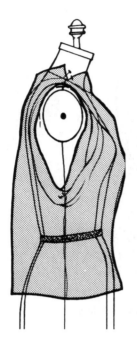

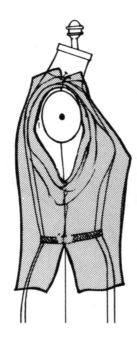

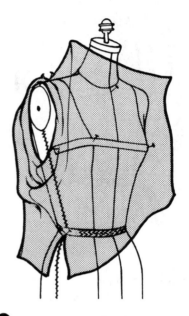

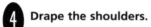

4 Drape the shoulders.

a. Hold the fabric at each end at the foldline of the fabric edge.

b. Swing the fabric up and onto the shoulders. Place anchor pins at this shoulder position.

c. Cowls will automatically form at the underarm.

NOTE: For deeper side seam cowl drapes, it will be necessary to form pleats at the shoulder.

5 Clip the fabric on the side seam, from the bottom of the bias line up to the waistline. Pin the bias line of the fabric to the side seam/waist position of the dress form.

6 Smooth and drape the fabric past the center front line until the grain of the fabric is parallel to the center front of the dress form.

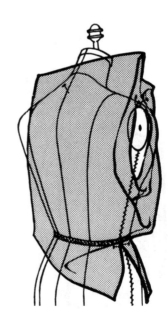

7 Smooth and drape the fabric past the center back line until the crossgrain of the fabric is parallel to the center back of the dress form.

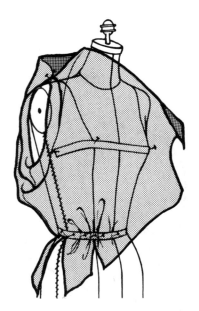

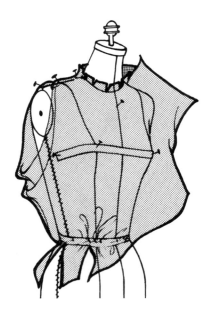

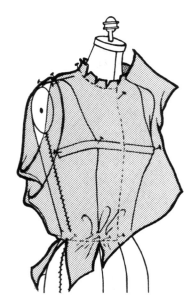

8 **Clip and pin the waistline in place** for the front and back.

NOTE: It will be necessary to form tucks, darts, or shirring as shown here when draping in the waistline.

9 **Clip the front and back necklines and drape in the shoulders.**

10 Mark all key areas:

a. Front and back.

b. Center front.

c. Center back.

d. Front and back waistline.

e. Shoulders and pleats.

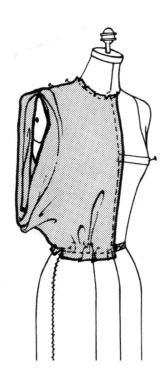

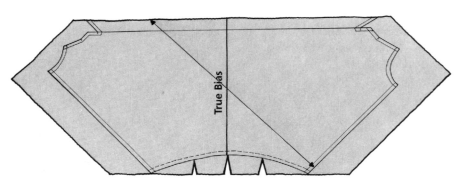

True Bias

11 **True up all lines.** Refer to The Basic Bodice, pages 57–60, for trueing up the shoulder, neckline, side seam, and waistline areas. Add seam allowances and trim excess fabric. At the underarm cowl foldline, determine the width and shape of the desired facing amount.

Chapter Twenty

Flounces,
Ruffles, and
Peplums

By studying the various draping steps in this chapter, the designer should be able to:

• Prepare and drape a circular piece of fabric into a relatively straight edge and create a cascading flounce.

• Determine the ratio of the length of the ruffle to the length of the seam into which it is being sewn.

• Prepare and drape a straight piece of fabric into almost any edge—necklines, armholes, or style lines—to create a ruffle.

• Trim and shape the outside style line to the desired design of a circular flounce or ruffle.

Designing Flounces, Ruffles, and Peplums

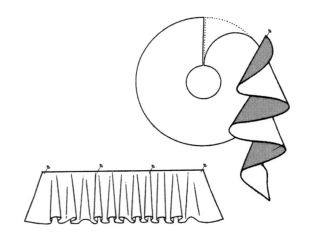

A **flounce** is an attached circular fabric piece that gradually flares and swells from a smooth seamline to a floating edge. Circular flounces generate floating fullness without bulking up the seamline. The smooth layer of a flounce at the seamline is constant, but the circularity and depth of the flounce pattern controls the finished waviness at the floating edge.

A **ruffle** is created by using a strip of fabric, doubled in length, which is gathered and sewn into a seam. Ruffles may be narrow or wide, arranged in single or multiple rows. Gathers are flexible and may adjust to a straight, curved, or angled seam.

Peplums are also created from a circle to form a short circular skirt attached to a bodice.

All three techniques inspire simple to elaborate design arrangements

The Circular Flounce

A circular flounce is a curving, cascading part of the design and can be draped into almost any edge—necklines, armholes, or style lines. Flounces are created correctly with a circular prepared fabric piece that is then draped into a relatively straight line, creating a cascading flow. The outside final shape is then formed by trimming and shaping in the desired design. A circular flounce can be draped by using one circle or several circles and can be designed with multiple or single layers.

The design of a circular flounce is the stuff of romance. Flounces recall a mood of elegance with a rich, dramatic, graceful flare.

  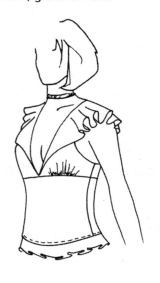

Circular Flounce: *Preparing the Fabric*

 Measure the style edge on the garment for the desired circular flounce:

a. Neckline flounce (an example is 18 inches, from center back neck edge to center front neck edge).

b. Large armhole flounce (an example is 24 inches, the entire circumference).

c. Princess seam flounce (an example is 17 inches, from the shoulder to the waistline).

2 Determine the amount of circle needed. Take the measurement from step 1, subtract 1 inch, and divide that new number by 6. This figure will be used for the next step.

a. Neckline flounce: 18" minus 1" = 17". Divide 17" by 6 to equal 2.8" or 2 3/4".

b. Large armhole flounce: 24" minus 1" = 23". Divide 23" by 6 to equal 3.8" or 3 3/4".

c. Princess seam flounce: 17" minus 1" = 16". Divide 16" by 6 to equal 2.6" or 2 5/8".

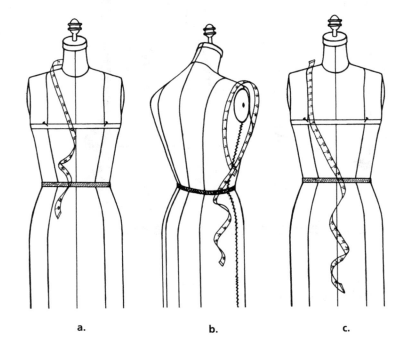

a.   b.   c.

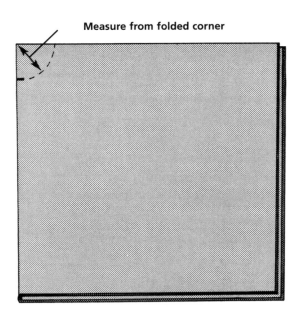

Measure from folded corner

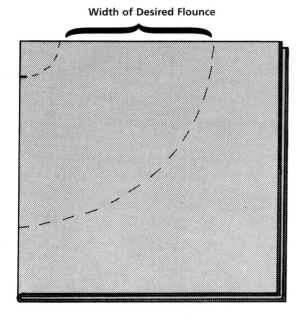

Width of Desired Flounce

3 Fold the muslin in half and then in half again in the other direction.

4 Measure down from the folded corner edge. Using a ruler or tape measure, mark the desired measurement. Draw this measurement as a quarter circle from folded edge to folded edge.

5 Determine the desired width of the flounce and add 2 inches. Draw this width parallel to the first circle.

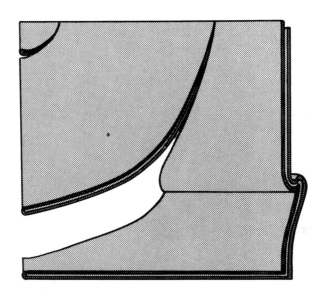

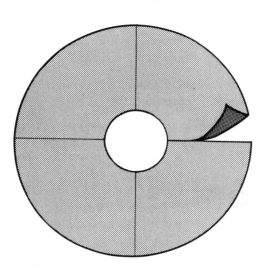

6 Cut out the fabric on the two circular lines.

7 Open the fabric, exposing a full circular fabric piece. Cut the fabric on one of the folds.

Circular Flounce: Draping Steps

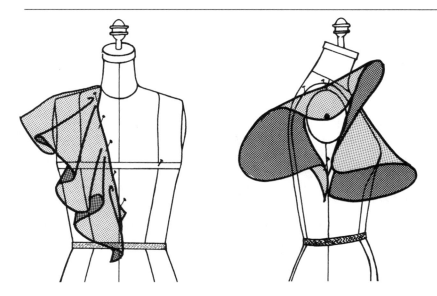

1 **Place the fabric circle on the dress form** along the desired styled edge. Pin approximately every inch.

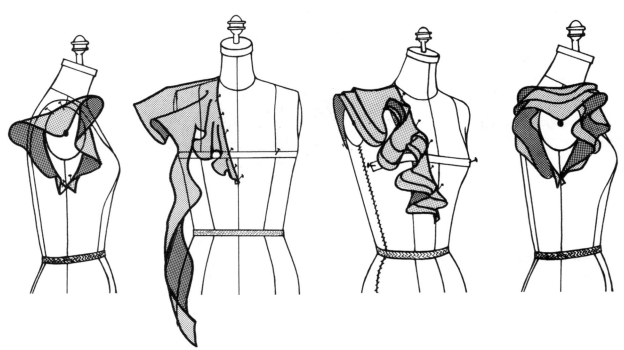

2 **Trim the outside edge of the flounce** into the desired shape of the design.

NOTE: There may be multiple layers required, depending on the design. Each layer is usually shaped and layered using different widths.

There are times when a designer may want more fullness in the flounce. In this case, apply the following pattern preparations.

Shirred Flounce: *Preparing the Fabric*

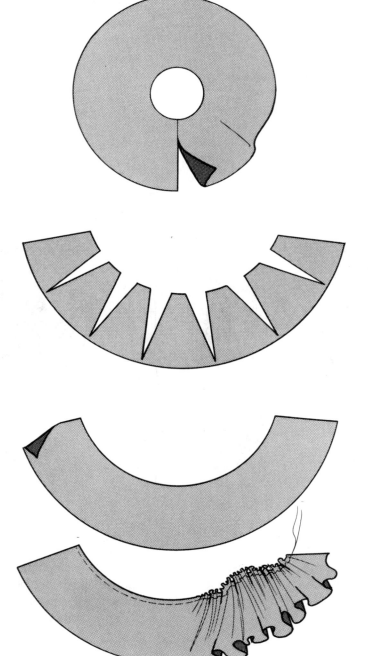

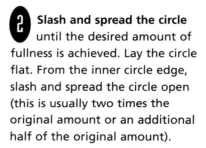
1 Fold the fabric, determine the circular measurement, and cut out the circle. Refer to Circular Flounce, pages 425–426.

2 Slash and spread the circle until the desired amount of fullness is achieved. Lay the circle flat. From the inner circle edge, slash and spread the circle open (this is usually two times the original amount or an additional half of the original amount).

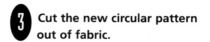
3 Cut the new circular pattern out of fabric.

4 Sew a row of gathers on the inner circle edge. Gather the circle until the inner circle length is the same as that of the seam it will be sewn into.

Shirred Flounce: Draping Steps

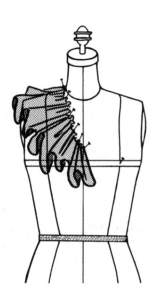

1 Place the gathered fabric circle along the desired style edge of the dress form. Pin approximately every inch.

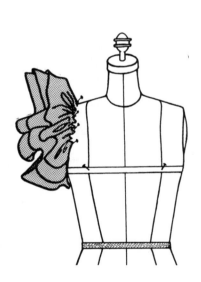 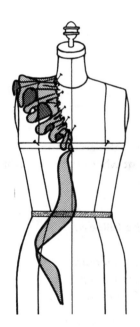 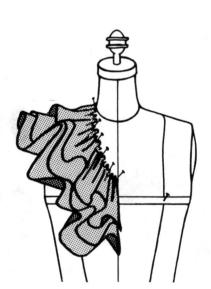

2 Trim the outside edge of the flounce until it represents the desired shape of the flounce design.

NOTE: Multiple layers may be required, depending on the design. Each layer is usually shaped and layered using different widths.

Ruffles

Ruffles can be the perfect solution for finishing a neckline, collar, skirt, or cuff. A ruffle is a straight piece of fabric gathered into a seam. Depending on the type of fabric and style, the ruffle can be designed in any width or length. However, the ratio for determining the length is 1 1/2 or 2 times the length of the seam it is to be sewn into.

Ruffles lend a graceful touch to inspire a softer, more romantic look in fashion.

Ruffles: Draping Steps

1 **Measure the area of the garment** where the ruffle will be applied.

2 **Add the fullness.**

a. Double the amount, using the measurement in step 1, for maximum fullness (2 to 1).

b. Add half the amount to the measurement from step 1, for less fullness (1 1/2 to 1).

3 **Determine the desired width.** This should be in proportion to the design of the garment.

Transfer the length and width measurements to the fabric. The width is placed on the straight of grain, so that the gathering will be done on the crossgrain. This ensures a clean and even fabric fullness.

NOTE: If the length measurement is longer than the width of the fabric, then the fabric length should be divided into sections.

5 Gather the ruffle into the same length as the area where the ruffle is desired. Pin the ruffle into the garment.

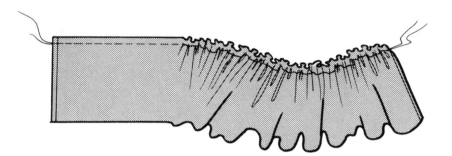

- A ruffle may be baby hemmed on the outer edge.

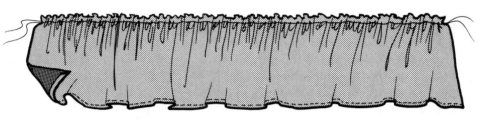

- A ruffle may be doubled in width and folded in half. Then, both raw edges are sewn into the desired styled area, and no hemming is required.

- A ruffle may have a double ruffle technique.

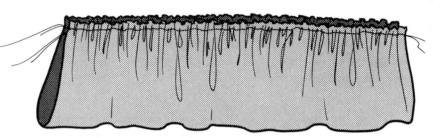

Notes

Peplums

A peplum is a short-fitted circular skirt attached to the waist seam of a bodice or jacket. Peplums are cut in a circle and then draped for a desired flare. A soft-draped peplum will often add a smashing touch to an otherwise traditional garment. The peplum moves in and out of the fashion limelight, but designers welcome this fashion emphasis periodically.

Peplums: Draping Steps

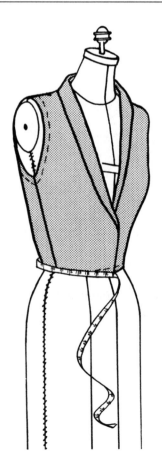

1 **Measure the style edge on the garment** for the desired peplum. In most cases, this is in a waist area of a jacket or dress.

2 **Determine the amount of circle needed.** Take the measurement in step 1, subtract 1 inch, and then divide that new number by 6. For example: 27" minus 1" = 26". Divide by 6 to equal 4 3/8".

Measure from folded corner

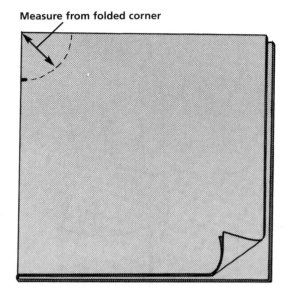

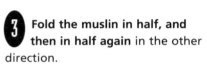

Desired Width

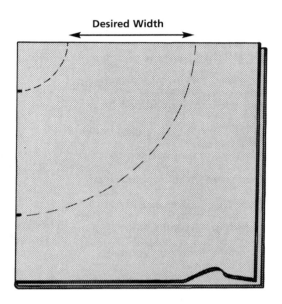

3 **Fold the muslin in half, and then in half again** in the other direction.

4 **Measure down from the folded corner edge.** Using a ruler or tape measure, mark the desired measurement. Draw this measurement in a quarter circle from folded edge to folded edge.

5 **Determine the desired width of the peplum.** Draw this width parallel to the first circle.

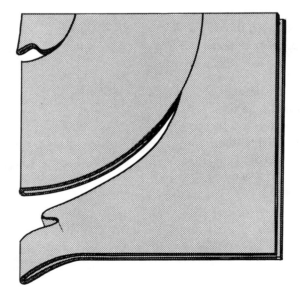

6 **Cut out the peplum** on the two circular lines.

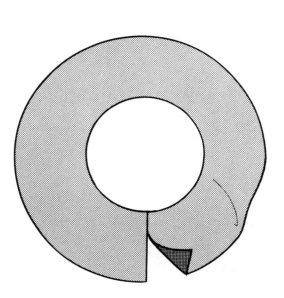

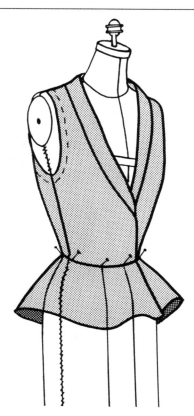

7 Open the fabric, exposing a full circular fabric piece. Cut the fabric on one of the folds.

8 Drape and pin the prepared peplum circle fabric along the desired style edge.

9 Check the peplum drape for the desired amount of circular fullness.

a. If more fullness is required, slash and spread from the outer edge to the styled edge.

b. If less fullness is required, slash and close from the outer edge to the styled edge.

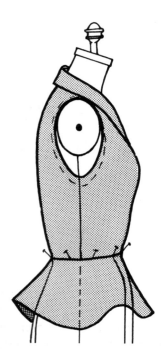

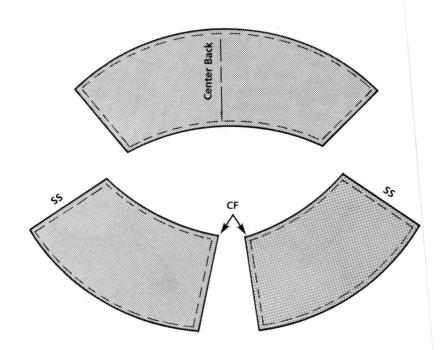

10 Pencil in the side seams. Following the side seam of the dress form, pencil the side seam position on the fabric.

11 Remove the peplum drape from the dress form. Cut the drape at the side seam.

12 Prepare a pattern piece for the front peplum (from center front to the side seam).

13 Prepare another pattern piece for the back peplum (from center back to the side seam). Usually center back is placed on the fold, and an opening is required for the front.

14 Return the peplum drape to the dress form. Pin the side seams together. Pin the peplum back to the garment. Check the peplum for correct length and movement.

Index